BEYOND GREED AND FEAR

Financial Management Association
Survey and Synthesis Series

BEYOND GREED AND FEAR

Understanding Behavioral Finance and the Psychology of Investing

Hersh Shefrin

OXFORD
UNIVERSITY PRESS

2002

OXFORD
UNIVERSITY PRESS

Oxford   New York

Auckland   Bangkok   Buenos Aires   Cape Town   Chennai
Dar es Salaam   Delhi   Hong Kong   Istanbul   Karachi   Kolkata
Kuala Lumpur   Madrid   Melbourne   Mexico City   Mumbai   Nairobi
São Paulo   Shanghai   Singapore   Taipei   Tokyo   Toronto

Library of Congress Cataloging-in-Publication Data
Shefrin, Hersh, 1948–
Beyond greed and fear : understanding behavioral finance and the psychology of investing /
Hersh Shefrin
p. cm. — (Financial Management Association survey and synthesis series)
Originally published: Boston: Harvard Business School Press © 2000.
ISBN 0-19-516121-1
1. Investments—Psychological aspects. 2. Stock exchanges—Psychological aspects.
3. Finance—Psychological aspects. I. Title. II. Series.
[HG4515.15 .S53 2002]]
332.6'01'9—dc21   2002010047

4 6 8 9 7 5 3

Printed in the United States of America
on acid-free paper

For Arna

Contents

Preface to the Oxford Edition

Behavioral finance is the study of how psychology affects finance. Psychology is the basis for human desires, goals, and motivations, and it is also the basis for a wide variety of human errors that stem from perceptual illusions, overconfidence, over-reliance on rules of thumb, and emotions. Errors and bias cut across the entire financial landscape, affecting individual investors, institutional investors, analysts, strategists, brokers, portfolio managers, options traders, currency traders, futures traders, plan sponsors, financial executives, and financial commentators in the media. This book is about recognizing the influence of psychology on oneself, on others, and on the financial environment at large.

I take some pride in the fact that *Beyond Greed and Fear* was the first comprehensive treatment of behavioral finance. However, the greatest satisfaction comes from witnessing the enormous growth that has occurred in the field since the book was first published in 1999.

As a field, behavioral finance is flourishing, not only in academia where financial issues are studied, but also in practice where behavioral concepts are coming to be routinely applied. One only need do a web-based search on "behavioral finance" to see how the field has virtually exploded.

Behavioral finance is now represented in almost every leading academic department of finance in the United States. Some universities, such as the University of Mannheim in Germany, have established institutes dedicated to the subject. The Social Science Research Network has a separate newsgroup devoted to behavioral and experimental finance. Behavioral papers are now routinely presented at every major academic finance meeting. Articles devoted to behavioral topics are winning Best Paper awards. Two notable instances are the Smith Breeden Prize and the William F. Sharpe Award. The Smith Breeden Prize was awarded to Kent Daniel, David Hirshleifer, and Avanidhar Subrahmanyam for the best paper published in the *Journal of Finance* during 1999. They wrote "Investor Psychology and Security Market Under- and Overreactions." The William F. Sharpe Award for Scholarship in Financial Research was awarded to Meir Statman and me for "Behavioral Portfolio Theory," which appeared in the *Journal of Financial and Quantitative Analysis* in 2000.

The *Review of Financial Studies* and the *Financial Analysts Journal* have devoted entire issues to behavioral finance, and the *Journal of*

Empirical Finance is planning a future issue, again dedicated to behavioral finance. The *International Library of Critical Writings in Financial Economics* is a compendium of edited collections in the various areas of finance. As a testament to its growing importance, a three-volume set on behavioral finance, which I was privileged to edit, appears in this collection, alongside more traditional areas such as corporate finance, futures markets, market efficiency, debt markets, options markets, and market microstructure.

Behavioral perspectives are routinely reported in major newspapers such as the *Wall Street Journal*. In January 2002, the *New York Times* profiled the work of Richard Thaler, one of behavioral finance's leading figures. In June 2001, the *Financial Times* devoted an entire section to behavioral finance. In 2002, public television's *The Nightly Business Report* devoted a whole program to behavioral finance. Well-known value manager and Forbes columnist David Dreman has organized the Institute of Psychology and Markets, along with a new journal, the *Journal of Psychology and Financial Markets*.

Many new papers and books are being written on behavioral topics. Shortly after *Beyond Greed and Fear* was published, two related behavioral books appeared, both by leading behaviorists. *Irrational Exuberance* by Robert Shiller is a highly acclaimed work, describing the psychological factors that produced a stock market bubble during the 1990s. *Inefficient Markets* by Andrei Shleifer contains a formal exposition of investor sentiment and its impact on security pricing.

Financial firms are increasingly applying behavioral concepts. At the forefront in basing their strategies explicitly on behavioral finance are Fuller & Thaler Asset Management, Dreman Value Management, Martingale Asset Management, and LSV Asset Management. In recent years the list of financial services firms that incorporate behavioral finance has grown to include American Skandia, Goldman Sachs, Merrill Lynch, Nuveen, Panagora, Putnam, Alliance Capital unit Sanford Bernstein, and Vanguard. A new mutual fund firm, Marketocracy, explicitly built its strategy on the concepts described in chapter 8. The use of behavioral concepts is not only confined to the United States; European financial institutions KBC Bank, ABN Ambro, J. P. Morgan Fleming Asset Management, and Robeco all run funds employing behavioral strategies.

Behavioral Finance: Key Message

People are imperfect processors of information and are frequently subject to bias, error, and perceptual illusions. The general lesson from

Beyond Greed and Fear is that psychology permeates the entire financial landscape. Since this book was first published, I have learned that many people continue to misconstrue the main message of behavioral finance. Many think that the main lesson from behavioral finance is about how to beat the market. This is a dangerous misconception.

On page 89 I specifically caution investors *not* to "use behavioral finance to make a killing." In chapter 1 and in my Final Remarks, I indicate that although behavioral errors do create abnormal profit opportunities for the smart money, these errors also introduce an additional source of risk, above and beyond fundamental risk. Many investors only hear half the message about behavioral finance—the part about abnormal profit opportunities. They miss the part about additional sentiment-based risk, meaning risk that stems from psychologically induced errors.

That additional profit opportunities are accompanied by additional risk is the moral of the story about the hedge fund Long-term Capital Management (LTCM), described on pages 5–7, 33–34, and 41–42. The people running LTCM were exceedingly smart. However, the high level of intelligence at LTCM did not prevent disaster. Overconfidence can trump intelligence. In the case of LTCM, overconfidence did trump intelligence.

Roger Lowenstein in *When Genius Failed* details the events that brought down LTCM in 1998. The biggest surprises to LTCM's traders did not come from unanticipated fundamental risk, but from unanticipated sentiment-based risk! On pages 50 and 51, I explain that overconfidence leads people to set confidence intervals that are too narrow, and as a result, overconfident people experience major surprises. Lowenstein tells us that LTCM calculated that on any single day its maximum loss was unlikely to exceed $35 million. On Friday, August 21, 1998, LTCM lost $553 million.

LTCM was built on the foundation of efficient market theory, where mispricing is small and quickly exploited by smart money, like them. Investors who are overconfident are inclined to take bigger risks than are prudent. Lowenstein reports that LTCM's large positions and especially its heavy use of leverage turned what on August 21, 1998, might have been small losses into huge losses.

A year before LTCM's collapse, behaviorists Andrei Shleifer and Robert Vishny published an article in 1997 in *Journal of Finance* entitled "The Limits of Arbitrage," arguing that hedge fund strategies of the sort followed at LTCM were vulnerable to risks stemming from the errors and emotions of other traders. Shleifer and Vishny emphasized that liquidity constraints would force hedge funds to sell assets at prices that were not only inefficient, but at market lows. Lowenstein writes that Bob Merton had read an early version of the paper and "pooh-poohed the notion." Ah, overconfidence.

One of the major lessons from behavioral finance is that investors should guard against overconfidence, and not pooh-pooh the magnitude of sentiment-based risk! That is why, on page 89, I state: "I think most investors would be better off holding a well-diversified set of securities, mainly in index funds, than they would be trying to beat the market." I say this not because I believe that skilled investors are incapable of beating the market. Instead, I think that most investors are overconfident about their vulnerability to psychologically induced errors, and although intelligent, not as intelligent as they believe themselves to be.

The Collapse of the Bubble: An Update

Behavioral analyses involves terms such as *framing, transparency, optimism,* and *overconfidence*. Psychology is ubiquitous and germane. In order to drive home this point, I would like to update some of the key events described in the book against the backdrop of events that have occurred since the book was first published. The events that have occurred since that time comprise an informal out-of-sample test and underscore the power of behavioral forces in financial decisions.

Beyond Greed and Fear went to press in August 1999, as the level of irrational exuberance in the market was approaching its peak. In chapter 4 (page 39 and the footnotes on pages 313–314), I mention that in December 1996, Federal Reserve chairman Alan Greenspan first used the phrase "irrational exuberance" when expressing his concern that excess optimism among U.S. investors would eventually lead to a prolonged bear market along the lines that the Japanese stock market had experienced since 1990. Behaviorist Robert Shiller chose the term "irrational exuberance" for the title of his book, and in so doing made the phrase a "familiar refrain." On pages 38–41, I use Shiller's analysis to explain why the U.S. stock market was in the midst of a major bubble. Figure 4–3 on page 39 depicts the point in graphic fashion.

As far as technology stocks are concerned, in chapter 10, page 133, I state: "On the strength of investors' imagination, and little else, Internet stock prices were propelled into orbit. According to Lipper Analytical Services, the best-performing mutual fund in 1998 was the Internet Fund, managed by Kinetics Asset Management." The fund manager was Ryan Jacob, whose story I return to below.

As *Beyond Greed and Fear* went to press, technology stocks began a dramatic advance. At the time, the technology-heavy Nasdaq Composite Index stood at about 2800. Yet, in the space of eight months, the Nasdaq soared above 5048. This rise amounted to an 80 percent increase, 142 percent when measured on an annual basis.

How did the story play out? The Nasdaq bubble burst in March 2000. The figure below plots the time path of the Nasdaq Composite, together with the S&P 500 and the Dow Jones Industrial Average. To facilitate the comparison, $100 is invested in each of the three indexes, beginning in January 1988, barely two months after the stock market crash of 1987. Was there a tech-stock bubble? The figure speaks for itself. Outside the period 1999 through 2002 the three indexes are quite close to one another. But within the eight-month period (August 1999 through March 2000), the technology stock bubble evolved and then burst.

As for Internet fund manager Ryan Jacob, mentioned above for being the best performing mutual fund manager in 1998, his experience essentially reflects the evolution and collapse of the bubble. In

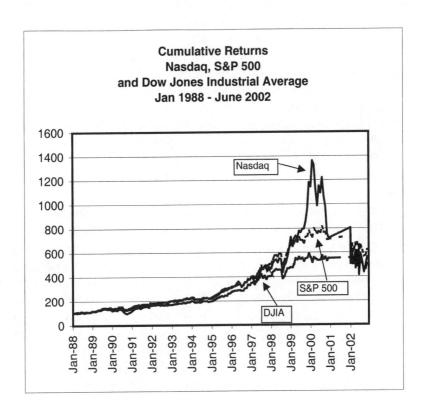

December 1999, Jacob left Kinetics Asset Management to launch the Jacob Internet fund. In August 2000 Lipper reported that year-to-date, the Jacob Internet was down 40 percent, and ranked last among 184 science and technology funds.

Scholars will study the late 1990s for some time to come. Here are two examples of issues already being investigated. The first involves pricing. In a working paper entitled "DotCom Mania: The Rise and Fall of Internet Stock Prices," Eli Ofek and Matthew Richardson analyze the role of short sale restrictions in respect to the overvaluation of Internet stock prices during the period January 1998 to November 2000. The second example examines the relationship between message posting on the Internet and trading volume and volatility. Werner Antweiler and Murray Frank at the University of British Columbia have written a working paper entitled "Is All That Talk Just Noise? The Information Content of Internet Message Boards." They report a strong relationship between the degree of message posting and the degree of both trading volume and volatility. Other studies on message board activity include "News or Noise? Internet Message Board Activity and Stock Prices" by Robert Tumarkin and Robert Whitelaw (*Financial Analysts Journal*, 2001), and "Yahoo for Amazon: Opinion Extraction from Small Talk on the Web" by Sanjiv Das and Mike Chen.

Real world events that occurred in the wake of the bursting bubble reinforce and confirm many points I make in the book. Initial public offerings or IPOs, constitute the subject matter of chapter 17. In the first paragraph of that chapter I state: "In the case of Internet stocks, the editor of one IPO newsletter has described investor activity as 'insanity.com' trading." The insanity continued through 2000, as VA Linux Systems set a new record for a first-day gain, rising 698 percent on December 9, 1999, to displace former IPO record holder theglobe.com (described on pages 245, 246).

A most remarkable example is the IPO of Palm, the firm that makes the Palm Pilot. In March 2000, Palm was spun out of 3Com. The first trading day for Palm's shares was March 2, 2000, a few days before the bubble peaked. Chapter 17 is entitled "IPOs: Initial Underpricing, Long-term Underperformance, and 'Hot-Issue' Markets." Long-term underpricing means that the initial offer price is too low, relative to the price set in the market on the first day of trading. Were Palm's shares underpriced? The offer price was $38. At that price, Palm held the record for the highest market capitalization of any high-technology IPO in United States history. Its associated $22 billion market capitalization made it the fourth-largest technology firm, behind Cisco Systems, Microsoft, and Intel, and the 49th most valuable firm in the U.S. On March 2, Palm opened at $165 a share. It closed the day at $95.

On March 2, 2000, 3Com retained 94 percent of Palm's shares. What is especially interesting is that at the end of the first day of trading, the market value of Palm's shares exceeded the market value of 3Com's shares by about $25 billion. In a working paper entitled "Can the Market Add and Subtract? Mispricing in Tech Stock Carve-Outs," Owen Lamont and Richard Thaler conclude that the market judged the non-Palm portion of 3Com to have negative value.

3Com structured its spinoff of Palm so that each 3Com stockholder would receive 1.5 shares of Palm for every share he or she held of 3Com. In describing this situation, Richard Thaler asked: Can the market multiply by 1.5? He noted that one can ask the same question about the relative valuations of Royal Dutch and Shell, that I discuss on page 7 in chapter 1. By the terms of their charter, the joint cash flows of Royal Dutch/Shell are split between Royal Dutch and Shell Transport so that Royal Dutch receives 1.5 times the cash flows that Shell receives. Yet, the relative market valuations of Royal Dutch and Shell frequently deviate from 1.5 by a significant amount.

Long-term underperformance means that an investor who buys and holds stock in the first few days that a firm's shares are traded publicly will earn inferior returns on average. In this respect, I note that at the close of trading on March 2, Palm, with fewer than 700 employees, had a market cap of $53.4 billion. At $165 per share, Palm had one of the highest market capitalizations in the United States. In respect to long-term underperformance, the price of Palm's stock went from its all-time high of $165 on March 2, 2000 to $1.11 on June 7, 2002. As to whether Palm's IPO took place in a "hot-issue" market, let me simply say that the IPO took place at the height of the bubble.

In chapter 5, I describe a key difference between the way individual investors form market predictions and the way institutional investors form market predictions. Individual investors suffer from extrapolation bias, and naively extrapolate recent trends. Institutional investors suffer from gambler's fallacy, and are overly prone to predicting reversals. For example, on page 46, I state: "In the wake of above average performance in 1995 and 1996, did the strategists predict that 1997 would feature below-average performance? Indeed they did. They predicted that the Dow would actually *decline* by 0.2 percent, well below the 8.6 percent annual rate that the Dow had grown between 1972 and 1996."

To predict a market decline in 1997, after two years like 1995 and 1996 when the Dow returned over 33 percent and 26 percent respectively, is to succumb to gambler's fallacy. The error involves going over-board. More appropriate is to predict that the Dow would rise by an amount closer to 8.6 percent—that is, to predict a lower increase than had occurred in the prior two years. In fact, as I point out in chapter 5, the Dow returned more than 22 percent in 1997.

Did strategists succumb to gambler's fallacy after the bubble burst? In December 2000, the *Wall Street Journal* elicited the market predictions of eight highly respected strategists. When these strategists were asked to state their predictions for the closing value of the S&P 500 at year-end 2001, the index had declined by 7 percent during 2000. The strategists' average forecast called for an increase in excess of 17 percent! In other words, gambler's fallacy continued. Just for the record: the S&P 500 returned −11.9 percent during 2001.

The message of chapter 16, "Corporate Takeovers and the Winner's Curse," is that because of hubris and overconfidence, the managers of acquiring firms often overpay for their targets. On page 328, I note that as I began work on the chapter in 1998, the computer firm Compaq was in the process of acquiring Digital Equipment Corp. The history of prior technology deals did not offer much in the way of promise for success. How did the merger turn out? Consistent with the hubris hypothesis, Compaq executives were surprised by the difficulty of integrating the two firms. This outcome appears to have been a primary factor in the resignation of Compaq's chief executive officer Eckhard Pfeiffer. It took Compaq more than a year to absorb Digital Equipment, during which time it lost valuable market share to Dell and Sun Microsystems.

At the time of my writing this new preface, Compaq has not recovered. However, this is not the end of the story. In 2002, Hewlett-Packard acquired Compaq in a shareholder battle that was front-page news. The battle pitted Carleton (Carly) Fiorina, CEO of Hewlett-Packard, against board member Walter Hewlett, son of William Hewlett, one of Hewlett-Packard's founders. I imagine that the outcome of that merger will be the subject of a future edition.

Acquisition activity peaked at $1.8 trillion in 2000, more than triple the level in the mid-1990s. Between 1995 and 2000, the average acquisition price in the United States rose 70 percent, to $470 million. Since that time, the extent of the winner's curse has become apparent. In April, 2002 AOL Time Warner Inc. wrote off $54 billion of "goodwill" to recognize AOL's overpayment for Time Warner. This was one of one of the largest writedowns in corporate history. Joining AOL Time Warner in the writedown category were Vivendi Universal SA of France, Cordiant

Communications Group, Boeing Co., Vodafone Group PLC., Tyco International Ltd., WorldCom Inc., and AT&T Corp. The appearance of AT&T on this list is especially interesting, in view of its long history experiencing the winner's curse: see pages 228–233 of chapter 16. Behaviorists stress that although people do learn, they learn slowly.

In chapter 18, "Optimism in Analysts' Earnings Predictions and Stock Recommendations," I pointed out that the games analysts play with investors have a "wink, wink, nod, nod character." Specifically, investors do not appear to appreciate the role that analysts' recommendations play in attracting investment banking business to their firms, so that what "investors hear is not always what analysts mean." The issues described in the first part of chapter 18 came to the fore as the prices of technology stocks plummeted after March 2000. As stocks peaked in March 2000, nearly 73 percent of all analyst recommendations were "buy" and "strong buy." Notably, at year-end 2000, the percentage of recommendations that were "buy" was still above 70 percent. The contrast between recommendations and performance was stark enough to attract the attention of Congress as well as the attorney general for the State of New York, Eliott Spitzer.

In the course of investigating Merrill Lynch, Spitzer's office uncovered some interesting facts. At the same time that Merrill analysts were issuing buy recommendations for particular stocks to the public, within their firm they were describing these same stocks as "crap" in email messages to each other. In 2002, Merrill Lynch agreed to pay $100 million in order to settle a case brought against them by the attorney general. Spitzer's office was particularly interested in the analysts covering technology stocks, such as Merrill's Henry Blodget, and Morgan Stanley's Mary Meeker, who had been dubbed "the queen of the dot-coms."

On pages 266 and 267 of chapter 18, I provide an example that took place in 1997, involving the stock of chip manufacturer Intel to describe biases in analysts' earnings estimates. The Spring 2001 issue of *Financial Management* contains an article titled "Is the Response of Analysts to Information Consistent with Fundamental Valuation? The Case of Intel," by Brad Cornell. He analyzes the market reaction to a press release by Intel on Thursday, September 21, 2000. The press release indicated that Intel's expected revenue for its third quarter would grow between 3 percent and 5 percent, not the 8–12 percent that analysts had been projecting. In response to news that was less than earth shattering, Intel's stock price dropped by 30 percent over the next five days! Intel's chairman, Craig Barrett, commented on the reaction, stating: "I don't know what you call it but an overreaction and the market feeding on itself."

One of the most interesting findings in Brad Cornell's analysis is that of the 28 analyst reports on Intel that he examined, not a single one contained a discounted cash flow model from which to infer fundamental value. Yet, in the week following Intel's press release, many analysts lowered their recommendations on the stock.

If analysts do not rely on discounted cash flow analysis to gauge whether a stock is fairly priced, what do they use? On pages 81–83, I discuss the heuristic "good stocks are stocks of good companies." In line with this heuristic, Cornell suggests that analysts rate the company instead of the investment; that is, they react to bad news in the same way that a bond-rating agency reacts to bad news by downgrading the firm's debt. In other words, analysts base their judgments on a heuristic that leaves them vulnerable to bias.

Chapter 14 provides an analysis of the behavioral elements that led to the Orange County, California, bankruptcy in 1994, the largest municipal bankruptcy in history. In December 2001 Enron, the seventh largest firm in the United States, filed for bankruptcy protection. Here too, behavioral elements were paramount. Enron management, apparently overconfident from its success in the natural gas business in the early 1990s, sought to repeat that success in markets where they lacked expertise. Enron invested more than $10 billion in ventures that produced a near-zero return. As a result, Enron returned less than its cost of capital to investors, thereby destroying shareholder value. Moreover, Enron executives employed an opaque framing strategy, obscuring the financial implications of their investments through the use of limited partnerships that were off-balance sheet items.

Enron's bankruptcy triggered widespread concern among investors about whether they could trust the information conveyed in corporate financial statements. Indeed in 2002, the entire accounting profession found itself in a crisis about the extent to which auditors permit firms to engage in opaque framing. Even worse, employees at Arthur Andersen, the accounting firm that audited Enron, had engaged in major modification and shredding of documents related to Enron. The U.S. Department of Justice filed suit, and a jury found the accounting firm guilty of obstructing justice. Arthur Andersen had also audited the financial statements for WorldCom, whose chief financial officer improperly booked $3.8 billion in expenses as capital expenditures, a maneuver that enabled the firm to report positive earnings in 2001 rather than a loss.

The issue of opaque accounting became a dominant theme in 2002. Although required by law to file financial statements with the Securities and Exchange Commission (SEC) that conform to Generally Accepted Accounting Principles (GAAP), many firms use different definitions of earnings for their news releases and forecasts than the GAAP-definition. The alternative definitions are known as "pro forma" earnings, to mark their "as if" nature. Typically, pro forma earnings only pertain to a subset of line items, mostly relating to operations, and exclude items such as restructuring charges. As a result, pro forma earnings often appear to be more favorable than GAAP earnings. More important there is no uniform definition of what pro forma earnings entail. The definition of pro forma earnings varies from firm to firm, thereby allowing firms to engage in opaque framing, if they wish. Interestingly, analysts forecast and track pro forma earnings. Notably, the focus of First Call's reports is pro forma earnings, not GAAP earnings. In an effort to make earnings more transparent, the SEC has been engaged in a major effort to prevent firms from using the pro forma definition in their news releases and forecasts.

New Research in Behavioral Finance

Having to send *Beyond Greed and Fear* off to press in the midst of a stock market bubble felt like turning in a mystery novel without the last chapter. Of course, psychological factors are always at work, but the last few years do seem to have been an extraordinary period in underscoring just how important psychological factors can be. In the remainder of the preface, I continue to discuss new developments in the context of existing chapters. However, instead of focusing on recent events, the updates will focus on recent contributions by academic scholars.

Part III of the book consists of three chapters about individual investors. Framing transparency is an issue of critical importance to individual investors, whose ability to process information is limited. Recent unpublished research identifies key factors that determine which stocks individual investors buy. (A copy of this study and other unpublished studies cited in this preface can be found at the authors' websites or downloaded from the Social Science Research Network—SSRN.) The study, entitled "All That Glitters: The Effect of Attention and News on the Buying Behavior of Individual and Institutional Investors," is by Brad Barber and Terrance Odean. Their study points to three indicators of attention: recent news, recent extreme price movements, and recent excess trading volume. In related work, Dong Hong and Alok Kumar ask a question that forms the title of their working paper: "What Induces Noise Trading Around Public Announcement Events?" Hong and Kumar suggest that at an aggregate level, investors exhibit a contrarian volume reaction that is primarily driven by price trends.

Odean and Barber tell us that companies that are in the news grab the attention of individual investors. And as I mentioned in the previous section, when the news about these companies pertains to earnings, the news tends to be framed in terms of opaquely defined pro forma earnings, rather than GAAP earnings. This is not to say that the evidence supports the idea that individual investors have the sophistication to make use of accounting information, even when it is transparently framed. Indeed, the evidence strongly supports the opposite contention: investors rely on very crude valuation heuristics rather than on fundamental analysis. As noted above in respect to Intel, even financial analysts schooled in fundamental analysis rely on heuristics!

Chapter 10 describes earlier work by Barber and Odean, whose research program offers some of the best evidence about the behavior of individual traders. Their new work has greatly added to our understanding. Consider the section "The Online Revolution" (pages 133–134), that discusses the impact on individual traders stemming from the Internet, overconfidence and the illusion of control. When I wrote this section, Barber and Odean had not yet written "Online Investors: Do the Slow Die First?" (*Review of Financial Studies*, 2002). Barber and Odean provide a fascinating account of the advertising strategies used by online trading firms in order to induce investors to trade online. These strategies appealed to a combination of overconfidence and the desire for control. Not all traders choose to trade online. Barber and Odean find that investors who chose to go online had experienced above average returns prior to going online, outperforming the market by 2 percent. Was the above average performance of online investors due to skill or luck? If it were due to skill, these investors would be expected to continue to outperform the market after going online. However, Barber and Odean find just the opposite. After going online, these investors traded more actively, took on more risk, and traded less profitably than they did prior to going online. They wound up underperforming the market by 3 percent.

Barber and Odean have also added to the findings about investment club performance described on page 131. In "Too Many Cooks Spoil the Profits: Investment Club Performance" (*Financial Analysts Journal*, 2000), they document that in the aggregate, investor clubs underperform not only the market, but also individual investors. Interestingly, investment club performance is related to gender. Brooke Harrington documents that clubs composed of a mix of women and men outperform clubs composed of only women or only men. Her paper is entitled "'Popular Finance' and the Sociology of Investing."

Do investors understand what they are doing? Do they think they have chosen well for themselves? In a study entitled "How Much Is Investor Autonomy Worth?" Shlomo Benartzi and Richard Thaler presented individuals saving for retirement with information about the distribution of outcomes they could expect from the portfolios they picked and also the median portfolio selected by their peers. Benartzi and Thaler found that a majority of their survey participants actually preferred the median portfolio to the one they picked for themselves.

In a separate article, "Excessive Extrapolation and the Allocation of 401(k) Accounts to Company Stock," (*Journal of Finance*, 2001), Benartzi analyzes the portion of 401(k) portfolios that employees devote to company stock. He identifies some of the major reasons why, in the aggregate, employees concentrate roughly a third of their portfolios in the stocks of the company for which they work. Specifically, Benartzi finds that employees purchase company stock after it has already gone up, effectively succumbing to extrapolation bias. He also suggests that employees treat the matching funds from a company, that are automatically invested in company stock, as an endorsement, that the automatic investment leads employees to hold an even larger share of company stock than they would have otherwise.

On page 26 I introduce the notion of mental accounting, and in chapter 10, on page 125, I discuss how the concept of mental accounting applies to portfolio choice. Two recent articles extend the ideas developed in this chapter. The first is "Behavioral Portfolio Theory" (*Journal of Financial and Quantitative Analysis*, 2000), by Meir Statman and me. The second is "Mental Accounting, Loss Aversion, and Individual Stock Returns" (*Journal of Finance*, 2001) by Nicholas Barberis and Ming Huang. Barberis has several recent pieces that are relevant to this discussion. In "Investing for the Long Run When Returns Are Predictable" (*Journal of Finance*, 2000), he analyzes what investors need to consider about the proportions of their portfolios to hold in stocks, given the limits of our understanding about the drivers of returns. In "Style Investing" (*Journal of Financial Economics*, 2002), he and co-author Andrei Shleifer analyze the ramications stemming from investors' tendency to categorize investments into groups, such as growth and value.

Chapter 9 is devoted to the disposition effect, especially "get-even-itis," the tendency to gamble by holding onto losers too long. On page 24, I mention the case of Nicholas Leeson, who lost Barings Bank over $1.4 billion because he could not come to terms with a loss and engaged in highly speculative currency trading in an attempt to get even. In February 2002, the *Wall Street Journal* reported the largest currency trading scandal since the case of Nicholas Leeson. One John Rusnak, a trader at Allied Irish Banks PLC, lost his firm $691 million, in an attempt to get even. The way to deal with get-even-it is to employ stop-loss orders, either explicitly or through a self-imposed rule. Apparently, neither Leeson nor Rusnak learned the lesson.

The behavioral elements that influence investment decisions are hardly unique to Americans. In an article entitled "What Makes Investors Trade?" (*Journal of Finance*, 2001), Mark Grinblatt and Matti Keloharju use data from the Finnish Central Securities Depository to analyze the behavior of Finnish traders. Grinblatt and Keloharju find strong evidence of get-evenitis. They differentiate between an extreme loss (in excess of 30 percent) and a moderate loss. Grinblatt and Keloharju report that an extreme capital loss makes it 32 percent less likely that an investor will sell a stock, whereas a moderate capital loss makes such a sale 21 percent less likely. The discussion in chapter 9 explains that this phenomenon reverses itself in December. Grinblatt and Keloharju report that in December, investors are 36 percent more likely to sell extreme losers than they are in the rest of the year. Interestingly, investors wait for the last eight trading days to sell extreme losers, almost the last minute.

On page 34 readers will find a section entitled "The Failure to Diversify." On pages 132–133, I describe the results in a working paper by Brad Barber and Terrance Odean, a paper that has now been published as "Trading Is Hazardous to Your Health: The Common Stock Investment Performance of Individual Investors" (*Journal of Finance*, 2000). Barber and Odean report that in their sample of 78,000 households with accounts at a major discount broker, the median number of stocks held was between 2 and 3.

One of the most striking findings in the Barber-Odean study involves the percentage of investors who managed to beat the market. When I ask people to guess what fraction of individual investors beat the market, the typical response lies between 5 percent and 20 percent. Barber and Odean find that 49.3 percent of investors beat the market before trading costs, and 43.4 percent beat the market after trading costs. This fact astonishes people, because they connect performance to skill. However, the market return serves to average the returns to all stocks; hence, half of stocks beat the market. And the average individual investor only holds 2 or 3 stocks. Lack of diversification leads about half of investors to beat the market before trading costs. At the same time, this lack of diversification produces a very wide range in performance, from –95 percent to over 11,000 percent, measured on annual basis.

The Barber-Odean study pertained to January 1991 through December 1996. Recent research by William Goetzmann and Alok Kumar documents that although investors have made some progress on this dimension, they continue to hold portfolios that fall far short of being well diversified. Their working paper is entitled "Equity Portfolio Diversification."

Chapter 11 describes the behavioral factors that influence retirement saving and spending. As I say on page 139, "investors need to overcome myopia and exercise self-control in order to save for retirement." On page 141, I indicate that most Americans have not been able to save adequately. A 2000 working paper by David Wise and Steven Venti, entitled "Choice, Chance, and Wealth Dispersion at Retirement," provides evidence that the dominant factor that determines the wealth households possess at retirement is their past saving rate. In the aggregate, the rate at which households save over their lifetimes is more important than the size of their medical bills, the impact of inheritances, and whether they have invested conservatively or aggressively over their lifetimes.

One of the most important recent developments in regard to retirement saving is a program developed by Richard Thaler and Shlomo Benartzi, called "Save for Tomorrow" (SMT). In January 2002, the *Wall Street Journal* and *New York Times* ran stories describing the program. In their paper, "Save More Tomorrow: Using Behavioral Economics to Increase Employee Saving," Thaler and Benartzi describe the characteristics of their plan, along with preliminary results.

The SMT plan has four ingredients, all designed to deal with issues identified in the behavioral literature. First, because people tend to accord future unpleasantness much less weight than immediate unpleasantness, employees are approached about increasing their contribution rates a considerable time before they begin to participate. Second, people hate situations where they perceive themselves as incurring losses. Consider the challenge of how to frame matters so that employees do not perceive a loss in their take-home pay. Thaler and Benartzi suggest that if employees join SMT, their contribution to the plan should begin with the first paycheck after a raise. Third, the contribution rate continues to increase on each scheduled pay raise until it reaches a preset maximum. In this way, inertia and status quo bias work toward keeping people in the plan. Fourth, the employee can opt out of the plan at any time.

Thaler and Benartzi report that the first implementation of the SMT plan took place in 1998 at a midsized manufacturing company. Prior to adoption, the company suffered from low participation rates as well as low saving rates. Thaler and Benartzi report three findings about the post-adoption period. First, 78 percent of those who were offered the SMT plan elected to use it. Second, 98 percent of those who joined remained in the plan through two pay raises, and 80 percent remained in the plan through the third pay raise. Third, the average saving rates for SMT plan participants increased from 3.5 percent to 11.6 percent over the course of 28 months. Thaler and Benartzi are in the process of applying the lessons of their successful pilot study to other firms.

Thaler and Benartizi constructed their SMT plan with great care. To be sure, automatic enrollment in 401(k) plans does not guarantee that employees will save more. This finding is described in the working paper entitled "For Better or For Worse: Default Effects and 401(k) Savings Behavior" by James Choi, David Laibson, Brigitte Madrian, and Andrew Metrick. These authors find that employees participants tend to become anchored at low default savings rates and in conservative default investment vehicles.

Chapter 12 describes how investment companies strategically use opaque framing in their interactions with investors. On page 171, I describe the game of opaque fees. In this regard, Brad Barber, Terry Odean and Lu Zheng have written a paper entitled "Out of Sight, Out of Mind: The Effects of Expenses on Mutual Fund Flows." The main point of the paper is that that mutual fund investors are more sensitive to salient in-your-face fees, such as loads and commissions, than they are to operating expenses. The authors document a negative relationship between fund flows and load fees, between fund flows and commissions charged by brokerage firms, but not between operating expenses and fund flows.

One of the most interesting applications of the ideas in chapter 12 involves the Masters 100 Fund run by well-known fund manager Ken Kam at Marketocracy. Ken Kam's strategy is based on the Olympic coins framework (gold, silver, and bronze), which I describe on pages 161–165. In that framework, the coins are weighted and represent intrinsic ability. Those who toss gold coins have more intrinsic skill than those who toss silver coins or bronze coins. Heads represents success. However, luck also plays a role—through luck alone, someone tossing a bronze coin may still toss a long sequence of heads. In chapter 12, I describe the odds of being able to filter out skill on the basis of past performance.

Marketocracy invites people to manage fictitious portfolios over the web and chooses the top 100 to manage real money—hence the name Masters 100 Fund. More than 50,000 people have signed up at the Marketocracy website to try their hand. Hence the sample is very large. Ken Kam argues that by selecting the top 100 performers from a universe of over 50,000, the odds favor Marketocracy being able to filter out investors whose success stems from superior skill or information rather than luck. The Masters 100 Fund was introduced in November 2001 and beat the S&P 500 by about 2 percent over the next two months. For the first five months of 2002 the fund was up by 7.5 percent. In contrast, the S&P 500 was down 6.5 percent in the same period, and the Wilshire 5000 was down 4.3 percent. Notably, the fund appears to be no more volatile than the S&P 500 or the Wilshire 5000. The *Wall Street Journal* ranked the fund as the top-performing fund among multi-cap core funds.

Chapter 15 describes issues involving the money management industry. I present a case, based on the experience of my own university, which is advised by the consulting firm Cambridge Associates. After *Beyond Greed and Fear* was published, I received a letter and Cambridge research paper from Ian Kennedy, Director of Research at Cambridge Associates. He writes in the hope of persuading me that "we are not entirely unenlightened on the issue of value-added by active management! I should add, however, that this paper, distributed to all our clients, has made no perceptible dent in the manager selection practices of the investment committees we work with. Because they are generally composed of very successful, intelligent people, they just *know* that they can identify superior active managers. At Cambridge Associates, we have a lively, running debate as to whether *anyone* could pick managers that would beat 'the market,' net of fees, over any extended period of time (e.g., ten years or more), and how one might reasonably go about trying to do so. I'm in the camp that thinks it *might* be possible, but is extremely difficult—and that the usual approach of the typical investment committee is absolutely doomed to failure (unless they just happen to get lucky.)"

The behavior of investment committees is a new area for researchers. John Payne and Arnold Wood have report the findings of a survey they conducted of investment committee members in a working paper "Optimizing Investment Committee Decision Making." The general behavioral decision literature documents that groups are effective when dealing with intellectual tasks where there is a correct answer, but are less effective when dealing with judgmental tasks where there is no objectively correct answer. Against this backdrop, Payne and

Wood find that investment committees report that they deal more frequently with judgmental tasks than tasks involving a correct answer, and that they feel being confident in their decisions. On average, they indicate that the probability of making a correct decision is 73 percent, a finding that is consistent with Ian Kennedy's remarks quoted in the previous paragraph.

I have intentionally left for the end updates to chapter 7, "Picking Stocks to Beat the Market" and chapter 8, "Biased Reactions to Earnings Announcements." I feel that academics and practitioners pay far too much attention to beating the market, and in consequence discount, or even overlook, the most important behavioral lessons discussed above.

I began chapter 7 by making clear that some people do consistently beat the market. In this respect, I mentioned the *Wall Street Journal's* contest that pitted the "pros" against the "darts." The newspaper terminated the contest in 2002, after more than a decade of operation. Over the contest period, the average annual return for the pros' stock picks was 10.2 percent, roundly trouncing the darts' return of 3.5 percent and the Dow Jones Industrial Average that returned 5.5 percent. Another example I mention on page 70 involves the stocks recommended on the television program "Louis Rukeyser's Wall Street," the continuation of "Wall $treet Week With Louis Rukeyser."

In chapter 7, I present evidence collected by Zacks that on average, stocks recommended by brokerage firms beat the S&P 500. At the same time, on pages 78–80 and 89, I indicated that the margin of outperformance was modest, and that the odds of picking a brokerage firm whose recommendations would outperform the market were no better than tossing a fair coin. These conclusions are reinforced in an article entitled "Can Investors Profit from the Prophets? Security Analyst Recommendations and Stock Returns," by Brad Barber, Reuven Lehavy, Maureen McNichols, and Brett Trueman (*Journal of Finance*, 2001).

Chapters 7 and 8 discuss what are called predictable patterns in individual stock returns. Most financial economists agree that stock returns exhibit momentum in the short term and reversals in the long term. However, there is disagreement as to whether or not this pattern signifies mispricing. Proponents of behavioral finance assert that it does signify mispricing, and proponents of market efficiency assert that it does not. Moreover, among proponents of behavioral finance there is a debate. Some argue that momentum stems from underreaction, while others argue that momentum stems from overreaction.

Since the book was published, Narasimhan Jegadeesh and Sheridan Titman have updated their pioneering 1993 study of momentum.

In "Profitability of Momentum Strategies: An Evaluation of Alternative Explanations" (*Journal of Finance*, 2001), they find that the conclusions of their earlier study remained robust in the post-sample period.

In "Price Momentum and Trading Volume" (*Journal of Finance*, 1999), Charles Lee and Bhaskaran Swaminathan provide additional insights. They suggest that in order to exploit a momentum-based strategy more effectively, investors should take trading volume into account. Specifically, investors should buy high-volume winners and short sell high-volume losers. They note that investors would have lost money by focusing on the low volume losers: historically, low volume losers have rebounded.

Mark Grinblatt and Bing Han have an intriguing paper entitled "The Disposition Effect and Momentum" (2001). They argue that momentum stems from the disposition effect, rather than underreaction or overreaction.

Momentum arises in many contexts. Consider stock splits. In an article entitled "What Do Stock Splits Really Signal?" (*Journal of Financial and Quantitative Analysis*, 1996), David Ikenberry, Graeme Rankine, and Earl Stice document that there is also positive drift associated with stock splits. They find that firms that split their stocks earn an average abnormal return of 7.93 percent in the first year, and 12.15 percent in the first three years. The three-year effect seems to be concentrated in value stocks. For growth stocks, the effect does not extend beyond the first year. In subsequent work, David Ikenberry and Sundaresh Ramnath demonstrate that firms who decide to split their stocks tend to be those for whom coverage by analysts in respect to earnings forecasts has been pessimistic. Their article is entitled "Underreaction to Self-selected News Events: The Case of Stock Splits" (*Review of Financial Studies*, 2002). In addition, Ikenberry and Ramnath find that firms who announce stock splits are much less likely to experience a decline in future earnings, relative to firms with comparable characteristics.

Researchers are also studying other securities to see whether the same issues occur there. In "The Long-Run Stock Returns Following Bond Ratings Changes" (*Journal of Finance*, 2001), Ilia Dichev and Joseph Piotrosdki find negative abnormal stock returns of between 10 and 14 percent in the first year following downgrades of corporate debt. They conclude that this effect stems from underreaction to the announcement of the downgrades, rather than from lower systematic risk.

In chapter 19, I argue that options markets also feature mispricing. In "Underreaction, Overreaction, and Increasing Misreaction to Information in the Options Market" (*Journal of Finance*, 2001), Allen Poteshman finds that options traders exhibit short-horizon underreaction to daily information, but long-horizon overreaction to extended periods of mostly similar daily information. Moreover, these misreactions increase as a function of the quantity of previous information that is similar.

For some years now, those who trade options and those who study options markets have realized that the traditional theory, based on Black-Scholes pricing, does not apply. One of the first articles to document the phenomenon is "Riding on a Smile" (*Risk*, 1994), by Emanuel Derman and Iraj Kani. The "smile" refers to the shape of the graph that plots "implied volatility" against exercise price for options having the same expiration date. Were options priced in accordance with the Black-Scholes formula, that graph would appear as a horizontal line, rather than something resembling a smile or a smirk. I propose a behavioral explanation for the smile effect in "Irrational Exuberance and Option Smiles" (*Financial Analysts Journal*, 1999). After my article appeared in print, I received a supportive message from Emanuel Derman, who heads the quantitative strategies group at Goldman Sachs, and whose work I cite above. He had read my article, and sent me a copy of his own current presentation on smiles, aptly titled "Fear and Greed in Volatility Markets."

Historically, U.S. stocks have exhibited momentum at short horizons and reversals at long horizons. These phenomena are not exclusively American. In "Contrarian and Momentum Strategies in Germany" (*Financial Analysts Journal*, 1999), Dirk Schiereck, Werner De Bondt, and Martin Weber establish that the same phenomenon has occurred for stocks that trade in Germany on the Frankfurt exchange.

The key question that investors want to know is how to use behavioral finance to pick stocks in order to beat the market. As I reminded readers at the beginning of this preface, the task is not easy. Louis Chan, Narasimhan Jegadeesh, and Josef Lakonishok, in "The Profitability of Momentum Strategies" (*Financial Analysts Journal*, 1999), point out that chasing momentum can generate high turnover and requires a strategy that focuses on managing trading costs.

On page 99 in chapter 8 I described the performance of Fuller & Thaler's Behavioral Growth fund. This fund effectively seeks to exploit momentum associated with delayed reactions to earnings surprises. Figure 8–2 shows the strong performance the strategy experienced since its inception in 1992. What has happened in the subsequent three years, since this book went to press?

For the full year of 1999, the return to Behavioral Growth was 65 percent, a full 10 percent above its benchmark index, the Russell 2500

Growth Index. The years 2000 and 2001 were very different, and Behavioral Growth underperformed its benchmark by about 10 percent in both of those years. From inception through March 31, 2002, Behavioral Growth has returned 6.6 percent per year, with the Russell 2500 having returned 3.9 percent over the same period.

According to proponents of behavioral finance, long-term reversals are a reflection of investor overreaction. In 1998 Fuller & Thaler began the Behavioral Value fund, to exploit long-term reversals. This fund is benchmarked against the Russell 2000 Value Index. From inception through March 31, 2002, the fund has returned 21.8 percent annually, and its benchmark has returned 14.7 percent. Notably, Behavioral Value underperformed its benchmark in both 2000 and 2001, as had Behavioral Growth.

On pages 70 and 81, I mention David Dreman, one of the most prominent spokesman for value investing. For the ten-year period ending in April 30, 2002, Dreman's largest fund, the Scudder-Dreman High Return Equity Fund, earned 15.94 percent. Notably in 1999, during the evolution of the Nasdaq bubble, the fund lost 13 percent of its value. In 2000, when the bubble collapsed, the fund gained 41 percent, and in 2001 it gained 1 percent. Over the most recent three-year period, the cumulative return has been 7.26 percent.

On pages 86 and 87, I discuss work by Josef Lakonishok, Andrei Shleifer, and Robert Vishny, work that has come to be known by the initials of the three authors—LSV. The three run a money management firm, LSV Asset Management. Their Large-Cap Value Fund is benchmarked against the Russell 1000. Since inception in 1994, the fund has returned 18.5 percent on an annual basis, before fees. In contrast, during this period, the Russell 1000 returned 14.8 percent, and the S&P 500 returned 14.6 percent. Except for 1998 and 1999, the LSV Large-Cap Value Fund has outperformed both indexes every year. In the three-year period ending March 31, 2002, the fund outperformed the S&P 500 by 13.7 percent. For the prior twelve-month period, the fund outperformed the S&P 500 by 14.9 percent.

In July 1998, Theo Vermaelen began to manage a fund for Belgian bank KBC, based on a behavioral strategy. The fund is called KBC Equity Buyback. Together with David Ikenberry and Josef Lakonishok, he wrote an article entitled "Market Underreaction to Open Market Share Repurchases" (*Journal of Financial Economics*, 1995), in which the authors argue that investors underreact when companies repurchase shares. Interestingly, corporate managers often announce that they are repurchasing shares because they think the shares of their firms are undervalued. The authors quote the chairman of Midland Resources, Inc, an American-based oil and gas concern, who said: "If you look at the amount of our reserves, we think (our stock) should be trading for about twice its current value. What it boils down to is, if you can buy a dollar for 50 cents, why not buy it?"

Ikenberry, Lakonishok, and Vermaelen found that when a company announced a share repurchase, on average it saw its stock go up by an average of 3.5 percent. However, the market underreacted in that the 3.5 percent run-up was too small, especially if the stock was a value stock. Over the next four years value stocks rose by 45.3 percent more than comparable firms that had not repurchased shares.

Vermaelen's buyback fund invests in value stocks, taking a position when managers announce share buybacks, claiming their stock is undervalued. At year-end 2001, the KBC Equity Buyback fund was up 36.7 percent. Theo Vermaelen tells me that in its first two years, his fund beat the S&P 500 by 35 percent and the Russell 2000 by more that 45 percent.

In academia debates about momentum and reversals continue. For example, in "Momentum and Autocorrelation in Stock Returns," Jonathan Lewellen argues that the momentum effect does not stem from underreaction (*Review of Financial Studies*, 2002), although the discussants of his paper, Joseph Chen and Harrison Hong claim to be unconvinced. Alon Brav and J.B. Heaton, in "Competing Theories of Financial Anomalies" (*Review of Financial Studies*, 2002), argue that it is difficult to discriminate between behaviorally based theories such as the De Bondt-Thaler overreaction effect, and rationality-based theories that account for the risk of structural change. Their discussant, Werner De Bondt, challenges their test, and counters that there is overwhelming evidence that many investors fail to infer the most basic investing principles, even after years of experience. In this respect, he cites his own work, which I discuss on pages 131–132.

Werner De Bondt has a point. One of the fundamental principles of finance is that risk and return are positively correlated, that if investors are to accept more risk, they will insist on higher expected returns. This principle is manifest in the core concepts of the *capital market line* and the *security market line*. The capital market line indicates the maximum expected return associated with any given return standard deviation, while the security market line indicates how the expected return to a security varies with its beta. Both of these graphs feature a positive slope, meaning that the higher the risk the higher the expected return.

On page 84, I report that even though investors may state that in principle, risk and expected return are positively related, in practice they form judgments in which the two are negatively related. In my editorial comment "Do Investors Expect Higher Returns from Safer Stocks than from Riskier Stocks?" (*Journal of Psychology and Financial Markets*, 2001), I provide additional evidence for this claim, based on surveys conducted with portfolio managers and analysts.

My survey results also show that investors attribute high expected returns and low perceived risk to the stocks of firms that are high in both market cap (size) and price-to-book (growth). In this regard, work by Gregory Brown and Michael Cliff provides evidence that stocks associated with high degrees of investor sentiment subsequently earn low returns at horizons of two to three years. Their paper is entitled "Investor Sentiment and Asset Prices."

After my editorial appeared on the Social Science Research Network (FEN), I received several messages from economists who also noted the negative correlation between expected returns and perceived risk. John Graham emailed me in connection with his own recent paper, written with Campbell Harvey, entitled "Expectations of Equity Risk Premia, Volatility and Asymmetry from a Corporate Finance Perspective." Graham and Harvey conducted a large survey of chief financial officers and found that the relationship between the CFOs' one-year expected risk premiums and their perceptions of expected risk is negative, not positive as traditional theory indicates.

Scott Smart, who teaches behavioral finance at Indiana University emailed with the following message: "I saw your paper arguing that people believe there is a negative relationship between risk and return on FEN recently. I thought you might like to hear a related story. Each year in my behavioral finance class, teams of students have to come up with a project to test some idea from behavioral finance. Last year a team did a survey of professors in different schools (business, law, music, and A&S) asking them various questions about their investments. One unexpected (to me) finding was that across every school in the university, the correlation between how risky people thought an investment was and how high they thought the return on the investment would be was negative. That relationship was true even in the business school, except for faculty in two departments . . . accounting and finance." On the basis of Scott Smart's observations, it is safe to conclude that finance and accounting faculty are adept at modeling their own judgments. As for modeling the judgments of others, that is a different matter.

Behavioral finance appears to be exploding. Academics will continue to write survey papers describing the evolution of behavioral finance. Indeed, in the last three years, several excellent surveys have actually appeared. Meir Statman wrote a thought-provoking piece entitled "Behavioral Finance: Past Battles, Future Engagements" (*Financial Analysts Journal*, 1999). David Hirshleifer surveyed the psychology literature that he judges to be especially relevant for financial economists; his article is entitled "Investor Psychology and Asset Pricing" (*Journal of Finance*, 2001). Nicholas Barberis and Richard Thaler wrote "A Survey of Behavioral Finance," which was commissioned for the *Handbook of the Economics of Finance*. Finally, let me mention an editorial that argues the case for the traditional perspective. Its author is Mark Rubinstein, and his editorial is entitled "Rational Markets: Yes or No? The Affirmative Case" (*Financial Analysts Journal*, 2001). Rubinstein's editorial is based on a debate between himself and Richard Thaler that took place at a Berkeley Program in Finance Symposium in November 2000.

Future Directions

What comes next? At the moment, great strides are being made in the application of behavioral concepts to corporate finance. I described some of the key issues in a recent article "Behavioral Corporate Finance" (*Journal of Applied Corporate Finance*, 2001). John Graham and Campbell Harvey have begun a research program that will prove to be of immense value. They are conducting widespread surveys of chief financial officers (CFOs) in order to determine the factors that the CFOs take into account when making decisions about capital budgeting, capital structure, the cost of capital, dividend policy, and the equity premium. Some of their findings are published in "The Theory and Practice of Corporate Finance: Evidence from the Field" (*Journal of Financial Economics*, 2001). Graham and Harvey report additional findings in their working paper, mentioned earlier, "Expectations of Equity Risk Premia, Volatility and Asymmetry from a Corporate Finance Perspective."

Chapter 17, on IPO pricing, is based on insights from the work of Tim Loughran and Jay Ritter. In "Why Don't Issuers Get Upset About Leaving Money on the Table in IPOs?" (*Review of Financial Studies*, 2002), Loughran and Ritter continue their research program on equity offerings. In their article, they provide a formal analysis to explain why corporate executives are willing to accept initial underpricing. The issue is one that I have treated informally on page 249, and deals with the difference between "in-the-pocket gains" and "opportunity losses."

Jeremy Stein laid the groundwork for a behavioral framework of corporate financial decisions, in "Rational Capital Budgeting in an Irrational World" (*Journal of Business*, 1996). Building on the Stein framework, Malcolm Baker and Jeffrey Wurgler have written "Market Timing and Capital Structure" (*Journal of Finance*, 2002). Baker and Wurgler report that firms tend to issue new equity when their existing equity is most likely to be overpriced. Moreover, they find that temporary fluctuations in market valuations lead to permanent changes in capital structure.

Malcom Baker, Jeremy Stein, and Jeff Wurgler wrote a paper entitled "When Does the Market Matter? Stock Prices and the Investment of Equity-Dependent Firms." The three authors document that stock prices will have a stronger impact on the investment of firms that need external equity to finance their marginal investments, than those that do not.

Baker and Wurgler have also studied dividend policy. In their paper "A Catering Theory of Dividends," they suggest that firms cater to investors by initiating or increasing dividends when behavioral factors increase the attractiveness of cash dividends in the eyes of investors.

There are additional papers in behavioral finance that I have not mentioned that are part of the rapidly growing debate. Below are some examples to indicate the direction of future research. Michael Cooper, Roberto C. Gutierrez Jr., and Allaudeen Hameed report that that momentum profits exclusively follow market gains and that contrarian profits are stronger following market losses. Their working paper is entitled "Market States and the Profits to Momentum and Contrarian Strategies." David Hirshleifer, James Myers, Linda Myers, and Siew Hong Teoh ask: "Do individual investors drive post-earnings announcement drift?" The question forms the title of their paper, and the answer they provide is no.

Where is the behavioral finance headed? Richard Thaler suggests that the end point is for behavioral elements simply to become part and parcel of regular financial analysis. He calls this state of affairs the end of behavioral finance (*Financial Analysts Journal*, 1999). Judging by the volume of work described above, the end of behavioral finance may be fast approaching.

Acknowledgments

I would like to express my gratitude to many people for their help on this book. I especially thank Richard Thaler and Meir Statman, from whom I have gained a great deal over the years. In the mid-1970s, Dick Thaler introduced me to behavioral heuristics, biases, errors, and framing. In the early 1980s, Meir Statman joined me in a collaborative effort to apply behavioral concepts to finance. Both Dick and Meir provided very useful comments on earlier drafts of this book. I am also indebted to Phil Cooley, who suggested the idea behind this book, Kirsten Sandberg, my editor at Harvard Business Press who first published the book; Paul Donnelly, my editor at Oxford University Press, the current publisher; my colleagues at Santa Clara University, Mario Belotti, Alex Field, Harry Fong, Atulya Sarin, Jerry Shapiro, Barbara Stewart, Robert Warren; and my academic colleagues at other institutions, Mark Carhart, Werner De Bondt, Ken Froot, William Goetzmann, Robert Hansen, Daniel Kahneman, Charles Lee, Lola Lopes, Terry Odean, Jay Ritter, Richard Roll, Robert Shiller, Jon Skinner, Paul Slovic, Bhaskaran Swaminathan, Jacob Thomas, and Kent Womack. I thank as well a host of practitioners, including John Watson (Financial Engines); Cadmus Hicks, William Kehr, Steve Peterson, Andrew Schell, and Brad Shaw (Nuveen); Rick Chrabaszewski (Zacks); Georgette Jasen (Wall Street Journal); Rick Dubroff and Martha Gosnay, (Wall $treet Week with Louis Rukeyser); Louis Radovic and Kim Rupert (MMS); Bob Saltmarsh (Silicon Graphics, Inc.); Frank Tesoriero (New York Cotton Exchange); Rick Angell, Chris Bernard, Sheldon Natenberg, and Al Wilkinson (Chicago Board of Trade); Russ Fuller and Fred Stanske (Fuller and Thaler Asset Management); Doug Carlson (Cambridge Associates, Inc.); Yakoub Billawalla, Ken Kam, and Kevin Landis (Firsthand Funds); Stan Levine (First Call); Tisha Findeisen and Patricia Sendgsen (Vanguard); Diana MacDonald (Bridge Information Systems); James Davidson (Hambrecht & Quist); Florence Eng (I/B/E/S); John Ronstadt (PaineWebber); Allan Eustis (National Weather Service); the Dean Witter Foundation, especially Sal Gutierrez and Kip Witter. I am grateful to individuals Ira Scharfglass, Jayne Scharfglass, and my tireless research assistant Chitra Suriyanarayanan. I am indebted to Bridge Information Systems, I/B/E/S International, MMS, and Zacks for data used in this book.

My biggest debt of gratitude goes to my dear wife, Arna, who provided editorial advice along with years of encouragement, support, and examples that illustrate behavioral phenomena.

PART *I*

WHAT *IS* BEHAVIORAL FINANCE?

Chapter **1**

Introduction

*W*all *$treet Week with Louis Rukeyser* panelist Frank Cappiello once explained that because of a "change in psychology," but "no change in fundamentals," he altered his stance on the market from positive to neutral.[1] Cappiello has plenty of company. The popular financial press regularly quotes experts and gurus on market psychology. But what do these experts and gurus mean? The stock answer is, "greed and fear." Well, is that it? Is that all there is to market psychology?

Hardly. Our knowledge of market psychology now extends well beyond greed and fear. Over the last twenty-five years, psychologists have discovered two important facts. First, the primary emotions that determine risk-taking behavior are not greed and fear, but *hope* and fear, as psychologist Lola Lopes pointed out in 1987. Second, although to err is indeed human, financial practitioners of all types, from portfolio managers to corporate executives, make the same mistakes repeatedly. The cause of these errors is documented in an important collection edited by psychologists Daniel Kahneman, Paul Slovic, and the late Amos Tversky that was published in 1982.

Behavioral finance is the application of psychology to financial behavior—the behavior of practitioners. I have written this book about practitioners, for practitioners. Practitioners need to know that because of human nature, they make particular types of mistakes. Mistakes can be very costly. By reading this book, practitioners will learn to

- recognize their own mistakes and those of others;

- understand the reasons for mistakes; and

- avoid mistakes.

For many reasons, practitioners need to recognize others' mistakes as well as their own. For example, financial advisers will be more

3

effective at helping investors if they have a better grasp of investor psychology. There are deeper issues too. One investor's mistakes can become another investor's profits. But one investor's mistakes can also become another investor's risk! Thus, an investor ignores the mistakes of others at his or her own peril.

Who are practitioners? The term covers a wide range of people: portfolio managers, financial planners and advisers, investors, brokers, strategists, financial analysts, investment bankers, traders, and corporate executives. They all share the same psychological traits.

The Three Themes of Behavioral Finance

The proponents of behavioral finance, myself included, argue that a few psychological phenomena pervade the entire landscape of finance. To bring this point out clearly, I have organized these phenomena around three themes. What are the three themes? And how does behavioral finance treat them differently than traditional finance does?[2] The answers are arranged by theme. I begin the discussion of each theme with a defining question.

1. Do financial practitioners commit errors because they rely on rules of thumb? Behavioral finance answers yes, and traditional finance answers no. Behavioral finance recognizes that practitioners use rules of thumb called heuristics to process data. One example of a rule of thumb is: "Past performance is the best predictor of future performance, so invest in a mutual fund having the best five-year record." Now, rules of thumb are like back-of-the-envelope calculations—they are generally imperfect. Therefore, practitioners hold biased beliefs that predispose them to commit errors. For this reason, I assign the label heuristic-driven bias to the first behavioral theme. In contrast, traditional finance assumes that when processing data, practitioners use statistical tools appropriately and correctly.

2. Does form as well as substance influence practitioners? By form, I mean the description or *frame* of a decision problem. Behavioral finance postulates that in addition to objective considerations, practitioners' perceptions of risk and return are highly influenced by how decision problems are framed. For this reason, I assign the label *frame dependence* to the second behavioral theme. In contrast, traditional finance assumes *frame independence*, meaning that practitioners view all decisions through the transparent, objective lens of risk and return.

3. Do errors and decision frames affect the prices established in the market? Behavioral finance contends that heuristic-driven bias and framing effects cause market prices to deviate from fundamental values. I assign the label *inefficient markets* to the third theme. In contrast, traditional finance contends that markets are efficient. Efficiency means that the price of each security coincides with fundamental value, even if some practitioners suffer from heuristic-driven bias or frame dependence.[3]

Just How Pervasive Are Behavioral Phenomena?

Behavioral phenomena play an important role in the major areas of finance: portfolio theory, asset pricing, corporate finance, and the pricing of options. These areas correspond to works recognized for Nobel prizes in economics, for the development of financial economics. To date, two such Nobel prizes have been awarded, to five recipients, for their contributions in finance.

In 1990 Harry Markowitz, Merton Miller, and William Sharpe shared the first prize. The Nobel committee recognized Markowitz for having developed portfolio theory, Miller for laying the basis for the theory of corporate finance, and Sharpe for developing the capital asset pricing model. In 1997, the committee recognized Myron Scholes and Robert Merton for having developed option pricing theory. I have drawn on recent comments by all five Nobel laureates in order to make the connection between their work and the insights from behavioral finance.

Why Is Behavioral Finance Important for Practitioners?

Practitioners are prone to committing specific errors. Some are minor, and some are fatal. Behavioral finance can help practitioners recognize their own errors as well as the errors of others. Practitioners need to understand that both are important. Here is a game, called the "pick-a-number game" designed to bring out the point.

In April 1997 the *Financial Times* ran a contest suggested by economist Richard Thaler.[4] The paper announced that the contest winner would receive two British Airways round-trip "Club Class" tickets between London and either New York or Chicago. Readers were told to choose a whole number between 0 and 100. The winning entry would be the one closest to two-thirds of the average entry.

The *Financial Times* provided the following short example to help readers understand the contest: Suppose five people enter the contest and they choose 10, 20, 30, 40 and 50. In this case, the average is 30, two-thirds of which is 20. The person who chose to enter 20 would be the winner.

What is the point of this pick-a-number game? The point is that if you are playing to win, you need to understand how the other players are thinking. Suppose you think everyone who enters the contest will choose 20, since that is the winning choice in the example. In that case, you should choose the integer closest to two-thirds of 20, or 14.

But you might reflect on this for a moment, and wonder whether most other entrants would also be thinking along these lines, and therefore all be planning to choose 14. In that case, your best choice would be 10. And if you kept rethinking your choice, you would eventually come down to choosing 1.[5] And if everyone thinks along these lines, the winning entry will indeed be 1.

But in a group of normal, even well-educated, people, the winning entry will not be 1. In the *Financial Times* contest, with two transatlantic round-trip tickets at stake, the winning choice was 13.[6] If everyone chose a 1, then nobody would have made a mistake in his or her choice. But if 13 is the winning choice, then most people are making mistakes. The real point of this game is that playing sensibly requires you to have a sense of the magnitude of the other players' errors.

The pick-a-number game illustrates two of the three themes of behavioral finance. People commit errors in the course of making decisions; and these errors cause the prices of securities to be different from what they would have been in an error-free environment.

Paul Gompers and Andrew Metrick (1998) document that between 1980 and 1996, there was a marked increase in institutional ownership and concentration of equities. This shift magnifies the possible market impact of mistakes made by a small group of people. As the next example illustrates, practitioners ignore the moral from the pick-a-number game at their peril.

Consider the case of Long Term Capital Management (LTCM), a hedge fund that received considerable publicity during the second half of 1998. Three of the partners in LTCM are extremely well known—John Meriwether, who pioneered fixed-income arbitrage at Salomon Brothers, and Nobel laureates Myron Scholes and Robert Merton, mentioned earlier.[7] LTCM had generated spectacular after-fee returns between 1994 and 1997.[8] At year-end 1997, LTCM held more than $7 billion of capital.

But 1998 turned out to be disastrous, as LTCM watched its $7 billion shrink to $4 billion. In September of that year, the Federal Reserve Bank of New York felt the need to organize a privately funded rescue plan in which fourteen major banks and brokerage houses contributed a total of $3.6 billion in exchange for 90 percent of LTCM's equity. Clearly, something had gone terribly wrong.

In fact, many things had gone wrong, but the following example is particularly illuminating. LTCM had taken large positions in two companies, Royal Dutch Petroleum and Shell Transport and Trading, that jointly owned the entity Royal Dutch/Shell. The shares of Royal Dutch Petroleum and Shell Transport trade on both the London Stock Exchange and the New York Stock Exchange. In a recent case study, Kenneth Froot and Andre Perolt (1996) point out that a corporate charter linking these two companies divides the joint cash flow of Royal Dutch/Shell between them on a 60/40 basis. Presumably, this should lock the ratio at which the shares of the two companies trade. In theory, the market value of Royal Dutch should be 1.5 times as large as the market value of Shell Transport. But as with the pick-a-number game, actual prices typically depart from what they would be in an error-free environment.[9]

Interestingly, the shares of Shell Transport have traditionally traded not at parity but at an 18 percent discount relative to Royal Dutch. When the discount widened beyond 18 percent, LTCM did a "pairs" trade. They took a long position in Shell Transport and a corresponding short position in Royal Dutch, anticipating a short-term profit when the discount reverted to its traditional value. But LTCM encountered the same fate as someone who chose a 1 in the pick-a-number game. It wasn't a winning strategy. As *Business Week* reported in its November 9, 1998, issue (Spiro with Laderman), the discount widened rather than narrowed.

We are not done with Long-Term Capital Management. As we shall see in later chapters, the experiences of that particular hedge fund offer many illustrations of behavioral phenomena.

How Behavioral Finance Developed

Behavioral finance burgeoned when the advances made by psychologists came to the attention of economists. As noted, many of the behavioral concepts described in this volume can be found in Kahneman, Slovic, and Tversky's 1982 volume. These authors' works play a central role in the field of behavioral finance.

Slovic's work emphasizes misperceptions about risk. Early on, he saw the relevance of behavioral concepts for finance and discussed it in two articles. The first, pertaining to stockbrokers, appeared in the 1969 *Journal of Applied Psychology*. The other, pertaining to analysts and individual investors, was published in the 1972 *Journal of Finance.*

Amos Tversky and Daniel Kahneman published two articles that had a profound impact on finance. Their 1974 article in *Science* (Tversky and Kahneman) deals with heuristic-driven errors, while their 1979 article in *Econometrica* (Kahneman and Tversky) deals with frame dependence.

These last two articles strongly influenced both my work with Richard Thaler on self-control and savings behavior, and my work with Meir Statman on the "dividend puzzle." The article addressing the dividend puzzle, so dubbed by the late Fischer Black, was published by the *Journal of Financial Economics* in 1984. Because he saw the limitations of the traditional approach to finance, Black enthusiastically supported the development of behavioral finance. As president-elect of the American Finance Association, he chose to include a session on behavioral finance that I was fortunate to chair at the 1984 annual meeting.

In July 1985, the *Journal of Finance* published two of the papers presented at that session. One paper, by Werner De Bondt and Richard Thaler, applied Tversky and Kahneman's notion of representativeness to market pricing. De Bondt and Thaler argued that investors overreact to both bad news and good news. Therefore, overreaction leads past losers to become underpriced and past winners to become overpriced. The second paper, by Meir Statman and me, applied Kahneman and Tversky's notion of framing to the realization of losses. We called this phenomenon the *disposition effect*, arguing that investors are predisposed to holding losers too long and selling winners too early. These two papers defined two different avenues for looking at the implications of behavioral phenomena, with one stream focusing on security prices and the other on the behavior of investors.

In effect, the behavioral perspective brought an organized body of knowledge to bear on an approach to trading that had already been practiced for some time. De Bondt and Thaler's work is in the tradition of Benjamin Graham and David Dodd's notion of value investing, first described in their classic 1934 work, *Security Analysis*. In the late 1970s, money manager David Dreman became well known for advocating the price-to-earnings ratio (P/E) as a value measure.

In the 1980s, scholars began to discover a host of empirical results that were not consistent with the view that market returns were determined in accordance with the capital asset pricing model (CAPM) and efficient market theory. Proponents of traditional finance regarded these findings as anomalous, and thus called them *anomalies*. The anomalies started with size—e.g., the small-firm effect—and kept on coming. Soon we had the January effect, the weekend effect, and the holiday effect. As they discovered new anomalies, scholars began to wonder whether traditional finance was incapable of explaining what determines security prices.

The Reaction from Traditional Finance

Behavioral finance and traditional finance differ sharply in respect to the three themes. So how have the proponents of traditional finance reacted? Consider first the reaction to the concept of frame dependence. In 1985, a year after the appearance of my article with Meir Statman on the dividend puzzle, the University of Chicago sponsored a conference to discuss behavioral finance.

Nobel laureates Merton Miller and Franco Modigliani developed the traditional theory of dividends. At the Chicago conference, Miller discussed the Shefrin-Statman approach. He acknowledged that our approach might apply to his own Aunt Minnie—an interesting story perhaps, but one of many interesting stories. In fact, Miller argued, the stories were too interesting: they were distracting and diverted the attention of scholars away from the identifying the fundamental forces that drive markets. He repeated this point in the published proceedings of the conference (Miller 1986).

One of the chapters in this book deals with the behavioral biases that led to the Orange County bankruptcy—the largest municipal bankruptcy in U.S. history—and to subsequent lawsuits that involved Merrill Lynch and many others. Merrill Lynch retained Miller's services to assist them with their defense. In a 1997 article, Miller and coauthor David Ross argued that the bankruptcy was entirely avoidable. They may well be right. But the bankruptcy did happen—largely, I would argue, because of a series of behavioral biases. And this leads me to suggest that these biases are not too distracting, at least if our purpose is to understand major events in financial markets.

Indeed, as I hope to make clear in this book through the use of numerous stories, behavioral phenomena are both ubiquitous and germane: ubiquitous because you will find them wherever people are making financial decisions; germane because heuristic-driven bias and framing effects are very expensive.

In a 1987 survey of the literature on market efficiency, Robert Merton (1987b) began by reviewing a classic 1965 article by Paul

Samuelson. He then moved on to discuss the challenges presented by Robert Shiller's (1981) work on stock market volatility, the De Bondt–Thaler overreaction effect, and the Shefrin-Statman treatment of loss realization.[10] At that time, Merton wrote that the evidence against market efficiency was "premature." He pointed to technical difficulties with Shiller's framework, weak statistical effects in the De Bondt-Thaler study, and an apparent contradiction between the prescriptions of De Bondt-Thaler and those of Shefrin-Statman.[11]

Robert Merton may well have been right that in 1987 it was premature to reject market efficiency. Since 1987, however, scholars have done much work studying phenomena that involve volatility, overreaction, and loss realization, and they have resolved some of the issues Merton raised. For example, in a 1998 article Terrance Odean (1998a) confirms the Shefrin-Statman claims about realizing losers; and Odean's study of investment performance finds no contradiction with the De Bondt–Thaler effect.[12] Certainly, the experience of Long-Term Capital Management, where Merton has been extensively involved, suggests a move away from the firm conviction that markets are efficient. However, I hasten to add that rejecting market efficiency is not the same thing as having absorbed all the lessons of behavioral finance.

Still, some tenaciously cling to the belief that markets are efficient. Eugene Fama (1998b), who pioneered work on the efficient market hypothesis, has written a more recent survey of the challenges to market efficiency presented by behavioral finance. In 1998, he published a portion of his survey in a University of Chicago Graduate School of Business magazine. The title summarizes his view: "Efficiency Survives the Attack of the Anomalies" (Fama 1998a). In this connection, I have heard Fama describe behavioral finance as nothing more than "anomalies dredging."

Fama's remark about "anomalies dredging" raises two issues. The first, narrower issue, addressed in chapters 7 and 8, is whether markets are efficient. With respect to Fama's specific concerns about market inefficiency and behavioral finance, I suggest that the weight of the evidence favors the behavioral point of view. The second, broader issue is whether there is more to behavioral finance than just market inefficiency. In other words, would heuristic-driven bias and frame dependence be irrelevant if markets were efficient? This issue will be discussed throughout the book, with the caveat that neither practitioners nor scholars can afford to ignore heuristic-driven bias and frame dependence. The mistakes are too expensive.

Stories and Quotations

Merton Miller and I agree that there are many interesting stories in finance. We disagree about what to do with them. Miller argues that we should ignore stories because they draw attention away from fundamental forces. I argue that we should embrace stories because they provide insight into the psychological forces that impact financial decisions and prices.

In this book, I describe a small number of behavioral concepts and a large number of behavioral stories. The power of behavioral finance is such that a few key concepts underlie many different stories. These stories span a lot of territory and illustrate how heuristic-driven bias and frame dependence affect the following:

- Wall Street strategists as they predict the market
- security analysts as they recommend stocks
- portfolio managers as they pick stocks
- hedge fund managers as they trade currencies
- investment bankers as they take companies public
- individual investors as they save for retirement
- financial planners as they advise investors
- corporate executives as they take over other companies

Stories are illustrative—aids to help readers gain insight into behavioral finance. Note that I do not base general claims on stories. Rather, it is the other way around. The literature on behavioral finance contains studies documenting general phenomena; I have selected stories to illustrate the general findings.

I quote extensively in the stories, mostly from the popular press. Quotations offer important insights into the thought processes of practitioners, and therefore into the underlying psychology. What people say provides a window into how they think, and how they think lies at the heart of behavioral finance.

Plan of the Book

I have organized the book around themes and applications. The rest of part I—chapters 2, 3, and 4—presents the three themes that underlie behavioral finance: heuristic-driven bias, frame dependence, and inefficient prices, respectively.

I have organized the remainder of the book around specific applications. I devote part II to applications that feature predictions about the overall market, stock returns, and earnings. Most of these applications concern different forms of heuristic-driven bias and the effect of these errors on market efficiency.

Part III presents applications that involve individual investors, such as selling at a loss, portfolio selection, and retirement saving. These applications deal mostly with frame dependence and heuristic-driven bias.

The applications discussed in the remainder of the book involve all three themes. In part IV I focus on the relationship among the money management industry and the investors they serve. This part deals with institutional investors: open-ended mutual funds, closed-end mutual funds, the management of fixed income securities, and the tax-exempt money management industry.

In part V I look at corporate executives and their relationships with analysts and investors. I discuss these relationships in several contexts: corporate takeovers, initial public offerings, seasoned equity offerings, and analysts' earnings forecasts and stock recommendations. Part VI is devoted to special topics in investment: options, futures, and foreign exchange.

Parts II through VI follow a particular format. Each chapter begins with a short case that illustrates the main message of that chapter. Then, in the remainder of the chapter, I present the general findings from the behavioral finance literature, as typified by the case. The upside of this technique is that it makes the application of behavioral concepts to finance very easy to see. The downside of the technique is *hindsight bias,* a behavioral error. Someone susceptible to hindsight bias views events, after the fact, as being almost inevitable. In presenting these cases, by no means do I wish to suggest that they needed to turn out the way they did. Rather, they happened to do so.

What's Next?

I have arranged the topics in a particular order. Readers will thus find some advantage in reading the chapters consecutively; however, this should not deter those who want to follow a different order. I say this with one caveat. Since the next three chapters focus on main themes of behavioral finance—heuristic-driven bias, frame dependence, and inefficient markets—which constitute the core concepts in the book, I strongly suggest that readers complete these chapters before moving on to the applications. With that, let's take up the first theme.

Chapter 2

Heuristic-Driven Bias: The First Theme

*T*his chapter discusses the following:

- availability bias
- representativeness, grade point average, winners, and losers
- regression to the mean and stock market prediction
- gambler's fallacy and stock market prediction
- overconfidence and expert judgment
- anchoring-and-adjustment and earnings forecasts
- aversion to ambiguity

The dictionary definition for the word *heuristic* refers to the process by which people find things out for themselves, usually by trial and error. Trial and error often leads people to develop rules of thumb, but this process often leads to other errors. One of the great advances of behavioral psychology is the identification of the principles underlying these rules of thumb and the systematic errors associated with them. In turn, these rules of thumb have themselves come to be called *heuristics*.

An Illustrative Example

Consider this question: Which is the more frequent cause of death in the United States, homicide or stroke? How do most people go about answering this question? The majority rely on recall, that is, by seeing how many events of each type come readily to mind. If people more readily recall instances of homicide than of stroke, then they will answer "homicide." This simple rule conforms to the principle known as *availability*—the degree to which information is readily available. A rule based on this principle is called an *availability heuristic*.

Heuristics are like back-of-the-envelope calculations that sometimes come close to providing the right answer. But heuristics may involve *bias*, meaning they may tend to be off target in a particular direction, and this can apply to an availability heuristic also. Most people rely on the media for their information about homicides and strokes. Suppose that the media tends to report one cause of death more than the other, because one is newsworthy and the other is not. Then people who rely on an availability heuristic may recall instances related to one type of death more readily than the other. Therefore, media coverage biases a rule based on recall.

What about error? Which is the more frequent cause of death, homicide or stroke? The answer is stroke. In fact, strokes occur *eleven* times as often as homicides (Slovic, Fischoff, and Lichtenstein 1979). People who rely on an availability heuristic tend to be amazed by this fact.

Let's look at these steps from a broader perspective:

- People develop general principles as they find things out for themselves;

- They rely on heuristics, rules of thumb, to draw inferences from the information at their disposal;

- People are susceptible to particular errors because the heuristics they use are imperfect; and

- People actually commit errors in particular situations.

Taken together, these four statements define *heuristic-driven bias*.[1]

Representativeness

One of the most important principles affecting financial decisions is known as *representativeness*. Representativeness refers to judgments based on stereotypes. The principle of representativeness was proposed by psychologists Daniel Kahneman and Amos Tversky (1972), and analyzed in a series of papers reproduced in the collection edited by Kahneman, Slovic, and Tversky (1982).

Consider an example involving admissions officers in universities. One measure of successful admission decisions is that students who are admitted perform well scholastically. Therefore, imagine a situation where an admissions officer is attempting to predict the grade point average (GPA) of some prospective students based upon their high school GPA levels.

Here are some actual data for undergraduates at Santa Clara University, based on students who entered the university in the years 1990, 1991, and 1992.[2] During this period, the mean high school GPA of students who entered as freshmen and graduated was 3.44 (standard deviation was 0.36). The mean college GPA of those same students was 3.08 (standard deviation 0.40). Suppose you are given the task of predicting the graduating GPA for three undergraduate students, based solely on their high school GPA scores. The three high school GPA scores are 2.20, 3.00, and 3.80. What are your predictions for the college GPAs of these students upon graduation?

In administering this question to large groups, I have obtained very consistent mean responses. Table 2-1 contains the mean predictions along with the actual results. The average predictions for the question are 2.03, 2.77, and 3.46, whereas the actual results are 2.70, 2.93, and 3.30, respectively. Notice that at both the low end and the high end, the predictions are too far from the mean of 3.08. That is, both the low (2.20) and high (3.80) high school GPAs result in college GPAs that are much closer to the mean than the predictions. These responses illustrate that people do not appreciate the extent to which there is *regression to the mean.*

Representativeness is about reliance on stereotypes. The simplest example based on this principle is to predict that college GPA will be the same as high school GPA. Now most people do not use as simple a rule as this one. But they do base their predictions on how *representative* a student appears to be. Thus a student with a high GPA in high school

Table 2-1

Actual GPAs are closer to the mean than predicted GPAs.

High School GPA	Predicted College GPA	Actual College GPA
2.20	2.03	2.70
3.00	2.77	2.93
3.80	3.46	3.30

is seen as representative of a good student. Notice that they are especially hard on students with low high school GPAs. What most people fail to appreciate is that students with the lowest high school GPAs may have experienced bad luck, and consequently will, on average, do better in college.[3] So, the heuristic involves bias; representativeness can be misleading. Again, people fail to recognize regression to the mean. Therefore, they are predisposed to making errors when they predict the future GPA of particular individuals.

A financial example illustrating representativeness is the winner-loser effect documented by Werner De Bondt and Richard Thaler (1985, 1987). De Bondt and Thaler find that stocks that have been extreme past losers in the preceding three years do much better than extreme past winners over the subsequent three years. De Bondt (1992) shows that the long-term earnings forecasts made by security analysts tend to be biased in the direction of recent success. Specifically, analysts overreact in that they are much more optimistic about recent winners than they are about recent losers.

Do you recognize any similarities with the GPA question above? De Bondt and Thaler base their argument on the misapplication of representativeness. In effect, I suggest that investors treat past losers like high school students with low GPAs, and past winners as high school students with high GPAs. Notice that the predictions are particularly pessimistic when it comes to the low GPA students. People tend to predict that a student with a low high school GPA will end up with an even lower college GPA, indicative of a "kick 'em when they're down" perspective.[4] As we shall see in chapter 4, the same phenomenon also appears to be at work when it comes to stocks. The returns to past losers are exceptionally high, suggesting that investors become unduly pessimistic about the prospects of these stocks.

Before leaving representativeness, let us consider one more example showing that although financial professionals may recognize regression to the mean, they may not apply it properly. Below is an excerpt from an interview that appeared in the August 18, 1997 issue of *Fortune* magazine, with global strategist Barton Biggs of Morgan Stanley and senior investment adviser Robert Farrell of Merrill Lynch (Armour, 1997). This interview occurred after two-and-one-half years of spectacular stock market returns. I have divided the excerpt into two parts. The first part sets the stage for a discussion about regression to the mean, and also for an issue that comes up in chapter 5 (on skewed confidence intervals). Here is the first part of the excerpt:

Biggs: My view is that we're at the very tag end of a super bull market. That means the prudent person who's thinking ahead toward retirement should assume that over the next five to ten years the total return from his equity portfolio is going to be in the 5%- to 6%-a-year range.

Fortune: NOT THE 15% TO 20% WE'VE COME TO LOVE AND EXPECT?

Biggs: Right. It's very late in the game.

Farrell: Trouble is, it's looked that way for a long time.

Biggs: Yes, but it's never looked as much that way as it does right now.

We will come back to the "late-in-the-game issue" a little later. For now, consider regression to the mean.

Farrell: It's been better to have been a novice than a professional the past few years, because people with the most experience have been the most cautious. But markets do regress back to the mean {return to their long-term average performance}, and I agree we are late in the ball game. This is the longest period we've ever had with such high returns from equities, and I can't believe it's a new era that will just keep going forever. I don't know if returns going forward will be 7% or 8%, but I'm pretty sure they will be below average.

This interview raises a number of very important issues. Look first at the last three sentences in Robert Farrell's remarks, where he predicts below-average returns. What's his rationale? Well, he says markets "regress back to the mean" and points out that this "is the longest period we've ever had with such high returns."

Is a prediction of below-average returns appropriate? Take another look at table 2-1, the GPA example. Would we predict that the student with the 3.80 high school GPA would end up with a college GPA *below* the mean of 3.08? I don't think so. Regression to the mean suggests that future returns will be closer to their historical average. But it doesn't say they will be *below* their historical average.[5]

Farrell's error, too low a prediction, stems from *gambler's fallacy*. If five tosses of a fair coin all turn out to be heads, what is the probability that the sixth toss will be tails? If the coin is fair, the correct answer is one-half. Yet many people have a mental picture that when a fair coin is tossed a few times in a row, the resulting pattern will feature about the same number of heads as tails. In other words, the representative pattern features about the same number of heads and tails. So, after a run of five heads, people tend to predict tails on the sixth toss, because of the representativeness heuristic. From their perspective, "a tail is due." But this reasoning is wrong, just as below-average returns are no more likely after "the longest period we've ever had with such high returns."

Gambler's fallacy arises because people misinterpret the law of averages, technically known as the "law of large numbers." They think the law of large numbers applies to small samples as well as to large samples. This led Tversky and Kahneman (1971) to facetiously describe gambler's fallacy as the "law of small numbers."

Let's go back to Farrell's remarks about future returns. Notice that he tells us he is "pretty sure they will be below average." Time will tell if he ultimately is right. I say ultimately because in the twenty-one months that followed the *Fortune* magazine interview, the S&P 500 returned more than 41 percent. But his statement that he is "pretty sure" leads us to the next issue—*overconfidence.*

Overconfidence

Here is a question for you.

The Dow Jones Industrial Average closed 1998 at 9181. As a price index, the Dow does not include reinvested dividends. If the Dow were redefined to reflect the reinvestment of all dividends since May 1896, when it commenced at a value of 40, what would its value have been at the end of 1998? In addition to writing down your best guess, also write down a low guess and a high guess, so that you feel 90 percent confident that the true answer will lie between your low guess and your high guess.

Ready? The answer to the preceding question is found in the title of a paper by Roger Clarke and Meir Statman (1999): "The DJIA Crossed 652,230 (in 1998)." If people were well calibrated, then 90 out of every 100 would find that the correct answer lay between their low and high guesses. But when I ask this question as part of a survey, virtually nobody finds that the true answer lies between his or her low and high guesses. For most, their high guesses are much too low. So most people are not well calibrated. Instead, they are overconfident.

When people are overconfident, they set overly narrow confidence bands. They set their high guess too low (and their low guess too high).

Hence, they get surprised more frequently than they anticipated. Later in this volume we will come across Wall Street strategists who, in the course of reviewing their predictions in the light of actual events, speak about being "humbled." In other words, they were overconfident in their predictions.

Anchoring-and-Adjustment, Conservatism

Next is a textbook problem in probability, designed by psychologist Ward Edwards (1964) that provides some insight into analysts' earnings revisions.

> Imagine 100 book bags, each of which contains 1,000 poker chips. Forty-five bags contain 700 black chips and 300 red chips. The other 55 bags contain 300 black chips and 700 red chips. You cannot see inside any of the bags. One of the bags is selected at random by means of a coin toss. Consider the following two questions about the selected book bag.
>
> 1. What probability would you assign to the event that the selected bag contains predominantly black chips?
>
> 2. Now imagine that 12 chips are drawn, with replacement, from the selected bag. These twelve draws produce 8 blacks and 4 reds. Would you use the new information about the drawing of chips to revise your probability that the selected bag contains predominantly black chips? If so, what new probability would you assign?

This problem is analogous to the tasks faced by financial analysts. The bag is like a company that in the future may operate in the black or in the red. So in accordance with generally accepted accounting colors, black chips stand for good future earnings, red for poor future earnings. Analysts start out with information that leads them to form their initial beliefs. In this case, beliefs concern the probability that the bag contains predominantly black chips. The most frequent answer given to the first of the two preceding questions is 45 percent. So, the bag of chips is like a company that appears more likely to generate poor future earnings than good future earnings.

The second question is a lot more difficult than the first. The drawing of 8 black chips and 4 red chips is akin to a positive earnings announcement. So now the question is how to react to a positive earnings announcement made by a company that has not been performing all that well.

When I administer these questions, I find that the two most frequent responses to the second question are 45 percent and 67 percent—the two most *salient* numbers in the problem—with 45 percent being the number of bags containing predominantly black chips, and 67 percent the fraction of black chips drawn with replacement.

Those who respond with 45 percent essentially do not know how to incorporate the new information. So, they stick with their initial beliefs. Since the "earnings announcement " is favorable, they *underreact*.

People who answer 67 percent (or thereabouts) focus on the fact that two thirds of the chips drawn with replacement are black. They ignore their prior information, in accordance with the representativeness heuristic. Do they overreact, underreact, or get it just right?

The correct answer to the second question is 96.04 percent. About 55 percent of those responding choose either 45 percent or 67 percent; The remaining responses are scattered. But most are well below 96 percent. In fact, most are below 75 percent. In other words, most people respond too *conservatively* to the new information in this problem. Perhaps they get anchored on to 45 percent and do not adjust sufficiently to the new information.

This is how security analysts react to earnings announcements: They do not revise their earnings estimates enough to reflect the new information. Consequently, positive earnings surprises tend to be followed by more positive earnings surprises, and negative surprises by more negative surprises. Of course, the unexpected surprises in store for analysts are also a manifestation of overconfidence because overly narrow confidence bands mean people get surprised more frequently than they anticipate.

Aversion to Ambiguity

Imagine that I offered you the choice between accepting a sure $1,000 or an even gamble in which you either win $0 or $2000. When I pose this question in MBA classes, about 40 percent of the students say they would take the gamble.

I describe this choice to students by telling them that there is a bag containing 100 poker chips, 50 black chips and 50 red chips; they can choose a sure $1,000, or a lottery ticket that pays $2,000 if a black chip is drawn at random from the bag but $0 if a red chip is drawn.

Now consider this variation. Imagine the bag contains 100 colored chips that are either red or black, but the proportions are unknown. Many people who are willing to gamble when the odds are even prefer to play it safe and take the sure $1,000 when the odds are unknown. This phenomenon is known as the *aversion to ambiguity*. People prefer the familiar to the unfamiliar.

Remember the Wall Street proverb about greed and fear? I note that the emotional aspect of aversion to ambiguity is fear of the unknown. The case of Long-Term Capital Management, discussed in chapter 1, provides an apt example of this phenomenon. Recall that on September 23, 1998, a $3.6 billion private rescue of LTCM was arranged. The Federal Reserve Bank of New York orchestrated this plan because of a concern that the failure of LTCM might cause a collapse in the global financial system. The November 16, 1998, issue of the *Wall Street Journal* describes the scene as the participants departed the meeting at which the deal was struck. The article attributes an interesting remark to Herbert Allison, then president of Merrill Lynch, a remark that typifies aversion to ambiguity as fear of the unknown. "As they filed out, they were left to ponder whether all this was necessary, and whether a collapse would really have jolted the global financial system. 'It was a very large unknown,' Merrill's Mr. Allison says. 'It wasn't worth a jump into the abyss to find out how deep it was.'"[6]

Emotion and Cognition

The issues discussed in this chapter involve cognitive errors, that is, errors that stem from the way that people think. But in describing ambiguity to aversion in terms of fear of the unknown, I suggest that some phenomena involve a combination of cognition and emotion. Of course, both involve mental processes, and may be physiologically linked, as opposed to being separate from each other. Scholars have produced ample evidence that emotion plays an important role in the way people remember events. So, phenomena involving the availability heuristic may reflect both cognitive and emotional elements. Here is an example.

In 1972, the Dow closed at 1020. In 1982 it closed at 1047, just 27 points higher than the value achieved a decade earlier. In between, it gyrated wildly, recording four years of negative growth. During this period, inflation reduced the purchasing power of a dollar by over 66 percent. A 1995 article in the *Wall Street Journal* quotes Russell Fuller, president of RJF Asset Management (now Fuller & Thaler Asset Management) in San Mateo, California, as follows: "'People like myself, who have been in the business since before the 1973–74 crash, we were terrified by that crash,' says Mr. Fuller, the money manager. 'That's a very low probability event. But many of the people in this business have spent the last 20 years worrying about that happening again.'"[7]

Summary

This chapter described the first theme of behavioral finance, heuristic-driven bias, and introduced some of the main heuristics upon which financial practitioners rely. Throughout the book, readers will encounter many instances of representativeness, anchoring-and-adjustment, overconfidence, availability bias, and aversion to ambiguity. These heuristics surface in many different contexts, such as analysts' earnings forecasts, investors' evaluation of mutual fund performance, corporate takeover decisions, and the types of portfolios selected by both individual and institutional investors. Because of their reliance on heuristics, practitioners hold biased beliefs that render them vulnerable to committing errors. In addition to the heuristics described in this chapter, readers will come across a host of others, such as excessive optimism, the illusion of validity, hindsight bias, the illusion of control, and self-attribution error. There are many examples of such errors in this book.

Chapter **3**

Frame Dependence: The Second Theme

*T*his chapter discusses the following:

- loss aversion, loss realization, and losing projects
- mental accounting, frame dependence, and facing risk
- hedonic editing and tolerance for risk
- self-control and dividends
- regret and pension fund allocation
- money illusion and inflation

Frame *independence* lies at the heart of the Modigliani-Miller approach to corporate finance. Merton Miller has a succinct description of frame independence. When asked to explain, in twenty-five words or less, the essence of his contributions with Franco Modigliani, he said: "If you transfer a dollar from your right pocket to your left pocket, you are no wealthier. Franco and I proved that rigorously."[1]

It is a matter of form whether a person keeps a dollar of wealth in the right pocket or in the left pocket. The form used to describe a decision problem is called its *frame*. When I speak of frame independence, I mean that form is irrelevant to behavior. Proponents of traditional finance assume that framing is *transparent*. This means that practitioners can see through all the different ways cash flows might be described. Yet many frames are not transparent but rather are *opaque*. When a person has difficulty seeing through an opaque frame, his decisions typically depend on the particular frame he uses. Consequently, a difference in form is also a difference in substance. Behavior reflects frame dependence.

Loss Aversion

In their landmark work on *prospect theory,* a descriptive framework for the way people make choices in the face of risk and uncertainty, Daniel Kahneman and Amos Tversky (1979) provide evidence of frame dependence. The starting point in their work is the role of "loss," an issue explored by Harry Markowitz (1952b). Kahneman and Tversky studied how people respond to the prospect of a loss. Here is one of their examples. Suppose you face a choice between (1) accepting a sure loss of $7,500, or (2) taking a chance where there is a 75 percent chance you will lose $10,000 and a 25 percent chance you will lose nothing. The expected loss in both choices is $7,500. Would you choose to take the guaranteed loss or take a chance? Most people opt for the latter. Why? Because they hate to lose! And the uncertain choice holds out the hope they won't have to lose. Kahneman and Tversky call this phenomenon *loss aversion.* They find that a loss has about *two and a half times* the impact of a gain of the same magnitude.[2]

It is not difficult to find real-world illustrations of loss aversion. In a manual for stockbrokers, Leroy Gross (1982) describes the difficulties investors face in coming to terms with losses.

> Many clients, however, will not sell anything at a loss. They don't want to give up the hope of making money on a particular investment, or perhaps they want to get even before they get out. The "get-evenitis" disease has probably wrought more destruction on investment portfolios than anything else. . . .
>
> Investors who accept losses can no longer prattle to their loved ones, "Honey, it's only a paper loss. Just wait. It will come back." (p. 150)

Some people learn about "get-evenitis" the hard way. Take the case of Nicholas Leeson. In 1995, Leeson became famous for having caused the collapse of his employer, 232-year-old Barings PLC. How? He lost over $1.4 billion through trading. In 1992, Leeson began to engage in rogue trading in order to hide errors made by his subordinates. Eventually, he incurred losses of his own, and "get-evenitis" set in. He asserts that he "gambled on the stock market to reverse his mistakes and save the bank."[3]

"Get-evenitis" also afflicts corporate executives' ability to terminate losing projects. For example, 3Com's popular Palm Computing products, the handheld organizers that access data with a stylus, had a predecessor—Apple Computer's more sophisticated Newton.[4] Apple

CEO John Sculley was thoroughly committed to the Newton, and made it the center of his personal vision for the computer industry. He coined the term "personal digital assistant" to describe the concept and argued that it would be a pivotal step in the convergence of three industries: computing, communications, and entertainment.[5]

Development of the Newton began in 1987, and the product was launched in 1993. But at $1000, it was much too expensive for the mass market. Moreover, because of initial failures in its handwriting recognition capability, cartoonist Gary Trudeau lampooned the Newton in his comic strip *Doonesbury*. Given the size and demographics of Gary Trudeau's readership, think about the impact the availability heuristic had on Newton's potential market.

By January 1994, it was apparent that sales were disappointing and the Newton was a losing project. But Apple did not terminate it. The company was committed to personal digital assistants. A year later, in January 1995, Apple had added enhanced features, and the year after that it came out with a backlit screen, but to no avail. In March 1997 Apple spun the Newton off into its own division, but this did little good, and six months later Apple folded the division back into its own organization. Through all this, the Newton remained a loser.

CEOs may come and go, but losing projects stay on. John Sculley "went"; he was replaced by Gil Amelio, who also came and went. In a dramatic comeback, Steve Jobs, Apple's cofounder and first CEO, replaced Amelio. Years before, Sculley had ousted Jobs. In January 1998, about ten years after its inception, CEO Jobs announced his decision to terminate the Newton project.

Concurrent Decisions

Here is another Kahneman-Tversky decision problem:

Imagine that you face the following pair of *concurrent* decisions. First examine both sets of choices, then indicate the option you prefer for each.

First decision: Choose

A. a sure gain of $2,400, or

B. a 25 percent chance to gain $10,000 and a 75 percent chance to gain nothing.

Second decision: Choose

C. a sure loss of $7,500, or

D. a 75 percent chance to lose $10,000 and a 25 percent chance to lose nothing.

The way that people respond to this problem tells us a lot about their approach to making decisions. Consider your own responses. Choosing *A* in the first decision would be the risk-averse choice. Most people find a sure $2,400 difficult to pass up. Although $10,000 is a lot more than $2,400, the odds of collecting it are only one in four. Hence, the expected value of *B* is $2,500, considerably less than $10,000. In fact, $2,500 is just a tad more than the guaranteed $2,400 offered in *A*.

Did you recognize the second decision? We encountered it before, in the previous section. Did you respond the same way as before? In my own experience, about 90 percent choose *D* in the second decision problem. They want the chance to get even.

The two decision problems together constitute a concurrent "package." But most people do not to see the package. They separate the choices into *mental accounts*. And that brings us to frame dependence.

Suppose you face a choice. You can take a 75 percent chance you will lose $7,600 and a 25 percent chance you will win $2,400. Or you can take that same chance and accept an additional $100. Which choice would you make? A no-brainer, right? It should be: This decision frame is transparent.

But sometimes the frame is opaque. Consider the decision problem at the beginning of this section. When I administer this problem to my MBA students, about half choose *A* & *D*: *A* in the first decision problem and *D* in the second. People who choose *A* & *D* end up facing a 25 percent chance of winning $2,400 and a 75 percent chance of losing $7,600. However, they could do better: They could choose the *B* & *C* combination, which would offer them a 25 percent chance of winning $2,500 and a 75 percent chance of losing $7,500. But most people don't see through the opaque frame. Therefore, they act as if they don't value $100. The opaque frame makes for a "brainer" instead of a no-brainer.

Hedonic Editing

In his stockbroker manual, Gross (1982) implicitly raises the issue of frame dependence within the context of realizing a loss. His essential point is that investors prefer some frames to others, a principle known as *hedonic editing*. Consider Gross's advice to stockbrokers:

> When you suggest that the client close at a loss a transaction that you originally recommended and invest the proceeds in another position you are currently recommending, *a real act of faith has to take place.* That

act of faith can more easily be effected if you make use of some transitional words that I call "magic selling words."

The words that I consider to have magical power in the sense that they make for a more easy acceptance of the loss are these: "Transfer your assets." (p. 150)

Why are "transfer your assets" magic selling words? Because they induce the client to use a frame in which he or she reallocates assets from one mental account to another, rather than closing a mental account at a loss.

Thaler and Eric Johnson (1991) propose a theory of hedonic editing for mental accounts. As part of a study, they administered a series of choice problems to subjects. You will find two of these problems below. Read the first problem, record your answer, and then move on to the next problem.

1. Imagine that you face the following choice. You can accept a guaranteed $1,500 or play a stylized lottery. The outcome of the stylized lottery is determined by the toss of a fair coin. If heads comes up, you win $1,950. If tails comes up, you win $1,050. Would you choose to participate in the lottery? Yes or no? Yes means you take your chances with the coin toss. No means you accept the guaranteed $1,500.[6]

2. Imagine that you face the following choice. You can accept a guaranteed loss of $750 or play a stylized lottery. The outcome of the stylized lottery is determined by the toss of a fair coin. If heads comes up, you lose $525. If tails comes up, you lose $975. Would you accept the guaranteed loss? Yes or no? Yes means you accept a $750 loss. No means you take your chance with the coin toss.

Let's consider how people usually respond to these questions. In the first choice problem, the majority prefer to take the guaranteed $1,500 over the gamble where they might get less. This could be viewed as a typical risk-averse response, because the average payoff to the lottery ticket is $1,500, the same amount involved in the riskless option. However in the second choice problem, many people choose the lottery over the guaranteed loss. This is decidedly a risk-seeking response, in that the expected payoff to the coin toss is a $750 loss, the same amount involved in the riskless option.

There is a lesson here: People are not uniform in their tolerance for risk. It depends on the situation. Some appear to tolerate risk more readily when they face the prospect of a loss than when they do not.

It is common for financial planners and investment advisers to administer risk tolerance quizzes in order to determine a degree of risk that is suitable for their clients. However behavioral finance stresses that tolerance for risk is not uni-dimensional. Rather it depends on several factors, one being recent experience facing risk. Here are two more examples developed by Thaler and Johnson that bring out the complexity of these issues.

3. Imagine that you have just won $1,500 in one stylized lottery, and have the opportunity to participate in a second stylized lottery. The outcome of the second lottery is determined by the toss of a fair coin. If heads comes up, you win $450 in the second lottery. If tails comes up, you lose $450. Would you choose to participate in the second lottery after having won the first? Yes or no?

4. Imagine that you have just lost $750 in one stylized lottery, but have the opportunity to participate in a second stylized lottery. The outcome of the second lottery is determined by the toss of a fair coin. If heads comes up, you win $225 in the second lottery. If tails comes up, you lose $225. Would you choose to participate in the second lottery after having lost in the first? Yes or no?

Now that you have recorded your yes or no answers, compare your response to choice 3 with your response to choice 1. From a dollar perspective, choices 1 and 3 are equivalent. In the framework of traditional finance, people should respond the same to both. Yet in practice, many "switch" their choices. When replicating the Thaler-Johnson study I have found that about 25 percent of the respondents are more willing to take the gamble in choice problem 3 than they are in the dollar-equivalent choice problem 1. Why?

Thaler and Johnson suggest that the answer involves hedonic editing, the way people organize their mental accounts. In choice problem 3, if people lose $450 they combine it with the $1,500 gain and experience the net position of $1,050—exactly the situation they are presented with in choice problem 1. But if they win, they do not net their two gains; instead, they savor them separately. According to Thaler and Johnson, the added attraction of experiencing gains separately inclines people to be more willing to gamble.

Thaler and Johnson found that in choice problem 2, over 75 percent chose to gamble rather than accept a sure $750 loss.[7] However, although example 4 is dollar-equivalent to choice problem 2, almost 50 percent switch their choice from taking a gamble in example 2 to playing it safe in choice problem 4. Thaler and Johnson suggest an explanation based on the way people experience losses. They note that people seem incapable of netting out moderately sized losses of similar magnitudes. So, a loss of $225 coming on top of a prior loss of $750 is especially painful. The added pain leads people to shy away from taking the gamble as framed in choice problem 4, relative to the frame in choice problem 2.

Cognitive and Emotional Aspects

People who exhibit frame dependence do so for both cognitive and emotional reasons. The cognitive aspects concern the way people organize their information, while the emotional aspects deal with the way people *feel* as they register the information.

The distinction between cognitive and emotional aspects is important. For example, the main cognitive issue in choice problem 3 is whether people ignore having just won $1,500 when deciding whether or not to take an even chance on winning or losing $450. Some do ignore the $1,500, whereas others see themselves as being $1,500 ahead. The cognitive and emotional aspects operate together, in that those who ignore the $1,500 *feel* a $450 loss as just that, a $450 loss. But those who begin by seeing themselves as $1,500 ahead instead experience a $450 loss as a smaller gain of $1,050. This difference affects behavior: Because of loss aversion, people who ignore having just won $1,500 are much less prone to accepting the gamble than those who see themselves as $1,500 ahead. Thaler and Johnson call this a "house money" effect.[8]

The term *frame dependence* means that the way people behave depends on the way that their decision problems are framed. Hedonic editing means they prefer some frames to others. That is the main insight to be gleaned from studying how people chose in the four preceding choices. In a financial context, hedonic editing offers some insight into investors' preference for cash dividends. When stock prices go up, dividends can be savored separately from capital gains. When stock prices go down, dividends serve as a "silver lining" to buffer a capital loss. Remember Merton Miller's succinct description of frame independence? Some investors prefer to keep dividends in their right pocket.

The following excerpt, taken from a *Forbes* magazine interview with closed-end fund manager Martin Zweig, describes how he came to realize the importance of dividends. It began with the fact that his fund was trading at a deep discount relative to net asset value (NAV), the value the shares would trade for if the fund were open-ended instead of being closed.

Then in 1986 we did a closed-end fund. . . . I always worried about discounts on closed-end funds. . . . The first nine months out of the gate, we were at a 17 percent discount. I was mortified. I sat down and did a lot of thinking. Bond funds at the time were selling at about parity. Stock funds were all at discounts. It didn't make sense, because stocks do better than bonds in the long run. And I realized bond funds pay interest. People like the certainty of an income stream. So I said, "Well, we're going to pay the dividend, whether we earn it or not." And we went to this 10 percent dividend policy. . . . The discount narrowed immediately. (Brimelow, 1998)

Self-Control

Self-control means controlling emotions. Some investors value dividends for self-control reasons as well as for reasons that stem from hedonic editing.

Martin Zweig talks about paying a dividend whether earned or not because people "like the certainty of an income stream." What does a reliable dividend have to do with self-control? Meir Statman and I (Shefrin and Statman 1984) argue that the answer involves the "don't dip into capital" heuristic. Older investors, especially retirees who finance their living expenditures from their portfolios, worry about spending their wealth too quickly, thereby outliving their assets. They fear a loss of self-control, where the urge for immediate gratification leads them to go on a spending binge. Therefore, they put rules into place to guard against the temptation to overspend.

"Don't dip into capital" is akin to "don't kill the goose that lays the golden eggs." But if you don't dip into capital, how do you finance consumer expenditures—Social Security and pension checks alone? Not necessarily—this is where dividends come in. Dividends are labeled as income, not capital. And investors tend to frame dividends as income, not capital. Again, this is frame dependence. Investors feel quite comfortable choosing a portfolio of stocks that feature high dividend payouts and spending those dividends.

Regret

Imagine someone who makes a decision that turned out badly and engages in self-recrimination for not having done the right thing. *Regret* is the emotion experienced for not having made the right decision. Regret is more than the pain of loss. It is the pain associated with feeling responsible for the loss.

For example, imagine someone who has a regular route to work. One day, for the sake of variety, she decides to try a different route. That particular day she winds up in an accident. Now, even if the odds of an accident were no different on the two routes, how will that person feel? Will she chastise herself, thinking "If only I had done what I always do and taken my regular route!" If so, she is experiencing the frustration of regret.

Regret can affect the decisions people make. Someone who feels regret intensely, does not have a strong preference for variety, and thinks ahead, may follow the same route to work every day, in order to minimize possible future regret.

Here is a financial example. Consider the choice of equity-fixed income allocation in a defined contribution retirement plan. In the January 1998 issue of *Money* magazine, Harry Markowitz explains what motivated his personal choice about allocation. As the Nobel laureate recognized for having developed modern portfolio theory, was he seeking the optimum trade-off of risk and return? Not exactly. He said, "My intention was to minimize my future regret. So I split my contributions fifty-fifty between bonds and equities" (Zweig 1998, 118). In other words, had Harry Markowitz selected a 100 percent equity allocation, and had stocks subsequently done terribly, it would have been to easy, in hindsight, to imagine having selected a more conservative posture—and this would give rise to considerable self-recrimination, meaning regret.

Regret minimization also leads some investors to use dividends, instead of selling stock, to finance consumer expenditures. Those who sell stock to finance a purchase, only to find that shortly thereafter the stock price soars, are liable to feel considerable regret. That is often at the heart of expressions such as "this is my half-million-dollar car."

Money Illusion

Frame dependence also impacts the way that people deal with inflation, both cognitively and emotionally. This is the issue of *money illusion*. Let us examine the following questions from a study by Eldan Shafir, Peter Diamond, and Amos Tversky (1997).

> Consider two individuals, Ann and Barbara, who graduated from the same college a year apart. Upon graduation, both took similar jobs with publishing firms. Ann started with a yearly salary of $30,000. During her first year on the job, there was no inflation, and in her second year, Ann received a 2 percent ($600) raise in salary. Barbara also

started with a yearly salary of $30,000. During her first year on the job, there was 4 percent inflation, and in her second year, Barbara received a 5 percent ($1500) raise in salary.

a. As they entered their second year on the job, who was doing better in economic terms, Ann or Barbara?

b. As they entered their second year on the job, who do you think was happier, Ann or Barbara?

c. As they entered their second year on the job, each received a job offer from another firm. Who do you think was more likely to leave her present position for another job, Ann or Barbara?

Most people indicate that Ann is better off, Barbara is happier, and Ann is more likely to look for another job. Now this is somewhat perplexing. If Ann is better off, why is she less happy and more likely to look for another position? Shafir, Diamond, and Tversky suggest that although people can figure out how to adjust for inflation, it is not a natural way for them to think. The natural way is to think in terms of nominal values. Therefore people's emotional reaction is driven by the nominal values, and those appear more favorable for Barbara than they do for Ann.

Summary

This chapter presents the second theme of behavioral finance, frame dependence, which deals with the distinction between form and substance. Framing is about form. In short, frame dependence holds that differences in form may also be substantive. It reflects a mix of cognitive and emotional elements. The cognitive issues pertain to the way that information is mentally organized, especially the coding of outcomes into gains and losses. There are several emotional issues, the most fundamental of which is that people tend to feel losses much more acutely than they feel gains of comparable magnitude. This phenomenon has come to be known as loss aversion. Therefore, people prefer frames that obscure losses, if possible—and engage in hedonic editing. People tend to experience losses even more acutely when they feel responsible for the decision that led to the loss; this sense of responsibility leads to regret. Regret is an emotion. People who have difficulty controlling their emotions are said to lack self-control. Some people use framing effects constructively to help themselves deal with self-control difficulties.

Chapter 4

Inefficient Markets: The Third Theme

This chapter discusses the following:

- representativeness, and the market's treatment of past winners and losers
- anchoring-and-adjustment, and the market's reaction to earnings announcements
- loss aversion, and the risk premium on stocks
- sentiment, and market volatility
- overconfidence, and the attempt to exploit mispricing

Cause and Effect

One of the most fiercely debated questions in finance is whether the market is efficient or inefficient. Remember the hedge fund Long-Term Capital Management (LTCM)? How did it advertise itself to investors? LTCM members promoted their firm as an exploiter of pricing anomalies in global markets. In this regard, consider the following heated exchange between Myron Scholes, LTCM partner and Nobel laureate, and Andrew Chow, vice president in charge of derivatives for potential investor Conseco Capital. Chow is quoted as saying to Scholes, "I don't think there are that many pure anomalies that can occur"; to which Scholes responded: "As long as there continue to be people like you, we'll make money."[1]

That last remark might not be the best way to win friends and influence people. But Scholes is correct about cause and effect—investors' errors are the cause of mispricing. Is the market efficient?

The fact is that from 1994 through 1997, LTCM claims to have success-fully made leveraged bets—bets that exploited mispricing identified by the option pricing theory for which Scholes and Merton jointly re-ceived the Nobel prize. In this regard Merton Miller, another Nobel laureate, is quoted as having said, "Myron once told me they are suck-ing up nickels from all over the world. But because they are so lever-aged, that amounts to a lot of money."[2] "Sucking up nickels" is indica-tive of inefficiency. Of course, then came LTCM's 1998 fiasco, but more on that later.

Effects Stemming from Representativeness

Let's begin with the De Bondt–Thaler winner-loser effect. De Bondt and Thaler (1985) argue that investors who rely on the representative-ness heuristic become overly pessimistic about past losers and overly optimistic about past winners, and that this instance of heuristic-driven bias causes prices to deviate from fundamental value. Specifically, past losers come to be undervalued and past winners come to be overval-ued. But mispricing is not permanent; over time the mispricing corrects itself. Then losers will outperform the general market, while winners will underperform.

De Bondt and Thaler (1989) present evidence in support of their claim. Figure 4-1 displays the returns to two portfolios, one consisting of extreme losers and the other of extreme winners. In both cases, the criterion used to judge performance is past-three-year returns. Extreme losers are the stocks that lie in the bottom tenth percentile, while the stocks that lie in the top tenth percentile are the extreme winners.

Figure 4-1 shows cumulative returns to the two portfolios for the sixty months after formation, relative to the overall market. Notice that the cumulative returns are indeed positive for losers, about 30 percent, and negative for winners, about –10 percent. De Bondt and Thaler sug-gest that this pattern signifies a correction to mispricing.

In traditional finance, the pattern depicted in figure 4-1 would re-flect compensation for risk. That is, losers would be associated with higher returns because they are riskier than the average stock; the op-posite holds for winners. But De Bondt and Thaler contend that an in-vestor who bought losers and sold winners short would have beaten the market by about 8 percent on a risk-adjusted basis. I discuss this issue further in chapter 7.

Figure 4-1 Cumulative Average Residuals for Winner and Loser
Portfolios of 35 Stocks (1–60 months into the test period)

Cumulative abnormal returns for two portfolios, one consisting of past losers and
the other consisting of past winners. Past losers subsequently outperform, while
past winners subsequently underperform.

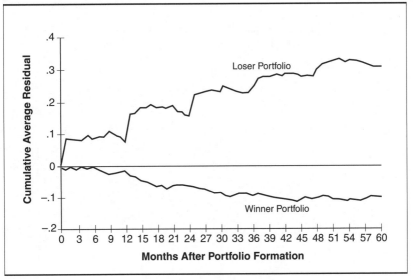

Effects Stemming from Conservatism

Analysts who suffer from conservatism due to anchoring-and-adjustment do not adjust their earnings predictions sufficiently in response to the new information contained in earnings announcements. Therefore, they find themselves surprised by subsequent earnings announcements. Unanticipated surprise is the hallmark of overconfidence. However, there is more at work here than plain overconfidence. Conservatism in earnings predictions means that positive surprises tend to be followed by positive surprises and negative surprises tend to be followed by negative surprises.

Does conservatism in analyst earnings predictions cause mispricing? If it does, then we should find that stocks associated with recent positive earnings surprises should experience higher returns than the overall market, while stocks associated with recent negative earnings surprises should earn lower returns than the overall market. Figure 4-2, taken from an article by the late Victor Bernard and Jacob Thomas (1989), summarizes the evidence.[3] The figure shows the behavior of

Figure 4-2 Cumulative Abnormal Returns (CAR) to Portfolios Based upon Standardized Unexpected Earnings (SUE)

What happens to stock prices after earnings surprises: price momentum is greater for bigger surprises. Cumulative abnormal return pattern is steeper with the magnitude of the surprise (SUE).

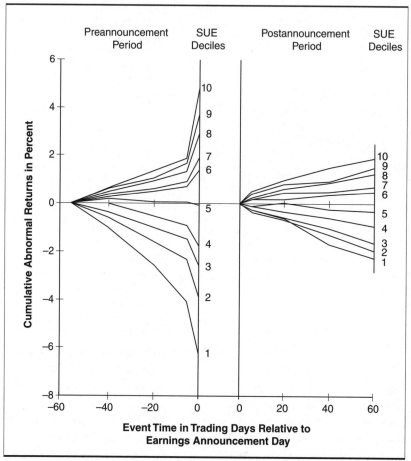

cumulative returns to portfolios formed based on the size of the most recent earnings surprise. In the sixty days following an earnings announcement, the stocks with the highest earnings surprises outperformed the overall market by about 2 percent, while the stocks with the most negative earnings surprises underperformed the overall market by about 2 percent.

Behavioral finance suggests that heuristic-driven errors cause mispricing. As an example, look at the pricing pattern depicted in figure 4-2. Traditional finance holds that this pricing pattern occurs because stocks associated with positive earnings surprises are riskier than the stocks associated with negative earnings surprises. In chapter 8, I discuss why this pricing pattern cannot be explained in terms of risk.

Effects Stemming from Frame Dependence

Does frame dependence have an impact on price efficiency? Shlomo Benartzi and Richard Thaler (1995) suggest that the answer is a strong yes. They argue that in the past, loss aversion caused investors to shy away from stocks; therefore, stocks earned very large returns relative to risk-free government securities.

Economist Jeremy Siegal documents that over the last two centuries the real return to stocks has been about 7 percent more than risk-free securities. From a theoretical perspective, a premium of 7 percent is enormous, and this differential has come to be called the *equity premium puzzle* (Mehra and Prescott 1985). To understand the character of the puzzle, consider the following question on risk tolerance.

> Suppose that you are the only income earner in your family, and you have a good job guaranteed to give you your current (family) income every year for life. You are given the opportunity to take a new and equally good job, with an even chance it will double your (lifetime family) income and an even chance that it will cut your (lifetime family) income. Indicate exactly what the percentage cut x would be that would leave you indifferent between keeping your current job or taking the new job and facing a 50-50 chance of doubling your income or cutting it by x percent (Barsky et al. 1997).

When I administer this question to general audiences, the average response comes out at about 23 percent. But the kind of response necessary to justify the historical equity premium is somewhere around 4 percent. The difference between 23 percent and 4 percent is not small. In fact, being willing to tolerate no more than a 4 percent decline seems very extreme, relative to the way people normally respond to the preceding question.

Shmuel Kandel and Robert Stambaugh (1991) suggest that people might be less tolerant of risks whose magnitudes are smaller than those described in the preceding question. However, I find that when the stakes are smaller, people actually become more tolerant of risk, not less tolerant.[4]

Benartzi and Thaler (1995) suggest that individual investors' historical reluctance to hold stocks may have stemmed from their evaluation horizons being too short. They call this reluctance *myopic loss aversion*. Benartzi and Thaler suggest that investors who are prone to myopic loss aversion can increase their comfort with equities by monitoring the performance of their portfolios less frequently, no more than once a year. It appears that investors who hold individual stocks monitor those stocks much more frequently than that. John Pound and Robert Shiller (1989) found that individual investors spent over a half-hour per day following the most recent stock they bought.[5] Nicholas Barberis, Ming Huang, and Tano Santos (1999) use the Thaler-Johnson "house money effect" discussed in chapter 3, to take the argument one step further. They suggest that after a market runup, the house money effect kicks in, raising investors' tolerance for risk, and lowering the equity premium. In a downturn the reverse occurs.

Departure from Fundamental Value: Short-term or Long-term?

One of the most striking claims of behavioral finance is that heuristic-driven bias and frame dependence can cause prices to deviate from fundamental values for long periods. Shiller (1979, 1981) argues that there is more volatility in stock markets and bond markets than would be the case if prices were determined by fundamentals alone. His analysis vividly illustrates the length of time stock price and fundamental value can part company.

Shiller computed what the fundamental value of stocks would have been over time for an investor who had perfect foresight about the future value of dividends. He then compared fundamental value and prices.[6] Figure 4-3 depicts the timelines for two indexes, starting in 1925. The figure is scaled to adjust for the long-term historical growth rate of stock prices. One line depicts the index for fundamental value, while the other shows the index for actual stock prices.

The years 1929 and 1987 were crash years, and, as I discussed in chapter 2, 1973 was the beginning of a long bear market. Consider how these events are portrayed in figure 4-3. Prior to 1929 and 1973, price lies well above fundamental value. Shortly after those years price falls below fundamental value. The lesson here is that prices move away from fundamental value for long periods, but eventually revert.

On December 3, 1996, Shiller, along with John Campbell, expressed his views about the market in joint testimony before the Board of Governors of the Federal Reserve system (Campbell and Shiller 1998). Apparently, their testimony had some influence. Two days later, on December 5, Alan Greenspan, chairman of the Federal Reserve Board,

Figure 4-3 Fundamental Value versus Actual Price, 1925–1999
Stock prices tend to stray from fundamental value for long periods of time. The
period after 1994 is especially striking.

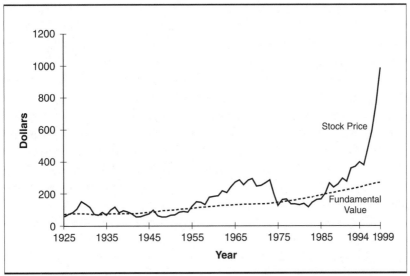

shocked global markets when he used the term "irrational exuberance"to describe the state of the U.S. stock market.[7]

What did Shiller and Campbell tell the Federal Reserve Board?
They explained that historically, when the dividend yield (D/P) has
been low and the price-to-earnings ratio (P/E) high, the return to holding stocks over the subsequent ten years has tended to be low. This
should not be surprising. The earnings yield is E/P, the inverse of P/E.
In a rationally priced market, dividend yields and earnings yields form
the basis of stock returns.[8] Recall the question in chapter 2 concerning
reinvested dividends and the Dow Jones Industrial Average. One of the
lessons from that question is that when it comes to long-run stock returns, compounded dividends swamp stock price.[9] The future course
of earnings and dividends would have to be dramatically better than in
the past to rationalize high subsequent stock returns in a low D/P and
E/P environment.[10]

To place the Campbell-Shiller argument into context, let me point
out that the historical mean for the dividend yield is 4.73 percent. But
in late 1996, it was an extremely low 1.9 percent. The historical mean
for P/E is 14.2. Moreover, for most of the time since 1872, P/E has
moved in the range of 8 to 20. Until recently, its peak of 26 dated back
to 1929; however, in December 1996, the P/E stood at 28. In their joint

testimony, Campbell and Shiller predicted that between 1997 and 2006, the stock market would lose about 40 percent of its real value.[11]

Shiller's 1981 work generated considerable controversy and has been the subject of many debates.[12] The central question asks: Do stock prices only change in response to fundamentals? Most of the debate has focused on technical details, which Robert Merton described in his survey of market efficiency (see chapter 1).

Merton wrote his survey in 1986 and published it in 1987. Of course, 1987 was a propitious year for debating questions about stock prices and fundamentals, given that the stock market crashed in October. Immediately thereafter, Shiller conducted a major investor survey to identify the information that led stock prices to lose 25 percent of their value in the course of a single day. Shiller (1990) documents that the market crash of 1987 occurred in the *absence* of any major news about changing fundamentals.[13]

With this in mind, I draw your attention to the extreme right of figure 4-3. Look at the period 1995 through early 1999, during which price rose well above Shiller's estimate of fundamental value. Note that figure 4-3 ends in January 1999, at which time the dividend yield on the S&P 500 had fallen further, to 1.26 percent.[14] The trailing P/E stood at a record 32.7![15]

Like Campbell and Shiller, some Wall Street strategists also placed the market's rise of 1995 and 1996 in historical context. For example, Edward Kerschner, a strategist at PaineWebber, had been bullish during the market's climb in 1995 and 1996 but then turned bearish. In a June 1997 article that appeared in *Barron's* he stated, "In '87 the market went to 135 percent of fair value, and in '73 we got to 155 percent of fair value." Kerschner went on to note that according to his P/E model, the market was 15 percent overvalued, making it the third most expensive market in a quarter of a century.[16]

In a related vein, Charles Lee, James Myers, and Bhaskaran Swaminathan (1999) have devised an intrinsic measure of the Dow Jones Industrial Average based upon the book-to-market ratio, the long-term return on equity, expected earnings growth, and interest rates. In mid-June of 1997, when Kerschner indicated that the market was 15 percent overvalued, the Lee-Myers-Swaminathan measure indicated that the Dow was 42 percent overvalued.

Kerschner has not been as steadfast in his stated view as some academic scholars have been. Strategists are subject to different pressures than scholars. During strong bull markets, bears become unpopular on Wall Street.[17] In early 1999, as the P/E of the S&P 500 hit a record high 32, the *Wall Street Journal* reported Kerschner's view as "[S]tocks may have gotten a little ahead of themselves . . . but he thinks the fundamentals dictate future stock gains."[18]

Overconfidence

Remember the case of Royal Dutch/Shell discussed in chapter 1? The market values of Royal Dutch and Shell Transport were misaligned relative to fundamental values. Yet, in attempting to exploit the mispricing, hedge fund Long-Term Capital Management (LTCM) managed to lose heavily. There is a moral to that story. Not every instance of mispricing leads to $20 bills on the sidewalk waiting to be picked up, or even to nickels, for that matter.

In fact, there are many behavioral lessons in the saga of LTCM. It does appear that their early success can be attributed to the exploitation of mispricing. At the same time, mispricing does get reduced as investors trade to exploit the associated profit opportunities. And investors do learn, albeit slowly; thus profit opportunities that had existed in 1994 through 1996 in the derivatives markets dried up in 1997. In response, LTCM began to take other kinds of positions, such as bets on the movements of foreign currency movements. Myron Scholes is reported to have been critical of these trades, asking his LTCM colleagues questions like "What informational advantage do we have over other traders?"

Scholes asked an eminently sensible question. Here is an analogy: "How good a driver are you? Relative to the drivers you encounter on the road, are you above average, average, or below average?"

Between 65 and 80 percent of the people who answer the driver question rate themselves above average. Of course, we all want to be above average, but only half of us are! So, most people are overconfident about their driving abilities. I suspect that investors are about as overconfident of their trading abilities as they are about their driving abilities.

There are two main implications of investor overconfidence. The first is that investors take bad bets because they fail to realize that they are at an informational disadvantage. The second is that they trade more frequently than is prudent, which leads to excessive trading volume. See my work with Statman (Shefrin and Statman 1994) and Terrance Odean (1998b).

A *Wall Street Journal* article describing the experience of Long-Term Capital Management quotes Nobel laureate William Sharpe.

"Most of academic finance is teaching that you can't earn 40 percent a year without some risk of losing a lot of money,"says Mr. Sharpe, the former Stanford colleague of Mr. Scholes. "In some sense, what happened is nicely consistent with what we teach."[19]

Proponents of behavioral finance, especially those who manage money, recognize that beating the market is no snap, and they try to avoid being overconfident. Russell Fuller and Richard Thaler operate Fuller and Thaler Asset Management. They manage a mutual fund, based on the De Bondt–Thaler effect, called Behavioral Value.[20] It may sound paradoxical, but Fuller believes that markets are, in the main, efficient. He tells me that many of the De Bondt–Thaler losers are, in fact, properly priced, that "most should be losers."[21] What's the lesson? Don't think the streets are paved with gold, or at least Wall Street anyway.

One other thing: Behavioral finance offers refutable hypotheses, but it does not have all the answers. De Bondt and Thaler predicted overreaction based on representativeness. But take another look at figure 4-1. It shows that a portfolio of extreme losers does outperform the market. However, a careful inspection of the figure shows that the effect is concentrated in the month of January. I know of nothing that suggests that people rely on representativeness in some months but not others.

Summary

This chapter covered the third theme of behavioral finance, *inefficient markets*, which is connected with the earlier two themes by cause and effect. Heuristic-driven bias and frame dependence cause prices to stray from fundamental values. Three examples are (1) representativeness as a cause of the winner-loser effect; (2) conservatism as a cause of post-earnings-announcement drift; and (3) mental accounting as a cause of a historical equity premium that has been too high, relative to the underlying fundamentals. But as I noted, prices can stray far from fundamental value, and for very long periods.

I conclude the chapter with a word of caution. The departure of price from fundamental value does not automatically lead to risk-free profit opportunities. In fact, the "smart money"may avoid some trades, although they have identified mispricing. Why? Because of nonfundamental risk, meaning risk associated with unpredictable sentiment.

PART *II*

*P*REDICTION

Chapter 5

Trying to Predict the Market

When it comes to predicting the market, how immune are Wall Street's strategists from heuristic-driven bias? Are they any different from the typical investor? And what illusions, if any, bias investors' predictions about where the market is headed?

This chapter discusses the following:

- strategists' susceptibility to gambler's fallacy

- evidence that strategists are overconfident

- which investors bet on trends

- how anchoring-and-adjustment, and salience, influence investors' predictions

- the key illusions that most people have about randomness, and why these illusions bias their predictions

- the impact of inflation on strategists' predictions of the market

Gambler's Fallacy: A Case Study

Consider the predictions that strategists made in January 1997. Let's start with some background. The years 1995 and 1996 had resulted in spectacular back-to-back returns of 34 percent and 20 percent on the S&P 500.[1] In the wake of the 1996 national elections, the S&P 500 soared 7.5 percent during November, a move that prompted Federal Reserve chair Alan Greenspan to ask whether "irrational exuberance has unduly escalated asset values."[2]

For Abby Joseph Cohen, cohead of the investment policy committee at Goldman Sachs, the market's strong performance corroborated the bullish forecasts she had consistently been making. These forecasts had led *Barron's* to describe her as the "virtual maven of the nineties' bull market."[3]

On January 1, 1997, the S&P 500 stood at 740. Cohen's target for the end of the year was 815 to 825, an 11.5 percent increase, predicated on projected earnings growth of 10 percent. Yet, the index ended the year at 970, up 31 percent!

Cohen had plenty of professional company in misgauging the market during 1997. In its issue of December 30, 1996, *Barron's* published the predictions of Wall Street's leading strategists for the mid-year and end-of-year values of the Dow Jones Industrial Average. In addition to Abby Joseph Cohen, this esteemed group included Marshall Acuff of Salomon Smith Barney, Charles Clough of Merrill Lynch, Edward Kerschner of PaineWebber, Elizabeth Mackay of Bear Sterns, David Shulman of Salomon, and Byron Wien of Morgan Stanley. Every single one underestimated the market's performance during 1997.

The Dow closed at 6448 in 1996 and at 7908 in 1997, a 22.6 percent increase. After the Dow surged by 33.5 percent in 1995 and 26 percent in 1996, could the strategists be faulted for not having anticipated a third spectacular year in a row? Not to my mind. But this does not mean that their predictions were free from bias.

Strategists are prone to committing *gambler's fallacy,* a phenomenon whereby people inappropriately predict reversal. In chapter 2, I pointed out that gambler's fallacy is regression to the mean gone overboard, and quoted Merrill Lynch's Robert Farrell in this connection. Remember, Farrell had predicted that future performance would be below average. What does regression to the mean suggest about predictions in the wake of above-average performance? It implies that future performance will be closer to the mean, *not* that it will be *below* the mean in order to satisfy the law of averages.[4]

Let's return to the strategists' 1997 predictions for the Dow. In the wake of above-average performance in 1995 and 1996, did the strategists predict that 1997 would feature below-average performance? Indeed they did. They predicted that the Dow would actually *decline* by 0.2 percent in 1997, well below the 8.6 percent annual rate that the Dow had grown between 1972 and 1996.[5]

General Findings

The instances of gambler's fallacy described above are not isolated cases. Werner De Bondt (1991) has examined the market predictions collected by the late Joseph Livingston since 1952. De Bondt reports that, in accordance with gambler's fallacy, these predictions consistently are overly *pessimistic* after three-year bull markets and overly *optimistic* after three-year bear markets. As for accuracy, De Bondt concludes that market predictions are not "particularly useful."[6]

So What? Prediction and Performance

Is there a downside to strategists succumbing to gambler's fallacy? That depends on how their predictions get used. Strategists also make recommendations about strategic asset allocation, the proportion of a portfolio devoted to equities, bonds, cash, and other assets. These recommendations are routinely available from sources such as *Dow Jones News Service* and *Business Week*. Not surprisingly, strategists' recommended equity allocations have a high positive correlation with their market predictions. So if strategists are unduly pessimistic in bull markets, the returns to the portfolios they recommend are less than they might have been.

Richard Bernstein, head of quantitative research at Merrill Lynch, suggests that the asset allocations recommended by Wall Street strategists do indeed reflect missed profit opportunities. In fact, he has developed an indicator based on the average recommended allocation to stocks. He issues a "buy" signal when this average drops below 50.4 percent, and a "sell" recommendation when it rises above 57.5 percent (R. Bernstein 1995). He considers the range in between as neutral. Consider the period between September 1997 and April 1998, when strategists increased their average equity allocation in a balanced portfolio from 48.1 percent to a four-year high of 54.5 percent. *Wall Street Journal* writer Greg Ip described Bernstein's perspective on this change as follows:

> Mr. Bernstein considers that negative for stocks, but not unduly so. Indeed, gurus aren't so much turning more bullish, as easing their entrenched bearishness.
>
> "Over the 13 years of data that we have, the average equity allocation is only 53.4%," says Mr. Bernstein, with the remainder in bonds or cash. But he notes that most survey participants consider a 60% stock allocation to be about neutral. "So through time, Wall Street is underweighted on equities. There's all this talk of the 'wall of worry.'"
>
> There it is. The people who have the greatest incentive to sell equities are habitually bearish.[7]

Kenneth Fisher and Meir Statman (1999b) confirm Richard Bernstein's claims. They find that for every 1 percent *decline* in the recommended equity allocation by strategists, the S&P 500 has *increased* by 26 basis points.[8]

Overconfidence

A study sponsored by PaineWebber, and administered by the Gallup Organization, found that experience is an important factor in investors' expectations about the market. The results were summarized as follows in the July 8, 1998, *Wall Street Journal:* "As stock prices hover at or near records, a new poll indicates that inexperienced investors expect considerably higher returns on their portfolios than do longtime investors—and are more confident of their ability to beat the market."[9]

This finding is very interesting. Inexperienced investors are more confident that they will beat the market than are experienced investors. Given the difficulty that many investors actually have beating the market, novice investors may be not just confident, but overconfident.

How is overconfidence reflected in the predictions people make? I discussed the general issue of overconfidence in chapter 2. In order to review the basic issue, and set the stage for a discussion of overconfident predictions, let us consider the following five-question quiz.[10] The first two questions pertain to general knowledge, and the remaining three to financial predictions.

You will be asked to give your best guess in answering each of the five questions. In addition to giving your best guess, consider a range—a low guess and a high guess—so that you feel 90 percent confident that the right answer will lie between your low guess and your high guess. Try not to make the range too narrow. Otherwise, you will appear overconfident. At the same time, try not to make the range between your low guess and high guess too wide. This will make you appear underconfident. If you are well calibrated, you should expect that only one out of the five correct answers does not lie between your low guess and your high guess.

1. How long, in days, is the gestation period of an Asian elephant?

2. How deep, in feet, is the deepest known point in the ocean?

3. Figure 5-1 provides the share price chart for a particular security over a forty-eight-month period. What is your prediction for the share price value six months beyond this forty-eight-month period?

4. Figure 5-2 provides the share price chart for a particular security over a forty-eight-month period. What is your prediction for the

Figure 5-1 Share Price

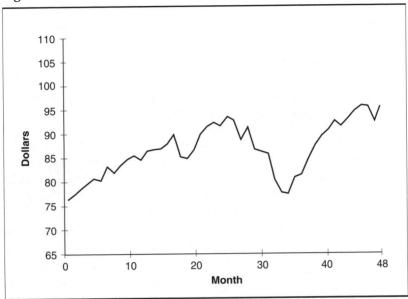

Figure 5-2 Share Price

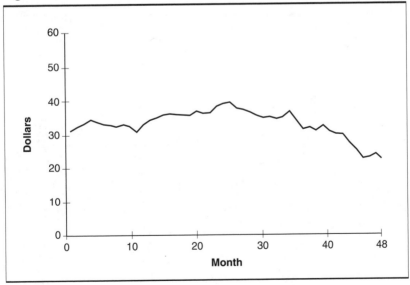

share price value six months beyond this forty-eight-month period?

5. Figure 5-3 describes the dollar change in share price for a particular security over a forty-eight-month period. What is your prediction for the average change in the share price, per month, for the six months beyond this forty-eight-month period?

The answers are (1) 645 days, (2) 36,198 feet, (3) $100.30, (4) $30.83, and (5) $0.83. Count an answer as a hit if the right response lies between your low guess and your high guess. Count an answer as a miss if the right response falls outside of the range between your low guess and your high guess. What score did you get?

Most people miss more than one out of the five questions in the preceding quiz. Actually, most miss four or even all five. Someone who is well calibrated should miss no more than one question. But the percentage of people who miss only one question is less than 1 percent. This means that the other 99 percent are overconfident. Overconfidence abounds.

Overconfident people get surprised more frequently than they anticipated. Take the strategists' predictions for 1997.[11] On June 20, 1997, the Dow closed at 7796, well above the expectations of all seven analysts. On June 23, *Barron's* reinterviewed them, recorded their reactions

Figure 5-3 Dollar Change in Share Price

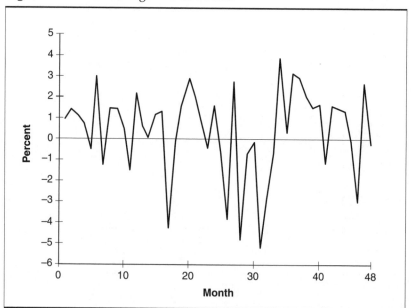

to how the market had behaved during the first half of the year, and collected their predictions for the remainder of the year.[12]

So how did the strategists react? In a word, *surprise*. The article quotes Smith Barney (now Salomon Smith Barney) stock strategist Marshall Acuff, who had the most optimistic prediction for the first half of 1997, as saying: "Certainly I've been surprised, everyone's been surprised. We've all been humbled."[13]

So, where did the strategists' June revisions indicate the Dow would close at the end of 1997? At 6995, *down* 10.3 percent from its June value of 7796. Gambler's fallacy? The Dow closed 1997 at 7908.

Do strategists learn? Well at the end of 1997, *Barron's* elicited the Dow predictions of eight strategists, six of whom were repeats from the previous year.[14] The average prediction was that the Dow would close 1998 at 8500, up 7.5 percent for the year. And what about Marshall Acuff, who, despite his optimism, expressed so much surprise in June 1997? He predicted that in 1998 the Dow would close at 8000, both at mid-year and at year-end, a 1.2 percent increase. In actuality the Dow closed on June 30 at 8952, up 13.2 percent, and ended 1998 at 9181, up 16.1 percent for the year. The surprises continued. Clearly, learning is a slow process.

Betting on Trends: Naive Extrapolation, Anchoring, and Underreaction

Questions 3 and 4 in the quiz on page 48 bear directly on the over-confidence associated with predicting the market. The questions are taken from a study by Werner De Bondt (1993) titled "Betting on Trends." In both questions, the security depicted is an S&P 500 index fund, although the forty-eight-month time periods differ. Three major findings emerged from De Bondt's study.

First, people tend to formulate their predictions by naively project-ing trends that they perceive in the charts. Second, they tend to be over-confident in their ability to predict accurately. Third, their confidence intervals are skewed, meaning that their best guesses do not lie mid-way between their low and high guesses.

What does skewness mean? It means that when the market has been going up, people think there is only a little room left on the upside in case they guess too low. But if they turn out to be wrong on the downside, then they would not be surprised by a large drop.[15]

Think back to the comments of Morgan Stanley's Barton Biggs, that I quoted in chapter 2. In August 1997, Biggs stated, "we're at the very tag end of a super bull market," and although it has looked that way for a long time, "it's never looked as much that way as it does right now." The situation Biggs faced in 1997 was similar to that depicted in figure 5-1, and his view at the time conforms with the average response to question 3. In the twenty-one months after Biggs made his remarks, the S&P 500 returned more than 41 percent.

In question 3 above, a person's best guess usually lies closer to his or her high guess than to the low guess. Perhaps the person is saying that since the stock has gone up by so much already, it can't possibly go up by much more. Peter Lynch (1989) calls this one of the "silliest (and most dangerous) things people say about stock prices." We could say the same of question 4, where a person's best guess lies closer to his or her low guess.

Why do people have skewed confidence intervals? De Bondt suggests that their predictions are anchored on the early history presented in the chart, a primacy effect. The effect of an anchor depends on just how salient past history is. Questions 3 and 5 in our overconfidence quiz are actually based upon identical data. Question 3 presents the data in terms of levels, while question 5 presents the data in terms of changes. Most people predict a higher change in share price for question 5 than for question 3. Why? As suggested by psychologist Paul Andreassen (1990), the early low share price values are less *salient* in figure 5-3, used in question 5, than they are in figure 5-1, used in question 3.

Heuristic Diversity

Oh, how straightforward the world would be if investors committed just one type of error in predicting the market. Alas, the world is not that simple. Those who bet on trends *extrapolate:* they bet that trends continue. Those who commit gambler's fallacy predict reversal. And both predictions stem from representativeness. For those who bet on trends, continuation is representative of what they perceive, while for those who commit gambler's fallacy, reversal is representative of what they perceive. The same heuristic, but different perceptions—that is what leads to these different predictions.

Interestingly, there are systematic differences in perceptions across groups, leading to systematic differences in their predictions. De Bondt (1998) points out that Wall Street strategists are prone to committing gambler's fallacy, whereas individual investors are prone to betting on trends.[16] The result is that in rising markets, we get to see headlines such as the following, which appeared in the *Washington Post* on November 25, 1998: "Joe Investor Beats the Mavens; Roller-Coaster Market Confounds Wall Street's Experts."[17]

Technical Analysis versus Fundamental Analysis: Addressing Sentiment

Ralph Acampora has served as Prudential Securities' director of technical analysis since 1990. In a November 20, 1998, appearance on the television program *Wall $treet Week with Louis Rukeyser*, Acampora described technical analysis in the following terms: "Well, it's what I do for a living is I'm basically a trend follower." In effect, betting on trends lies at the heart of technical analysis. It therefore should come as no surprise that the predictions of technical analysts and those of fundamental analysts often conflict, sometimes dramatically. Here is a short case that highlights some of the differences.

In early 1997, Acampora accurately predicted that the Dow would close 1997 at 8000 after hitting a high of 8250.[18] He continued to be bullish throughout 1997, predicting in August that the Dow would cross 10,000 by June 1998. At the same time, he expressed concern that a bear market was in store for the second half of 1998. His next *Wall $treet Week with Louis Rukeyser* prediction, made on January 2, 1998, was for a high of 8600 on the Dow, a low of 6000, and a close of 7300.[19] In making this forecast, Acampora had stated: "I think the sentiment out there is there's too much optimism, and I think this is the year for contrarians."

Now *sentiment* is a very important concept in behavioral finance. A consistent theme in this book is that sentiment is the reflection of heuristic-driven bias. As we shall see, fundamentalists and technicians both address issues of sentiment, but in quite different ways.

The first half of 1998 followed Acampora's general script. By July 20, the Dow had reached 9367. But then it began to tumble, closing at 8883 for July.

Keep in mind that Ralph Acampora is a technical analyst. By and large, technical analysts predict the continuation of trends until a clear reversal pattern develops. That is, they follow the maxim "the trend is your friend," qualified by "trees don't grow to the sky." In late July 1998, chart patterns were changing. Support lines associated with the Dow's movement in 1998 were being approached. Was sentiment changing? The number of stocks whose prices were on the decline was growing, leading technical indicators of breadth to signal that a reversal pattern was underway.

During an August 3 appearance on CNBC, Acampora warned of a "stealth bear market" in which small to midcap stocks would be more vulnerable to a downswing than blue-chip stocks. The very next day he eliminated the word *stealth*, as the Dow declined by nearly 300 points to 8487. In fact, Acampora was in the process of being interviewed by

CNBC, predicting that the Dow would fall by 20 percent from its recent high, when it fell by 60 points. The interview ended abruptly when Acampora declared: "This is going down. It's going as I'm talking. Got to run."

Interestingly, the CNBC interview with Acampora, which took place at 2:45 P.M. Eastern time, appears to have induced the media to attribute the market decline to his pronouncements. The August 10, 1998, issue of *Barron's* described the events as follows: "Prudential Securities' Ralph Acampora, a once-obscure practitioner of the voodoo art of technical analysis, basked in the national limelight for more than the requisite 15 minutes after he was credited/blamed for helping trigger Tuesday's thrashing by bearish comments he made on CNBC late in the trading session. (Critics dub him 'Ralph Make 'em Poorer.')"[20]

It seems that a gauntlet had been thrown, and it was time to duel. In an apparent attempt to counterbalance the concerns stemming from the drop in the market and the negative pronouncements emanating from Acampora, Abby Joseph Cohen emphasized to the Goldman Sachs sales force, and later to the press, that the underlying fundamentals had *not* changed. Specifically, she pointed out that she saw no deterioration in second-quarter earnings for 1998, a justifiable price/earnings ratio given the unusually low inflation and interest rate environment, and the prospect of stabilization in Asia during 1999.[21] Strategists Edward Kerschner of PaineWebber and Thomas Galvin of Donaldson, Lufkin & Jenrette reinforced this analysis.

What we have here is a classic confrontation between those whose market predictions are based on technical analysis and those whose predictions are based on fundamental analysis. In fact, on August 6, 1998, the *Wall Street Journal* concluded its coverage of Cohen's remarks by stating: "As for others' more pessimistic views, she professed to pay 'very little attention to what others may be saying,' explaining that she focuses on fundamentals instead of the charts and other statistical material that form the basis for work by technicians like Prudential's Mr. Acampora."[22]

Remember the moral of the pick-a-number game described in chapter 1? Technical analysts seem to attribute a more important role to sentiment in their market predictions than do fundamental analysts.[23] Nevertheless, there is one point on which both agree. Sometimes markets reflect changes in sentiment quite apart from any change in fundamentals. Tuesday, August 4, 1998, appears to have been such a time. A day later the *Wall Street Journal* pointed out that there appeared to have been no apparent news about changing fundamentals, specifically stating "And the sell-off suggested a fundamental shift in mood among investors, not because of its magnitude or breadth, but because there was no precipitating bad news."[24]

As I noted in chapter 4, sentiment can influence market prices for prolonged periods. After the Dow declined to 8051.68 on Friday, August 28, *Barron's* rounded up the usual suspects to interview. In the August 31 issue, Abby Joseph Cohen is described as having "swiftly pronounced last week's market slide a sentiment-propelled overreaction."[25] But on the next Monday, the Dow dropped by 512.62 points to 7539.07, 19.5 percent off its July 17 peak and within a whisker of the "bear market" threshold of 20 percent that Acampora had predicted several weeks earlier.

Illusions About Randomness: Lessons to Be Learned from Coin Tosses

Most people have a poor intuitive understanding about the character of random processes and how to predict the future behavior of these processes. Therefore, let me discuss some key lessons about the character of coin tossing and then apply those lessons to predicting the market.

I usually divide students in my MBA classes into two groups. I ask everyone in the first group to take a coin, toss it one hundred times, and record the sequence of heads and tails that result. I ask everyone in the second group to imagine that they are tossing a coin, and to record the outcome of an imaginary sequence of one hundred tosses.

Then I collect the responses of each group, and analyze each student's response according to the number and length of the *runs* they have generated. What is a run? Here is a quick example. Imagine a family in which the first three children were boys, and the fourth child was a girl. This family had a run of three boys. For coin tosses, a *run* is defined as a sequence where consecutive tosses result in the same outcome. So, if someone started out tossing three heads, and had a tail on the fourth toss, then the first three tosses would constitute a run of three heads.

What is the point of asking half the group to toss a real coin and the other half to do so only in their imagination? Simply this: The imaginary tossers do not generate enough long runs. In a hundred real tosses it is unusual to experience as many as thirty runs of length one, and likewise no run longer than four. Yet, the records of most imaginary tossers feature too few runs of length five or more. That is, the records of most imaginary tossers feature too many runs of length one or two.

The real tossers are often surprised to see long runs during their tosses because their experience is at odds with their intuition about random sequences of coin tosses.[26] Rather, their intuition conforms to the law of small numbers. People believe that most strings of coin tosses feature about the same number of heads and tails; hence, they expect short runs. That is why most people fall prey to gambler's fallacy. I think the situation with the market is analogous. Through 1998 the S&P 500 has experienced four consecutive years of gains in excess of 20 percent—quite a run!

For most, an equal proportion of heads and tails corresponds to what they view as the representative toss of a fair coin. Representativeness, in this case synonymous with stereotype, is one of the most common and widespread heuristics. It frequently serves as the basis for how people make predictions. This sometimes works well, and sometimes not.

Consider the following experiment. Suppose that I plan to toss a fair coin one hundred times. Before each toss, you have an opportunity to bet on whether the coin toss will turn up heads or tails. I agree to pay you $1 for each correct prediction and nothing for each incorrect prediction. So, what procedure would you use to arrive at your prediction?

When I play this version of the game in MBA classes, students' predictions usually feature about fifty percent heads and fifty percent tails, in accordance with what they imagine randomness to have produced. Then we play a second version, where the coin is a little worn on one side, thereby changing the odds slightly: I tell them that the probability of heads has increased from 50 percent to 51 percent. When I ask how people would change their prediction patterns, most say that they might change one or two of their tails to heads, but nothing more. Then I ask how people would change their prediction pattern if the probability of heads moved from 51 percent to 55 percent. Most change a few more tails to heads. But is this the right way to predict?

The optimal prediction pattern for all versions of this game is to *predict heads every time.* This surprises most people, because their instincts are to make their prediction representative of the process they are trying to predict. However an optimal forecast is much less variable than the process being predicted. The key to optimal forecasting is to minimize the likelihood of mismatching; yet a variable forecast does just the opposite.

De Bondt (1991) emphasizes that for all but the shortest-term predictions, statisticians find it difficult to do more than extrapolate the historical rate of growth.[27] Remember Ralph Acampora's eighteen-month prediction for the Dow, made in August 1997? Bullish until June 1998 and then bearish, big time. The Dow has behaved like that in the past. Not this time. The Dow closed 1998 at 9181, up 16.1 percent for the year. But that is not the point. The point is that an efficient forecast does not exhibit as much volatility as Acampora's forecasts.[28]

Technical analysts are prone to making excessively volatile predictions because they are like generals who continually fight the last war. Here is an example to illustrate what I mean by that. The August 31, 1998, issue of *Barron's* quotes Richard Russell, respected editor and publisher of the *Dow Theory Letter*, as having said: "Past history suggests that most bear markets wipe out at least half of the preceding bull market."[29] You may ask, what's wrong with that? The point is that markets behave a lot like coin tosses. Coin tosses produce interesting patterns, but past patterns provide little if no guidance about how to predict the patterns of the future.

Inflation

In chapter 3 I discussed *money illusion*, the difficulties presented by inflation. It turns out that inflation also impacts the prediction errors of Wall Street strategists. For Goldman Sachs's Abby Joseph Cohen, the biggest surprise for 1997 was the change in expectations about inflation and the subsequent impact on equity prices. In June 1997 she stated: "If inflation is low, there is a willingness to pay a higher price/earnings multiple for whatever earnings are being generated. More importantly, there is great confidence in the durability of the economic cycle and the profit expansion."[30]

Inflation exerts an important effect on equity valuation. Why? There are two reasons. The first is money illusion; the second is that due to anchoring-and-adjustment, people underreact to changes in inflation.

Abby Cohen is correct that price/earnings ratios are higher in periods of low inflation. But this may be the result of a behavioral bias. During the 1970s, inflation was high, nominal interest rates were high, and stock prices were low. At the time, Franco Modigliani and Richard Cohn (1979) argued that financial analysts were *undervaluing* equities by not taking proper account of inflation in their valuation formulas. Modigliani and Cohn suggested that analysts were mismatching real and nominal variables, discounting real earnings at nominal rates. Of course, that leaves us with the question of whether the reverse phenomenon, *overvaluation*, occurs in periods of falling inflation. In analyzing forecasts that extend back to 1952, De Bondt (1991) finds that it does.

Robert Shiller (1995) argues that inflation is very salient for most people, but that they significantly overweight the *importance* of inflation. Why? Because inflation is much more salient when it comes to the prices people pay than the incomes they receive.

Summary

Wall Street strategists are prone to committing a variety of behavioral errors and biases: gambler's fallacy, overconfidence, and anchoring.

Gambler's fallacy stems from two sorts of confusion. First, people have very poor intuition about the behavior of random events. With gambler's fallacy, they expect reversals to occur more frequently than actually happens. The second source of confusion stems from the reliance on representativeness. People tend to base their predictions and probability judgments on how representative an event is. Alas, predictions based on representativeness exhibit too much volatility.

Sentiment reflects the aggregate errors and biases in the market. As such, the presence of sentiment adds to the difficulty of accurately predicting the market. But most people are overconfident about their ability to complete difficult tasks successfully. Therefore, they are surprised more frequently than they anticipate. Moreover, overconfidence seems to increase with the difficulty of the task. In fact, people who regard themselves as experts tend to be the worst offenders.

Some experts use fundamental analysis and others use technical analysis. One reason why fundamental analysts tend to be surprised is that they underweight the impact of sentiment. On the other hand, technical analysts are often surprised because their reliance on representativeness leads them to make excessively volatile predictions. But fundamental analysts and technical analysts do have one major characteristic in common: They both are slow to learn.

In predicting the future, people tend to get anchored by salient past events. Consequently, they underreact. Finally, most people—including Wall Street strategists—have difficulty taking inflation into proper account.

Chapter **6**

Sentimental Journey: The Illusion of Validity

Many investors believe that there is a negative relationship between the predictions made by newsletter writers and the subsequent moves in the market. Is the relationship they perceive truly valid, or is it nothing more than an illusion? Are these investors prone to the "illusion of validity?"

This chapter discusses the following:

- why people mistakenly think that it's possible to make money by betting against the market predictions contained in advisory newsletters

- confirmation bias leading to overconfidence: why investors are prone to the *illusion of validity*

- how the predictions of newsletter writers have historically responded to changes in market conditions

The Logic of Going against Sentiment

What is the supposed logic that leads some investors to bet against sentiment, or at least against the prevailing views of advisory newsletter writers?[1] To gain some insight into this question, consider the behavior of the market during the first quarter of 1998.

In those three months the Dow Jones Industrial Average rose over 1000 points to surpass 9000 for the first time. This remarkable increase, of almost 14 percent, was even more astonishing because it followed three consecutive years of extraordinary increases in the market. So in April 1998, the *Wall Street Journal* announced the retreat of bearish sentiment. The headline read: "The Final Bears May Be Giving Up: Bulls'

Victory Prompts Fears." Fears of what? Greg Ip, the author of the article writes:

> Wall Street strategists, individual investors and investment advisers are all registering their greatest optimism on stocks in years.
>
> And that could spell trouble.
>
> Traditionally, market sentiment is seen as a contrarian indicator. Markets rise, the theory goes, as bears become bulls and put money into the market. The market peaks when there are no bears left and everyone is invested.[2]

So, there we have it, in that last paragraph: The logic behind the view. If there are no bears left, the market must top out. And how do we know how many bears there are relative to bulls? Because Chartcraft, Inc., tracks them. Chartcraft compiles the forecasts of stock market newsletters, and reports the summary data in its publication *Investors Intelligence*. *Investors Intelligence* has been publishing this data since 1963. Chartcraft classifies newsletter writers into three distinct camps: bullish, bearish, and those who are optimistic for the long term but expect a near-term correction. As we shall see below, some refer to the correction camp as "chickens."

The relative size of the three groups provides a sense of the *sentiment* of newsletter writers. To measure the degree of optimistic sentiment in the market, *Investors Intelligence* computes an index called the Bullish Sentiment Index. To define the index, let the number of Bulls denote the number of bullish newsletter writers and the number of Bears denote the number of bearish newsletter writers. Now define the Bullish Sentiment Index as

$$\frac{\text{\# Bulls}}{\text{\# Bulls } + \text{ \# Bears}}$$

As Ip mentioned, practitioners of technical analysis treat the Bullish Sentiment Index as a contrarian indicator. *Investors Intelligence* explains the rationale underlying this view as follows: "Since most advisory services are trend followers, they are most bearish at market bottoms, and least bearish at market tops."[3]

Ip writes: "the bearish portion of advisory newsletters has fallen below 25% in the past two weeks, hitting a six-year low."[4] That's why technicians who believe that the Bullish Sentiment Index is a contrarian indicator, sense there may be trouble ahead.

The Evidence Concerning the Bullish Sentiment Index

Greg Ip is no stranger to the sentiment index. A year earlier, on May 12, 1997, he described the sentiment of newsletter writers and portfolio managers when the market quickly dropped in March and April and then recovered just as rapidly.[5] Ip noted that at the time of the market's March peak, bulls outnumbered bears 51 percent to 30 percent. A month later, when the market bottomed out, bears outnumbered bulls 41 percent to 35 percent. As the saying goes, the market climbed a "wall of worry." These events provide confirming evidence for betting against the Bullish Sentiment Index. But was this case typical?

To answer this question, consider figure 6-1. I have adapted this figure from two papers, one by Michael Solt and Meir Statman (1988), and the other by Roger Clarke and Statman (1998). The figure plots subsequent percentage annual changes in the Dow against the current value of the sentiment index. If the case described in Ip's article is typical, then we ought to find that the data in the graph are clustered as follows: Low values of the Bullish Sentiment Index, at the left-hand side of the graph, give rise mostly to subsequent increases in the Dow; and high values of sentiment, at the right, give rise mostly to decreases.

But what does figure 6-1 show? It shows that low bullish sentiment is followed about as often by increases as by decreases. The same is true for high bullish sentiment. Bullish sentiment does *not* serve to signal

Figure 6-1 Percentage Change in Dow Jones Industrial Average versus Percentage of Bulls

Annual percentage change in Dow Jones Industrial Average subsequent to reading of Bullish Sentiment Index. Statistical analysis indicates the absence of a significant relationship.

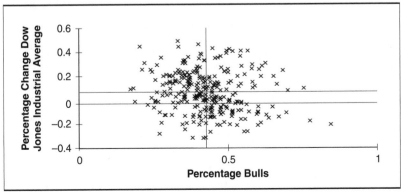

anything *at all* about future market performance. The Bullish Sentiment Index is about as likely to predict how the market will move in the future as a coin toss![6]

Denial

The evidence presented by Solt and Statman (1988) is now over ten years old. When this evidence first appeared, John Dorfman surveyed the reaction for the *Wall Street Journal*. And what was that reaction? In a word, denial.

> Michael Burke, editor of *Investors Intelligence,* says the indicator caused the newsletter to be "100% bullish" in July 1982, a month before the beginning of the five-year bull market that saw stock prices triple. In 1987, he says, it advised subscribers to get out of stocks in August—near the market's peak and two months before the crash. "We were up 40% for the year," Mr. Burke says.
>
> Profs. Solt and Statman argue, however, that such successes don't prove the rule. "The index is useless," they write, "not because it does not provide some good forecasts, but because it also provides so many bad forecasts."
>
> Mr. Burke of *Investors Intelligence* says that while he has no specific criticisms of the Solt-Statman methodology, he feels the professors "arbitrarily used" the data. A different way of looking at the data could lead to a different conclusion, he contends.[7]

Louis Rukeyser's Sentimental Journey

Why do investors continue to believe that the sentiment index is useful despite strong evidence to the contrary? They do so because they focus on the evidence that confirms their views but overlook evidence that is contradictory. *Investors search only for confirming evidence; and they ignore disconfirming evidence.*

Here is an entertaining example that illustrates the bias, taken from the popular television program *Wall $treet Week with Louis Rukeyser*. On February 6, 1998, as the Dow was rising rapidly, Louis Rukeyser took a few moments to trace the relationship between the sentiment of newsletter writers and the subsequent performance of the market. He referred to this retrospective as a "sentimental journey." Here is the beginning of Rukeyser's portrayal of that journey:

> Let's take one of our periodic looks at why every self-respecting market technician treats the sentiments of his colleagues with contempt,

as we track the embarrassing records of market advisers. So come along as we are "Gonna Take a Sentimental Journey."

In 1963, the very first year *Investors Intelligence* conducted its poll of market newsletter writers, bulls were at an all-time low of less than 9 percent; with nearly 78 percent chickens looking for a correction; and almost 14 percent outright bears.

You betcha. The Dow proceeded to rise 250 points in twenty-one months. Ten years later, nearly 62 percent of those polled thought the market would head even higher. And what came to pass? You guessed it. Down 470 points in 23 months.

Figure 6-2 provides a graphical representation of Rukeyser's entire retrospective. One line represents the percentage of bulls, and the other line represents the point rise in the Dow Jones Industrial Average. The data is arranged so that the percentage of bulls and the *subsequent* point gain are vertically aligned.

Notice that figure 6-2 consists only of evidence that confirms the usefulness of the Bullish Sentiment Index. Graphically, the events traced out by Rukeyser show that whenever the curve representing the percentage of bulls declines, the curve representing the point move in the Dow goes up.

Louis Rukeyser ends his journey with a very important question: "[Y]ou can't win them all, but can't these guys win any of them?"

Figure 6-2 Louis Rukeyser's Sentimental Journey

Along Louis Rukeyser's sentimental journey, the Dow Jones Industrial Average increases when newsletter writers are bearish and decreases when they are bullish.

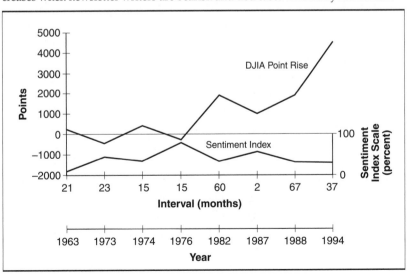

Rukeyser doesn't tell us. But he could have selected different events and told a very different story, such as the one illustrated in figure 6-3. This figure, which depicts percentage changes rather than points, shows that newsletter writers can get it right at least some of the time.

So What's the Big Deal?

So what if newsletter writers are unable to predict where the market is headed? Is that a problem? Well, it means that investors who rely on the advice in these newsletters to time the market will be trading too frequently, generating trading commissions but not helping themselves. A study by Brad Barber and Terrance Odean (1998a) finds that individual investors who trade the most frequently have the poorest-performing portfolios.

Analogous remarks apply to the stock selection advice in newsletters. Economist Andrew Metrick (1999) has analyzed stock recommendations of newsletter writers. The May 12, 1998, issue of the *Wall Street Journal* quotes Metrick as saying: "After trading costs, on average they would have lagged behind the market. There doesn't seem to be a lot of evidence that the stock selection of these newsletters is any good."[8]

Confirmation Bias: The Illusion of Validity

Psychologists Hillel Einhorn and Robin Hogarth (1978) have studied the general issue of why people persist in beliefs that are invalid, that is, why they succumb to the *illusion of validity.* Einhorn and Hogarth suggest that people do so because they are prone to search for confirming evidence, not disconfirming evidence. Consequently they not only may come to hold views that are fallacious, but they may be overconfident as well.

In his sentimental journey, Louis Rukeyser effectively makes the statement, If advisors are bearish, the market is more likely to go up than go down. Notice that this statement has the form "If P, then Q." Most people experience great difficulty assessing the validity of statements that have this form, which is why they accept false statements as true.[9] The root cause is that people use a heuristic[10] that leads them to search for confirming evidence (where P and Q hold) instead of the logically correct search for disconfirming evidence (where P and not-Q hold).[11]

Einhorn and Hogarth provide a general framework for their discussion of the illusion of validity. Here is a description of that framework, applied to the contrarian hypothesis for the Bullish Sentiment Index. Assume four types of situations. (1) periods when the Bullish

Sentiment Index was high, (2) periods when the Bullish Sentiment Index was low, (3) periods when the market rose, and (4) periods when the market fell. Match these situations according to the arrangement in table 6-1.

Table 6-1 depicts four types of event combinations associated with the claim that the Bullish Sentiment Index is a contrarian indicator. Notice that the two diagonal cells are labeled as "hits." A hit occurs when an event takes place that validates the contrarian theory. Either sentiment is bearish and the market subsequently rises (a *positive* hit), or sentiment is bullish and the market subsequently falls (a *negative* hit). Notice that all of the event combinations depicted in Louis Rukeyser's sentimental journey are hits.

The off-diagonal entries relate to events that go *against* the Bullish Sentiment Index's being a contrarian indicator. All of the events described in figure 6-3, the journey Louis Rukeyser did *not* take, fall into the off-diagonal cells.

Suppose that we focus our attention on the full history of the Bullish Sentiment Index and allocate events into the four cells in table 6-1. If most of the event combinations fell into the diagonal cells, we would conclude that the contrarian view of the Bullish Sentiment Index is valid. If most of the events fell into the off-diagonal cells, we would conclude that investment advisers appear to have impressive forecasting ability. If the events fall evenly across diagonal and off-diagonal cells, then we would conclude that the Bullish Sentiment Index is useless as a tool to forecast the market.

So where do most of the events fall? As Solt and Statman (1988) showed, event combinations are evenly distributed across the diagonal and off-diagonal cells in table 6-1. This is why the sentiment index is useless as a forecasting tool. Recall that Michael Burke, editor of *Investors Intelligence,* is alleged to have said that Solt and Statman used the data arbitrarily. But to avoid succumbing to the illusion of validity, they followed the general procedure prescribed by Einhorn and Hogarth.

Table 6-1

	Market Subsequently Rises	Market Subsequently Falls
Bullish sentiment low	Positive hit	False negative
Bullish sentiment high	False positive	Negative hit

Figure 6-3 Sentiment Index versus Percentage Change in Dow Jones Industrial Average

Along the alternative journey, the Dow Jones Industrial Average increases after newsletter writers have become more bullish and decreases after they have become more bearish. For each observation, the interval associated with the change in the Dow is 12 months.

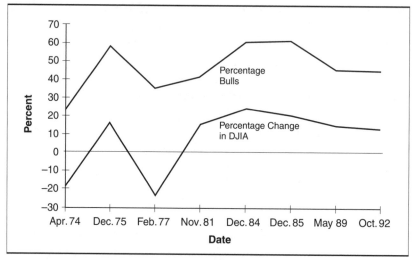

Naive Extrapolation and Nervous Bullishness

The sentimental journey suggests that advisers are most bullish at market tops and most bearish at market bottoms. However, if you take a careful look at figure 6-1, you will see that the index is no more effective at the extreme right (bullishness) or extreme left (bearishness) than it is in the middle of the range.[12]

By now you may be wondering about the existence of a valid connection between sentiment and the market. Well, a connection does exist. Bullishness increases after the market has gone up; bearishness increases after the market has gone down. For the period 1972 through 1997, a 10 percent increase in the Dow has on average been followed by an 8.3 percent increase in the proportion of bulls. Even Michael Burke recognizes this. He is quoted in the April 13, 1998, issue of the *Wall Street Journal* as having said, "It's hard to stay bearish when the market goes up all the time."[13]

The sentiment index does a good job of predicting the past. It only has difficulty predicting the future. Indeed, bullishness appears to have a backward-looking horizon of about twelve months. The two most recent months exert the strongest impact on bullish sentiment, with the market movements in the other ten months exerting a moderate influence. Not surprisingly, market moves from three months ago affect the degree of bullish sentiment today more than market moves of the same magnitude twelve months ago.

The logic behind treating the Bullish Sentiment Index as a contrarian indicator seems compelling. Most investors are trend followers, or so the logic goes, and believe in technical analysis proverbs such as "the trend is your friend" and "don't fight the tape." Hence, we might naturally expect newsletter writers to be trend followers as well. But are they?

Clarke and Statman (1998) analyze how sentiment responds to moves in the market. Keep in mind that bulls forecast that the recent upward trend in the market will continue, while bears and chickens predict that the recent upward trend will reverse. Suppose that during the preceding four weeks the S&P 500 index increased by 1 percent. Clarke and Statman find that this leads to a 1.23 percentage increase in bulls, as some bears and chickens change their perspective. Specifically, the bears decline by 1.18 percent and the chickens by 0.05 percent.

Although the behavior described in the preceding paragraph conforms to the idea that newsletter advisers naively extrapolate trends, the situation is more complex. Advisers responded differently to that same 1 percent increase in the S&P 500 had it occurred during the preceding twenty-six weeks, as opposed to the preceding four weeks. Now the chickens register a 0.4 percent increase, which is even larger than the 0.3 percent increase in bulls. Clarke and Statman refer to this phenomenon as *nervous bullishness.* There is heuristic diversity. Unlike the response to a four-week increase, where the migration in sentiment is from bears to bulls, the response to a twenty-six increase is a migration from bears to an even combination of bulls and chickens.[14]

How did the 1987 crash affect the sentiment of advisers? Not surprisingly, the general level of bullishness fell dramatically. However, Clarke and Statman report that once bullishness adjusted to its new lower level, the reaction of sentiment to changes in the S&P 500 was pretty close to what it had been prior to the crash. Before the crash, an increase of 10 percent in the S&P 500 led to a 7 percent increase in the Bullish Sentiment Index. After the crash, the same 10 percent increase led to a 6.4 percent increase.[15] In chapter 4, I mentioned that behavioral finance does not have all the answers. Clarke and Statman had hypothesized that the crash would make the sentiment more responsive to changes in the S&P 500. But the evidence refuted their hypothesis.

Interestingly, newsletter writers find it more difficult to spot market trends when the market is highly volatile. Consequently, volatility serves as a moderating influence, leading these writers to become, relatively speaking, less bullish during up markets and less bearish during down markets.[16]

The fact remains that the Bullish Sentiment Index provides no guidance as to where the market is headed next. The index is more of a rearview mirror than a front windshield. Were the past to provide an accurate guide about where the market was headed, then the index, as a reflection of the past, could prove useful. Alas, the past is a poor indicator of the future, and hence so is the Bullish Sentiment Index.

Whose Sentiment?

There is no universally accepted sentiment index. The Bullish Sentiment Index is a misnomer in that it only reflects the views of the writers of advisory newsletters. The American Association of Individual Investors (AAII) monitors the sentiments of small investors. *Investors Intelligence* does the same for the writers of advisory newsletters. Richard Bernstein's index (see chapter 5) is based on Wall Street strategists' allocations. Some technical analysts use the Call/Put ratio to measure sentiment. In chapter 13, I discuss the extent to which the discount on closed-end funds serves as a sentiment index. And many money managers, such as Martin Zweig, have developed sentiment indicators of their own. Kenneth Fisher and Meir Statman (1999b) compare several of these and show that they behave quite differently from one another.[17]

Summary

Technical analysts continue to treat the Bullish Sentiment Index as a contrarian indicator. Why do they succumb to the illusion of validity? Because the logic seems so appealing. Because others believe it. Because the popular financial press continues to perpetuate the myth. Because selective sentimental journeys, especially when presented by successful and entertaining commentators, can be very persuasive. And because in the end, technical analysts have not learned to validate their views. They emphasize evidence that confirms their own point of view, and overlook evidence that disconfirms their point of view. Consequently, they end up with a biased view *and* an overconfident attitude to boot. These biases are deeply ingrained: Learning is a slow process.

Chapter **7**

Picking Stocks to
Beat the Market

*E*ither market efficiency is an illusion or mispricing is an illusion.
In a landmark article, Eugene Fama (1970) argued that financial
markets are *efficient*. Market efficiency holds that unexploited profit opportunities do not lie around for very long, just as a $20 bill does not lie
for long on a crowded sidewalk.

Recall that the third theme of behavioral finance is *inefficient markets*. In recent years scholars have produced considerable evidence that
heuristic-driven bias and frame dependence cause markets to be inefficient. I mentioned in chapter 1 that scholars use the term *anomalies* to
describe specific market inefficiencies. For this reason, Fama character-
izes behavioral finance as "anomalies dredging."

This chapter discusses the following:

- the evidence that recommended stocks have consistently beaten
  the market

- the riskiness attached to recommended stocks

- the role of risk in the market efficiency debate

- the implications of heuristic-driven bias for value investing and
  momentum-based strategies

- the roles played by regret and hindsight bias

Some managers have beaten the market consistently. Two examples come to mind.[1] The first pertains to the television program *Wall
$treet Week with Louis Rukeyser,* which first aired in 1970. Stocks recom-
mended on that program have beaten the market by 4 percent per year.

The second example is the "Pros vs. Darts" contest that the *Wall Street Journal* has run since January 1990. In this contest, four security analysts (pros) each select a single stock. Four *Wall Street Journal* staffers throw a dart at a sheet of stocks. The contest winner, pros or darts, is determined by the performance of the respective selections over the subsequent six-month period. Not only have the pros' recommendations trounced the darts, but they beat the S&P 500 and Dow Jones Industrial Average as well, by 5 percent a year.

According to the efficient market school, investors cannot rationally expect to *beat* the market, except by taking on more systematic risk *than* the market. Active money managers disagree. Some, such as David Dreman, argue that these errors and biases create profitable opportunities for those who recognize them. In his book *Contrarian Investment Strategies: The Next Generation,* Dreman (1998) states: "Nobody beats the market, they say. Except for those of us who do."

There are two sides to the market efficiency debate, and one side is wrong. Either money managers such as Dreman are subject to the *illusion of mispricing,* or the efficient market school is subject to the *illusion of market efficiency.*

I argue that the evidence goes against market efficiency. Much of this evidence pertains to the long-term success of value investing, momentum investing, and the reaction to changes in security analysts' recommendations. To be sure, one of the main contributions of behavioral finance has been to explain the long-run success of value investing in terms of heuristic-driven bias, rather than risk.

At the same time, there are subtle issues. The meaning of market efficiency is that prices reflect fundamental values, not "you won't find $20 bills lying along crowded sidewalks." This is important. As I stressed in chapter 4, the "smart money" traders typically *stop short* of exploiting all of the mispricing they identify. Why? They conclude that it's not worth the risk. There are limits to arbitrage.[2] For example, investors who are convinced that value investing almost always outperforms a growth-based strategy, may experience a rude shock.

One other note. Knowing that prices are inefficient and exploiting that inefficiency are two different things. A lot of people seem to think that the message of behavioral finance is that beating the market is a no-brainer because errors cause mispricing. Well, it's not easy money; just the opposite, in fact. One of the main messages of behavioral finance is that heuristic-driven bias and frame dependence get in the way. There was a lot of California gold waiting to be discovered in 1849, but how many prospectors actually got rich? Precious few.

Do Brokerage House Recommendations Beat the Market? Yes, but . . .

In his survey of market efficiency, Robert Merton (1987b) describes many ways of looking for evidence of inefficient prices. One way is to see whether professionals beat the market. Stock-picking advice is one of the major services investors buy when they deal with a full-service brokerage firm. If mispricing is an illusion, then stock-picking advice should be worthless. Have brokerage house recommendations beaten the market? Yes, but—yes, they have, but with a lot of noise.

In June 1986, the *Wall Street Journal* and Zacks Investment Research began a joint study to investigate the value of this advice. In their study they track the performance of stocks recommended by brokerage firm analysts and compare that performance against the Dow and the S&P 500. Results were initially issued on a quarterly basis.

Some of the brokerage houses in the *Wall Street Journal*/Zacks study issue monthly "buy" lists. Other firms do not issue such lists but communicate their opinions by rating all the stocks they followed. Typically, these ratings range from "1" for a strong buy to "5" for a strong sell.[3]

The study tracks the recommended stocks from about fifteen brokerage houses at any one time. The firms selected include local, regional, and national brokerages.[4] Over the course of time, the identity of firms in the study has changed as brokerage houses have merged or gone out of business.

A 1990 *Wall Street Journal* article describes the procedure used to evaluate the recommended stocks.

> The study assumes that an investor buys every strongly recommended stock and sells all others, even if they are designated as holds or weak buys. Equal dollar amounts are put into each stock; portfolios are rebalanced monthly to keep the amounts equal. All buying and selling is on the last trading day of each month. Commissions and taxes are disregarded, mostly to make it easier to compare the results with market indexes. Dividends are included.[5]

The *Wall Street Journal*/Zacks study offers some intriguing lessons. Thirty months into the study, journalist John Dorfman wrote: "Stocks recommended by major brokerage houses have done, on average, no better than the market as a whole. That means investors could have done as well plunking their money into a mutual fund that mimics

Standard & Poor's 500-stock index."[6] As figure 7-1 illustrates, this pattern continued through 1989.

The period 1990 through 1992 was an entirely different matter. During these three years, recommended stocks returned over 72 percent, more than double the 35.9 percent return of the S&P 500. Now John Dorfman was communicating an entirely different message. In a 1993 *Wall Street Journal* article he wrote:

> Taken your broker to lunch lately?
>
> Maybe you should. Major brokerage houses tore up the track in stock-picking last year.
>
> Fourteen out of 15 major brokerage houses beat the overall stock market with their "recommended lists" of stocks to buy, according to a quarterly study by *The Wall Street Journal* and Zacks Investment Research of Chicago.[7]

Figure 7-1 Recommended Stocks versus S&P 500,
June 1986–December 1989

From the inception of the study through December 1989, stocks recommended by major brokerage houses did no better than the S&P 500.

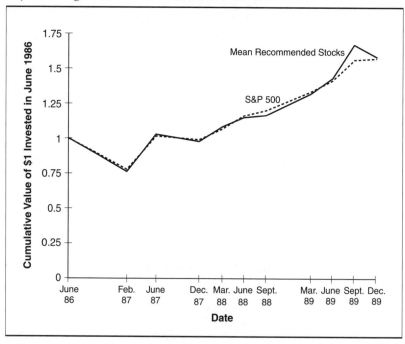

Where does that leave us? It leaves us in need of more data. Fortunately, we have some, and it's better data too. Starting in 1993, some improvements were made to the study. First, performance was tracked monthly, rather than quarterly. Second, a theoretical 1 percent commission was added for trades associated with changes to the recommended stock list. Third, only recommendations made by noon Eastern time are priced at that day's close. Recommendations made in the afternoon are priced at the following day's close.

Consider what the sixty months of monthly data from January 1993 through December 1997 indicate, as shown in figure 7-2. On a cumulative basis, the recommended stocks slightly, but consistently, outperformed the S&P 500. For the five-year period as a whole, they returned 165 percent, somewhat larger than the 151 percent returned by the S&P 500.[8] In other words, the recommended stocks beat the market by 106 basis points per year.[9]

Figure 7-2 Recommended Stocks versus S&P 500, January 1993–December 1997

Over the five-year period January 1993–December 1997, the recommended stocks slightly, but consistently, outperformed the S&P 500 on a cumulative basis.

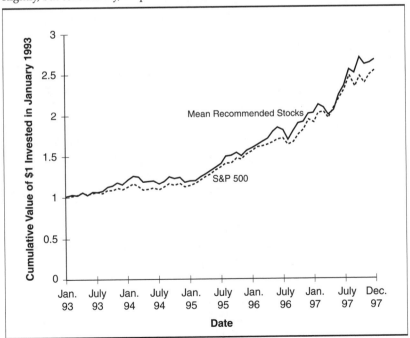

What Happens When an Analyst Changes a Recommendation?

Interesting things result. Kent Womack (1996) finds that not only does the market price immediately react to the announcement that an analyst has changed his or her recommendation on a stock, but the adjustment continues for a substantial period thereafter. This phenomenon is hardly in keeping with market efficiency.

Womack studied the period 1989–1991.[10] Here is a short illustrative example taken from his database.[11] Tom Kurlak is a Merrill Lynch analyst who follows Intel. Back on February 1, 1989, Kurlak upgraded his intermediate-term rating on Intel from the second highest recommendation of "accumulate" to the highest, "buy." The price of Intel shares jumped by $1.25 to $27.25, on volume of 3.4 million shares, compared with average daily volume of about 2 million shares. Intel also increased relative to the market: The Dow Jones Industrial Average closed down 4.11 that day, at 2338.21.

Is this event consistent with market efficiency? Possibly. It may be that Kurlak was providing new information to the market, and the price jump represented the appropriate adjustment to fundamental value. According to *Dow Jones News Service*,[12] Kurlak's upgrade stemmed from a changing inventory picture. But Intel's stock displayed significant post-recommendation drift. It outperformed the S&P 500 in each of the next five months: Intel rose 11.5 percent, while the S&P 500 rose 8.8 percent.

The preceding scenario is typical of Womack's findings for what takes place on average. On the day of the recommendation change, and for two days thereafter, there is a large jump in the price of the stock. Moreover, the change is in the direction forecast by the analyst who altered his or her recommendation. But the surprising thing is the existence of significant post-recommendation drift. On average, the price of a stock that is upgraded to "buy" goes up by 5 percent, relative to a comparison benchmark group. Analogously, the price of a stock that is downgraded to "sell" drops by 11 percent.

Market efficiency holds that price adjusts virtually immediately to new information. Post-recommendation drift is not a property of efficient prices. So, where does that leave us?

Risk

There are still many questions left to answer, the chief one centering on risk. Did the recommended stocks beat the market because they were riskier? Does a change in recommendation affect the riskiness of a stock? In particular, do stocks that have been upgraded to a "buy" become more risky? They would have to in order for the post-recommendation drift identified by Womack to be consistent with market efficiency.

A lot depends on what we mean by *risk*. If by risk we mean beta, the recommended stocks were actually less risky than the S&P 500. Suppose that some investor holds the recommended stocks from a particular brokerage firm, say, Merrill Lynch. Imagine that in January 1993, this investor formed his portfolio by purchasing the stocks recommended by Merrill Lynch, and then updated his portfolio monthly, as Merrill changed its recommendations. What would the beta of this portfolio have been over the five-year period January 1993 through December 1997? The answer is 0.90. For the seventeen brokerage firms in the *Wall Street Journal*/Zacks study, the average beta was 0.94. It thus appears that recommended stocks both outperform the S&P 500 and have lower risk.

However, this does not close the issue of whether or not markets are efficient. In recent years a belief has sprung up that as a risk measure, beta is dead. Does this mean that the practitioners and academics who for all those years thought beta to be the correct risk measure were committing a cognitive error? Let me add that the recommended stocks were more volatile than the S&P 500 during the period 1993–1997. The volatility of the S&P 500 was 3.05 percent per month, lower than for *any* of the seventeen recommended stock portfolios. The volatility of the average recommended stock portfolio was 3.77 percent.

Recently other measures of risk have been proposed. These alternative risk measures are based on firm characteristics such as market capitalization (size) and price-to-book. Price-to-book is routinely used to label stocks as "growth" or "value." Growth stocks have high price-to-book ratios, while value stocks are the opposite. Related measures are used in this connection as well, such as price-to-earnings and dividend yield.

In a pair of papers, Eugene Fama and Kenneth French (1992, 1996) consolidate a large literature and suggest that smaller stocks with low price-to-book ratios are riskier than larger stocks that have high price-to-book ratios. However, Kent Daniel and Sheridan Titman (1997) find that although stock returns are indeed related to characteristics such as size and price-to-book, the characteristics do not seem related to traditional measures of risk. Nevertheless, it is interesting to ask whether we can identify the styles brokerage firms use to recommend stocks.

Specifically, do the recommended stocks beat the market because the recommendations are for small firms with low price-to-book ratios?

In a series of articles, John Dorfman provides some insight into many of these questions. When it comes to style, we see a tendency to focus on momentum, the recommendation of "glamour" stocks, with a wide dispersion when it comes to size. Dorfman states:

> [T]he brokerage-house crowd is trying to pick stocks with fast earnings growth, a good "story," and already-high popularity among investors. The buy 'em-while-they're-hot method is one legitimate approach to investing, and can work well for nimble traders. . . .
>
> [T]he brokerage-house favorites are priced like caviar.
>
> Start by comparing stock prices with the dividends the stocks pay.
>
> Over the decades, stocks have usually sold for about 24 times dividends. When the overall market exceeds 33 times dividends, it's traditionally viewed as a danger zone.
>
> Currently, the overall market is at 44 times dividends. The Equity Opportunity List at Everen Securities Inc., Chicago, sells for 100 times dividends. The U.S. Priority List at Goldman, Sachs & Co. goes for 93 times dividends. The average for brokerage-house recommended lists is about 64 times dividends, says Rick Chrabaszewski at Zacks.
>
> Another familiar gauge is the price/earnings ratio, which is a stock's price divided by the company's per-share earnings. Over the years, a P/E of about 14 has been average. A P/E below 10 is generally considered quite low, and a P/E above 20 is often considered high.
>
> These days, the average stock's P/E is about 18. The average for stocks on brokerage houses' recommended lists is about 19, and five houses studied have average P/E ratios above 20.[13]

Turning to size, we find considerable dispersion. The following excerpt from another column describes the situation.

> In the first quarter, only two firms, both from St. Louis, were able to beat Standard & Poor's 500-stock index. The "Focus List" at A.G. Edwards Inc.'s A.G. Edwards & Sons chalked up a return of 3.2%, while the "Best Buys" list at Edward D. Jones & Co. was up 3.1%. The S&P 500 was up 2.7%, including dividends.
>
> The two St. Louis firms picked the largest stocks among the 17 houses, with typical market values of more than $18 billion and $27 billion, respectively. That turned out to be smart: Big-capitalization

stocks were in favor, as investors sought their relative safety and stability.

By contrast, the median market capitalization (share price times shares outstanding) of the stocks recommended by the other 15 firms in the study ranged from $13.8 billion at Salomon Brothers Inc. (a unit of Salomon Inc.) down to $387 million at Wheat First Butcher Singer Inc., according to Rick Chrabaszewski of Zacks.

Most brokerage houses fared far worse than the St. Louis pair. Small-capitalization stocks (those with market capitalization under about $750 million) were treated rudely, and technology stocks were bruised. Many brokerage houses have a healthy sprinkling of both on their recommended lists, and they paid for it.[14]

So, did the recommended stocks beat the market because they were smaller and had lower price-to-book ratios than the market? Apparently not.

Momentum

A common phenomenon in the three types of analyst recommendation studies (*Wall Street Journal*/Zacks, *Wall $treet Week with Louis Rukeyser,* and Pros vs. Darts) is *momentum.* The stocks that get recommended are those that have recently done well. In an important study Narasimhan Jegadeesh and Sheridan Titman (1993) document the existence of a momentum effect.[15] Jegadeesh and Titman attribute this effect to the fact that investors underreact to the release of firm-specific information, a cognitive bias.[16]

We have already encountered underreaction. In chapters 2 and 4, I discussed the phenomenon of post-earnings-announcement drift—that security analysts underreact to the earnings announcements of firms. As figure 4-2 demonstrates, earnings announcements carry an associated momentum effect. In fact, I devote the next chapter entirely to this issue.

One thing about momentum is that it requires turnover in order to implement. Do brokerage firms leave their recommendations in place for a long time, or do they change them frequently? With respect to the *Wall Street Journal*/Zacks study, Dorfman states:

> [B]rokerage houses often act as if most customers were short-term traders. Rick Chrabaszewski of Zacks recently analyzed the turnover rates on brokerage-house recommended lists in the past three years

and in the first half of 1997. He found that most brokerage houses are fickle, changing their minds frequently about which stocks are their favorites. Among 16 houses in the study, nine had turnover rates of 100% or more in 1996. Eleven houses are on track to exceed 100% turnover in 1997.

Such frequent additions and deletions from the recommended list could lead to adverse tax consequences for people who follow the firms' advice. And it may be emblematic of a general tendency to overtrade—always a temptation for brokers and brokerage houses, which earn a good chunk of their revenue from trading commissions.[17]

The study seeks to control for brokerage commissions but not for taxes. Of course, taxes are not an issue for tax-deferred accounts.

Does momentum represent mispricing? Not all agree that it does. Market efficiency proponents argue that with all those technical analysts looking at relative strength, if it were, mispricing would produce the equivalent of many $20 bills lying on the sidewalk waiting to get picked up. Hence, supporters do not rule out the fact that momentum represents an unobserved risk factor.

Style and Performance

The variation in performance across brokerage firms is wide. Figure 7-3 displays the best, worst, and median cumulative performance in the *Wall Street Journal*/Zacks study, as well as that of the S&P 500. Moreover, the brokerage firms in the study do not display strong herding behavior in the stocks they recommend. In fact quite the opposite. Notably, of the roughly 300 stocks recommended by the firms in the study, only a handful tends to be uniformly recommended by all.[18]

Does the difference in performance stem from risk? Did brokerage firms that combined momentum trading with small capitalization and low price-to-book perform best?

Consider Dorfman's descriptions of the principles used to pick stocks at the top three firms: PaineWebber, Raymond James, and A.G. Edwards.

Top performer PaineWebber tended to choose stocks that feature high price-to-book ratios and low dividend yields. John Dorfman wrote: "Its average stock pick sells for 3.3 times the company's book value, or assets minus liabilities, per share—the highest 'price-to-book' ratio among the 10 firms. And the average dividend yield (dividends as a percentage of the per-share stock price) was only 1.6%, the lowest

Figure 7-3 Performance Range Recommendations by Different Brokerage Firms, January 1993–December 1997

The cumulative track records for the best, worst, and median performers in the Zacks/Wall Street Journal study, during the five-year period January 1993–December 1997, relative to the S&P 500.

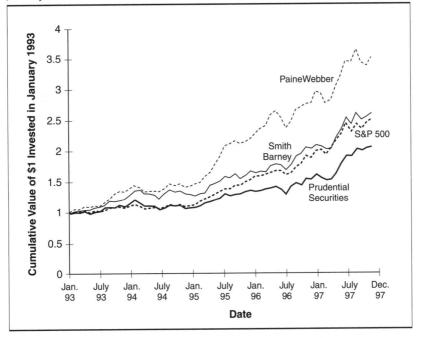

in the field. Edward Kerschner, the firm's chief strategist, says that's because the PaineWebber Group unit is emphasizing 'ruler stocks,' or stocks whose earnings go up as straight as a ruler. The firm thinks such issues should shine as other companies' earnings falter this year or next."[19]

In August 1994 Dorfman quoted PaineWebber's research director Ann Knight as saying that her firm is "sticking with two themes": corporate restructuring and heavy European exposure. He also wrote that PaineWebber tended to pick the most-volatile stocks, stating, "Its selections tended to show price swings 39 percent wider than those of the overall market."[20]

Second-place finisher Raymond James and third-place finisher A.G. Edwards followed very different strategies than PaineWebber. Both focused on small cap stocks. Those selected by Raymond James were the second most volatile. Dorfman described A.G. Edwards's approach as follows: "A.G. Edwards tends to select the stocks of relatively small companies, often not widely followed on Wall Street, that meet traditional 'value' criteria. For example, it likes stocks that sell at a low multiple of the company's 'book value,' or assets minus liabilities per share. It also favors stocks that pay good dividends. The average dividend yield of its recommended stocks is 3.7%, the second highest in the group after Smith Barney's 4.1%."[21] In a later article, Dorfman noted: "The St. Louis firm's "value" orientation has worked well during and after the crash. But it hasn't always worked. Before the crash, in the final stages of the great bull market, Edwards was an also-ran.[22] In terms of price to book and dividend yield, the contrast with PaineWebber could not be more striking.

Small/value outperformed the pack over the 11-year period 1988–1998 inclusive. But, small/value stocks did not lead the pack over the 6-year period 1993–1998. In fact, for the longer period, 1988–1998, the three brokerage houses switched position, with Raymond James emerging on top, followed by PaineWebber and A.G. Edwards.

Be it five years after the 1987 crash, ten years after the crash, before the crash: What do the close performance of A.G. Edwards and PaineWebber tell us? One thing it tells us is just how noisy realized returns are. Indeed during the five-year period 1993–1998, overall winner Raymond James placed seventh in a field of 13. This is important, as investors are prone to ask, "what have you done for me lately?"

Here is another indication of that noise. Consider whether winners repeat on a monthly basis. At the end of each month, divide the brokerage firms into two groups, the top 50 percent and the bottom 50 percent for that month. If performance were completely random, then the chance of making it into the top half during the next month is a fifty-fifty proposition. But if winners tend to repeat, then a firm that placed in the top half last month should stand a better-than-even chance of making it into the top half the next month as well. Over the sixty months between January 1993 and December 1997, there was a 49.4 percent chance that a winner in one month would repeat in the following month: not only close to even, but on the wrong side.

Behaviorally-Based Theories

The proponents of market efficiency hold that there are enough well-informed investors to seize all unexploited profit opportunities. The evidence from behavioral decision-making studies is that people learn slowly. Are there enough quick learners to eliminate mispricing in financial markets? That is an empirical issue.

In the 1980s, academic studies of security pricing specifically based on the findings described in the behavioral decision-making literature began to appear. These studies provided support for "value investing," an idea described in considerable depth by Benjamin Graham and David Dodd (1934) in their classic book *Security Analysis*. The logic behind value investing, as explained by Graham (1959), is as follows: "The market is always making mountains out of molehills and exaggerating ordinary vicissitudes into major setbacks." (p. 110). In other words, investors overreact to negative news.

Money manager David Dreman, who began to argue in 1978 that stocks with low P/E ratios were undervalued, provided further support for value investing. Dreman used the term *investor overreaction hypothesis* to describe the tendency of investors to become unduly pessimistic about the prospects for low P/E stocks. Since the crowd avoided them, investing in low P/E stocks became a *contrarian* strategy.[23]

Academics Werner De Bondt and Richard Thaler (1995) describe how in 1985 (p. 394) they "extended Dreman's reasoning to predict a new anomaly." De Bondt and Thaler hypothesize that because of representativeness, investors become overly optimistic about recent winners and overly pessimistic about recent losers. Hence, De Bondt and Thaler propose buying past losers and selling past winners.

De Bondt and Thaler define winners and losers according to past performance over the three previous years. Their study focuses on extreme winners and losers—the top and bottom 10 percent. As I discussed in chapter 4, extreme past losers tend to outperform the market over the subsequent five years by about 30 percent, and extreme past winners tend to underperform by about 10 percent. (See figure 4-1.) According to De Bondt and Thaler, too little smart money takes advantage of the profit opportunities created by investors who are misled by representativeness.

The evidence supporting the P/E and winner-loser strategies described above are based on realized returns, not on the way that investors formulate return expectations and perceptions of risk. It does appear that low P/E stocks and past losers tend to outperform the market. But do investors actually have low expectations for the future returns on these stocks? Or are low P/E stocks simply riskier?

A Tale of Two Stocks

Michael Solt and Meir Statman (1989) wrote that the *stocks of good companies are bad stocks*. In a 1995 article, Statman and I amplified the argument (Shefrin and Statman 1995). Why do investors appear to cling to the idea that good stocks are the stocks of good companies, and vice versa?

Is the answer any more complicated than representativeness? In investors' minds, good companies are representative of successful companies, and successful companies generate strong earnings, earnings that in turn lead to high returns. On the other hand, poor companies are representative of low earnings and disappointing returns. Investors shun the stocks of poor companies as a group, and therefore they come to be underpriced.

To understand this point, let us examine two companies, Dell Computer and Unisys. Dell has a strategy that is simple to describe. They sell custom-made computers directly to their customers. In June 1997, investors were looking at a company whose sales had risen by 47 percent in the previous fiscal year, and whose earnings per share had doubled. The stock had been soaring, providing a rate of return of 161 percent over the preceding three years. It goes without saying that Dell Computer is representative of a successful company.

Unisys is the product of a 1986 takeover by Burroughs of Sperry Univac. Both were struggling computer companies at the time, and after the merger they became one large, struggling computer company. In June 1997, the picture did not look as rosy for Unisys as it did for Dell. Unisys had lost billions of dollars since 1990, its market share had fallen, its stock price was depressed, and it had been unable to achieve stable revenue growth. Its CEO at the time, James Unruh, had announced his resignation. In order to enable the company to survive, Unruh had lead four major downsizings, amounting to a 70 percent reduction in the workforce. I would venture to say that Unisys is representative of an unsuccessful company.

Now the question is, How do investors form their return expectations for these two stocks? What does the capital asset pricing model (CAPM) have to say? In June 1997, the beta for Dell was 1.6, and for Unisys it was 1.9. The three-month Treasury bill was yielding 5.16 percent at that time. If, for the sake of argument, we take the equity premium to be its historical 8.7 percent, then investors would have expected Dell stock to return 19.1 percent, and Unisys to return 21.7 percent.

From an efficient market perspective, beta may not reflect all the risk to which these stocks are exposed. We would have to check the exposure of the two stocks to the various risk factors. For example, being a value stock, Unisys might be exposed to additional risk because it had an especially high value for book-to-market equity. As for Dell, the price of its stock did not just soar on a three-year basis: the rate of return in the first six months of 1997 was 48.6 percent. Given this momentum, Dell might be exposed to risk captured by a momentum factor.

In June 1997, I conducted a survey to elicit investors' expectations about returns for the stocks of eight technology companies. There were twenty-nine respondents, all living and working in Silicon Valley, and all familiar with technology; most were working in that industry. Their ages ranged from 25 to 40, and the median income of the group was $80,000 per year. All were students in the MBA program at Santa Clara University, were at a stage in the program where they were familiar with standard investment concepts, held individual stocks, and were familiar with the two companies.

The respondents expected that Dell would return 20.9 percent in the period July 1997 through June 1998, a little larger than the 17.6 percent predicted by the CAPM. But what about Unisys? Here the story was quite different. The respondents indicated that they expected its stock to return 6.3 percent over the period July 1997 through June 1998.

According to market efficiency, this would suggest that the respondents regard Unisys to be a *very safe stock*, so safe as to only require a risk premium of just over 1 percent! From the behavioral perspective, investors expect a low return on Unisys stock because Unisys is representative of a bad company, and investors believe that stocks of bad companies are bad stocks.

Were these return expectations generated by considerations of risk or representativeness? Which explanation sounds more plausible? To me, it seems clear that representativeness is more plausible than risk.

Evidence from Executives and Analysts

It may be that the subjects in my survey had it all wrong. But if so, they had plenty of company. Every year since 1982, *Fortune* magazine has conducted an annual corporate reputation survey. In the *Fortune* survey sell-side analysts, buy side analysts, corporate executives, and members of boards are asked to rate companies in their industry on a variety of attributes. One attribute concerns the company's stock in terms of *value as a long-term investment* (VLTI). Respondents rate each attribute, including VLTI, on a scale of 0 to 10.

In the *Fortune* survey published in March 1997, Unisys stock received a very low score of 4.0 on VLTI. In contrast, Dell received a

6.57.[24] Is some general phenomenon at work here? In examining the VLTI responses for the full range of *Fortune* magazine surveys, Meir Statman and I (Shefrin and Statman 1998) find the following: Respondents expect that past winners will continue to be winners and that past losers will continue to be losers. Respondents also expect that high P/E stocks will outperform low P/E stocks.[25]

It is noteworthy that analyst recommendations feature the same patterns. In examining the behavior of recommendations tracked by First Call, Meir Statman and I find the same effects. Analysts recommend the stocks of past winners (high P/E stocks) more highly than they do the stocks of past losers (low P/E stocks).

Advocates of market efficiency maintain that losers are riskier than winners, and low P/E stocks are riskier than high P/E stocks. Is this reflected in investors' risk perceptions? To address the issue, I included some risk perception questions in the investor expectation surveys that I disseminated. My subjects did perceive that losers are riskier than winners. And they perceived that low P/E stocks were riskier than high P/E stocks.

On its own, my survey results offer support for market efficiency—but not when return expectations are taken into account. Taking account of return expectations, I find that investors believe riskier stocks to have *lower* expected returns.

The Best of Stocks, the Worst of Stocks?

The Dell-Unisys story offers additional insights. Like the *Fortune* magazine survey respondents, analysts have been more favorably disposed toward Dell than Unisys. In June 1997 the consensus recommendation for Dell was between a buy and a strong buy, but closer to buy. For Unisys, it was between sell and neutral, but closer to neutral. However, since most analysts are known to mean sell when they say neutral, we can safely interpret the recommendation for Unisys to have been a sell.

Behavioral explanations such as the one advanced by De Bondt and Thaler (1985) postulate that investors overreact. When investors are pessimistic, they are overly pessimistic; when they are optimistic, they are overly optimistic. For instance, at the end of June 1997 Dell stock was a winner. During the preceding three years, it had returned 150.5 percent. On the other hand, Unisys was a loser, having returned a negative 2.8 percent.

What were the experiences of Dell and Unisys between July 1997 and June 1998? Dell continued to soar, returning an astonishing 216 percent, prompting *Fortune* magazine journalist Andy Serwer (1998) to wonder whether Dell would be "crowned stock of the decade, as in the best-performing stock of the S&P 500." As for Unisys, over the same period it returned 270.5 percent, beating Dell by 54 percent.

Overreaction and Underreaction

The winner-loser effect is puzzling in that if winners and losers are defined in terms of one-year past returns, rather than three-year past returns, an underreaction effect emerges, not an overreaction effect.[26] See Navin Chopra, Josef Lakonishok, and Jay Ritter (1993). What we seem to have is overreaction at very short horizons, say less than one month (Lehmann, 1990), momentum possibly due to underreaction for horizons between three and twelve months (Jegadeesh and Titman 1993) and overreaction for periods longer than one year (De Bondt and Thaler 1985, 1987, 1990). This phenomenon is quite complex, and does not lend itself to easy explanations. Chapter 8 will address some of the explanations that have been put forward.

The Three-Factor Model

Proponents of market efficiency have their own theory about value investing. That theory is the Fama-French three-factor model (Fama and French 1992, 1996). Of the three factors, one pertains to book-to-market (the inverse of price-to-book), one to size, and the third to the return on a proxy for the market portfolio. These factors represent sources of systematic risk, meaning risk that is priced.

In the three-factor framework, the average small stock is riskier than the average large stock, and therefore tends to earn a higher return. Consider a security whose return behaves more like a small stock than a large stock. A portion of its return will reflect the premium that small stocks earn over large stocks. The same statement applies to a security whose return behaves like a value stock, where value is measured by book-to-market. Securities that are neutral when it comes to size and book-to-market would earn the market return on average.

According to the efficient market school, size and book-to-market reflect systematic risk, meaning risk that requires compensation in the form of higher expected returns. If this is the case, then what we should find is that investors perceive small-value stocks to be riskier than large-growth stocks.[27] And we do, which on its own lends support to market efficiency. But investors consistently expect large-value stocks to outperform small-growth stocks. Likewise, analysts tend to recommend growth stocks more favorably than they do value stocks. In the efficient-market paradigm, expected return and perceived risk should be positively related, not negatively related.

Is beta dead? The existence of three factors, rather than one, implies that beta is at least crippled. But the casualty is *traditional* beta. At this point, you might be wondering what other beta there might be. Statman and I (Shefrin and Statman 1994) propose the notion of a *behavioral beta*. We analyze how the concept of beta needs to be adapted to reflect mispricing as well as fundamental risk. The traditional beta is defined relative to a proxy benchmark for the market portfolio, and is a suitable risk measure for a world where prices are efficient. But for a behavioral beta, the benchmark portfolio needs to change so that it tilts in the direction of underpriced securities and away from overpriced securities.

I suggest that *tilting* is why size and book-to-market give rise to factors that explain realized returns. Consider the book-to-market factor HL, the difference between the returns to high book-to-market stocks minus the returns to low book-to-market stocks. Does this seem like it captures the effect of tilting? How about factor SB, the return to big stocks minus the return to small stocks?—doesn't this capture the effect of tilting as well? Kent Daniel, David Hirshleifer, and Avanidhar Subrahmanyam (1999) argue that this is the case.

Misinterpreting the Evidence about Overreaction and Underreaction

Fama (1998a, 1998b) claims to be unpersuaded by the evidence coming out of behavioral finance. He raises concerns about both methodology and issues of interpretation. On the methodology side, he argues that behavioral finance needs to impose a clearly defined alternative hypothesis to market efficiency, one that is narrowly constructed. By this, I think he means that a useful theory tells us that only a small set of well specified phenomena are possible. A less useful theory tells us only that many vaguely defined phenomena are possible. That is why Fama suggests that behavioral finance adopt a specific alternative such as *overreaction.*

Fama contends that the anomalies literature has not accepted the discipline of an alternative hypothesis, although he does refer to one exception, presented in a paper by Josef Lakonishok, Andrei Shleifer, and Robert Vishny (1994). These authors propose that investors use sales growth and earnings growth as measures of past performance and that ratios involving stock prices, like P/E and book-to-market equity, proxy for future performance. They suggest that many firms having a high P/E or a low book-to-market equity will have experienced strong past earnings and sales growth. Lakonishok, Shleifer, and Vishny call companies with strong past performance and expected future performance *glamour stocks.* They suggest that investors form expectations by naively extrapolating past performance. Consequently, glamour stocks come to be overpriced, and poor performers eventually come to be underpriced. This leads investors to predict that value stocks will outperform glamour stocks, a prediction that can be tested and refuted if the data do not support it.

Lakonishok, Shleifer, and Vishny test the prediction that value stocks outperform glamour stocks. They do not test the hypothesis that investors naively extrapolate past performance. But because we look at expectations data, Statman and I can test the prediction about investors' expectations. What we find is that investors attach higher expected returns to stocks that have experienced higher past sales growth (or earnings growth) (Shefrin and Statman 1998).[28]

Fama makes two important points about a well-specified alternative hypothesis, especially one such as overreaction. First, this particular hypothesis, if formulated to hold regardless of horizon, will be rejected by the data. This we already know from the results on momentum. Second, Fama argues that because of random variation, realized returns will differ from expected returns, and expected returns are the focus of market efficiency. What market efficiency does predict about the spectrum of returns across securities and time is that they will exhibit no systematic deviation from their efficient means. And this leads him to make a novel interpretation of the findings on overreaction and underreaction.

Fama (1998a, 1998b) argues that "apparent overreaction of stock prices to information is about as common as underreaction." Moreover, this is "[c]onsistent with the market efficiency hypothesis that the anomalies are chance events" (1998a, p. 16).

It seems to me that this argument would make sense if about as many stocks displayed long-term underreaction as long-term overreaction, or if about as many stocks displayed short-term underreaction as short-term overreaction. But that's not what we see. Rather, what we find is apparent underreaction at short horizons and apparent overreaction at long horizons.[29]

Regret and Hindsight Bias

The data on return expectations tell us that investors are quite consistent in the mistakes they make. Investors believe that large-growth stocks will outperform small-value stocks. They tend to believe that past winners will continue as winners, past losers will continue as losers, and strong revenue growth in the past will lead to strong revenue growth in the future. A byproduct of this is that investors expect to earn higher returns on stocks they perceive to be less risky.

Efficient market theory predicts that mispricing is eliminated for the same reason that people pick up $20 bills lying on the sidewalk. But these errors are very difficult to override, even when you know about them. To appreciate just how difficult, consider the following excerpt from a January 1988 *Wall Street Journal* column by Barbara Donnelly, who had interviewed both De Bondt and Thaler about investing in losers.

> "It's scary to invest in these stocks," says Prof. Thaler. "When a group of us thought of putting money on this strategy last year, people chickened out when they saw the list of losers we picked out. They all looked terrible. . . ."
>
> [A]dds Prof. De Bondt, "The theory says I should buy them, but I don't know if I could personally stand it. But then again, maybe I'm overreacting."[30]

There are two other behavioral phenomena lurking in these quotations: regret and hindsight bias. Some losers will continue to be losers, maybe most of them. The De Bondt–Thaler strategy may not work in any given year. If it doesn't work, hindsight bias may well set in. It will look obvious that these stocks were going to bomb. And the investors who bought losers will probably feel like fools and experience the pain of wishing they could turn back the clock and do it all over again.

Summary

The weight of the evidence—the success of value investing over the long term, post-earnings-announcement drift, and post-recommendation drift—all go against market efficiency. As I emphasized in chapter 4, this reflects a cause-and-effect relationship. Heuristic-driven bias causes prices to depart from fundamental values.

Fama's defense of market efficiency would have us believe that representativeness-based errors are nothing more than random chance, or that there are enough investors immune to these errors to exploit them and correct any mispricing in the process. The latter, I believe, is the nub of the issue—whether the market holds enough smart money, enough investors able to learn quickly and overcome biases.

The evidence suggests that not enough smart money exists to eliminate market inefficiency. Representativeness, regret, and hindsight bias are very powerful, and most people are overconfident. The idea that self-interest will induce most people to learn to avoid errors is an empirical proposition, not a universal truth; furthermore, the evidence hardly supports it. In fact, most people are subject to the illusion of validity described in chapter 6. They emphasize evidence that confirms their views and downplay evidence that does not. Even proponents of market efficiency may not be immune from the illusion of validity.

At the same time, it is harder to beat the market than most people think. That is an important reason why the moral of this chapter is *not* that investors can use behavioral finance to make a killing. I think most investors would be better off holding a well-diversified set of securities, mainly in index funds, than they would be trying to beat the market. In other words, they would be better off acting as if Fama were right, that markets are efficient.

In truth, real-world performance is complicated. Stocks recommended by the major brokerage houses and those endorsed on the television program *Wall $treet Week with Louis Rukeyser* did beat the market—and *not* by investing exclusively in small-cap value stocks. In fact, just the opposite: recommendations emphasized momentum investing, large cap, and growth.[31]

The moral of the story, for most investors, is not to be overconfident. Markets may fail to be efficient, but that doesn't mean it's easy to beat the market—either by oneself or by relying on the advice of some guru. This statement applies even to the recommended stocks tracked by the *Wall Street Journal*/Zacks study. If an investor picked just one brokerage firm in 1986 and stayed with it for the duration, the odds of beating the market were no better than even. Why? Because only half the brokerage firms recommended stocks that beat the market.

What about investing based on learning some behavioral finance? Well, understanding the relevance of representativeness means having a little knowledge, and you know what they say about a little knowledge: It's a dangerous thing.

Chapter 8

Biased Reactions to Earnings Announcements

*M*ispricing is complicated. Sometimes mispricing results in reversals, while at other times it results in momentum.

Momentum and reversals coexist, despite lying at diametrically opposite ends of the spectrum. The academic scholars participating in the market efficiency debate have been grappling with what this coexistence means. Proponents of market efficiency view these phenomena as nothing more than random deviations from efficient prices. On the other hand, proponents of behavioral finance view them as systematic departures from efficient prices.

To shed additional light on the coexistence issue, I devote this chapter to post-earnings-announcement drift, a phenomenon that involves both reversals and momentum. What underlies reversals and momentum associated with earnings announcements? Are they nothing more than random disturbances? Or are they systematic, an effect caused by heuristic-driven bias? I believe that the evidence supports heuristic-driven bias stemming from conservatism—anchoring-and-adjustment—overconfidence, and salience.

This chapter discusses the following:

- a case that enables us to get a closer look at both momentum and price reversal
- the academic literature dealing with post-earnings-announcement drift
- the experience of one particular money management firm whose trading strategy is based on post-earnings-announcement drift
- recent theoretical work addressing momentum and overreaction

Case Study: Plexus Corporation

Plexus Corporation, located in Neenah, Wisconsin, is a contract provider of design, manufacturing, and testing services. Plexus develops, assembles, and tests a variety of electronic component and subsystem products for major corporations in industries such as computer, medical, automotive, and telecommunications.

At the beginning of 1997 Plexus was an $87 million company being followed by a single analyst, Robert W. Baird and Co. A year later, its analyst coverage had expanded from one to five, owing to a series of major earnings surprises. The surprises gave rise to price momentum, which was then followed by a sharp reversal.

Brief history: For the quarter ending December 31, 1995, Plexus's earnings per share (EPS) were 11¢. The EPS forecast for December 31, 1996, was for slightly less than double that amount. During the first week of January 1997, a report from Robert W. Baird & Co. said the company was on track to meet, or possibly exceed, its first-quarter earnings projection, which would reflect earnings growth of 26 percent from the prior year.

The first surprise: On January 16, 1997, Plexus registered a significant surprise when it reported earnings of 40¢. How did the market react that day? Volume was certainly dramatic. The day before the announcement, volume stood at 19,200 shares. On the day of the announcement, volume jumped to 420,500, and then on the subsequent three days volume was 718,400, 391,000, and 142,600 respectively.

But on the day of the announcement, the closing price only jumped $2.00 a share, from $25.50 to $27.50. Over the following three days, it climbed only a little more, to $28.75. Unlike the change in volume, the price change could hardly be called dramatic. Perhaps this was because the increase had already been anticipated. On Friday, December 20, the stock closed at $17.75, a little less than its all-time high of $19.00. Yet when the market reopened the following Monday, the stock soared to $26.00 on a volume of 54,800 shares. (See figure 4-2.)

Expanded coverage: As the market value of Plexus grew, so too did its analyst coverage. A month after the January surprise, on February 10, Stephens Inc. initiated coverage of Plexus Corp. with a "buy" rating. A report on *Dow Jones News Service* stated: "In a research note, the firm said Plexus should see rapid earnings growth in 1997 from its focus on increasing operating efficiency, reducing fixed costs and improving cash management. Stephens estimated Plexus will earn $1.60 a share in fiscal 1997 and $2.00 a share in fiscal 1998. The company's fiscal year ends in September. The firm set a 12-month price target of 40."[1]

The second surprise: Notice that Stephens's annual earnings forecast is four times the most recent quarterly number. Indeed, the consensus estimate for the second quarter was for 40¢. How did that quarter actually turn out? Were the two analysts right? It turns out there was a second surprise. Instead of being off by 100 percent, as they were previously, analysts were only off by 20.9 percent this time.

On April 16, the date of the announcement, Stephens responded by changing its recommendation from a "buy" to a "strong buy." The market's reaction was interesting: Prices declined on the news. Actually, prices had begun to decline a couple of days before earnings were announced, and continued to fall slightly during the three days after the announcement. But the dip was minor and temporary.

The value of Plexus shares rose steadily over the next months. The June 2 issue of *Barron's* reported that money manager James O'Shaughnessy had included Plexus in his "growth picks."[2] Other analysts, such as Nesbitt Burns and A.G. Edwards, initiated coverage of Plexus. How did their earnings forecasts fare against the actuals?

Subsequent surprises: The answer is one surprise after another. The First Call mean estimate for the quarter ending June 30 was for 51¢ a share. But on July 17, earnings were reported at 56¢, an 11.8 percent surprise. For the quarter ending September 30, the surprise was even larger, 15.4 percent. But in the final quarter of 1998, although there was a surprise, something different happened. The surprise turned out to be negative.

Graphical recap: Figure 8-1 from I/B/E/S displays the time path of analysts' earnings predictions, actual earnings, and stock price.

Figure 8-1 makes it apparent that earnings surprises had been consistently positive for five consecutive quarters. Notice the path of the stock price. It climbed steadily throughout this period until October. However, during October prices began to fall. And then they fell quite dramatically on December 18, from a postsplit price of $25 a share to $14, the largest percentage decline that day *for any stock traded on any U.S. exchange.* The reason? A preannouncement of lower earnings from Plexus's management.

Just prior to December 18, First Call reported that its survey of the five analysts following Plexus featured a consensus earnings estimate of 30 cents a share for the company's first quarter, meaning the quarter ending December 31, 1997. However, Plexus preannounced that because of slower than anticipated sales growth, earnings for the quarter would instead be between 21 cents and 24 cents.

Analysts' reactions to the negative surprise (preannouncement): How did the analysts who follow Plexus react? The excerpts below, from the

Figure 8-1 Plexus Corporation Quarterly Earnings Surprise

Plexus had five consecutive quarters of positive earnings surprises. Although the sixth quarter appears to show a positive surprise, the surprise was actually negative, stemming from a preannouncement. The figure shows the adjusted analysts' forecasts, not the original forecasts. The price path exhibits momentum along the positive earnings surprise trajectory, followed by a sharp decline after the disappointing preannouncement. The general finding features three consecutive quarters of earnings surprises, accompanied by abnormal returns in the same direction, followed by an earnings surprise in the opposite direction with an accompanying price reversal. *Source:* I/B/E/S International.

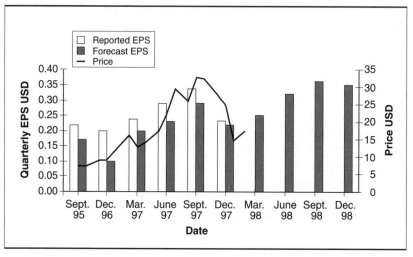

December 19 issue of the *Milwaukee Journal Sentinel,* capture their views.[3] The first quotation indicates surprise at the extent of the price drop.

> "The degree of punishment here is really high," said Matthew J. Desmond, equity analyst at Red Chip Review, a publication in Portland, Ore., that researches and writes about small-company stocks.[4]

The next set of remarks describes the nature of the drop-off in sales:

> "This is the first real earnings disappointment this company has had," said Scott Alaniz, securities analyst at Stephens Inc. in Little Rock, Ark. Slightly more than half of the shortfall occurred because Motorola Inc. moved some of the work Plexus had been doing in-house. . . . Motorola represents about 6 percent of Plexus' sales, down from about 12 percent before the work was pulled, said Paul S. Shain, research director at Robert W. Baird & Co.

Motorola represents the biggest risk of this type among Plexus' customers, Desmond said. The company's other big accounts, such as IBM and General Electric Corp., don't have the capacity to bring the work that Plexus does in-house.

Next, we learn how analysts revised their earnings forecasts, in reaction to the preannouncement.

Shain lowered his rating and earnings estimates for Plexus after the announcement Thursday. Now, he said, he expects Plexus to earn $1.10 per share for fiscal 1998, down from his previous estimate of $1.37. He also lowered his estimate for 1999 to $1.50 a share, from $1.75. "The near-term revenue disruption will likely continue into the second quarter, creating difficult comparisons for the remainder of the year," Shain said.

Finally, we return to the issue of the market's reaction, or should I say overreaction, which appears to be at odds with the analysts' views:

But analysts thought there were other reasons for the pounding Plexus' stock received.

"It's just a real touchy market. Geez, you sneeze and it turns into a nightmare," Desmond said. Investors generally are nervous about the technology sector, and they've been spooked by other earnings surprises that initially appeared to be isolated.

"People are finding out they're linked together," Alaniz said. Plexus was more alluring than many of its peers because it didn't have a lot of exposure on the computing or communications equipment side, and because it is more diversified with medical, industrial and other customers, Alaniz said. "That's another reason why this is a real shock," he said.

First Call reports that after the preannouncement, analysts revised their estimates to 22¢. In the end, earnings for the last quarter of calendar 1997 came in at 23¢ a share.

General lessons: Most of the general lessons to be learned from Plexus's experience can be seen in figure 8-1. There are two things to look at: (1) the pattern of earnings, and (2) the simultaneous price pattern reflecting momentum and subsequent reversal. Starting with a large positive earnings surprise in January 1997, what we see is that analysts *underreacted* to actual earnings. The revised earnings forecast of

$1.60 per share for fiscal year 1997, made in January 1997, turned out too low by almost 20 percent. Analysts underreacted in the sense that they continued to be positively surprised for the next two quarters. However, then they seem to have overreacted, predicting 30¢ a share, when the reality was 23¢. Hence, the earnings surprise was negative four quarters later.

Prices climbed steadily during the first three quarters of calendar year 1997, giving rise to momentum in the wake of a positive earnings surprise. Prices declined during the fourth quarter.

Given the comments by analysts quoted above, it seems reasonable to ask whether the news was sufficiently dire as to justify this price response. In other words, did the market overreact to the preannouncement? Recall Matthew Desmond's earlier remark, that investors were concerned about misinterpreting a permanent earnings decline as temporary. Comparing earnings per share for the two quarters ending in December, one in 1996 and the other in 1997, we find that their actual earnings were about the same. But so were the stock prices. So, did investors revise their expectations about Plexus's growth all the way back to the rates of January 1997? Certainly the analysts did: their revised forecasts for fiscal 1998 were actually less than $1.60.

Post-Earnings-Announcement Drift

The case of Plexus is highly representative of a phenomenon called *post-earnings-announcement drift.* The late Victor Bernard (1993) describes the general phenomenon as one where "analysts' forecasts tend to underreact to earnings information" and "market prices underreact to analysts' forecasts." (p. 322)

Scholars Richard Mendenhall (1991) and Jeffrey Abarbanell and Victor Bernard (1992) present evidence that analysts underreact to earnings information when they revise their forecasts. Their work, pertaining to Value Line quarterly earnings forecasts, finds that analysts do not sufficiently revise their forecasts. One positive surprise tends to be followed by another, and then by yet another.

In his survey of the literature on post-earnings-announcement drift, Bernard (1993) discusses evidence concerning market prices underreacting to analyst forecasts. He explains that the postannouncement stock prices for firms that have reported "good news" tend to drift up, whereas the prices for firms that have reported "bad news" tend to drift down. The identification of "good news" firms and "bad news" firms is accomplished using a criterion with the acronym *SUE*, which stands for *standardized unexpected earnings*. SUE is computed by taking the quarterly earnings surprise and scaling by the standard deviation of earnings surprises for that quarter.

For example, on April 16, 1997, Plexus announced that its earnings for the quarter ending March 31, 1997, were 24¢ a share. Since the analysts' consensus estimate had been for 20¢, the earnings surprise of 4¢ constituted a 20.9 percent surprise. I/B/E/S reported that this surprise had a SUE value of 8.44. This means that the typical surprise, which is a single standard deviation, was about 2.5 percent. The size of the April 16 Plexus surprise was 8.44 times as big as its typical surprise for earnings announcements.

In academic studies, the earnings forecast used to compute SUE is based on a simple forecasting rule. Take the quarter for which the forecast is being made, say, the first quarter. Now look at the history of all previously available first-quarter earnings for a given firm and compute the average growth rate for those earnings, on a year-over-year basis. This gives the average growth rate for first-quarter earnings from one fiscal year to another. To form a forecast for next year's first-quarter earnings, take this year's actual first-quarter earnings and multiply by one plus the average growth rate.

Suppose we were to arrange all companies into ten groups (deciles) according to their SUE values. Imagine forming two stock portfolios: one based on the highest of the most recent SUE values, and the other based on the lowest. The highest SUE values are, of course, the ones associated with extreme good earnings news, whereas the lowest SUE values are associated with extreme bad earnings news.

Once formed, how did those portfolios perform relative to the stocks of companies of comparable size (measured in terms of market value of equity)? Over the sixty days that followed the earnings announcement, the stocks of the highest SUE firms returned 2 percent more than their comparably sized peer group. The stocks of the lowest SUE firms returned 2 percent less than their peer group. Hence, a trading strategy of shorting the lowest SUE portfolio and using the proceeds to take long positions in the highest SUE portfolio would have earned 4.2 percent more. Call this 4.2 percent an *abnormal* return. Moreover, this trading strategy was even more successful for small and medium-size firms, which earned about 10 percent more than their peer group. I discussed these results in chapter 4; see figure 4-2.

Victor Bernard and Jacob Thomas (1989, 1990) and James Wiggins (1991) find that the returns to the trading strategy just described have a marked pattern. First, the abnormal returns are not earned all at once. Instead, they are spread over time. The largest effect occurs just after the announcement associated with an earnings surprise. Historically, it has been 1.32 percent, relative to the peer group. Next comes a delayed effect associated with the subsequent announcement one quarter later, and yet another delayed effect associated with the announcement two quarters later. On average, these have been 0.70 percent and 0.04 percent, respectively.

Think about what this pattern implies. It pays to hold stocks that have experienced recent large positive earnings surprises, because the market does not fully adjust to the good news. Instead, the market adjusts over the three quarters that follow an announcement.

There are two additional interesting features about the SUE-based trading strategy. First, it would not have worked if attempted for yet one additional quarter: Such an attempt would have produced a negative abnormal return of –0.66 percent. Second, the abnormal returns all tend to be concentrated in the first three trading days that follow the earnings announcements. They are not spread out evenly throughout the quarter.

Clearly, Plexus was a high SUE firm in 1997; its stock was a high performer for the first three quarters of the year, then turned down for the last quarter. In this respect, Plexus's experience is representative of the general pattern described by Bernard (1993). The one area where it does not fit the pattern concerns the three trading days following announcements. The large price moves in Plexus's stock were hardly concentrated during the three trading days following the announcements. In fact, those days were more volume events than price events.

Why does the trading strategy based on SUE lead to positive abnormal returns? One possible reason might be risk. If this explanation were valid, then the stocks of high SUE companies would have to be riskier than the stocks of low SUE companies. If true, the abnormal returns are nothing more than fair compensation for holding long positions in the stocks of high SUE companies.

But this explanation is difficult to justify. To begin with, Bernard (1993) reports that the SUE-based trading strategy generated positive abnormal returns for twenty-two consecutive years, from 1965 through 1986. (If that's risk, let's have more of it!) Moreover, the general phenomenon is concentrated in the three days following announcements. For the risk-based explanation to be valid, the stocks of high SUE companies would have to experience an increase in risk only on those days.

Trading on a Behavioral Bias:
Fuller and Thaler Asset Management

Another possibility is that the abnormal returns from the SUE trading strategy are hypothetical, and disappear if transaction costs are factored in. But the returns are not hypothetical.

Consider the experience of RJF Asset Management, now Fuller and Thaler Asset Management (F&T), one of the few firms that promotes itself as being a leader in behavioral finance. Fuller and Thaler manages a mutual fund called Behavioral Growth, which consists of the stocks of high SUE companies. It held the stock of Plexus Corp. throughout 1997.[5] The trading strategy underlying Behavioral Growth is the same as that of F&T's Small/Mid Cap Growth.

F&T started its Small/Mid Cap Growth Fund in January 1992. On an annual basis, the F&T Small/Mid Cap portfolio returned 28.4 percent, gross of fees, to its investors over its first seven years. In contrast, the Russell 2500 Growth Index returned 11.7 percent, and the S&P 500 index returned 19.5 percent. Figure 8-2 shows the cumulative difference between investing a dollar with F&T's Small/Mid Cap Growth in

Figure 8-2 Cumulative Performance of Fuller & Thaler
   Small/Mid Cap Growth Fund, January 1992–January 1999

Cumulative returns to a Fuller & Thaler trading strategy, designed to exploit post-earnings-announcement drift. Results are shown relative to the Russell 2500 Growth Index, which serves as the fund's benchmark. During the seven-year period, the Fuller & Thaler fund returned 28.4% per year gross of fees, while the Russell 2500 Growth Index returned 11.7%. Fees amount to 1.9% per year.

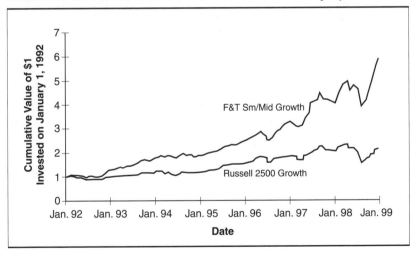

January 1992 and investing that dollar in the Russell 2500 Growth index. Over seven years, a dollar invested in F&T would have been worth $5.69 in December 1998, whereas a dollar invested in the Russell 2500 would have been worth only $2.13.

Behavioral Growth's long-run performance is consistent with the point made by Bernard (1993) that a SUE-based strategy consistently outperforms its peer group. F&T's Small/Mid Cap Growth portfolio outperformed the Russell 2500 index in six out of the seven years, 1992 through 1998 inclusive.

The data in figure 8-2 are based on actual trades net of commissions, but before management fees. These data also suggest that the superior performance of a SUE-based strategy is not due to risk. The monthly return standard deviation of the F&T Small/Mid Cap portfolio is almost identical to that of the Russell 2500, approximately 5.2 percent.

Which Behavioral Biases?

F&T's president, Russell Fuller, explained his trading philosophy in the January 5, 1998, issue of *Barron's*.[6] Fuller's view is that both analysts and investors are slow to recognize the information associated with a major earnings surprise. Instead, they overconfidently remain anchored to their prior view of the company's prospects. That is, they underweight evidence that disconfirms their prior views and overweight confirming evidence.[7] Consequently, both analysts and investors interpret a permanent change as if it were temporary; thus, the price is slow to adjust. F&T would buy a stock soon after a major positive earnings surprise and hold it until the positive earnings surprises diminished or disappeared.

Overconfidence and anchoring definitely appear to be part of the explanation underlying post-earnings-announcement drift. But there are other biases that may also contribute. Bernard (1993) mentions the work of Paul Andreassen (1990) and Andreassen and Steven Kraus (1990) on the importance of salience for financial predictions. See also Eli Amir and Yoav Ganzach (1998). These authors document the tendency for investors to place little weight on changes to a series, unless the recent changes are salient and attributable to a stable, underlying cause. The case of Plexus serves as an apt illustration. In January 1997, the time of the 100 percent earnings surprise, the major financial press contained virtually no stories describing what had caused the surprises. The same pattern continued throughout most of the year. Most of the stories simply reported the magnitude of the surprise but little more. However in December, when Plexus preannounced that earnings would be lower than expected, the loss of business from Motorola was highly salient. As can be seen from the earlier press excerpts, coverage went beyond merely reporting the magnitude of the earnings revision.

Some Theories

The return pattern in post-earnings-announcement drift is part of a more general phenomenon involving momentum in the intermediate term and overreaction in the long term. There have been several theories put forward seeking to explain why this pattern comes about.

In the first theory, Nicholas Barberis, Andrei Shleifer, and Robert Vishny (1998) hypothesize that analysts and investors have difficulty interpreting information about earnings. They suggest that analysts shift back and forth between two different mind-sets. In their first mind-set, analysts think that the rate of change is temporary. This means that they expect that earnings growth will revert. This is their mean-reverting mind-set. In their second mind-set, analysts believe that earnings are in a growth-spurt phase and that earnings growth will soar. This is their continuation mind-set. According to this theory, analysts are prone to have a mean-reverting mind-set. Therefore, when a permanent positive change in the earnings picture takes place for some company, analysts fail to recognize it. The first positive surprise will tend to be followed by a few more. However, after a succession of such changes, analysts will rethink their position and shift to a continuation mind-set. In doing so, however, they extrapolate past growth rates—they bet on trends. Therefore, they overreact. They wind up with a Goldilocks-like problem: Their first reaction is too cold, and their second reaction is too hot. According to this argument, analysts and investors are just too coarsely calibrated to deal effectively with the middle case.

The second theory, by Kent Daniel, David Hirshleifer, and Avanidhar Subrahmanyam (1998), is a little different. Theirs is not an underreaction-based explanation. Rather, they argue that analysts and investors suffer from a combination of overconfidence and *self-attribution bias*. Self-attribution bias occurs when people attribute successful outcomes to their own skill but blame unsuccessful outcomes on bad luck.

According to the theory, the combination of biases leads investors to underreact to information obtained from public sources and overreact to either information or analysis they arrive at on their own. To see how this applies to post-announcement-earnings drift, consider what happens when a company experiences a streak of good news. Suppose that an analyst has managed to uncover the first bit of good news as private information.[8] Having made a good call, the analyst's confidence grows and he becomes more overconfident. Therefore, he recommends a larger position in the stock to the investors he advises. As chance would have it, the streak of good news leads investors to earn a handsome abnormal profit. Note that the higher stake leads the price to jump as well, thereby giving rise to a momentum pattern. Emboldened further, the analyst recommends a larger share. And the momentum continues—that is, until the arrival of bad news. At this time the analyst's overconfidence disappears, and the price drops dramatically, giving rise to an overreaction pattern.

Harrison Hong, Terence Lim, and Jeremy Stein (1999) have proposed a third theory. In their theory, no single investor is in possession of all relevant information. Instead, the information is distributed across different investors. Moreover, cognitive limitations prevent investors from using market prices to infer what others know. Therefore, dispersed information diffuses slowly. The result is momentum. The authors hypothesize that wider analyst coverage and a larger investor base will help speed diffusion.

To test their theory, Hong, Lim, and Stein examine how the strength of the momentum effect varies with the number of analysts following a firm and with firm size. They find that the momentum effect is smaller for larger firms that are more closely followed.[9] They also find that analyst coverage is more pronounced for stocks that are past losers than for stocks that are past winners.

Although these theories are all motivated by behavioral concepts, they differ from one another. Daniel, Hirshleifer, and Subrahmanyam posit that momentum stems from overreaction, whereas the others propose that it stems from underreaction. A key aspect of this difference is that the behavioral traits hypothesized in these papers have not been documented in psychological studies. Rather, the authors have used behavioral bits and pieces to string together their own behaviorally motivated explanations. The explanations are interesting, but I see a flashing yellow light here. In the past, when economists have developed their own psychology, the result has been both bad psychology and bad economics.

Summary

Scholars have produced ample evidence that a trading strategy based on post-earnings-announcement drift has consistently generated positive abnormal returns. What causes intermediate-term momentum but long-term overreaction—is it random chance or heuristic-driven bias? This question has been prominent in the debate on market efficiency. The answer is heuristic-driven bias.

Both analysts and investors react to earnings announcements the way a poor heating system reacts to a sharp drop in winter temperature. At first, the reaction is too slow—the interior temperature stays low for too long and people freeze. Eventually the interior heats up, but instead of turning off at the desired temperature, the heating system overshoots and people boil.

A combination of overconfidence, together with anchoring-and-adjustment leads investors and analysts to adapt insufficiently to the arrival of new information. The result is conservatism. Permanent changes in circumstances get mistaken for temporary ones, at least up to a point. Salience is key here. If the earlier history is especially salient, the information about recent change will be underweighted. If the recent information about change becomes more salient, it will be over-weighted.

PART III

INDIVIDUAL INVESTORS

Chapter 9

"Get-Evenitis":
Riding Losers Too Long

*P*eople appear to be predisposed to "get-evenitis." Are they?

Get-evenitis refers to the difficulty people experience in making peace with their losses. I first discussed get-evenitis in chapter 3, when I introduced the concept of loss aversion. Meir Statman and I (Shefrin and Statman 1985) coined the term *disposition effect*, as shorthand for the *predisposition toward get-evenitis*. In this chapter, I describe the extent to which the disposition effect permeates the investment landscape.

This chapter discusses the following:

- instances of loss aversion in equity markets, mutual fund management, and real estate
- the documentation of loss aversion in the general financial literature

Case Study 1: Cy Lewis

Get-evenitis afflicts both sophisticated and unsophisticated investors. In this first case, I present a sophisticated investor.

Alan "Ace" Greenberg, currently Bear Stearns Company's chairman, believes that "the definition of a good trader is a guy who takes losses."[1] This view almost prevented him from rising to the head of Bear Stearns. His predecessor, Salim "Cy" Lewis, was known for his resistance to take a loss, holding on to every stock he bought.[2] The two clashed. At one point in the 1960s, Mr. Greenberg was able to convince Mr. Lewis to permit him to take losses, but only by threatening to resign. "Before then, he wouldn't let me sell," Mr. Greenberg recalls. "From then on, he let me sell anything I wanted to."

Case Study 2: Investors in Steadman Mutual Funds

Next, consider investors who are not quite as sophisticated as Cy Lewis. Some of the most insightful and entertaining examples of loss aversion have involved holders of Steadman mutual funds. According to quarterly ranking data from Lipper Analytical Services, between June 30, 1994, and April 15, 1997, at least one of the four Steadman funds has had the worst ten-year returns.

Through the 1950s, 1960s, and early 1970s, Melvin Klahr, a math instructor at Broward Community College in Pembroke Pines, Florida, invested about $1,000 in Steadman American Industry and a predecessor fund. In June 1997 his position was worth about $434. His last Steadman purchase was at the end of 1974. Had he placed $1,000 in the average capital-appreciation fund at that time, his position would have appreciated to $29,000 in June 1997. But Klahr stubbornly continues to hold onto his Steadman shares. Why has he not been able to bring himself to sell them?

Mr. Klahr says: "'Cause I'm so stupid. . . . Every time I think about selling it, I think, oh, I think it's going up a bit more." To be sure, the Steadman funds do have their moments. In January 1997, Steadman American Industry and Steadman Associated were up 13.6 percent and 14.7 percent, respectively. This placed them in the top four of diversified stock funds for the month.

In spite of this kind of occasional performance, Klahr does not see his resistance to selling his Steadman position as rational. "Maybe I don't need a financial planner so much as I need a psychiatrist," he says.

Loss Aversion: The General Phenomenon

Although psychiatric intervention might be a bit of an extreme, the aversion to selling at a loss definitely has very strong psychological roots. In chapter 3, I indicated that the phenomenon of get-evenitis is central to prospect theory, the framework developed by Daniel Kahneman and Amos Tversky (1979). Investors who behave in accordance with prospect theory do not mark their assets to market, at least internally. Rather they keep track of their trades in terms of gains or losses relative to the price they originally paid.

Think back to Cy Lewis and Melvin Klahr. Both exhibit loss aversion. Mentally, neither marks to market. Both are eager to get even before they will close out a position. Both suffer from get-evenitis.

Case Study 3: Charles Steadman's Strategy

Get-evenitis leads people to take chances in order to avoid taking a loss. I have already discussed Steadman shareholder Melvin Klahr. But let's also look at Charles Steadman, the late manager of the Steadman funds. He too experienced losses, and his path to those losses is intriguing.

William Steadman, Charles's older brother, started Steadman funds in the 1950s. According to the *Wall Street Journal*, when William died in the 1960s, Charles took over and acquired the right to manage several other mutual funds. Some did well, and assets in all of the Steadman funds together reached $160 million.

A few years ago, the performance of the funds deteriorated, but not abysmally. But then Steadman became ensnared in a legal issue with state securities regulators and the Securities and Exchange Commission. Although the SEC lost a lawsuit against Steadman, it has for the most part blocked the majority of Steadman funds from selling new shares to the public. New inflows did not offset redemptions; thus, as a proportion of money managed, expenses soared. In a January 1997 regulatory filing, two of the funds reported expenses of 25 percent of assets a year, compared to an average of 1 to 2 percent for most stock funds.

How did Mr. Steadman react? To try and earn more than his huge expenses, Mr. Steadman used leveraged, risky investments. On Dec. 31, 1996, Steadman Associates had 16.7 percent of its portfolio invested in Intel Corp. warrants. These warrants gave an investor the right to buy Intel stock at a fixed price. Because it is a leveraged instrument—like a call option—the return to a warrant tends to be quite volatile. If Intel were to close below the exercise price when the warrant expired, then the warrant would expire worthless.

In an April 1997 article, Robert McGough of the *Wall Street Journal* reported that Mr. Steadman came into 1997 with high hopes. In January, Charles Steadman wrote to shareholders that the "performance in 1997 should be reasonably good, and the fund will continue to participate in stocks of high-quality companies. . . . [U]pward movement of stock prices is strongly correlated to the extensive transformation of the national economy from technological discovery and accompanying increased output that we have experienced in recent years, a phenomenon which I disclosed to you a year ago."[3]

Case Study 4: Investing to Fund College Education

Real-world events have a lot of texture, more so than the simple questions involving prizes and probabilities that I discussed in chapter 3. This next case offers a considerable amount of detail to help you understand the context, range of emotions, and unpredictability associated with real-world decisions.

Reality looks much more obvious in hindsight than in foresight. People who experience hindsight bias misapply current hindsight to past foresight. They perceive events that occurred to have been more predictable before the fact than was actually the case. As we study case 4, which involved a real estate investment, I will ask you a series of questions to mitigate the effect of hindsight bias. Some of the questions pertain directly to hindsight bias.

Bill and his wife are in their early thirties and have just had their first child. A good friend of theirs named James has been actively investing in real estate for the last several years. James has displayed a knack for finding undeveloped property that looks like a mess but has great potential. After purchasing a property, James's formula has been to clean it up, divide it into parcels, and resell it at a substantial profit (without adding any structures to the land). In the last three years, James has been able to resell most of his properties for between one and two times what he paid for them. Since his initial purchases were made with borrowed funds, a common practice in real estate investment, James has been earning an extremely high rate of return.

Several years ago James had encountered some personal problems, and Bill was very helpful and supportive during that time. Since then, James has always tried to repay Bill for his kindness in whatever way he could. Last year James recommended that Bill join James by investing in a small rural tract, which Bill did. This year James had been able to sell the tract for 75 percent more than their initial investment. Bill and his wife bumped into James one evening, and James was quite enthusiastic about another deal, predicting: "You'll want to go in with us on this."

With the birth of their child, Bill and his wife have begun to think about setting aside more money for the future, particularly in respect to funding their child's college education. They know that even when the returns on an investment look attractive, those returns can turn out to be quite modest once inflation and taxes are taken into account. They are wondering whether the deal mentioned by James might be a suitable investment for funding their child's future college education.

Later when they meet with James, he tells them the details. A development company that has just declared bankruptcy purchased Clear Lake Development and is eager to sell. James believes that the property has great potential for retirees. It lies in a rural area, on the shore of a lovely lake.

The price tag for Clear Lake would be $205,000, and James suggests that they go in jointly, as equal partners. That is, James would invest $102,500, and so would Bill and his wife. James plans to follow his usual formula. After subdivision, he would sell all the lots within a year or so, for a total of $459,000. Bill and his wife currently have $17,500 in savings, and James assures them that he can arrange for them to borrow the remaining $85,000 at an attractive interest rate. James says that he is a great believer in leverage because it can offset inflation and taxes that really eat into initial returns.

1. On a scale of 1 to 10, how would you rank Clear Lake as an investment whose purpose is to fund college education in fifteen years? Here 10 means *extremely suitable* and 1 means *entirely unsuitable*.

During the first few months, Bill has been making payments on his $85,000 loan. In addition, he is no longer earning a return on the $17,500 of his own money that he invested. When he sees James a few months later, Bill asks him how Clear Lake is doing. James replies that a small glitch has come up.

Apparently, the property had never been surveyed properly, and he has now commissioned a survey. However, no lots can be sold until the survey is complete, and the survey is taking more time than he anticipated. Moreover, the original $85,000 loan has come due and must be renewed. Renewal is not a problem, but the bank only wants to renew the loan for $75,000. Consequently, Bill will have to come up with the additional $10,000 himself. James is clearly embarrassed, but he also remains upbeat about the ultimate success of the project. Fortunately, Bill and his wife have been able to save exactly $10,000 in recent months, and so have the necessary funds.

2. If you were in Bill's situation at this point, how would you react emotionally? Would you be *worried?* or *anxious?* Or would you be patient, believing that most investments incur some glitches here and there and that you are better off having minor problems than

major ones? How might you feel, if you found yourself in this situation: worried, anxious, or patient?

3. If you were Bill or his wife, would you begin to experience any feelings of regret? Specifically, would you feel that anyone should be blamed?

4. If you answered yes, whom would you blame most: yourself, James, or the situation?

5. Think about how the scenario has unfolded so far. At the outset, how obvious does it seem to you that it would have gone this way? That is, were any telltale indications present? How would you answer this question on a scale of 1 to 10, where 10 is *very obvious*, and 1 is *impossible to predict*?

Time passes. In fact, a full year has passed since Bill made his initial investment in Clear Lake. In a conversation, James apologizes that it has taken a year for things to get moving, but says that they now are on the move. He realizes that this has been a period of negative cash flow for Bill, but James says he can work things out so that Bill and his wife won't have to make any more payments on their loan. He, James, will handle the financing details. Moreover, to speed up sales, he will put up a model home on one of the lots. However, he thinks he can take care of the associated costs without asking Bill to contribute additional funds.

The next time Bill sees James, James tells Bill that he has good news and bad news. The good news is that the model home has been built and sold. The bad news is that the sale has not stimulated additional interest in Clear Lake. James says that he feels just terrible that he brought Bill into this venture, and is concerned that it will turn into a cash drain for Bill before too long. Therefore, he proposes taking over Bill's interest in Clear Lake, including all further interest payments, and asks Bill if he would like to sign his interest over to James. If Bill does so, he basically pulls out of this investment. In the event of a further cash drain, Bill would avoid the *extra loss*. But if the investment turns profitable, Bill *loses out on the chance to lower his loss, recover his investment, or make a positive return.*

6. Put yourself in Bill's shoes. How would you react to James's proposal? You are aware that James is more knowledgeable about the real estate market than you are, but you don't think that he would take advantage of you. He is too good a friend. However, you have

now invested $27,500 in Clear Lake. If you sign over your interest to him, you will have to come to terms with a $27,500 loss. If you keep your interest, you risk losing more money. But by keeping your interest you might also recoup your investment if lot sales pick up. What would you do at this stage?

    a. Tell James you understand that he is trying to help you and come to terms with a loss by signing your interest over to him.

    b. Remind James that he said that this was going to pay for your child's college education, and you still expect it to do that (in other words, you want to keep your interest).

7. Imagine that *six* years have passed from the time Bill made his initial investment. As in question 6, James proposes that you sign your interest over to him. In this connection, James also tells you that one of the real estate agents selling Clear Lake lots has offered to purchase all the remaining unsold lots for $35,000. Together with the $8,900 received from the sale of the lot with the model home, the total amount received for *all* the lots would amount to $43,900. Imagine that James informed you that he had decided to accept the real estate agent's offer, and then offered you the opportunity to sign your interest over to him. As in question 6, this offer includes James's taking full responsibility for all future interest payments associated with the loans that were taken out to enter the deal. Would this additional information change your answer to question 6? What would you do in this case?

    a. Tell James you understand that he is trying to help you and sign over your interest

    b. Remind James that he said that this was going to pay for your child's college education, and you still expect it to do that (in other words, you want to keep your interest).

Typically, people who have read the case about Bill and his wife do not think that Clear Lake is a particularly good investment for funding a child's college education. However, once committed financially, they become very reluctant to pull out. When problems begin to develop, they become a little anxious. The majority begins to experience feelings of regret and blame themselves. When James proposes taking over their interest, very few accept his offer in the circumstances I described in question 6. A few more accept the circumstances described in question 7. However, many do not. They cannot *come to terms with the loss.*

This is a real-world case. So how did it actually turn out? In the end, the real estate investment that went sour did not prevent Bill and his wife from sending their child to college. Chelsea Clinton entered Stanford in 1997 as part of the Class of 2001. By now, you may have recognized the major players in this case: Bill and his wife are President Clinton and Hillary Rodham Clinton. Clear Lake is Whitewater, and James is the late Jim McDougal. Note that the dollar sums I described are quite close to the actual amounts.

James Stewart, in his 1996 book *Blood Sport*, reports that Jim McDougal did offer, on more than one occasion, to take over then-governor Clinton's interest in Whitewater. He also reports that the Clintons declined those offers. In what seems to have been a strong case of get-evenitis, Hillary Rodham Clinton is quoted as saying to Susan McDougal, Jim McDougal's wife: "Jim told me that this was going to pay for college for Chelsea. I still expect it to do that!" (p. 133)

It appears that President and Mrs. Clinton suffered from a particularly bad case of get-evenitis. Their failed Whitewater investment eventually became the responsibility of Vincent Foster, a White House aide who committed suicide. The subsequent uproar led the White House chief counsel at the time, Bernard Nussbaum, to explain to President Clinton that he had a choice: Either take his financial records from Whitewater and appear before a Congressional panel, which would involve a personal and political cost to be borne immediately; or take his chances with the appointment of an independent counsel who would most likely cast an extremely wide investigative net.

As we all know, President Clinton took his chances with an independent counsel, and eventually ended up having Kenneth Starr investigate his Whitewater deal and much more. In early 1998, a scandal erupted involving a sexual relationship between the president and a White House intern, Monica Lewinsky. At the time, the president was defending himself in a suit filed by a woman named Paula Jones, who had accused him of harassment during his term as Arkansas governor.

While being deposed in the Paula Jones lawsuit, President Clinton was asked, under oath, if he had had a sexual relationship with Ms. Lewinsky. As we all know by now, he had in fact been involved with Ms. Lewinsky. At the time of the deposition, he faced a choice. He could take an immediate loss (embarrassment at the minimum) or deny the affair and take the gamble that he would not be caught. Being loss averse, he took the gamble.

When the media broke the story of the affair, the president faced a choice: Admit publicly at once to the relationship; or deny involvement and take his chances.

Is there some kind of pattern here? Being loss averse, Clinton denied his involvement, wagging his finger at the television cameras and proclaiming: "I want you to listen to me. . . . I did not have sexual relations with that woman, Miss Lewinsky."

Several months later, he faced Kenneth Starr in a grand jury proceeding and under oath admitted to an inappropriate relationship. By this time, the political establishment was hoping and expecting that the president would address the nation and apologize for deceiving them during the preceding seven months. President Clinton had two courses of action: Address the nation and apologize for his behavior, thereby taking an immediate loss; or admit to some measure of responsibility but make no apology, and instead attempt to refocus the debate by attacking the independent counsel. Even if you did not know how these events eventually turned out, how would you bet at this stage?

As we are aware, the case eventually moved to the floor of Congress, and in December 1998, the House passed two articles of impeachment, one for perjury and the other for obstruction of justice. William Jefferson Clinton thus became only the second president ever to be impeached by the House of Representatives. In 1999 the Senate tried President Clinton and acquitted him on both charges.

In April 1999 the judge in the Paula Jones case cited President Clinton for civil contempt, because he lied under oath. As this book goes to press there are media reports that Kenneth Starr is preparing to indict the president at some point. So the case may not be over. But whatever the eventual outcome, the lesson is clear.

Plenty of Company

Our list of people who suffer from loss aversion now includes the former head of Bear Stearns, a long-time investor in mutual funds, the manager of a group of mutual funds, and President and Mrs. Clinton. Earlier in the book we saw how loss aversion led to the collapse of Barings Bank, and prevented the executives of Apple Computer from terminating the Newton project in a timely fashion (see chapter 3). Later in the book, we shall encounter instances that are more dramatic. However, the evidence about the prevalence of loss aversion among investors goes beyond anecdote and laboratory experiments.

Meir Statman and I (Shefrin and Statman 1985) suggest that people generally sell their winners too early and hold their losers too long. Realizing a loss is painful, despite the possibility of a tax advantage. An investor who recognizes the tax benefit but finds the psychological cost too painful experiences a self-control problem. Some investors find ways to realize tax losses eventually, notably, by using December as a deadline.

Recent work by Terrance Odean confirms that this is so. Odean (1998a) reports his findings on the disposition effect based on a study of approximately 163,000 customer accounts at a nationwide discount brokerage house.

For each trading day and individual account, Odean looked at the value of all the stock positions that corresponded to capital gains. Some of these gains would have been realized on that day, and others would not. Odean compared the fraction of all gains sold on this particular day with the fraction of losses realized.

Investors who are loss averse realize more of their paper gains than they do their paper losses. It turns out that from January through November, investors realize gains 1.68 times more frequently than they realize losses. This means that a stock that is up in value is almost 70 percent more likely to be sold than a stock that is down. Only in the month of December do investors realize losses more rapidly than gains, though only by 2 percent.

Which stocks do investors trade the most frequently? They trade stocks that have outperformed the market in the two years prior to the transaction. But although investors tend to realize their smaller losses, they continue to hold on to their larger losses. Perhaps investors act like Melvin Klahr, waiting for their paper loss to disappear. One of the big surprises in Odean's study is that investors sell the wrong stocks. They receive subpar returns from the losers they keep. But the losers they sell subsequently do great.

In a similar vein, Jeffrey Heisler (1994) provides empirical evidence about the impact of loss aversion on futures traders. His data consist of over 2,000 individual futures account–trading histories, containing more than 19,000 trades, covering the period November 1989 through October 1992. The study deals with the behavior of off-floor traders in the Treasury Bond futures market of the Chicago Board of Trade. Heisler found that off-floor traders hold initial paper losses longer than trades that show initial paper gains. Significantly, he finds that when traders hold losers, their trading activity is nonprofitable. Only

24 percent of the accounts in his sample show a profit over the period he studied. On average, off-floor traders lose $17 per contract traded.

Finally, remember the third case, concerning Steadman's strategy? The example may be an outlier, but Steadman's approach is typical for mutual fund managers. Keith Brown, Van Harlow, and Laura Starks (1996) report that fund managers who find themselves in the middle of their comparison group by midyear subsequently increase the risk of their fund's portfolio during the second half of the year. For further details see chapter 12, on open-ended mutual funds.

Summary

Most people exhibit loss aversion: They have great difficulty coming to terms with losses. Consequently, people are predisposed to hold their losers too long, and correspondingly sell their winners too early. I provided several examples of the phenomenon in this chapter. However, there are others to be encountered elsewhere in this volume. Some pertain to money managers. Other examples pertain to decisions by corporate executives who, reluctant to terminate losing projects, instead throw good money after bad.

Chapter 10

Portfolios, Pyramids, Emotions, and Biases

*H*arry Markowitz, the pioneer of modern portfolio theory, played it both ways. Markowitz developed the theory of mean-variance portfolios, one of the pillars of traditional finance. But he also developed the basic ideas that underlie frame dependence and loss aversion. And when it came time to choose his own retirement portfolio, Harry Markowitz played it the behavioral way (see chapter 3).

Most investors do the same. Playing it the behavioral way means that they base their portfolio choices not on mean-variance principles but on frame dependence, heuristic-driven bias, and something I call the *emotional time line*. In this chapter I describe how these three elements together shape (1) the kinds of portfolios that investors choose, (2) the types of securities investors find attractive, (3) the relationship that investors form with financial advisers, and (4) the biases to which investors are subject.

This chapter discusses the following:

- the emotional time line—how emotions affect risk tolerance and portfolio choice over time
- why the combination of emotion and framing induces many investors to structure their portfolios as "layered pyramids"
- how a well-designed security must fit naturally into a layered pyramid
- the role of regret in the investor-advisor relationship
- how heuristic-driven bias inhibits investors from diversifying fully, and induces them to trade too frequently

The Emotional Time Line

Why is it important to discuss emotion in a chapter on portfolio selection? Emotions determine tolerance for risk, and tolerance for risk plays a key role in portfolio selection. Note that investing takes place along a time line. In short, investors experience a variety of emotions as they

- ponder their alternatives,

- make decisions about how much risk to bear,

- ride the financial roller coaster while watching their decisions play out,

- assess whether to keep to the initial strategy or alter it, and

- ultimately learn the degree to which they have achieved their financial goals.

Psychologist Lola Lopes (1987) identifies the major emotions along the time line and discusses the way that these emotions influence risk bearing. According to folklore, greed and fear drive financial markets. But this is only partly correct. While fear does play a role, most investors react less to greed and more to *hope*. Fear induces an investor to focus on events that are especially unfavorable, while hope induces him or her to focus on events that are favorable. In addition to hope and fear, that apply *generally*, investors have *specific* goals to which they aspire.

To what kind of goals do investors aspire? Typical goals include purchasing a home, funding children's college education, and having a comfortable retirement.

Think of the emotional time line as a line where time advances from left to right. Investment decisions lie at the left, and goals lie at the right. Investors experience a variety of emotions along the time line as they make decisions at the left, wait in the middle, and learn their fate at the right. Hope and fear are polar opposites, one positive and the other negative. Picture positive emotion above the time line and negative emotion below it. What happens above the time line as time progresses from left to right? Hope becomes anticipation and is then transformed into pride. Below the line, fear becomes anxiety[1] and is then transformed into regret. You may recall from chapter 3 that Harry Markowitz talked about the importance of regret when planning his own retirement, saying "my intention was to minimize my future regret." [*Money* magazine, January 1998, p. 118.]

Hope and fear affect the way that investors evaluate alternatives. Fear causes investors to look at possibilities from the bottom up and ask, How bad can things get? Hope gets investors to look at possibilities from the top down and ask, How good can it get? In Lopes's terminology, the bottom-up perspective emphasizes the desire for security, whereas the top-down perspective emphasizes the need for potential on the upside. Lopes tells us that these two perspectives reside within all of us, as opposite poles. But they tend not be equally matched: One pole usually predominates.

Barbara O'Neill (1990) has compiled an interesting collection of financial planning cases. The title of her book is *How Real People Handle Their Money*. Here is an example from her casebook, describing the situation of one particular couple, Barbara and Leon Smyth.[2]

> If they lived in a big city, instead of a rural area, you could probably call them "yuppies." Barbara and Leon Smyth, ages 35 and 37, are a two-career couple who earn a combined \$45,300.[3] They have a son, aged 14, from Leon's previous marriage. . . . Like many married couples, the Smyths have different attitudes about money. While Barbara is most concerned about safety of principal, Leon's major objective is future growth and he says he's willing to assume some risk to achieve financial gain. [Case study # 21]

The dominant emotion in Barbara is fear, and it leads her to emphasize security. For Leon, the dominant emotion is hope, and it leads him to emphasize potential. One of the great contributions of Lopes is to establish how the interaction of these conflicting emotions determines the tolerance toward risk. If there were one important point to take away from this chapter, this would be it!

Portfolios, Goals, and Risk Tolerance

What about the Smyths' portfolio? Does it reflect the emotional profile of Leon and Barbara with respect to security, potential, and aspiration? The Smyths have two major financial assets: a money market account and a growth mutual fund in a custodial trust that is earmarked to fund their (Leon's) son's college education.

Financial planners often suggest that investors form portfolios using a layered pyramid. Figure 10-1 offers a representative example from a book by Ginita Wall (1995). The pyramid is structured to address the needs associated with security, potential, and aspiration. At

Figure 10-1 A Portfolio as a Layered Pyramid

A typical layered pyramid that financial planners use to advise clients about building portfolios. Movements from bottom to top involve moving to riskier assets. Movements from right to left involve higher yield. *Source: The Way to Save,* Ginita Wall, 1993.

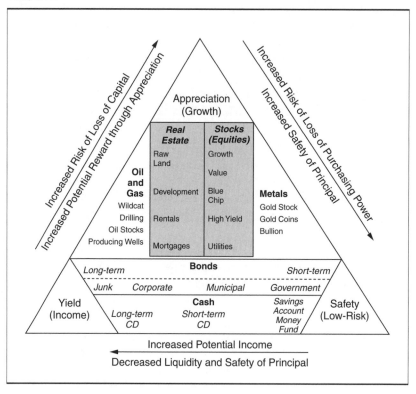

the bottom of the pyramid are securities designed to provide investors with security. These include money market funds and certificates of deposit. Further up the pyramid come bonds. Financial planners often suggest that investors earmark particular investments for specific goals. A common example is to use zero coupon bonds to fund the goal of providing for children's college education. Climbing up one more layer in the pyramid takes us to stocks and real estate. As Wall indicates, these are intended for appreciation, upside potential.

At the pinnacle of the pyramid lie the most speculative investments, such as out-of-the-money call options and lottery tickets, intended for a shot at getting rich. Lopes describes planning as "applied hoping," and she quotes Robin Pope (1983), who discusses the psychological value of such investments. Pope states that "after deciding to devote a fraction of the housekeeping funds to a weekly lottery ticket, housekeepers can dream from age nineteen to ninety-nine that they will become millionaires after the next drawing" (p. 156).

Without question, anticipation has value. Economist George Lowenstein (1987) reports an experiment where undergraduate students evaluated how much a kiss from a movie star of their choice was worth to them, depending on when the kiss was received. The students valued a kiss that would come in three days time as being worth more than a kiss received immediately, in three hours, or in one day. Why pay to wait? The opportunity to anticipate the experience.

Jonathan Clements writes a regular column for the *Wall Street Journal* called "Getting Going" that focuses on individual investing. In his column, he frequently quotes financial planners on the issues being discussed in this chapter. For example, a December 1997, column contains the following interesting characterization of the pyramid pinnacle: "'With my clients, we set up mad-money accounts,' says Deena Katz, a financial planner in Coral Gables, Fla. 'That's the money they use to buy hot stocks and go to Vegas. You should make a conscious decision about how much you're going to speculate with.'"[4] Clements recommends keeping the speculative portion of a portfolio below 5 percent. But he clearly recognizes the key emotion driving speculation. In his July 2, 1996, column he lumped lotteries and actively managed stock funds together, choosing as his headline "Hope Springs Eternal." Whereas anticipation is the manifestation of hope along the emotional time line between decision and outcome, anxiety is the manifestation of fear.

In Lopes's framework, the relative strengths of these two emotions, in conjunction with aspiration, determine tolerance for risk. In the context of portfolio selection, risk tolerance determines the allocation between the layers of the pyramid. The relative strengths of hope, fear, and aspiration determine the allocation between stocks and bonds.

Kenneth Fisher and Meir Statman (1997) analyze the nature of the advice that mutual fund companies provide to investors about the appropriate mix of stocks, bonds, and cash in their portfolios. These companies encourage investors who are more tolerant of risk and who have enough time to emphasize stocks in their mix. Financial planners provide similar advice. Of particular interest is the advice they offer when a major goal is financially within reach. In this situation, many planners recommend that investors consider shifting completely out of stocks.

Jonathan Clements discusses the issue of goal horizons in his December 2, 1997, column, in which he makes clear that the issue concerns whether a portfolio without stocks could deliver the returns required to achieve the investor's goal. He states:

> Would you be able to reach your investment goals with those sorts of annual returns? If not, then you really need to have at least some of your money in stocks, which have delivered over 10% a year on average since year-end 1925, according to Ibbotson Associates, the Chicago research firm.
>
> "If you're saving for college or retirement, stocks are really the only way to go," argues Alan Cohn, a financial planner in Bala Cynwyd, Pa. "There's nothing else that will provide you with that high rate of return."
>
> On the other hand, if you don't need high returns, then maybe you shouldn't take the risk of being in stocks.
>
> "We always invest for the lowest level of equity exposure possible," says Harold Evensky, a financial planner in Coral Gables, Fla. "Some of my friends would disagree with that. They would say, if you can live with an all-equity portfolio, you should be all-equity. We say, if all you need is 60% stocks to meet your goals, we should go for 60% stocks."[5]

What is the logic of avoiding equities? This is hardly a mean-variance argument. Mean-variance efficiency prescribes reducing the riskiness of a portfolio by shifting the allocation from stocks and bonds to cash but leaving the relative proportions of stocks and bonds intact. But mean-variance efficiency is ill equipped to deal both with goals and with the attendant psychological factors attached to them.

What about the emotional elements? Well, when a major financial goal is within reach, fear and aspiration combine to favor a conservative strategy. But suppose a conservative strategy virtually guarantees that an investor's aspirations will be unmet. In this case, the desire to increase the probability of reaching her goal will induce an investor to hold equities. There is also a time horizon issue involved. Clements continues:

> How long will you be investing?
>
> Wall Street's conventional wisdom suggests that the older you are, the less you should have in stocks. But in truth, the key factor isn't your age, but how long you will be investing. If you plan to buy a

home next month, for instance, you would be a fool to have your house down payment sitting in stocks, no matter how young you are.

Mr. Evensky offers this rule of thumb: Don't put money into stocks unless you are more than five years from your goal. Suppose your son is nine years from college. Initially, you might put some of junior's tuition money into stocks.

But once college is within five years, lighten up, preferably unloading the shares when the market is booming. "I'm always looking for a five-year window, during which I can decide when to sell," Mr. Evensky says.[6]

What is going on here? Again, the "five-year rule" is hardly a mean-variance strategy. Again, emotional variables drive the behavior. Think about how an investor would feel if he

1. had sufficient resources to achieve a major goal that was less than five years away by investing in safe fixed income securities, but

2. continued to allocate these resources heavily in equities; and

3. at the end of the horizon for his goal, his equity investments had declined in price, and his goal had moved out of reach.

The dominant emotion in such a case would be regret. Hence moving out of stocks within five years of an attainable goal is a regret-avoidance strategy.

Frame Dependence: Mental Accounts and Priorities—Is Safety First?

Lopes (1987) discusses a splendid metaphor for portfolio choice: J. Anderson's (1979) description of how subsistence farmers allocate their land between low-risk food crops and high-risk cash crops. Farmers first take care of subsistence needs, and then they plant cash crops. Theirs is a very risky portfolio. Why? It is the only way they have a chance at meeting the goals to which they aspire. Is there an analogy with investors? Here is Clements again, this time from his January 7, 1997, column:

A lot depends on your financial situation. If you can barely afford to make the house down payment, it would be nice to take greater risks so that you earn higher returns. But if the market turns against you, the consequences could be dire.

On other hand, if you have more than enough money to make the house down payment, shooting for higher returns is less of a risk, because you could still make the down payment even if you suffered some investment losses. Because you do have plenty of money, however, there's also less incentive to try for higher returns.

Indeed, it's one of the ironies of investing. The rich can afford to take risks, but they don't need to. The poor need to take risks, but they often can't afford to.[7]

To what extent do investors think about their portfolios in layers, with the bottom layer earmarked for security and the top layer earmarked for potential? I ran a small survey asking eighty-one investors a series of questions that bear on this and related points. In the main, I found that investors, like the subsistence farmers described earlier, do think in terms of layers based on security and potential.[8] Less than 20 percent indicated otherwise. Of those that do layer their portfolios, 70 percent concentrate on security first, before investing for potential. Respondents are even stronger in saying that they are willing to take a fair amount of risk on the upside, once they have adequate protection on the downside.[9]

A Meeting of the Ways

The emotion-based perspective of risk tolerance is very different from the perspective adopted in mean-variance analysis. Yet, the two are beginning to come together, as investors begin to use sophisticated software to make investment decisions. For example, investors can now use the Internet to obtain investment advice about their 401(k) plans. A major Internet provider of 401(k) advice is the firm Financial Engines, cofounded by Nobel laureate William Sharpe. Financial Engines software enables 401(k) investors to access the same mean-variance algorithms that Sharpe developed for institutional money managers.

But do investors think in mean-variance terms? Do they conceptualize their risk tolerance as the maximum increase in return variance that they could accept in return for a 100-basis-point increase in expected return? A June 29, 1998 article in *U.S. News & World Report* describes the performance measurement criterion—and it's neither the mean nor the variance—displayed in the Financial Engines software.

The most compelling feature is that a user's expected returns are expressed as probabilities—for example, the system might say, "You have a 41 percent chance of reaching your goal of $80,000 per year in retirement."

By adjusting risk, contribution level, and retirement age, a user can see how different combinations affect the chance of succeeding. (Kaye and Ahmad 1998).

Lopes repeatedly stresses that when individuals consider aspiration, they focus on the probability of achieving at least the *aspiration* level. So being told that there is a "41 percent chance of reaching your goal" is precisely what they want to know. Hence, we have a meeting of the ways. Financial Engines software will furnish investors with mean-variance portfolios. But investors will evaluate the risk attached to those portfolios in terms of fear, hope, and aspiration.[10]

Security Design

British Premium Bonds resemble index-linked certificates of deposit, but with a twist. Holders of these government bonds are assured of receiving their principal. But in lieu of interest, they receive tickets to monthly lotteries that carry prizes between £50 and £250,000. A Premium Bond packages a very safe security with a lottery ticket, and it is very popular. What accounts for the attraction?

Most investors do not choose securities by ascertaining where the risk-return profiles place the securities on the mean-variance frontier. Rather, investors' choices stem from their emotional reaction to the features promised by the securities. Those that promise safety appeal to investors whose primary emotion is fear. Securities that promise potential appeal to investors whose primary emotion is hope. But many investors are driven by both emotions; Lopes calls them "cautiously hopeful." Think about British Premium Bonds in this light: Perhaps the popularity of these bonds stem from the fact that they address both emotional needs.

What types of securities appeal to these investors? Below are two examples, taken from a paper by Statman and me titled "Behavioral Portfolio Theory" (Shefrin and Statman 1999). Dean Witter proposes what they call the Principal Guaranteed Strategy, which they describe as follows:

"Mr. Stewart" has $50,000 to invest and a time horizon of 10 years. He is looking to add stocks to his portfolio for growth, but is concerned with protecting his principal. Based on his objectives and risk tolerance, "Mr. Stewart's" Dean Witter Account Executive structures the

Principal Guaranteed Portfolio below, which includes "buy" rated stocks from Dean Witter's Recommended List.

To "protect" Mr. Stewart's $50,000 investment, the Principal Guaranteed Strategy calls for the purchase, for $24,951, of a zero coupon bond with a face value of $50,000 maturing in ten years. This leaves $25,049 for stocks and brokerage commissions.

The Principal Guaranteed Strategy has a payoff pattern that appeals to both fear and hope. The bond portion ensures that, if held the full ten years, the payoff will not fall below the $50,000 initial purchase price, while the stock portion offers a chance for a gain.

Here is another example. Life USA, an insurance firm, offers Annu-a-Dex. Annu-a-Dex provides a guaranteed return of 45 percent over a seven-year horizon. An additional amount might be paid based on the performance of the stock market. Life USA describes the payoff as follows:

> [Y]our principal will increase by 45% in the next seven years, market correction or not. And if the market does better than that, you get half the action. All without downside risk. You get the ride without the risk.

Annu-a-Dex is appealing to an investor whose aspiration level is 45 percent above current wealth. The payoff distribution has a floor at the aspiration level, and it offers some measure of upward potential beyond that level.[11]

Regret, Responsibility, and Financial Advisers

Regret is a painful experience that has already come up for discussion a couple of times. To help understand its impact on individual investors, consider the following example.

In March and early April 1997, the stock market experienced a substantial decline. At the time, there was a lot of concern expressed in the financial press about whether a crash might be at hand. Suppose that a conversation took place between you and your friends George, John, and Paul.

George had a lot of his portfolio in stocks, and on the basis of his own analysis decided to sell his stocks and buy certificates of deposit (CDs).

John was in the same situation as George, and like him, switched out of stocks and into CDs. However, John based his decision on his financial adviser's recommendation rather than on his own analysis.

Paul has traditionally held CDs. In fact, he follows a CD rollover rule (rolling over the proceeds from a maturing CD into a new one). He had been holding some CDs that had just matured. Paul thought that the market would rebound, and he considered changing his usual practice by purchasing mutual fund shares instead of renewing his CDs. But in the end, he decided to renew his CDs.

Subsequently, the market has appreciated by 15 percent. All three investors held CD portfolios during this period. All would have been better off by buying stocks.

Now consider this: whose self-image do you think suffers the most?

- George, who traded out of stocks and into CDs based on his own analysis
- John, who traded out of stocks and into CDs based on his adviser's recommendation
- Paul, who renewed his CDs
- nobody—self-image plays no role in these situations

When I ask this question to my classes, the typical responses I receive are as follows. About 70 percent choose George, 12 percent choose John, virtually no one chooses Paul, and 18 percent choose "nobody."

The vast majority choose George because he has no one to blame for a decision gone wrong. George must accept one hundred percent of the responsibility. Meir Statman and I discussed this issue in an article we wrote for *Psychology Today* (Shefrin and Statman 1986). Presumably George, John, and Paul all regret their decision to go with CDs: After all, in hindsight all three recognize that they would have been better off had they gone with stocks. But most judge George's pain to be the worst.

John, on the other hand, gets to blame his adviser. I would argue, in fact, that the shifting of responsibility from John to his adviser is one of the main services for which John's adviser gets paid. Hand-holding may be every bit as important as traditional advice, if not more so.

Hardly anyone picks Paul because Paul followed what for him was a *conventional* strategy. Daniel Kahneman and Amos Tversky (1982) argue that people who deviate from what is for them a conventional way of acting become especially vulnerable to the pain of regret if things go badly. Why? Because regret is counterfactual. If Paul were to deviate from his conventional behavior pattern and things were to go wrong, it would be so easy to imagine having done the conventional thing. And the ease of imagining taking the appropriate action is what triggers the emotion of regret.

In this example, both George and John take actions and soon after learn that their action resulted in a situation not to their liking. In short-term situations, regret is mainly associated with the taking of an action. However, when people are asked to think back over their lives, reflect on their regrets, and indicate what caused them the most regret—the things they did, or those they didn't—what do most of them say? Psychologists Thomas Gilovich and Victoria Husted-Medvec (1995) find that people most regret the things they didn't do. When it comes to the long-term, we most regret inaction.

Having a financial adviser enables the investor to carry a psychological call option. If an investment decision turns out well, the investor can take the credit, attributing the favorable outcome to his or her own skill. If the decision turns out badly, the investor can protect his or her ego and lower the regret by blaming the adviser. This phenomenon involves *self-attribution bias.* The investor attributes favorable outcomes to skill, and unfavorable outcomes to either somebody else, or just plain bad luck.

Regret is intertwined with hindsight bias, in which a person regards the events that happened as much more inevitable than they looked before the fact. For example, take Bernard Baruch, the legendary financier from the 1920s and 1930s. Martin Fridson (1998) reports that when Baruch wrote his memoirs in the 1950s he recalls having warned of the impending stock market crash of 1929. But looking back at his 1929 writings, he appears to have been as bullish as anyone was. Memory plays tricks on us. William Goetzmann and Nadav Peles (1994) find that mutual fund owners recollect that their funds performed much better than was in fact the case. Goetzmann and Peles attribute this tendency to *cognitive dissonance.* Not wanting to judge themselves harshly, investors simply remember beating the market.

Regret and hindsight bias come together in the selection of loser stocks for a portfolio. As I discussed in chapter 3, a portfolio of losers historically outperformed the market by 19 percent on a cumulative three-year basis. But when losers continue to lose, their continued poor performance looks inevitable in hindsight; and it is easy to imagine having avoided them. Indeed in chapter 7, I noted that Werner De

Bondt and Richard Thaler, who discovered the winner-loser effect, found that people, including themselves, were *fearful* of investing in loser stocks.

Heuristic-Driven Bias and Portfolio Selection

Individual investors are especially prone to heuristic-driven bias. Here is some intriguing evidence from a survey of individual investors conducted by De Bondt (1998). A group of forty-five investors were recruited at a conference organized by the National Association of Investment Clubs. Two thirds were men. The average investor in the group was fifty-eight years old, had been trading stocks for the previous eighteen years, and had a financial portfolio (excluding real estate) worth $310,000 that was 72 percent invested in stocks. He or she spent seven hours per week thinking about his or her investments, time that included viewing the television program *Wall $treet Week with Louis Rukeyser.*

Over a period of twenty weeks, De Bondt tracked the group's forecasts for the future performance of both the Dow Jones and their own stocks. Four of his findings are especially fascinating. (1) Investors were excessively optimistic about the future performance of shares they owned, but *not* about the Dow Jones. (2) They were overconfident in that they found themselves surprised by the price changes to their stocks more frequently than they had anticipated. (3) Their stock price forecasts were anchored on past performance: During an uptrend for one of their stocks, investors thought there was little room left for movement on the upside but a lot of room on the downside. The reverse held true for downtrends.[12] (4) They underestimated the degree to which their stocks moved in tandem with the market. In other words, they underestimated beta.

Equally interesting are the *attitudes* that De Bondt's investors expressed. (1) When it comes to picking stocks, they certainly do not believe in throwing darts. (2) Investors stated that they believe a solid understanding of a few firms is a better risk-management tool than diversification. (3) Not only do investors reject the notion that beta measures risk, they reject the fact that risk and return are positively related.

De Bondt's survey informs us that individual investors

- display excessive optimism,

- are overconfident,

- discount diversification, and

- reject there being a positive tradeoff between risk and return.

In the next few sections, I take up these issues in detail.

Optimism

Let's return to O'Neill's (1990) book of financial planning case studies. Those studies provide a sense of how eclectic, and problematic, the portfolios of individual investors can be. Her examples cover a multitude of sins such as inadequate insurance coverage, the failure to diversify, and excessive risk taking.

Why do so many people appear to have inadequate insurance coverage? Included in her group are the Smyths, whose case we discussed earlier. They lack long-term disability insurance. And the Smyths have plenty of company, especially from people in their twenties. This is one case of insufficient fear. O'Neill points out that the "twentysomethings" are seven times more likely to experience an extended disability than they are to die young. Presumably, they are unduly optimistic.

In fact, excessive optimism is a well-studied phenomenon, especially among people in their teens and early twenties. Psychologist Neil Weinstein (1980) found that people in this age group systematically think that they are less likely to experience bad outcomes, and more likely to experience good outcomes, than their peers. In replicating Weinstein's study, I have found that the same phenomenon holds true for people between the ages of 25 and 45, though to a lesser degree than for the younger cohort.

Overconfidence: Too Much Trading

Outside their 401(k) plans, many investors earn mediocre returns because they trade too much. A study by Brad Barber and Terrance Odean (1998b) finds that individual investors tilt their portfolios toward high-beta, small-capitalization value stocks.[13] Barber and Odean examined the trading histories of 60,000 investors over the six-year period ending in 1996. They found that during this time, individuals managed to beat the value-weighted market index by 60 basis points, although that was gross of trading costs. Trading costs ate up 240 basis points of returns. Not surprisingly, the individuals who traded most fared the worst, underperforming the index by 500 basis points.

Why do individual investors trade so much when the net effect is to reduce their returns? Clearly, they believe they can pick winners. But Barber and Odean suggest that investors are overconfident in their abilities. There is good reason to expect that this is the case, since overconfidence is ubiquitous, especially when difficult tasks are involved. Investors may also overrate their abilities. As noted in chapter 4, I asked my MBA students to rate themselves as drivers relative to the general population. Only 8 percent rated themselves below average; 65 percent rated themselves above average. The 65 percent figure may actually be low. Kahneman and Mark Riepe (1997) report that the general figure is more like 80 percent.

There is at least one additional explanation for why people trade so much. Lopes (1987) suggests that people are motivated to master their environment, and it is unpleasant to believe that one has no control, especially when chance and skill elements coexist. The trading of stocks fits this bill. Investors who are high in the desire for control and suffer from the illusion of control are prone to trade frequently.

The Online Revolution

Overconfidence, desire for control, and the illusion of control appear to be especially acute when it comes to online trading, Internet stocks, and day trading.

Online trading has made it cheaper and easier for individual investors to trade stocks. Between 1996 and 1998 the average commission charged per trade by the ten largest online trading firms dropped by about 75 percent. The amount of assets managed online went from near zero to about $100 billion in 1997. On June 1, 1999, in a move that may dramatically change the brokerage industry forever, Merrill Lynch broke from its traditional, high-cost, full-service approach and announced its intention to enter the low-cost business of online trading.

In 1998, Internet stocks captured investors' attention, especially those of online traders. On the strength of investors' imagination, and little else, Internet stock prices were propelled into orbit. According to Lipper Analytical Services the best-performing mutual fund in 1998 was the Internet Fund, managed by Kinetics Asset Management. It had a return of 196 percent.

Overconfidence and optimism appear to be particularly severe among day traders, the online traders who have abandoned regular jobs to trade full time from their personal computers. The lure of day trading has soared with the appearance of best-selling books and Web sites devoted to the subject.

Some things never change. Statman and I (Shefrin and Statman 1993b) discuss the evolution of the 1933 Securities Act and the 1934 Securities Exchange Act as a response to the fate that befell optimistic, overconfident traders in the 1920s.[14] Legislators enacted limits on margin and suitability requirements as a means of mitigating insufficient self-control (gambling addiction) and heuristic-driven bias. On January 27, 1999, Securities and Exchange Commission chair Arthur Levitt warned that online trading was like "a narcotic" to many online traders.[14] The technology may have changed over the last seventy years, but human psychology has not.

Generally speaking, most online investors are between 25 and 45 years old. In 1998, about 75 percent of online traders were men; the most active online cohort was the 30–34 age group. Investors in this age group are especially prone to optimism and overconfidence. A PaineWebber study found that younger investors were more optimistic than older investors were. (See chapter 5.)

As for gender, Barber and Odean (1998a) describe the differences between the trading patterns of men and women. Barber and Odean's data come from a large discount brokerage firm, consist of individual investors' trading records, and cover the period February 1991 through January 1997. During this period, the performance of the stocks picked by men and stocks picked by women were about the same. But men traded 45 percent more than women. And men chose stocks in smaller companies, having higher price-to-book, and higher betas. As a result men earned 1.4 percent less on a risk-adjusted basis. The numbers are even more dramatic for single men and single women. Single men traded 67 percent more but earned 2.3 percent less, on a risk-adjusted basis.

The Failure to Diversify

The failure to diversify is by now a well-documented phenomenon. One investor who computes mean-variance efficient portfolios for a living confided to me that he had but one stock in his individual retirement account (IRA). Needless to say, I was curious as to which one. The answer? Microsoft. He told me, "I let Bill Gates manage my IRA."

Virtually all academic studies of individual investors' portfolios find that they only contain a few securities. For example, an early study by Blume, Crockett, and Friend (1974) found that 34.1 percent of investors in their sample of 17,056 investors held only one dividend-paying stock, 50 percent held no more than two stocks, and only 10.7 percent held more than ten stocks. A Federal Reserve Board survey on the financial characteristics of consumers showed that the average number of stocks in the portfolio was 3.41 (Blume and Friend 1975). More recently Martha Starr-McCluer (1994), an economist at the Federal Reserve Board in Washington, reports similar findings based upon the Survey of Consumer Finances, sponsored by the Federal Reserve Board.

Lease, Lewellen, and Schlarbaum (1976) surveyed investors who held accounts with a major brokerage company and found that the average number of stocks in a portfolio ranged from 9.4 to 12.1, depending on the demographic group.

While we know that there are only few stocks in the typical portfolio, it is possible that diversification is accomplished through bonds, real estate, and other assets. However, evidence by Mervyn King and Jonathan Leape (1984), as well as most of O'Neill's case studies, indicates that limited diversification is observed even where assets other than stocks are included.

It is abundantly clear that individual investors have a very primitive understanding of what constitutes a well-diversified portfolio. In *The Investment Club Book,* John Wasik (1995) indicates that the National Association of Investors Corporations (NAIC), which represents 8,000 stock-picking clubs, advises that portfolios include no fewer than five stocks. The NAIC calls this the *Rule of Five.* The theory is that of the five stocks, one will probably be a loser, three will produce mediocre returns, but the fifth will be a real winner!

Of course, the number of securities in the portfolio is not the sole determinant of the proximity to mean-variance efficiency. Jacob (1974) and others have shown that an investor can reduce unsystematic risk significantly with only a few securities by a judicious selection of securities. However, Blume and Friend (1978) report that the actual degree of diversification for 70 percent of the investors in their study was lower than suggested by the number of securities in the portfolios.

Naive Diversification

Shlomo Benartzi and Richard Thaler (1998) have written a most intriguing study of the way many investors approach diversification in their 401(k) accounts. They present strong evidence that individuals divide their money evenly across all the choices their 401(k) plan makes available. So, if their plan offers them one bond fund and one stock fund, they will split their contributions fifty-fifty. This is what Harry Markowitz acknowledged doing in his own retirement account (1998).

If there are three choices, a money market fund, a bond fund, and a stock fund, then investors will split their contributions three ways equally. Benartzi and Thaler call this heuristic the $1/n$ rule, and characterize it as *naive diversification*.

The heuristic is important because depending on how the choices are structured, individuals can end up taking too little risk or excessive risk, relative to their risk tolerance. Somebody whose employer offers a plan that has two bond funds and one stock fund will end up with one third of their allocation in equities. However, the reverse will be true for someone who works for a company like TWA that offers a plan with more stock funds than bond funds.

Home Bias: Familiarity Does Not Always Breed Contempt

Although U.S. stocks only account for 45 percent of global market value of equity, U.S. investors tend to concentrate their holdings in U.S. stocks. This phenomenon is called the *home bias*. Ken French and James Poterba (1993) point out that in 1989 U.S. investors held less than 7 percent of their portfolios in foreign securities. Moreover, Europeans concentrate their portfolios in European stocks, and Japanese concentrate in Japanese stocks. Why?

In a word, familiarity. Remember the aversion to ambiguity discussed in chapter 2? In unfamiliar situations, the predominant emotion tends to be fear. Foreign stocks are less familiar than U.S. stocks. Perhaps familiarity also explains why, in their portfolios, people tend to overweight the stocks of companies they work for. Gur Huberman (1997) points out that U.S. investors concentrate their holdings in the Baby Bells—the former Bell operating companies—of their own region. Of course, investors who shun the Baby Bells of other regions, like investors who shun foreign stocks, give up some of the benefits of diversification.

Summary

The major factors driving portfolio selection are much more complex than the mean and variance of future returns. This chapter described how frame dependence, heuristic-driven bias, and the emotional time line together shape (1) the kinds of portfolios that investors choose, (2) the types of securities investors find attractive, (3) the relationship that investors form with financial advisers, and (4) the biases to which investors are subject.

The key emotions pertain to fear, hope, and the aspirations attached to investor goals. Heuristic-driven bias stems from a variety of phenomena: naive diversification rules such as the "Rule of Five" and the "$1/n$" heuristic, hindsight bias, excessive optimism, overconfidence, self-attribution bias, and fear of the unfamiliar.

Chapter **11**

Retirement Saving: Myopia and Self-Control

When it comes to planning for retirement, Americans delude themselves.

Anyone wanting to plan successfully for retirement recognizes the need to accomplish a series of key tasks.

1. Identify financial needs during retirement.

2. Save an appropriate amount over time.

3. Select a portfolio of assets with a risk-return profile that is appropriate for reaching their retirement goal.

4. Have procedures in place to prevent those assets from being consumed too early.

This chapter discusses the following:

- why investors need to overcome myopia and exercise self-control in order to save for retirement

- why investors find dividends attractive, and use frame dependence to save more

- how investors use mental accounting and dollar-cost averaging to save and manage the risk in their portfolios

What are the psychological phenomena in question? First comes *myopia*, leading to shortsightedness and low tolerance for risk. Low risk tolerance primarily stems from *loss aversion*. Next comes *overconfidence*: Investors seem pretty blasé about having sufficient resources in place for retirement, despite the absence of clear retirement plans. Third,

139

inadequate saving is essentially a *self-control* problem that occurs because the *temptation* to consume now is especially strong. *Exercising self-control* involves the *cultivation of good habits,* and good saving habits make good use of mental accounting. That is, good savings habits exploit frame dependence.

The chapter is organized around the household life cycle that begins with the road to retirement—the working phase when accumulation occurs, the onset of retirement, and culminates with the retirement phase itself. At each stage of the life cycle, I discuss the psychological impediments to saving adequately for retirement and present frame dependence–based measures that can be used to overcome these impediments. To introduce the main ideas, I begin with a short case.

Case Study: Myopia and Facing the Road to Retirement

Ira Roth and his wife, Jeannie,[1] are working professionals between the ages of 20 and 50. Ira, age 45, is vice president in charge of global operations for a well-known technology company based in Southern California. Jeannie, age 40, is a stay-at-home mom who looks after the couple's two young daughters.

Ira Roth has been able to save successfully and has accumulated a substantial amount in his regular IRA. Together with the funds in his 401(k) plan and some taxable investments, he and Jeannie have substantial financial resources set aside for retirement. But they also want to retire early, by the time Ira reaches age 55, and are unclear whether their nest egg will enable them to do so. This is the main reason they decided to consult a financial planner. But they have another reason. Ira's father, Max, just retired at age 65, and quickly came to the shocked realization that his total financial assets amounted to just $30,000.

Max Roth suffered from myopia when it came to planning his retirement, a common occurrence. His lack of foresight spurred Ira and Jeannie to assemble a financial plan for themselves. They will be helping Max out but do not want their daughters to have to do the same for them.

Financial planners routinely ask their clients to answer questions that indicate the extent to which the clients' financial affairs are in order. For example, a client might be asked to answer a series of questions such as the following:

To what extent do you agree or disagree with the following three questions? Answer each question on a six-point scale, where 0 denotes unsure, 1 denotes completely disagree, and 5 denotes completely agree.

1. I am on track with my retirement planning, and I am confident of a comfortable retirement.

2. I know what my living costs will be after retirement.

3. I know what my pension and Social Security benefits will be in retirement.

The Roths' financial planner posed these questions to them. Ira's responses were 2, 2, and 1. In effect, he disagreed with all three statements. On the other hand, Jeannie responded with 4, 3, and 4: She agreed somewhat or was neutral. In this respect, Ira and Jeannie straddle the typical case. The mean responses to these questions are 3.5, 2.3, and 2.0 respectively.[2]

Look at the declining pattern in these responses. Despite feeling somewhat on track, most people know neither what their needs will be nor what their means will be once they reach retirement. These responses are consistent with the findings of a *Wall Street Journal*/NBC News poll conducted in December 1997 by the polling firms of Peter D. Hart and Robert M. Teeter.[3] They found that although 42 percent of the 2,013 people they surveyed were confident that they will have enough money to live in retirement, 57 percent did not know how much they need to save in order to reach their retirement goal. But of the 55 percent who are saving for old age, 26 percent had accumulated no more than $10,000.

The Hart-Teeter results are similar to findings in the general academic literature. Consider the personal financial assets of the median family headed by someone between the ages of 55 to 64. James Poterba, Steven Venti, and David Wise (1996) report that in 1991 that family had personal financial assets amounting to only $8,300. Almost 20 percent of such families had no financial assets at all, let alone enough to fund a comfortable retirement.

Self-Control: Facing Temptation along the Road to Retirement

Why do so many people lack the self-control necessary to set aside adequate financial resources for retirement? In articles published in the 1980s, Richard Thaler and I (Thaler and Shefrin 1981; Shefrin and Thaler 1988) suggested that a major factor is insufficient self-control. The needs of the present make themselves felt through emotion. Those needs have a strong voice and clamor for immediate attention. In contrast, the needs of the future have a much weaker voice, expressing themselves more through thought. Most people feel the urge to satisfy their immediate needs, but they only think about satisfying their future needs.

The temptation to satisfy present needs is everywhere. Tantalizing stimuli generate impulses that call for a gratification response. Saving for retirement while at the same time facing temptation requires inordinate amounts of willpower. Most people do not have that much willpower. So what should they do? It's actually what they should *not* do: They should not face temptation at the same time that they save. They should not place themselves in situations where they make the thin voice of retirement saving compete for a portion of take-home pay with the shouts for food, entertainment, and vacation travel. The voice for retirement saving will get drowned out. What is required is a system like that used in golf. Retirement saving needs some form of handicap.

The right type of handicap for retirement savings involves money "coming right off the top," so that retirement needs do not compete directly with those for food, entertainment, and travel. Retirement saving is more likely to get accomplished through a regimented routine rather than through discretion. That is a crucial feature of 401(k) plans and 403(b) plans: Funds are automatically deducted from gross income.

Investors benefit because these retirement savings programs are both tax deferred and framed in terms of an employer contribution as well as an employee contribution. If it takes the stimulus of a reduction in one's current tax bill to generate the emotion required to induce participation in the company's 401(k) plan, then fine—whatever works.

Some people also use IRAs to save. And we learn one very important lesson about 401(k) plans and IRAs from Poterba, Venti, and Wise (1996). IRAs and 401(k) plans are the major vehicle through which people increased their retirement saving between 1984 and 1991. These authors use the Survey of Income and Program Participation (SIPP) to track the composition of household assets from 1984 through 1991. The households in SIPP contributed to a 401(k) plan or an IRA, or to both. For families with a 401(k) plan but no IRA, the median value of their total financial assets rose from $8,566 to $9,808 from 1987 to 1991. However, the portion of their assets outside their 401(k) plan fell slightly, from $2,587 to $2,498.

A similar pattern held for those households who were not eligible for a 401(k) plan but did contribute to an IRA. Total financial assets rose from $20,686 in 1984 to $27,094 in 1991, but most of the increase occurred in their IRA accounts. Non-IRA assets rose only slightly, from $13,098 to $13,355. Note that IRA contributors tended to be wealthier than non-IRA contributors.

Mental Accounting: Saving along the Road to Retirement

Not all saving takes place in 401(k) plans and IRAs. But saving rarely holds its own in the battle for regular take-home pay. Those who do manage to save additional funds do so by dividing their money into different mental accounts.

Here is an example to help get the point across. Imagine that you will receive a *special* bonus over and above your regular compensation. This bonus will be paid out of the ordinary cycle; it will be paid monthly over the course of a year and will increase your *after-tax* take-home pay by $500 a month for the next twelve months, for a total of $6,000. Think about how your family's consumption might change as a result of this special bonus. Specifically, by how much would you expect your family's monthly consumption to increase during the next year? Notice that you are being asked what you honestly think would happen, which may or may not be the same thing as what you would ideally like to have happen.

Now suppose that your $6,000 (after-tax) bonus will be paid to you in one lump sum. Think about whether you would treat the bonus money any differently now, especially with respect to your expenditures in the month immediately following receipt of the bonus.

What happens if the $6,000 is not a bonus but an inheritance? Imagine that a distant relative has died and left you a small inheritance with an after-tax value of $6,000. You will not receive the money for five years. During that time the money will be held in a unit investment trust (UIT), where it will be invested in conservative interest-bearing securities. At the end of five years, you will receive the $6,000 plus interest. By how much would you expect your family's consumption to rise over the next twelve months because of this gift?

Given these three possibilities, how do people tend to respond? Thaler and I posed these questions in a survey of MBA students in 1987. I repeated them ten years later and obtained essentially the same results. I also surveyed a group of professionals who work in the financial services industry and found that they respond in the same way. Figure 11-1 depicts the results for 204 individuals surveyed between 1996 and 1998.

Figure 11-1 Monthly Consumption Spending as a Function of How the Bonus Is Received

How much of a $6,000 windfall people decide to save depends on the form in which they receive the money. The spikes at the left indicate that most people are inclined to save the entire $6,000 when it arrives as an inheritance in the future, but they consume it quickly when it arrives as part of regular income.

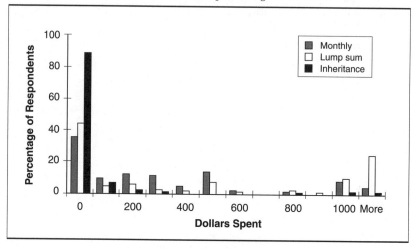

Begin with the three spikes at the left. These spikes depict the percentage of respondents who plan to save the entire bonus. Notice that this percentage is lowest when the bonus arrives in their regular take home pay, and highest when it arrives as an inheritance. At the right of the figure, notice something else: Some people tend to spend a sizable chunk of their bonus when it arrives as a lump sum.

Figure 11-1 shows that people treat the $6,000 bonus differently, depending on the form in which they receive the money. Part of this difference is due to the way that they allocate the money internally. If the bonus arrives as part of their regular paycheck, they tend to allocate it to their *current income* account. This account gets used to fund regular expenses. If it arrives in a lump sum, then people tend to react in one of two extreme ways. Either they place it off limits at once, by allocating it to a *wealth* account; or they treat themselves to a large purchase of some sort or another, placing the remainder into a wealth account.

Finally, if they perceive the money as arriving at some point in the future, then it enters their *future income* account. This account is usually way off limits to consumption. Almost 90 percent of the sample save the entire amount. Many of these folks hold large liquid assets. They could draw these down in anticipation of the time when the inheritance will arrive as cash in hand. But most don't. They use mental accounting to help them to both save money and safeguard their past savings from being accessed too early.

This example serves to illustrate how people engage in self-discipline. They use crude rules, based upon associations they find helpful. One of the common themes discussed in this volume is that people tend to categorize. They use *mental accounts* to help themselves simplify complex problems. In this case, they build on that mental accounting structure by developing rules that help them deal with their impulses.

Not everyone is fortunate enough to get a bonus. But most of us pay income taxes. And many use the Internal Revenue Service (IRS) to provide themselves with a simulated bonus. How? We overwithhold during the year, and receive a sizable check from the IRS at tax-filing time. In my own survey of investors, I find the average *planned* income tax refund to be between $800 and $900. For some, this is just precaution. They are somewhat uncertain about what their income will be, and prefer not to have an unplanned expenditure on April 15.

Others consciously use overwithholding as a self-control device, knowing that they will save the refund, whereas they would spend the money if it appeared in their regular paycheck. One investor in my survey received a $25,000 income tax refund in the previous year, and was planning for a $12,500 refund the next. That $25,000 could be earning a return! Oh, and what does this particular investor do for a living? He's a financial planner. I think he understands the concept of foregone interest. But he is willing to pay the cost in order to discipline himself.

Myopic Loss Aversion: Taking Risk along the Road to Retirement

There are at least two different ways that myopia can plague investors saving for retirement. We have already encountered the first way: insufficient attention to retirement because it seems so far off. The second way concerns investors' attitudes toward facing risk. Many investors choose portfolios that are too conservative for the goals to which they aspire. The question is why.

Here is an example that enables us to get to the heart of the issue. Consider a lottery whose outcome is determined by the toss of a fair coin. If the outcome of the coin toss is heads, you win $2,000. If the outcome of the coin toss is tails, you lose $1,000. If you had the opportunity to play this stylized lottery exactly *once*, would you?

Losing $1,000 can hurt, even when you stand an even chance to make $2,000. Less than 40 percent of those I survey indicate that they would take this bet. Perhaps the size of the stakes has something to do with it. What happens if we go with lower stakes—say, $100 instead of $1,000 and $200 instead of $2,000? It does make a difference. Now 60 percent say that they would take a chance. But that still leaves 40 percent on the sidelines, fearful of losing $100.

Would a repeated bet make accepting the gamble more attractive? Suppose the offer includes playing the lottery exactly twice, keeping the stakes at $100 and $200. Up to 70 percent would go for the two-shot gamble.

Finally, what would happen if instead of a two-shot gamble, we offered the opportunity to play the lottery 100 times in a row? The proportion of takers in my sample climbs from 70 percent to 90 percent.

Notice what has happened to people's tolerance for risk as we went through all four possibilities. In each case, respondents became more tolerant of taking the risk. In particular, tolerance for risk increased as the number of repetitions of the gamble went up. Why? And what is the general principle at work here?

Shlomo, Benartzi and Thaler (1995) suggest that people respond to the preceding questions as they do because of *myopic risk aversion*—or, to put it more accurately, *myopic loss aversion*. Those that turn down the first bet do so because the $1,000 loss looms larger than the $2,000 gain. Similarly, for those reluctant to take the same bet with the smaller stakes, the risk of losing $100 outweighs that of winning $200.

People evaluate one-shot gambles in isolation from other decision problems and record the possible outcomes for each of these gambles in a separate mental account. But playing the smaller stakes gamble multiple times offers a form of *time diversification*, where people feel that the law of averages is on their side. Now they only need a head to be tossed on one of the two rounds, and they will end up registering a gain. Their chance of incurring a loss is still 25 percent. But the probability they will gain has risen from 1 in 2, to 3 in 4. Of course, the magnitude of a loss, if it occurs, has doubled from $100 to $200. But the maximum gain has also doubled, from $200 to $400.

There are two separate and important issues involved in the above example. First, many people cannot tolerate the risk inherent in this gamble. Now what drives their low tolerance for risk in this situation? One thing is their low tolerance for loss, their fear of loss. Given that the odds of a loss are even, those who turn down the opportunity to play are telling us that they fear the pain of a $100 loss more than the pleasure of a gain of twice the magnitude.

Second, those that turn down the one-shot gamble but accept the multiple-shot risk display *myopic loss aversion*. That is, they frame every gamble they face in isolation from all others. Yet people face small gambles of one sort or another all the time. Most such gambles are independent of one another. In this sense, people continually experience the advantage of the law of averages for small gambles. But people don't frame that experience in an integrated way. Instead, they frame every gamble as a one-shot deal rather than as one more turn on the multiround gamble road of life.

The offer of a two-shot version of the lottery induces people to frame the gamble in multiround terms. In effect, this stretches the perceived time horizon of the problem, making people less myopic. Moving from two rounds to one hundred rounds makes people less myopic still—and less averse to single-round losses.

Benartzi and Thaler (forthcoming) suggest that many investors hold overly conservative portfolios. Why? Because they overfocus on the potential for short-term losses. Myopic loss aversion leads investors to hold too little in equities and too much in fixed-income securities. Horizon is critical. When looked at in months, stocks have made money 62 percent of the time since 1926, with the average loss having been almost as large as the average gain. But when looked at in five-year segments, stocks made money 90 percent of the time, and the average loss was only 63 percent the size of the average gain.

Loss aversion is perhaps the major element that drives investors' tolerance for risk. Now, loss is partly *perception*, and therefore is subject to framing. The expression "If someone hands you a lemon, make lemonade" concerns the reframing of a loss. Investors perceive a loss as having to sell something for a lower amount than they bought it for. People fear having to realize what they regard as losses.

Kenneth Fisher and Meir Statman (1999a) discuss the fact that an important element in time diversification is the ability to postpone, or avoid altogether, the realization of a perceived loss. This is one reason why some investors favor Treasury securities over stocks. Holders of Treasurys need never recognize a perceived loss on their bond purchases as long as they are willing to hold those Treasurys to maturity.

That is why some financial planners recommend the use of "ladders"—purchasing a series of Treasurys of different maturities, and continually replacing those that mature. Although the market value of a laddered portfolio may fluctuate over time, and investors may even find that the value of their portfolio dips below the purchase price, they need not focus on this fact. For them, having a ladder enables them to frame their outcomes as being one gain after another rather than a capital loss. After all, the capital loss reflects an *opportunity cost* for them, not an *out-of-pocket* cost. And as Thaler pointed out in his classic (1991) article, out-of-pocket costs loom much larger than opportunity costs.

Myopic loss aversion leads investors to choose portfolios that are overly conservative. But myopia is not the only factor operating on portfolio selection, and its effect can be cancelled by excessive optimism. Excessively optimistic investors may select portfolios that are unduly aggressive. Benartzi and Thaler conducted their study in the early 1990s, before the dramatic surge in stocks that began in 1995. As I discussed in chapter 5, those investors who have experienced a bear market are considerably less optimistic than those who have not.

Dollar-Cost Averaging: Acting Prudently along the Road to Retirement

Financial planners are big on dollar-cost averaging, a practice closely related to myopic loss aversion and time diversification. Here is how financial planner Ginita Wall (1995) describes the practice in her book *The Way to Invest*.

> Dollar-cost averaging is a fancy term for investing money over time. In dollar-cost averaging, you invest a set amount each month, acquiring more shares when the price is low and fewer shares when the price is higher. The result is a lower cost per share than if you bought a set number of shares each month. . . .
>
> Dollar-cost averaging has an added advantage, especially with an automatic investment plan, when you invest a set amount each month. It helps keep you from panicking when markets go down. You can be delighted that the market has dropped and you are able to acquire so many more shares that month, rather than become frightened and pull all your money out of fund just when the market reaches bottom. . . .
>
> Let's say you received a hefty bonus, so you want to add $5,000 to your mutual fund investments. If you do so all at once, you run the risk that the market will fall, and you will have invested at the wrong time. . . . On the other hand, if you put $500 into the fund each month for the next ten months, each time the market dips, you'll cheer. . . .
>
> Dollar-cost averaging for lump sums may not make sense in the early stages of a bull market, or in a bear market that promises quick recovery. When prices are climbing rapidly, you will benefit far more from investing your money early, taking full advantage of the early

growth in value, rather than spending your investment over several months and losing out on the early price surge. (pp. 77–82)

Finance academicians have criticized the practice of dollar-cost averaging for years. See George Constantinides (1983) and Michael Rozeff (1994). But as Statman (1995a) points out, the standard critique misses the important framing advantages offered by dollar-cost averaging. These advantages are implicit in the description provided by Wall above.

Consider a variant of Wall's $5,000 bonus example. Suppose that an investor in receipt of a bonus considers investing half the amount this month and the remaining half the next month. Let the current share price be $50. In this case, the investor purchases 50 shares this month. Imagine that the share price falls dramatically during the month, to $12.50. By following the dollar-cost-averaging rule at the beginning of the next month, the investor purchases an additional 200 shares. The average price per share is $31.25, the midpoint of $50 and $12.50. But the investor does not buy the same number of shares in the two months. Therefore the average cost to the investor on a per share basis is actually lower than $31.25, because more shares are purchased when the price is less. In this example, the average cost per share is $20, the ratio of the total expenditure $5,000 to the number of shares purchased, 250.

So $20 is less than $31.25, which is something that a dollar-cost averager can take comfort in. Remember how Wall described it: "The result is a lower cost per share than if you bought a set number of shares each month." Had the investor bought the same number of shares in the two months, the cost per share would have been $31.25. So, is there anything wrong with that? That is, if an investor measures the $20 he paid against a reference point of $31.25, then what's wrong with generating a guaranteed gain?

To answer this question, consider a variation of a problem presented by Rozeff (1994). Suppose that the investor with the $5,000 bonus compares two strategies: (1) investing the $5,000 in stock immediately, the lump-sum strategy; and (2) parking $2,500 in cash and following a two-month dollar-cost-averaging strategy. For the sake of illustration, let the expected monthly return on the stock be 1 percent, and the monthly return standard deviation be 1 percent. The yield on cash is zero.

If the investor follows the lump-sum strategy, he can expect to have $5,100.50 at the end of the two-month horizon. If he uses dollar-cost averaging, then he can expect to have $5,075.50. This illustrates Wall's cautionary note about investing early in bull markets. Of course, only a crystal ball can say before the fact that prices are about to climb rapidly. The fact is that the expected return to dollar-cost averaging is less than the expected return to lump-sum investing. But so too is the risk. A little arithmetic shows that the return standard deviation of the former strategy is $56.57 while that of the latter is $72.13.

Is this the academician's complaint, lower risk? Actually, it's not. The academician's complaint is that an investor who puts 75 percent of his bonus into stocks right away and keeps the remaining 25 percent in cash for the entire two-month horizon can expect to do as well as with dollar-cost averaging, but with less risk. The 75/25 strategy has a return standard deviation of $54.10.

Why is dollar-cost averaging riskier? To answer that question, consider a slightly different problem. Suppose a second investor has $2,500 to invest. She can put 50 percent into stocks and 50 percent into cash, and keep the position for two months. Or she can hold the $2,500 in cash for the first month and then invest it all in stocks for the second month. Which is the riskier strategy?

A typical investor prefers the first strategy because it seems less risky. And the first strategy *is* less risky. Now suppose that we give the same investor an additional $2,500 of stock that must be held for two months, and ask her whether that would change what she does with the first $2,500. Most investors do not see why having an additional $2,500 in stock would affect their preferences for what to do with the first $2,500.

But this is a framing issue. In this frame the typical investor says she prefers to split the first $2,500 evenly between cash and stock for the two months, rather than lurch from 100 percent cash to 100 percent stock at the end of the first month. But it turns out that the first strategy gives her the same result as the first investor's lump-sum strategy with $5,000, and the second gives her the same result as his dollar-cost averaging. If both investors are identical in their views about risk, their different choices will stem from frame dependence.

Of the two frames, the first is more common. In this frame, dollar-cost averaging is attractive for the same reason that people prefer multiple bets to one-shot risks: It mitigates loss aversion. Moreover as Statman (1995a) argues, financial loss is usually accompanied by regret. Lump-sum investors are likely to blame themselves more than dollar-cost averagers if the stock takes a dive shortly after they bought it. Why? Regret is especially painful if the action that was taken is perceived as departing from what is habitual, or what Kahneman and Tversky (1982) call conventional. By its nature, dollar-cost averaging is habitual, like making a mortgage payment on the first of every month. But lump-sum investing is not routine, and it appears to be less prudent than the cautious step-by-step approach of dollar-cost averaging. A lump-sum investor leaves himself more vulnerable to regret than a dollar-cost averager.

As Wall pointed out, dollar-cost averaging has other benefits as well. First and foremost, investors who adopt dollar-cost averaging cultivate an excellent saving habit. Why? Because dollar-cost averaging mimics the regular deposits in a defined contribution plan. Second, it serves as an anti–panic device when stocks fall.

Dividends: Safeguarding That Retirement Nestegg

Cash dividends have two tax disadvantages relative to capital gains. They are usually taxed at a higher rate, and those taxes cannot be deferred. Taxes on capital gains can be deferred by not selling the appreciated stock.

Nonetheless, many investors prefer stocks that pay dividends. Why? This is an issue that Statman and I addressed (Shefrin and Statman 1984). Until now, I have been discussing retirement savings from the perspective of someone still working. But to understand the major reason why investors find dividends attractive, let's move on to retirement. Suppose that you are retired and that you use three sources to fund your expenditures: Social Security (funds 20 percent of monthly expenditures); defined benefit pension plan (funds 45 percent of monthly expenditures); and dividends from two individual stocks, a utility stock and a bank stock. Together, the dividends from the two stocks fund 35 percent of your monthly expenditures. Moreover, these are the only stocks in your portfolio.

Imagine that by sheer coincidence, the utility and the bank both experience financial distress at the same time; the value of both stocks has declined by 50 percent in the past three months, and both firms have decided to omit the next quarterly dividend. You have a choice: Either you can let your consumption expenditures decline by 35 percent over the next three months, or you can sell some of your stock and spend the proceeds on consumption.

When I ask this question in surveys, over 70 percent of the respondents indicate that in this situation they would cut their consumption

rather than sell stock.[4] Is this the behavior of people who have difficulty delaying gratification? I don't think so. In fact, these people appear to have the opposite difficulty. During their working years, they
have cultivated habits to safeguard their savings against a lapse in self-
control, a lapse that might lead them to dip into their savings too early.
One such habit is the rule "don't dip into capital." The way to use this
rule, and fund consumption expenditures out of a portfolio, is to hold
dividend-paying stocks and consume the dividends.

This goes with the mental accounting framework described earlier.
People often control their spending by financing consumption from
their current-income accounts. Dividends are income, just like bond
coupons and salaries. The cost of not controlling expenditures can be
expensive. People might outlive their assets, a frightening thought for
some. The additional tax burden associated with cash dividends appears to be worth the price for most. The additional discomfort of cut-
ting consumption for three months, rather than dipping into capital,
also appears to be worth the price.

Using dividends to finance consumption is much more common
among retirees than in the general investor population. In a survey
conducted in 1986, Robert Shiller and John Pound (1989) asked respondents to indicate the extent to which they agree with the following
question: "I use dividend income for day-to-day expenses of living, but
avoid selling stock except to reinvest the proceeds." On a scale of 1 to 7,
where 1 connotes strongly agree, the average response was 3.29. When
I administered the Shiller-Pound survey to a new sample in 1998, I obtained a similar response, 3.35, which I interpret as very mild agreement. But I also administered the previous "if retired don't dip into
capital" question to this same group. And over 88 percent indicated
that *if they were retired*, they would cut consumption before dipping into
capital.

As I mentioned in chapter 3, dividends offer the opportunity to engage in *hedonic framing*. Hedonic framing involves the allocation of
money across separate mental accounts for the purpose of producing
the most pleasant psychological response. One instance of hedonic
framing involves the "silver lining" effect, where a small positive outcome is used to partially counterbalance a loss that is much larger.

Shiller and Pound also asked investors the extent to which they
agree with the following statement about such an effect for dividends:
"I am left with a larger silver lining in the event of a stock price decline.
That is, even if the stock price later goes down I still have the consolation of knowing I will get my money back eventually in the form of

dividends." The median response they received was 3.41. The average score for the respondents in my sample was 3.09: They agreed with this statement somewhat more strongly than did the original Shiller-Pound sample. In fact, 25 percent registered strong agreement.[5]

Retirement Spending: How Comfortable?

People exhibit great variation in the amount of planning they do for retirement. As a result, they vary greatly in the type of retirement they experience.

Douglas Bernheim, Jonathan Skinner, and Steven Weinberg (1997) used the Panel Study of Income Dynamics and Consumer Expenditure Survey to study how people adjust their consumption expenditures around the time they retire. They divided people into sixteen groups according to the actions they took in two respects during the six years leading up to retirement: the rate at which people accumulated wealth, and the rate at which they replaced one source of income with another.

Figure 11-2 shows the results for three groups of people. You will see that there are three curves in the figure. Each curve shows what happened to the growth rate of consumption expenditures in the years around retirement. The left side of the figure depicts what occurred before retirement, while the right side indicates what happened after retirement.

The top curve in the figure pertains to the "high fliers," the top 6 percent or so. High fliers accumulated wealth and replaced income the most quickly. The bottom curve pertains to the group I call "unprepared," the bottom 6 percent. These people accumulated wealth and replaced income at the slowest rate. The middle curve shows what happened to the median group.

Not surprisingly, the high fliers maintain a steady growth rate in their consumption before retirement, but increase their consumption rapidly once they retire, especially with respect to travel and entertainment.

Remember the case of Max Roth, Ira Roth's father? He is a typical member of the unprepared, those who do not think ahead to retirement even when it looms in front of them. The day they retire they usually go into shock. As figure 11-2 makes apparent, their consumption expenditures sink like a stone the day they retire. They must rely exclusively on Social Security checks and, if they were fortunate

Figure 11-2 Growth Rate of Consumption Expenditures around Date of Retirement

People vary greatly in their preparation for retirement. Some, the high fliers, save aggressively during their working years, searching out income sources that will replace their wages and salaries when they retire. These people plan to spend more in retirement than they did while working. At the other end of the extreme are people who are completely unprepared for retirement. They do not make any adjustments, even when the onset of retirement is very near. They greet retirement by slashing their consumption spending dramatically. The median case lies in between the two extremes. The average person cuts personal spending noticeably at the onset of retirement.

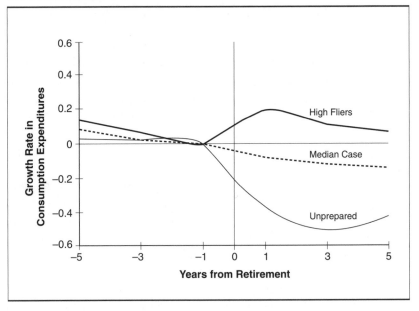

enough to work for a company that offered a pension plan, on pension checks.

The median group falls between the two extremes. Members in this group reduce their consumption expenditures at retirement.

Bernheim, Skinner, and Weinberg suggest that mental accounting drives the behavior of these groups. People fund consumer expenditures out of their current-income accounts. Those who have replaced income as retirement approached can afford to increase their consumption when they retire. Those who have not will cut consumption, in some cases drastically. These results are consistent with the earlier discussion concerning the use of dividend income.

Economist Laurence Levin (1992) used the Longitudinal Retirement History Survey to study how people budget their income across different types of consumer expenditures in the years around retirement. The expenditure categories he examined in his study are groceries, eating out, charity, social club dues, entertainment, gifts, transportation, and vacations.

Levin found very strong evidence of mental accounting. Retirees appear to control their spending by using rules that identify which portions of their wealth are off-limits when it comes to spending in particular categories. Levin divided wealth into several components: current income, liquid assets, home equity, and future income. He finds that liquid assets, home equity, and future income are off-limits for all consumption expenditures except eating out and vacations. All other categories are funded from current income.

When retirees use assets to fund consumption, they use liquid assets. They very rarely use home equity or borrow against future income. Most retirees are reluctant even to downsize their homes in order to increase their consumer expenditures. In fact, the high fliers actually increase the value of their home equity.

The reluctance to spend anything except current income is striking. Suppose we take a typical retiree, give him an extra $1,000 in current income per year, and then see how much of it he spends. Suppose the answer is $840. Imagine that instead of giving him the money in the form of current income, we give it to him as a liquid asset, say, a certificate of deposit. How much would we have to give him in order to induce the same $840 increase in consumer expenditure? Levin's answer is $26,000. Such is the reluctance to dip into assets!

The $26,000 figure refers to Levin's entire sample. However, the unprepared group is much more willing to use liquid assets to fund consumer expenditures than other groups. Why? There are probably two reasons. First, they are already in dire straits. Second, their lack of preparedness is an indication that they have failed to cultivate the habits required to achieve a more comfortable retirement. Those with ample resources never touch their assets, except to eat out and take vacations.

Summary

A great many people find that they lack the foresight and self-control necessary to save adequately for retirement. But the spectrum is wide. Some people learn the keys to successful retirement planning. They understand that they need to deal with framing effects and behavioral biases.

There are some aspects of mental accounting that are detrimental to accumulating retirement wealth, and other aspects that are helpful. Mental accounting can lead people to invest too conservatively by causing them to suffer from myopic loss aversion. At the same time, mental accounting can be constructively used to distinguish different categories of wealth, thereby helping people both to save money and thereafter to safeguard that money from being injudiciously spent.

Dollar-cost averaging is intriguing from a behavioral perspective. It combines the cultivation of good savings habits to deal with temptation, framing effects that reduce the pain of loss, and conventionality that mitigates feelings of regret.

PART IV

INSTITUTIONAL INVESTORS

Chapter 12

Open-Ended Mutual Funds: Misframing, "Hot Hands," and Obfuscation Games

*T*hink about a legendary mutual fund manager. Whose name comes to mind? Peter Lynch?[1]

There are many lessons to be learned from Lynch's experience managing Fidelity's Magellan Fund. These lessons concern the way *misframing* and heuristic-driven bias combine to confuse investors about the relative contributions of skill and luck in fund performance. Investors invariably attribute excessive weight to skill, and consequently they tend to overweight the importance of an individual fund's track record. Moreover, open-ended mutual funds companies tend to play to investors' weaknesses by inducing opaque frames.

This chapter discusses the following:

- the nature of Peter Lynch's record as a mutual fund manager, and his attitude towards investing

- the framing effects and heuristics that lead individual investors to attribute too much importance to the role of skill, and too little luck, in fund performance

- a series of games, called obfuscation games, that the mutual fund industry uses to induce opaqueness into the frames of individual investors

Case Study: Peter Lynch's Salient Record at Magellan

Peter Lynch managed the Fidelity Magellan Fund for thirteen years, from 1977 until 1990. During that period, Magellan's performance was nothing short of amazing. A $1000 investment in Magellan in 1977 would have grown to $28,000 in 1990, an astonishing 29.2 percent return per year. Moreover, Magellan's performance was consistent, beating the return on the S&P 500 in all but two of those years. And as far as the competition was concerned, the race was not even close: Magellan's nearest rival earned 23.2 percent during this period.

Peter Lynch's record is a salient aspect of mutual fund history. What are the implications, if any, of such a record? Has it generated availability bias, leading investors to believe that mutual fund managers beat the market more than they do? Has it led investors to believe, in error, that successful fund managers have *"hot hands,"* meaning that successful performance tends to persist from year to year?

Let it not be said that Peter Lynch believes that markets are efficient. When he took over at Magellan, he set himself the remarkable goal of beating other no-load funds by 3 to 5 percentage points a year. Not only did he manage to achieve his goal, but he also made beating both the competition and the market look like a snap.

In his book *One Up on Wall Street,* Lynch (1989) describes the process that led him to choose some of his winners: "Taco Bell, I was impressed with the burrito on a trip to California; La Quinta Motor Inns, somebody at a rival Holiday Inn told me about it; Volvo, my family and friends drive this car; Apple Computer, my kids had one at home and then the systems manager bought several for the office."

To be sure, Peter Lynch did additional research; and he was very organized in the way he treated the information he obtained. He kept a series of notebooks that synthesized what he learned from such diverse sources as *Value Line Investment Survey,* quarterly reports, and meetings with company executives. These notes were then boiled down into what he called a "two minute monologue" that focused on a few key variables such as net worth, stock price, sales, and the profit picture.

Peter Lynch was always clear about the importance he attached to holding the stocks of companies whose situations were transparent. He once said, "Investing is not complicated. If it gets too complicated, go on to the next stock. I give balance sheets to my fourteen-year-old daughter. If she can't figure it out, I won't buy it."[2]

Well, if it's really that straightforward, then mutual fund managers should have little difficulty beating the market. Yet they do. Vanguard offers an index fund, the 500 Index Portfolio, that tracks the S&P 500. Vanguard reports that in the twenty-year period 1977 through 1997, the 500 Index Fund outperformed more than 83 percent of all mutual funds.[3] During 1997, the 500 Index Fund actually beat most, over 90 percent, of the diversified U.S. equity mutual funds. For the year, the S&P 500 returned 32.61 percent, in comparison to the 24.36 percent return on the average equity mutual fund.

If investing is as simple as Peter Lynch suggests, then something is not adding up. Indeed, Lynch suggests that amateur investors should have little difficulty beating the professionals if they stick to companies they know, use common sense, and do a little basic research. For instance, he advocates that they invest in companies they work for, or whose products they use. And Lynch cautions them to stay away from companies they don't understand and to avoid trying to time the market. He claims that this gives amateurs a leg up on professional investors, who tend to be removed from the companies in which they invest, instead relying on analysts' reports. In other words, Peter Lynch urges investors to succumb to *familiarity bias*.

Lynch told Gerard Achstatter of *Investor's Business Daily* that he honed his skills for making risky decisions by playing bridge and poker: "They help you understand the rules of chance. . . . If the upside isn't terrific, maybe I should fold my hand."[4]

Some Rules of Chance

To be sure, the rules of chance play a critical role when it comes to open-ended mutual fund performance. So let's engage in some "thought experiments" to help us think about the relevant rules of chance.

The first thought experiment has you opening up a roll of shiny quarters, just obtained from your bank. Suppose that you give one of these coins to me and I toss it ten times. Each time I toss it, the coin turns up heads. What would your reaction be after the tenth head? Incredulous? Suspicious? If so, why? Is tossing ten consecutive heads that extraordinary?

Well, the odds of ten consecutive heads from a fair quarter are about one in a thousand. But whether or not the outcome is extraordinary depends on the context. Suppose that this experiment involved you, me, and nobody else. Then you would have every right to be suspicious that my having tossed ten consecutive heads was attributable to more than plain luck. I would not be in the least offended if you asked to inspect the coin closely to see, for example, whether or not it was two-headed.

Perhaps the situation with mutual fund managers is similar. Fund management involves both skill and luck. If a particular manager performs well consistently, then you could be forgiven for attributing his success more to skill than to luck. But would you be right? To answer this question, consider a second thought experiment.

In your mind's eye, imagine three types of coins—one gold, one silver, and one bronze. Every coin has a head appearing on one side and a tail on the other. In 1998, the number of mutual funds listed in the Mutual Fund Quotations section of the *Wall Street Journal* was about 5,000.[5] Suppose that we give a coin to each of the 5,000 managers. One third of these managers receive a gold coin, one third receive a silver coin, and the remaining third receive a bronze coin. Now we ask each manager to toss his or her coin ten consecutive times. Each time a manager tosses a head, we pay him $1. If he tosses a tail, we pay him nothing.

Can you see where we are going with this? In order to keep track of how the 5000 managers are doing, we use the imaginary *Eveningscore* service. *Eveningscore* tracks and publishes the dollar payoff to each manager, but it does not record what type of coin he was using. *Eveningscore* also publishes summary statistics to evaluate managers' coin-tossing abilities.

To facilitate comparison, *Eveningscore* uses a benchmark. What amount of money do you think would serve as a reasonable benchmark in this experiment? Well, if the coins were all fair, then the average manager should toss five heads and five tails, thereby earning $5. So why don't we go with that amount?

Eveningscore reports that of the 5,000 coin-tossing managers, 1,905 beat the benchmark, which is about 38 percent. Moreover six of the managers posted perfect records: ten heads in a row.

Now armed with the track records of these 5,000 managers and the *Eveningscore* summary data, suppose we try and pick the winners of the next ten-toss game. What do the rules of chance tell us here? Remember that we know the managers' track records, and we know that managers toss three different types of coins. But we don't know whether any or all of the coins are fair.

Suppose that all of the coins were fair. If this were the case, how many managers should we expect to beat the *Eveningscore* benchmark? Would you guess 1,905? If not, would you guess more than 1,905 or fewer?

The correct answer is 1,885. If 5,000 managers each tossed a fair coin, then we should expect that 37.7 percent of them would beat the benchmark. And what about using past track records to choose which manager to back next? Well, if every manager uses a fair coin, regardless of its color and metallic composition, track record becomes useless.

Note that I have *not* told you that in the second thought experiment the fund managers were all tossing fair coins. I only provided you with some information about how they performed, and related the results to the rules of chance.

Biased Predictions Based upon Track Record

In reality, a mutual fund manager's track record is critical. It should come as no surprise that during Peter Lynch's thirteen-year tenure, Fidelity Magellan became the largest mutual fund in the world, with its assets growing from $20 million to $14 billion.

In practice, investors bet on past performance.[6] *Wall Street Journal* columnist Jonathan Clements wrote an article titled "Looking to Find the Next Peter Lynch"—in which he argues that Lynch's success has led investors to overstate the chances of finding skilled managers. In particular, Clements describes the process by which high-performing mutual fund managers attract the attention of journalists, and what follows as a result.

> If a manager specializes in, say, blue-chip growth stocks, eventually these shares will catch the market's fancy and—providing the manager doesn't do anything too silly—three or four years of market-beating performance might follow.
>
> This strong performance catches the media's attention and the inevitable profile follows, possibly in *Forbes* or *Money* or *Smart Money*. Unfortunately for the journalists involved, our fund manager is less interesting than most podiatrists. Surely, sir, you have an intriguing hobby? Maybe, sir, you could tell us an anecdote to illustrate your investment style?
>
> By the time the story reaches print, our manager comes across as opinionated and insightful. The money starts rolling in. That's when blue-chip growth stocks go out of favor. You can guess the rest.
>
> Too harsh? Maybe I have seen too many star managers come and go. When they go, they tend to go gently into that good night, a performance whimper rather than a spectacular bust.

I think of managers such as Gabelli Asset Fund's Mario Gabelli, Janus Fund's James Craig, Monetta Fund's Robert Bacarella, Parnassus Fund's Jerome Dodson, Pennsylvania Mutual Fund's Charles Royce, as well as Fidelity Asset Manager's former manager Bob Beckwitt and Fidelity Capital Appreciation Fund's former manager Tom Sweeney.[7]

Clements is careful not to suggest that the performance of mutual fund managers is akin to tossing a fair coin. In fact, he notes: "Past performance may be a guide to future results. But it's a mighty tough guide to read."

Why is past performance so difficult to evaluate? To understand the reason, let's go back to our coin-tossing analogy. Remember that managers use three types of coins—gold, silver, and bronze. Imagine that of the three types, only the silver is fair. The gold coin is weighted toward heads, and the bronze coin is weighted toward tails. Specifically, the odds of tossing a head are 55:45 when using a gold coin and 45:55 when using a bronze coin. Only the silver coin offers even odds.

Now, suppose that we glance through *Eveningscore* and spot a manager who has tossed seven heads, thereby beating the benchmark by two. If we knew that this manager was actually tossing a gold coin, then it would make sense to back him in the next round. If you are going to back just one manager, then that is the best you can do—back a gold-coin tosser.

But we don't know who the gold coin tossers are. So if we are only armed with track records, then given the track record (beat benchmark by 2), what are the odds that this manager is tossing a gold coin? The lowest number you should guess is 33.3 percent since one third of the managers are randomly assigned gold coins. The highest number is, of course, 100 percent, but that is too high because bronze-coin tossers too can toss seven heads. Where in the range 33.3 to 100 would you put your answer?

The correct answer is 46.5 percent: better than 33.3 percent, but well below 100 percent. And what about the odds that this money manager, the one with the seven-head track record, will beat the benchmark next time? The probability that he will beat his benchmark next time is 41 percent—better than 38 percent, but not by much.

What about the chances of the coin tossers' doing at least as well as they did in the first round of ten tosses? Alas, the odds of repeating the previous performance are only 20 percent.

Even when mutual fund managers differ in their ability to produce winning performance, picking future winners based on past track record is very dicey because of the rules of chance. The gold-coin tossers are mixed together with lots of tossers of silvers and bronzes; and many of the managers tossing silvers and bronzes are likely to beat the benchmark. So sifting out the gold nuggets from the silvers and bronzes is a crude art, not a science. That is the nub of the issue.

Most investors do not understand that picking future mutual fund winners is a crude art. To begin with, they do not *frame* the evaluation problem correctly. Remember our two thought experiments? In the first experiment, we evaluated how likely it would be for *me* to toss ten heads in a row. In the second experiment we handed each of 5,000 managers a coin, and we asked how likely it would be for *at least one of them, but no one in particular,* to toss ten consecutive heads. The point of these experiments is that what is a remote event in the first experiment is highly likely in the second. Investors need to frame the evaluation problem using the second thought experiment. But they use a *heuristic* whereby they *isolate* on the manager whose performance they are evaluating. Consequently, they attribute too much of performance to skill, and not enough to luck.

Representativeness

Here is a third thought experiment. Suppose that in the past, a particular fund manager is known to have beaten her benchmark two thirds of the time. Consider three possible short-term track records for her fund's most recent performance. Each record is a string of B's and M's. A "B" denotes "beat or met benchmark," whereas an "M" denotes a "missed benchmark." The possible short-term records are (1) BMBBB, (2) MBMBBB, (3) MBBBBB.

Which of these three track records do you think is the most likely? Most people—about 65 percent, in fact—believe that the second track record is the most probable. However, the first track record is actually the likeliest of the three. The second track record was obtained from the first when the manager (first) missed her benchmark (an M), followed by BMBBB.

Most people get the wrong answer because they rely on representativeness to assess likelihood. Notice that the second track record has a success rate of two thirds, the same rate as the manager's long-term success rate. So, the second track record most closely *represents* the manager's long-term performance. But *representativeness* and *probability* are not synonymous. Hence, representativeness can be a misleading guide to likelihood assessment, as in this case.

In the most likely track record, BMBBB, the manager met or beat her benchmark 80 percent of the time. Representativeness leads investors to misjudge how often departures from one's own average performance occur. Hence, investors are too quick to attribute track records such as BMBBB to skill rather than luck. Representativeness compounds the misframing problem, leading investors to attribute too much performance to skill rather than luck.

Was Peter Lynch Just Plain Lucky?

So, was Peter Lynch just plain lucky all those years? I put that question to Bob Saltmarsh, who served as treasurer of Apple Computer and was responsible for investor relations when Lynch was managing Magellan.[8] Recall that Apple was one of the stocks in Magellan's portfolio.

Saltmarsh told me that he found Peter Lynch very different from other mutual fund managers. In describing his interactions with Lynch, Saltmarsh says: "His questions were different. They were more focused and insightful. In particular, he stayed away from techno-questions, and told me: 'I only buy what I understand.'"

Saltmarsh recalls a particular encounter that took place at a Cowan & Co. investor conference during the autumn of 1987. At that time, Apple's sales had doubled very quickly to $4 billion, and consequently Apple found itself with between $700 million and $800 million in cash. Saltmarsh had been meeting with many fund managers at the conference, but Lynch was alone in probing Apple about its cash position. He asked Apple the same question in nine or ten different ways. Saltmarsh was uncertain what issue Lynch was trying to expose, and finally just asked Lynch what it was he wanted to know. The response? "Will you be another G.M.? Is that money burning a hole in your pocket? Will you stick to your knitting, or will you go off and try something that you don't understand?"

Given Lynch's thirteen-year track record, he may well have been using a "gold coin": it would be silly to rule out the role of skill. Indeed since Peter Lynch retired from Magellan in 1990, three other managers have run the fund: Morris Smith, Jeffrey Vinik, and Robert Stansky. Yet Magellan has not beaten the S&P 500 since 1993–1998.[9]

Do Winners Repeat?

If skill is a factor in mutual fund performance, then we should expect to find that winners repeat. Successful mutual fund managers should continue to be successful, at least on average. A basketball player who seems to make every basket he shoots is said to have "hot hands." Successful mutual fund managers should also have hot hands. Do they?

What do we know about persistence? The earliest study is by Michael Jensen (1968), who studied performance over the period 1945–1964. He found that mutual fund managers, both as a group and individually, do *not* have hot hands.

Jensen refrained from telling investors to forget about managers beating the market. Rather he said that a fund could only be expected to return more than the market *if* it held a portfolio that featured more systematic risk than the market. What Jensen did was to take the raw return to a fund and subtract out a portion that reflected the compensation for taking risk. He called the residual "alpha," and it has come to be known as "Jensen's alpha." In effect, Jensen established a benchmark to compare the performance of different mutual funds. Alpha is the amount by which a fund's return exceeds the benchmark. Essentially, Jensen found that all mutual fund alphas were indistinguishable from zero.

Since Jensen's pioneering work a number of studies have appeared that suggest that some mutual fund managers may indeed have hot hands. Richard Ippolito (1989) finds evidence of significant positive Jensen alphas net of expense fees, but not load charges. Mark Grinblatt and Sheridan Titman (1989) also provide evidence in this vein. William Goetzmann and Roger Ibbotson (1994a) document a hot-hand effect in that winners repeat. Daryll Hendricks, Jayendu Patel, and Richard Zeckhauser (1993) also find that winning performance persists. Mark Carhart (1997) provides the clearest evidence about the character of persistence. However, at least one recent study, by Elton Gruber, Sanjiv Das, and Matt Hlavka (1993), finds no evidence of positive alphas.

Goetzmann and Ibbotson examined the period 1976 through 1988. They divided this period into six two-year time periods and looked at measured performance in two ways—raw returns and Jensen's alpha. In any two-year period, a fund is categorized as a *winner* if its return was above the median. In the absence of a hot-hand effect, the chance of a winner's repeating between successive two-year periods is 50 percent. Goetzmann and Ibbotson found that the probability that a winner repeats is actually 60 percent.

Carhart's study offers the clearest portrayal of persistent mutual fund performance. The study covers the period 1962 through 1993, and it includes all known equity funds during this period. For each of these years, Carhart divides funds into ten groups based on the return they earned in the previous twelve months, net of all operating expenses and security-level transaction costs, but excluding sales charges.

Consider the top 10 percent performers in any given year. If managing a mutual fund involved as much skill as tossing a fair coin, then we would expect these managers to perform no differently the following year. In other words, we would expect these managers to arrange themselves quite uniformly over the ten performance groups the next year.

Is this in fact how they find themselves arranged the next year? Not exactly. Figure 12-1 contrasts the actual arrangement with a uniform arrangement. The figure shows that group 1, the top performers, are more likely to find themselves in the top-performing group the next year than in any other group. So, winners do tend to repeat! Indeed, top performers are almost twice as likely to be top performers the following year, as compared to managers in any other group. Notably, the situation is much the same no matter which group we look at. The members of each group are most likely to find themselves in the same group next year as they are now. However, Carhart finds that this is a single-year phenomenon. Except for the worst performers, the ranking distribution for mutual fund managers after two years tends to be uniform.

What explains this one-year hot-hand phenomenon? Is it skill? Or could it be risk? Do top performers simply hold riskier portfolios than other managers, thereby earning higher returns on average?

Unfortunately, measuring risk is not as straightforward as it used to be when Jensen's mutual fund study appeared back in 1968. At that

Figure 12-1 Where the Top Ranked Funds from Last Year End Up a
Year Later

There is a weak "hot hands" phenomenon for mutual funds. The top-performing funds in a given year are more likely to repeat as winners the following year than random chance would suggest. The effect lasts for one year and then disappears.

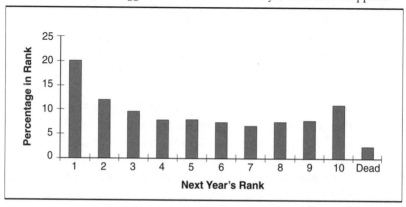

time, risk was measured by beta—the extent to which a portfolio moved with the market. However, for the reasons discussed in chapter 7, risk measurement is now based on factor models. In addition to a proxy for the market portfolio, Carhart uses size, book-to-market, and a short-term momentum variable as factors. However, as you may recall from chapter 7, I suggest that size and book-to-market serve as factors that capture mispricing rather than risk.

Carhart finds that the four factors explain mutual fund performance for all but the bottom 10 percent. The worst performers underperform relative to what the factors predict. So, where does that leave us: Is performance determined by risk, or by skill in picking winners? Grinblatt, Titman, and Russ Wermers (1995) find that about 77 percent of mutual fund managers use momentum strategies, meaning that they purchase stocks that have recently gone up. But they also find that this tendency is not particularly large. In addition, Grinblatt, Titman, and Wermers find that mutual fund managers tend to display herding behavior with respect to stocks that have recently gone up: They move in to buy past winners at the same time. However, they don't herd when it comes to selling past losers.

As noted in chapter 7, there does appear to be a short-term momentum effect for stock returns. Stocks that have gone up recently are more likely than other stocks to continue to go up. Is the momentum strategy that managers follow enough to drive the persistence effect? Carhart (1997) suggests not. He suggests that these funds "accidentally end up holding last year's winners. Since the returns on these stocks are above average in the ensuing year, if these funds simply hold their winning stocks, they will enjoy higher one-year expected returns, and incur no additional transaction costs for this portfolio. With so many mutual funds, it does not seem unlikely that some funds will be holding many of last year's winning stocks simply by chance (p. 73)."

Risk and Mutual Fund Ratings

Rating mutual fund ratings is no trivial manner. Investors can find these ratings in *Business Week, Barron's, Consumer Reports,* and various Morningstar publications. Ratings are rarely based on raw returns alone, especially returns from the previous year. For example, Morningstar prepares a mutual fund scorecard for *Business Week* that adjusts returns for risk, where risk is measured by downside volatility. Interestingly, the A-rated funds in *Business Week*'s 1997 scorecard actually earned 0.9 percentage points less than the S&P 500; this is because they exhibited less downside volatility than the index. In fact, the Vanguard

Index 500 Fund, which closely tracks the S&P 500, only received a grade of B+.

A grade of B+ for a fund that outperformed 90 percent of all mutual funds in 1997, and 83 percent of all mutual funds over the previous 20 years, may seem odd. Don Phillips, president of Morningstar explains it this way. "When you look at funds by risk-adjusted returns, you are not necessarily looking at the most profitable funds, but the most comfortable funds."[10]

Obfuscation Games

As you may recall from chapter 10, the importance of comfort should not be underestimated. But it leaves investors vulnerable to the obfuscation games played by the mutual fund industry, games designed to exploit frame dependence. Recall from chapter 3 that psychologists Tversky and Kahneman (1986) classify decision frames into two categories—transparent and opaque. The purpose of obfuscation games is to make investors' decision frames opaque rather than transparent. And these games appear to be successful.

Obfuscation games work because mutual fund investors are subject to the standard cognitive limitations described in this volume. Recent studies by the Investment Company Institute reveal that most mutual fund investors do not rely on their own judgment to choose funds, but on the judgment of advisers. The ICI reports that nearly 60 percent of investors own funds purchased only through a broker, insurance agent, financial planner, or bank representative. In contrast, 22 percent are pure "do-it-yourselfers" who purchase through the direct-market channel; that is, they purchase directly from the fund companies themselves or through discount brokerages.

A related study by Vanguard shows that most mutual fund investors lack expertise. Vanguard administered a twenty-question knowledge test to a broad group of users and found that investors fared very poorly on the test. More than three in five failed to answer even half the questions correctly. The average score was 49 percent, and only 3 percent scored 85 percent or higher.[11]

Mutual fund investors also exhibit selective memory. William Goetzmann and Nadav Peles (1994) found that investors have biased recollections of how well their funds performed in the past. Investors wear rose-colored glasses, meaning they think that their funds did much better than was actually the case. Goetzmann and Peles attribute this tendency to the psychological phenomenon known as *cognitive dis-*

sonance. Rather than feel uncomfortable about how poorly past choices turned out, investors reconstruct the past.

So, mutual fund investors are vulnerable to obfuscation games. What are these games? They come in several varieties. Goetzmann and Ibbotson describe some of them in a 1994b paper. Some of these games are akin to what magicians do: make some items, like rabbits, appear out of nowhere and other items, like eggs, vanish before our eyes.

In the first game, which I call the *incubator fund game,* fund companies maintain a group of "incubator funds." These funds appear out of nowhere. They are closed to outside investment, but those that are successful are brought to market. Why is this a game? Because it capitalizes on the same misframing phenomenon that was discussed earlier in connection with the thought experiments. Investors tend to frame their evaluation of performance by focusing on the fund in isolation rather than on the whole group of incubator funds. When there are many new funds being incubated, the likelihood that some will perform well by chance alone is very high. Unfortunately, investors are prone to interpret good performance by an incubator fund as evidence of skill rather than luck. Consequently, they fail to recognize the tendency for these funds to regress to the mean in terms of future performance.

The second game is called *hiding the losers*. Suppose a company is managing many funds, and some of them have been poor performers. What to do? Whisk the losers off by merging them into other funds. Jonathan Clements illustrated the point in a column aptly titled "Abracadabra, and a Putnam Fund Disappears."[12]

The disappearing fund was the $334 million Putnam Strategic Income Trust. Since its inception in 1977, its cumulative return of 153 percent was well below the 324 percent earned by the S&P 500, and it earned more than the index in only three of those years. It was merged into the tiny Putnam Equity Income Fund, which had less than $1 million in assets.[13] Clements quotes Don Phillips, publisher of *Morningstar Mutual Funds:* "That's a classic case of burying a bad record."

Next comes the game of *opaque fees*. A *Wall Street Journal* article by Charles Gasparino describes an address by Securities and Exchange Commission chair Arthur Levitt at a conference sponsored by the Investment Company Institute.[14] Although fees are discussed in mutual fund prospectuses, they are nowhere near as salient to investors as performance. One reason for this is that fees are expressed in percentage terms, not dollars. In contrast with average performance expressed as a percent, the fees look small. But when expressed in dollars, fees get compared against a different benchmark—regular expenditure items—where they look sizable. Consequently, investors pay little attention to the long-term impact of percentage-based fees.

In a 1997 article, John Bowen Jr. and Meir Statman discuss the *benchmark game.* This game is about assigning funds to categories and then measuring performance relative to benchmarks. Lipper Analytical Services compiles the benchmark performance reported in the *Wall Street Journal.* Bowen and Statman provide an example. For the year ending June 20, 1996, the Vanguard 500 Index Fund earned a 24.3 percent return, whereas the Vanguard Index Small-Cap Index Fund earned a 24.6 percent return. The 500 Index is in the growth and income category, whereas the Index Small Company Fund is in the small-company growth category. How about the grades? Despite the raw returns, the Vanguard 500 Index Fund received a grade of A, whereas the Small Company Fund received a D. Professors who assign grades to their students in such fashion would invariably find themselves in serious trouble, and clearly should have chosen instead a career rating mutual funds.

Benchmark performance is not risk adjustment, but style adjustment. Given what we know about risk, and about investors' comprehension about the meaning of risk, is it clear that style should be relevant for investors' financial interests? I suggest not. But given that investors care about style, so too should mutual fund managers.

As I discussed in chapter 10, investors do not understand diversification at all well. They misinterpret *variety* for diversification, and pick many different kinds of funds as a result. Thus, by offering a variety of styles, flavors, and colors the mutual fund industry capitalizes on this behavior pattern. Investors buy lots of different kinds of funds. Categorical comparisons by means of benchmarks cater to this behavior.

Of course, there will be times when investors wonder whether the emperor wears clothes. After a year like 1997, when 90 percent of funds underperformed the S&P 500, managers may find it difficult to deflect investors' attention back to the benchmark—a point made by *Barron's* writer Andrew Bary:

> In putting their 1997 performances in the best light, many money managers will compare their funds with other mutual funds. That's what Fidelity loves to do. "Your fund beat the average growth fund tracked by Lipper," is how many annual reports will begin. This comparison holds dubious value because it measures a fund against mediocre competition.
>
> It's like a .260 hitter calling himself a star because he plays on a

last-place team. The true comparison for the vast majority of funds should be the S&P 500.[15]

Another game is *masking the risk*—another concern that Gasparino mentions in his article about the SEC's Levitt. There are different versions of this game. One involves including derivatives in the portfolio that affect the risk in ways investors do not understand. Another concerns the behavior of some managers halfway through the year. At this point, there will be some managers who find that their funds are underperforming relative to their benchmarks. What should they do? Remember chapters 3 and 9, which discussed how people behave when they perceive themselves in "loss territory"? These managers increase their risk exposure, hoping to at least break even. Keith Brown, Van Harlow, and Laura Starks (1996) report that fund managers finding themselves in the middle of their comparison group by midyear increase the risk of their fund's portfolio during the second half of the year.

The final game, called *come out with all guns blazing*, involves managers of new funds. New funds tend to have riskier portfolios. Those that do well, thereby garnering attention, tend to reduce their risk exposure after becoming established. Consider the Technology Value Fund run by Firsthand Funds in San Jose, California. This fund concentrates in technology stocks; it is the only fund based in Silicon Valley, where most of the companies in which it invests are also located.

Firsthand Funds used to be called Interactive Investments. It was started in 1994 with very little money and produced very impressive returns in its first two years—61 percent in both 1995 and 1996. *Investor's Business Daily* gave Technology Value a grade of A+, based on its cumulative three-year return of 216 percent, the highest for all funds.

The fund became available to the public in December 1994. One year later, it had $900,000 under management. In December 1996, this amount had grown tenfold to $9 million. By December 1997, the amount of assets under management was $195 million. Now what were we saying about whether investors base their decisions on past performance?

In mid-June 1997, Technology Value received a five-star rating from Morningstar, Inc. But the rating was ambivalent because Technology Value concentrates its holdings in just a few high-technology stocks, and this makes it more risky than even a sector fund. The following quotation, which appeared in a June 13, 1997, *Wall Street Journal* article, captures the ambivalence: "High risk accompanies Technology Value fund's hot performance. 'I don't see why people should take a chance on them,' says Russ Kinnel, head of equity-fund research at Morningstar. 'If you buy a hot fund with high expenses with a high-risk approach, don't be surprised when you get burned,' Mr. Kinnel warns."[16]

Not four months later, Kinnel's words proved prophetic when problems in the Asian economies hit the stocks in Technology Value's portfolio particularly hard. For the fourth quarter of 1997 the fund underperformed its peer group and was down 18.72 percent.

The folks who run Firsthand Funds pay no attention to security risk. Instead, they concentrate on how the combination of technology and competitive advantage are likely to impact future earnings growth. In this respect, the fund managers rely on the fact that they have both strong technical backgrounds as well as business backgrounds.

In a 1997 interview that appeared in *Barron's*, Kevin Landis described Firsthand's approach: "It makes sense that you have this fund in Silicon Valley, run by two people who worked in these industries, plugging into a network of industry professionals providing great input, doing fundamental research and buying great companies at great prices. People love the story, and it seems to work."[17]

Does anything in this approach, about concentrating on companies you can understand, where you may have an informational advantage, sound vaguely familiar? Landis was explicit. "We were real adherents of the Peter Lynch philosophy of investing in what you know."

Summary

We have come full circle, back to Peter Lynch, the salient Peter Lynch. Most people tend to misinterpret what his success means. To be sure, there does seem to be something of a hot-hands effect, some persistence in mutual fund managers' performance. But most investors will misread what this performance says about the future. Because they use the wrong frame and rely on the heuristic of representativeness, they will tend to attribute too much of that success to skill rather than luck. Moreover, these biases will leave them vulnerable to a host of games played by the mutual fund industry.

Chapter **13**

Closed-End Funds: What Drives Discounts?

The prices of closed-end funds present a puzzle for market efficiency.

In a closed-end fund, the number of shares is fixed after the initial offering. Therefore, the only way investors can buy shares in the fund is to purchase them from some other investor. Open-end funds are different. In an open-end fund, the number of shares is not fixed, and investors purchase shares directly from the investment company running the fund. In this case, the investment company simply issues more shares to meet investor demand.

The closed-end puzzle illustrates opaque framing, heuristic-driven bias, and an inefficient market—in short, all three themes in behavioral finance. The chief feature of the puzzle is that closed-end fund prices systematically deviate from fundamental values. In this respect, fundamental value is measured by *net asset value* (NAV), which is defined as the per-share market value of the securities in the closed-end fund portfolio.

Because fund shares trade on organized exchanges, just like the shares of corporations, the market value of the closed-end fund shares may differ from NAV. When the market value of closed-end fund shares exceeds NAV, the shares are said to trade at a premium. If market value is less, the shares trade at a discount.

Money magazine's Wall Street correspondent, Jordan Goodman, suggests that fixing the number of shares offers closed-end funds managers the opportunity to make investment decisions without the distraction of dealing with purchases and redemptions faced by their open-end mutual fund counterparts. This brings us to the point about closed-end funds being a puzzle, as well as an embarrassment. The puzzle is that closed-end funds often trade at values quite different from NAV. The embarrassment, at least to fund managers and fund boards, is that the funds trade at discounts more often than not.

This chapter discusses the following:

- a case illustrating the movement of discounts over time
- the four parts of the closed-end fund puzzle
- sentiment as an explanation of the closed-end fund puzzle
- the impact of heuristic-driven bias on the prices of country funds
- how dividends affect discounts on closed-end funds

Case Study: Nuveen Closed-End Bond Funds

John R. Nuveen and Company is a major financial firm specializing in municipal bonds.[1] The November 29, 1993, issue of *Barron's* reports that in that year, Nuveen accounted for approximately 42 percent of the $45 billion municipal bond closed-end fund market.[2] In April 1998 Nuveen managed fifty-seven different closed-end funds. Among them is the Nuveen Premium Income Municipal Fund (NPI), which is a national fund, meaning that it holds municipal bonds from a variety of states. The key attraction of these bonds is that the interest the bonds pay is not subject to federal income tax.

Consider the behavior of NPI shares between July 1988 and July 1992. As figure 13-1 illustrates, the price of NPI started out at $15 a share, declined to $14 shortly thereafter, and rose to $17.25 by July 1992. This represented an 8 percent annual return over those four years.

An important factor driving these returns was the general movement of interest rates. In August 1988 the ten-year Treasury bond was trading at 8.64 percent. The rate rose to 9.32 percent in February 1989 and then began to decline, eventually falling to 6.71 percent at the end of July 1992.

Looking at figure 13-1, we can see that the share price of NPI rose dramatically from early 1990 through midyear 1992. Investors who bought NPI shares in February 1990 would have earned 14.36 percent per year by the end of July 1992. But had they bought at the end of May 1992, investors would have earned a remarkable 31.8 percent per year over the next two months!

In August 1992, Nuveen introduced a new closed-end fund, Nuveen Premium Income Municipal Fund 2 (NPM). The history of NPM illustrates some of the key features associated with closed-end funds.

Figure 13-1 Share Price, NPI, July 1988–July 1992
How the price of Nuveen Premium Income Municipal Fund (NPI) performed between its introduction in 1988, at a price of $15, and July 1992. Shortly after its introduction, the price declined below $15 for several months.

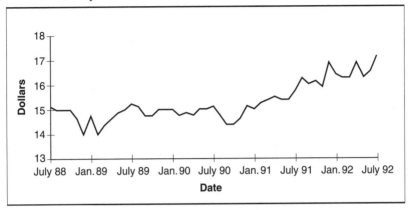

First, the environment was positive for mutual funds. Interest rates were falling, and municipal bond funds were earning high returns. Investor sentiment appeared quite positive. NPM began trading on August 17, 1992, at $15 per share. This represented a *premium* of 6.8 percent, relative to NAV.

Figure 13-2 traces out the behavior of the NPM share price between August 1992 and March 1998. Notice how similar figures 13-1 and 13-2 are to each other. The shares of both funds trade around their initial offer prices, decline below the offer price within the first few months, and then rise through time. As we shall see, this pattern is typical of many closed-end funds.

The time frame depicted in figure 13-2 was a very interesting period. Let's start with the period through December 1993. After initially trading at $15, the price of NPM fell to $13 and then rose back to $15 as 1993 progressed.[3] As can be seen from the figure, NPM shares started to fall dramatically in November 1993, in reaction to general interest rate movements. The Treasury bill rate had fallen below 3 percent in September 1993. But because of Federal Reserve Board policy, it rose to 3.2 percent in November.

At the start of 1994, the price of NPM stood at $14.12. This represented a 9.2 percent *discount*. In early January, an article titled "Quarterly Mutual Funds Review: Closed-end Bond Funds Look Cheap" appeared in the *Wall Street Journal*. The article described the general environment for municipal bond funds, and began as follows:

Department stores aren't the only place for after-Christmas sales. Bargains also beckon in publicly traded bond funds.

"There are lots of bargains around in such funds," says Thomas Herzfeld, president of Thomas Herzfeld Advisors, a Miami firm specializing in publicly traded mutual funds. "This is hunting season for closed-end bond funds."

Among Mr. Herzfeld's favorites are Nuveen Insured Premium Income Municipal 2 and Nuveen Premium Income Municipal 4, currently at discounts of 7.6% and 9.7%, respectively. These tax-exempt bond funds came to market last year at $15 a share—a 6.8% premium—and now trade at about $13 a share. Their assets, meanwhile, have edged up in value, and should continue to gain on rising investor demand as the tax season approaches, he says.

Of course, the outlook for interest rates may justify bond funds' discounts, and there's no guarantee their cheap prices won't get even cheaper in the future. The apparent bargains may accurately reflect real risks lurking in these funds, some analysts say.[4]

Figure 13-2 makes it dramatically clear that in hindsight, "some analysts" turned out to be right. The Federal Reserve Board was about to hike interest rates seven times in twelve months. By October 22, the price of NPM had dropped to $11.50, and its discount had gone to 13.8 percent.

Figure 13-2 Share Price, NPM

How the price of Nuveen Premium Income Municipal Fund 2 (NPM) performed between its introduction in August 1992, at a price of $15, and March 1998. Shortly after its introduction, the price declined below $15 for several years.

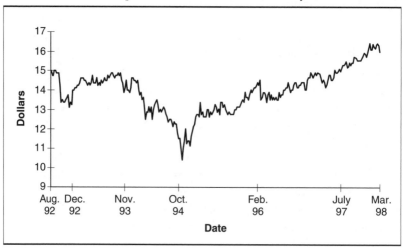

Over the next two years, the discount gradually narrowed. On February 23, 1996, it stood at 7 percent. On July 11, 1997, it was down to 4.1 percent. In 1998, much to the relief of the fund board, NPM was again trading at a premium—0.4 percent.

The General Phenomenon:
A Puzzle in Four Parts

The experience of NPM relative to other closed-end funds is quite typical. Charles Lee, Andrei Shleifer, and Richard Thaler (1991) describe what they call the *closed-end fund puzzle*. The puzzle has four parts.

1. The average closed-end fund is initially priced at a premium of 10 percent.

2. Within 120 days of being brought out, the average fund is trading at a discount of 10 percent.

3. The magnitude of the discount is not stable; it varies through time.

4. When a closed-end fund is either liquidated or converted into an open-end fund, the share price tends to rise and the discount tends to shrink.

How can we explain the closed-end fund puzzle? Let's begin with the first part of the puzzle.

Part 1: The experience of Nuveen closed-end funds provides some insight. Nuveen sells its funds to individual investors through adviser-based channels. Investors who rely on advisers tend to have limited knowledge about financial matters. Investors with limited knowledge would typically trade securities through a full-fee broker, for example, rather than use a discount broker who provides no advice. Naturally, investors pay more through full-fee brokers than they do through discount brokers, with the difference in fee representing the value of the counseling services and advice. Essentially, the same issue applies to the initial offering of a closed-end fund. These funds carry an up-front "load." However, as Bary explained, these funds are framed as being "no-load"—a clear instance of frame dependence. Bary writes:

> While many brokers will say new closed-end funds are "commission-free," the reality is quite different. Rather than the broker charging the investor directly, the commissions, typically totaling 6%–7%, are deducted from the fund proceeds.

A fund that comes to market, for instance, at 15 will typically start with just $14 in assets. After an initial period during which underwriters support the stock price, the closed-end funds tend to drop down to their NAVs. Because of the tendency of new funds to erode in price, many pros advise investors to stick with older issues.[5]

Part 2: Kathleen Weiss Hanley, Charles Lee, and Paul Seguin (1996) also make the preceding point. They suggest that the fund manager will usually support the fund price in the market for a short while after the offering and then reduce that support gradually to mask the nature of the initial premium. This explains why the premium tends to be transformed into a discount within the first 120 days.

Part 3: But the removal of support does not explain why funds typically trade at a discount. Lee, Shleifer, and Thaler (1991) suggest that the explanation involves investor sentiment. Pessimism drives up the magnitude of the discount.

In a 1993 *Forbes* magazine article, Mary Beth Grover recommended that smart investors not purchase closed-end funds when they are initially offered, but instead purchase those funds when they already trade at a discount. She stated:

> When your broker calls, flogging initial public offerings of closed-end funds at a cut rate, don't bite.
>
> With the public appetite for equities and bonds voracious, marketers of closed-end funds are churning out initial public offerings like never before. The total of newborn closed-ends this year will be in the neighborhood of $17 billion, according to Newark, N.J.–based Securities Data Co. That's a trebling in three years.
>
> When Wall Street is pushing anything this strongly, investors need to be skeptical. The closed-end boom is a case in point. There are thousands of mutual funds that can be bought at net asset value and dozens of existing closed-end trusts selling at discounts. So why pay a premium of 6% or 7% in brokerage commissions to buy a newly minted fund? (Grover 1993)

Notice Grover's statement about sentiment, namely that "marketers of closed-end funds churn out those funds when the "public appetite" is "voracious." Smart investors will wait to purchase these funds until the funds move to a discount. However, as we saw with the discount on Nuveen's NPM fund, the magnitude of the discount has been quite variable over time. This illustrates the third part of the puzzle, that investor appetites are more voracious at some times than others. So even sophisticated investors face risk when buying at a discount. In fact, closed-end funds may need to trade at a discount most of the time, in order to compensate smart investors for the risks associated with holding these funds.

Bary makes a similar point in his *Barron's* article dealing with municipal bond closed-end funds:

> After several years as one of the hottest investments, closed-end municipal bond funds have gone cold lately. . . .
>
> [I]ssuance of new funds has virtually ground to a halt after running at a quarterly pace of more than $2 billion up until mid-year. Through Friday, just four funds, totaling $200 million, had come to market since the start of the fourth quarter.
>
> More important for investors, prices of most funds have come under pressure lately, with some declining 10% or more since the start of November.
>
> "The Wall Street underwriters have been relentless in bringing new funds to market," says Thomas Herzfeld, president of Thomas Herzfeld Advisors, a Miami firm specializing in closed-end funds. "They and the fund managers got greedy and they brought clone after clone to market. There's simply a glut." . . .
>
> It had gotten to the point where the market was seeing not only clone funds, but also clones of clones of clones. John Nuveen, for instance, has offered six different funds called Nuveen Premium Income Municipal Fund. The like-sounding names make it tough even for pros to keep the funds straight.
>
> Several other factors contributed to the recent losses in the $45 billion market, most notably the recent spike in interest rates.[6]

According to Lee, Shleifer, and Thaler, discounts on closed-end funds as a whole serve as a sentiment index. The widening of premiums signals investor optimism, and the widening of discounts signals investor pessimism. As a general matter, the discount on any particular fund may reflect something specific to that fund, rather than overall investor sentiment. Yet the discount on Nuveen's NPM fund did track the average discount on national municipal bond funds quite closely. Table 13-1 illustrates the point, for key dates between August 1992 and January 1998.

When NPM went public in August 1992, the average discount for national municipal bond funds was 1 percent. In October 1994, when

Table 13-1 Co-movement of Discount on NPM and Average Discount on National Municipal Bond Funds

Date	Premium/Discount on NPM	Average Discount on National Municipal Bond Funds
August 17, 1992	6.8	–1.0
January 3, 1994	–9.2	–3.2
October 24, 1994	–13.8	–9.9
February 26, 1996	–7.0	–5.1
July 14, 1997	–4.1	–2.0
January 26, 1998	0.4	0.1

the discount on NPM was near 14 percent, the average national municipal bond fund was trading at a discount of about 10 percent. In January 1998 both NPM and the average fund were trading at premiums of less than 1 percent.

Part 4: The fourth part of the closed-end fund puzzle involves the fact that the discount narrows when the fund is either liquidated or converted into an open-end fund. In itself, this is not surprising. However, what is surprising is that investors in closed-end funds that do trade at deep discounts have been reluctant to push forcibly to have those funds opened up. This manifestation of investor *inertia* was described in a May 1997 *Los Angeles Times* article.

> When open-ending provisions come up for a vote, many investors fail to cast ballots or blindly check off the actions recommended by the directors. It doesn't help that funds routinely require "supermajority" approval of open-ending proposals, mandating a "yes" vote by anywhere from 67% to 80% of outstanding shares.
> John M. Cunningham, an investment advisor in Wayne, Pa., was among a group of investors who in March tried unsuccessfully to convert the closed-end Templeton Global Income Fund into an open-end portfolio. "Some of my own clients didn't even act on the proposal; they didn't even read the proxy materials to notice that my name was in there," he said. "That's how uninterested some people are."[7]

Is There Learning?

Over time, the public's appetite for new closed-end funds did wane. In 1996, only four new closed-end funds were brought to market, down from 126 three years earlier. Investors began to learn, as did the sponsors and syndicates that bring out the funds and sell them.

After 1994, sponsors began putting more effort into understanding the biases and framing issues affecting investors. Individual investors are subject to *extrapolation bias,* meaning they bet on trends. During a period of rising interest rates, investors become unduly pessimistic about the prospects for closed-end bond funds.

Fund sponsors like Nuveen began to realize that investors had a very poor understanding of how closed-end bond funds work. During the 1980s and early 1990s, investors had successfully bet on a trend. But they did not understand that interest rates move in cycles. So, after their experience in 1994, investors began to bet that the future trend would be down.

In the face of this pessimism, the closed-end fund "universe" came to realize the need for investor hand-holding—education, explanation, and consolation. And it had an effect on some parts of the closed-end fund puzzle. The "load framed as a no-load" strategy for initial public offerings of closed-end bond funds has disappeared. Now the sponsor bears all the initial expenses, covering the investment house concession fee and brokerage commissions, and recouping through future fees.

Nevertheless, despite the innovations of sponsors, the puzzle is still with us. For example, in order to address investors' growing reluctance to pay an initial premium and watch it turn into a discount shortly thereafter, one fund tried a new twist. The Dessauer Global Equity Fund, which was introduced in May 1997, stated in its prospectus that after eighteen months, if its shares trade at a discount of 5 percent or more for fifteen straight days, then the fund will convert to open-end format. Such a conversion, however, is not likely since enough investors understand that the fund trades at net asset value when opened. Hence, they would start to purchase shares in the fund at the five percent discount, as the fifteen day period ended, thereby causing the discount to fall below five percent.

So how did the discount on the Dessauer Global Equity Fund behave in practice? When it was first offered on May 30, 1997, at $12.50 a share, the fund traded at a 5 percent premium. By October 1997, the premium had fallen to 2 percent, and at year-end 1997 the fund was trading at a 16 percent discount. For the first ten months of 1998, the discount averaged 7.8 percent. And what happened as the eighteen-month horizon approached? Between October 9 and November 13, 1998, the fund's discount fluctuated between 8.3 percent and 16.7 percent. As the end of the horizon approached on December 1, the discount fell back to 8.5 percent. On February 26, 1999, it was 6.2 percent.

Sentiment

One of the most intriguing aspects of the argument by Lee, Shleifer, and Thaler (1991) is that the discounts on closed-end funds serve as an indicator of individual investors' sentiment. They point out that over 90 percent of closed-end fund shares are held by individual investors, suggesting that the narrowing of discounts reflects increased optimism on the part of these investors.

Interestingly, small stocks too are largely held by individuals rather than institutions. For instance, about 75 percent of the smallest firms (lowest decile) are held by individuals. The return to small stocks should go up, on average, when individual investors become more optimistic. If closed-end fund discounts serve as an indicator of sentiment, then a narrowing of these discounts should occur together with an increase in the return to small stocks. In fact, that is what Lee, Shleifer, and Thaler find.

The connection between closed-end fund discounts and small stocks extends to IPOs, a subject I discuss in chapter 18. Lee, Shleifer, and Thaler point out that if the number of new IPOs goes up when individual investors become more optimistic, then a narrowing of discounts should coincide with an increase in IPOs. They do find that this is the case.

Certainly, the popular financial press is aware of the connection between the returns to small stocks and the frequency of IPOs. Below is an illustration from the *Wall Street Journal:*

> Underwriters say the pace of IPO registrations appears to favor an even stronger fourth quarter, provided the demand for small caps continues.
>
> So far this month, 41 IPOs have gone public, generating first-day gains averaging 17.6%, the strongest one-day average since the 25.2% gains of May 1996, says Securities Data Co. More than 77% of the deals in the past three months have been priced within or above their originally targeted price ranges, compared with 64% at the beginning of the year and 88% during last spring's IPO frenzy.[8]

The article by Lee, Shleifer, and Thaler (1991) generated a heated academic debate. The June 1993 issue of the *Journal of Finance* contained a critical comment by Nai-Fu Chen, Raymond Kan, and Merton Miller. They suggested that the relationship between fund discounts and small-firm returns is neither robust over time nor impacted by the degree of institutional ownership. The same issue contained a reply by the original authors, who were joined by Navin Chopra. In their reply, the authors demonstrated that for 90 percent of small-firm stocks, lower institutional ownership stocks do better than higher institutional ownership stocks when discounts narrow.

Bhaskaran Swaminathan (1996) has extended the Lee, Shleifer, and Thaler analysis and investigated the issues they raise in greater depth. He replicates their findings for a broader data set, obtaining additional findings that are consistent with closed-end fund discounts being an indicator of sentiment. For instance, he finds that the discounts serve as better predictors of future returns to the closed-end funds than returns to the underlying assets (NAV). He notes that the discounts have a much stronger relationship with returns to small stocks than returns to large stocks. And he finds that the information embedded within discounts is not subsumed by other variables such as the default premium on bonds, the term premium on Treasury, book-to-market ratios, and dividend yields.

But Swaminathan also finds that discounts are informative about the future value of corporate earnings and macroeconomic fundamentals. This leads him to question whether the discount on closed-end funds is a pure sentiment index. He suggests that discounts may be driven both by sentiment and by fundamentals.

Country Funds

Country funds offer some vivid examples of how sentiment is perceived in closed-end fund discounts. Consider the following excerpt from a *Barron's* article entitled "Closed-End Mania Is Ba-a-a-ack."

> One convenient way to buy a package of foreign stocks is via closed-end funds that are denominated in dollars and listed on the New York Stock Exchange. Unlike mutual funds, these single-country and regional funds boast a fixed number of shares that trade at a premium or discount to their underlying net asset value.
>
> Last week, discounts shrank and premiums rose. In the latest

mania for country funds, 30 of them hit 1993 highs and many posted huge percentage gains. According to Michael Porter, who covers country funds for Smith Barney Shearson, their average premiums to NAV now are flashing a warning signal.[9]

A dramatic example involves the Germany Fund. Figure 13-3 below illustrates how the price of this fund behaved in the period July 1986 through April 1998. Take a close look at this figure. Can you tell from the chart when the Berlin Wall fell?

Most people guess that the spike in figure 13-3 marks the day, November 9, 1989, when the Wall came down. That would not be a bad guess. But actually, the peak came several months later.

In retrospect, what proportion of that spike appears to have been sentiment as opposed to fundamentals? You decide. In jumping from a price of $13.75 to $24.50, the premium went from 17 percent to *100 percent!*

A taste of the exuberance associated with this price movement can be gleaned from a January 1980 *Wall Street Journal* article titled "Capital Floods into Germany at Frantic Pace." Consider the following excerpt, showing that not only individual investors got caught up with the excitement of the moment.

Figure 13-3 Share Price of Germany Fund

Price path for the Germany Fund, a closed-end country fund. Looking at this figure, can you pick out about when the Berlin Wall came down? Is there a lesson from the rapid rise and subsequent decline in the chart?

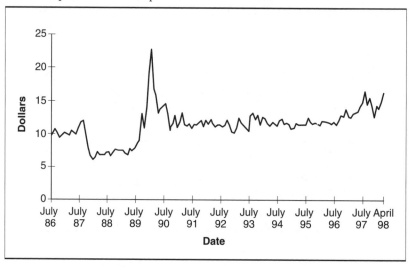

Germany Fund, a publicly traded U.S. fund that invests in German stocks, has soared to where it trades at a sky-high 37% premium to the value of its holdings.

Michael Tintelnot, a managing director at Deutsche Bank Capital Management USA Corp., the New York–based institutional money-management arm of Deutsche Bank AG, is scheduled today to make a presentation on bond portfolios to a U.S. public pension fund. But on Friday, Mr. Tintelnot says, the chairman of the fund's investment committee called to ask if he would also talk about Germany Fund. Mr. Tintelnot told him Germany Fund was primarily designed for individual investors. "He replied: 'That's fine, but can you do something like that for us?'" Mr. Tintelnot recalls.[10]

Lee, Shleifer, and Thaler (1991) emphasize that sentiment is like background noise, affecting whole classes of securities—closed-end funds, small cap stocks, and IPOs. The end of the cold war, with the fall of the Berlin Wall as its symbolic event, had implications far beyond the price of the Germany Fund. If we looked at the price histories for the closed-end country funds in Italy, Spain, Thailand, and the Republic of China, we would observe similar patterns. That is, they all exhibited spiked patterns at the same time.

The spike is the most *salient* feature in figure 13-3. Indeed, the fall of the Berlin Wall was a highly salient event. Are premiums and discounts affected by the saliency of events? Are the investors who trade closed-end country funds subject to availability bias?

In a fascinating study, Peter Klibanoff, Owen Lamont, and Thierry Wizman (1998) suggest that discounts on closed-end country funds, which are traded on U.S. exchanges, are in fact affected by the saliency of news events in the U.S. press. What these authors did was measure saliency by looking at the column width of stories that appeared on the front page of the *New York Times.*

Here is an example from their study, involving the First Israel Fund. On December 18, 1992, a three-column *Times* story appeared with the following headline: "Israel Expels 400 from Occupied Lands; Lebanese Deploy to Bar Entry of Palestinians." In the week that followed the appearance of this article, the discount on the fund widened from 14.87 percent to 15.55 percent.

Three columns are less salient than six columns. The September 14, 1993, story announcing the peace accord between the government of Israel and the Palestine Liberation Organization (PLO) was six columns wide. Its headline was "Mideast Accord: The Overview; Rabin and Arafat Seal Their Accord as Clinton Applauds 'Brave Gamble.'" During the week this story appeared, the premium on the New Israel Fund jumped from 1.7 percent to 7.7 percent!

Klibanoff, Lamont, and Wizman argue that in the absence of salient news, country fund prices are sticky, meaning that investors underreact to news that is not salient—news that does not appear on the front page of the *New York Times* but that is germane to underlying NAV. For example, consider the period just prior to the appearance of the December 19, 1992 story on Israel's expulsion of the 400 Palestinians. There were no front page stories about Israel between December 11 and December 18. During this seven-day period, the NAV of the New Israel Fund declined from $14 to $13.95, yet the price of the fund was unchanged at $11.88.

Figure 13-4 displays the price path of the New Israel Fund. The salient news events are not difficult to identify. Moreover, like the Germany Fund, the contribution of sentiment relative to fundamentals is clear, at least in hindsight.

Events that occur in foreign countries usually receive more press coverage in the country in which they occur than in the United States. Hence the salience of those events is typically different in the foreign country. For the most part, the NAV of a fund is determined on the

Figure 13-4 Price of New Israel Fund

Price path for the New Israel Fund, a closed-end country fund. Looking at this figure, can you pick out about when Itzhak Rabin and Yasser Arafat shook hands on the grounds of the White House? Is there a lesson from the rapid rise and subsequent decline in the chart?

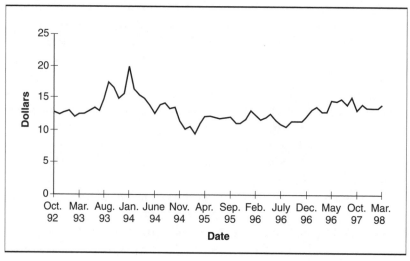

home country market, and these market features are less vulnerable to the sentiment of American investors than they are to home country investors. But closed country funds traded in the United States are more vulnerable to the sentiment of American investors than they are to home country investors. In fact, work by James Bodurtha, Dong-Soon Kim, and Charles Lee (1993) demonstrates that the premiums on U.S. closed-end funds tend to move in tandem with the return on U.S. markets; however, changes in the net asset values of these funds do not.

Jeffrey Pontiff (1997) compares the volatility of closed-end fund returns in the Lee, Shleifer, and Thaler (1991) study with the volatility of the returns to the fund's underlying assets. Given figures 13-3 and 13-4, which do you think is more volatile—the return to holding the fund or the return to holding its underlying assets? Pontiff finds that the return to holding the fund is 64 percent more volatile than the return to the underlying assets.

More Puzzles

There are yet more puzzles associated with closed-end funds.

Dividends: In Bary's article for *Barron's,* discussed earlier, the following intriguing statement appears: "The closed-end market drives efficient-market theorists crazy because similar funds can trade at appreciably different prices."[11] Table 13-2 illustrates the point using the three Nuveen Premium Income Funds discussed earlier.

Notice that the yields, taxable equivalent yields, and fifty-two-week market returns of the three funds are quite similar to one another, yet the discounts are markedly different. Moreover, although the annual total return on NAV also differs across the three funds, this does not explain the discounts. NPI has both the lowest annual return on NAV *and* the lowest discount. Only the difference in dividend seems to explain the discount pattern.

Because people think about money in segregated terms rather than in integrated terms, dividends are important. Remember the comments made by closed-end fund manager Martin Zweig, whom I quoted in chapter 3? As was discussed in that chapter and in chapter 11, dividends get evaluated in their own mental accounts. Investors find high, stable dividend payouts attractive; all else being equal, the fund with the superior dividend profile will feature a higher price.

In his *Barron's* article, Bary raises two other interesting points, both pertaining to frame dependence. The two points involve leverage and rights offerings.

Table 13-2 Comparing the Characteristics of Three Nuveen Municipal Bond Closed-End Funds

	NPI	NPM	NPT
Yield	6.58%	6.58%	6.43%
Taxable equivalent of yield	10.28%	10.28%	10.05%
Annual total return on NAV	5.92%	8.28%	7.53%
Taxable equivalent total return	9.63%	11.89%	10.93%
Share price	$14.500	$14.125	$12.688
Premium/discount	–4.1%	–7.0%	–10.5%
52-week market return	7.9%	9.7%	8.2%
12-month dividend	$0.0804	$0.0773	$0.0680

Leverage: First, municipal bond fund companies often use leverage in their closed-end funds. They achieve leverage by issuing both common stock and preferred stock, split, say, two shares of common for each share of preferred. In usual circumstances, the yield curve will be positively sloped, and the rate on municipal bonds will be higher than the short-term interest rate. The leveraged fund will set the preferred dividend equal to the short-term interest rate. Since the holders of preferred stock receive a lower rate than the holders of common stock, this structure enables the fund to augment the dividend it pays to common stockholders. And as I discussed elsewhere, some investors care a great deal about dividends. But leverage also leads to volatility. A 100-basis-point decline in the long-term rate leads the dividend to fall by 150 basis points.[12]

Bary asks: "Given the risks, why do funds bother to use leverage? Because without leverage, they'd have a hard time staying competitive with the larger, open-ended muni-fund market."[13] Do fund shareholders understand the leveraged character of their holdings? Well given the way the leverage is structured, do you think that investors are presented with a transparent frame or an opaque frame?

Rights offerings: Second, closed-end funds tend to use rights offerings in order to add assets. Now, rights offerings are framed to appear attractive, offering each fund shareholder an opportunity to pay less than the current price to acquire more shares. But other than the fund's shareholders, who makes up the difference? Nobody. Therefore, the share price of the fund should fall immediately after the rights offering. Although it seems that no shareholder is being coerced into purchasing more shares, the fact is that shareholders who do not purchase additional shares find that the value of their fund holdings will decline as a result of the purchases by other shareholders.

Summary

The fact that closed-end funds trade at prices far from *net asset value* has long been a puzzle for proponents of market efficiency. The puzzle has four parts. The underlying determinants of the puzzle are heuristic-driven bias and frame dependence. In particular, heuristic-driven bias manifests itself in the form of investor sentiment, and volatile investor sentiment is the main driver behind discounts. This is particularly evident in the case of country funds, where salience is an issue. However, there are other puzzles. Fund shareholders have been apathetic about voting to eliminate discounts through open ending. There is also wide variation in discounts across similarly structured funds.

Chapter **14**

Fixed Income Securities: The Full Measure of Behavioral Phenomena

When it comes to interest rates, investors are especially slow learners.

In 1938, Frederick Macaulay published a book that described how interest rate movements were both puzzling and notoriously difficult to predict. Little has changed since 1938, at least in this respect. But some have been slow to learn what Macaulay pointed out more than fifty years ago.

This chapter discusses the following:

- how overconfidence, gambler's fallacy, and betting on trends set the stage for disaster in the case of the Orange County Investment Pool

- how conservatism, hindsight bias, loss aversion, and regret came into play during and after the crisis that led Orange County to declare bankruptcy

- the theoretical issues that underlie the expectations hypothesis of the term structure of interest rates

- the evidence suggesting that the expectations hypothesis fails

- why underreaction to changes in inflation, stemming from anchoring-and-adjustment, interfere with the expectations hypothesis

This chapter covers some of the successes and failures associated with the management of fixed income securities, first by presenting a case and then by discussing some general issues associated with yield curves. The case, which focuses on the first behavioral themes of heuristic-driven bias and frame dependence, details the experiences of the Orange County Investment Pool. It is exceedingly rich in behavioral phenomena.

The discussion of general issues focuses on the third theme, market inefficiency. Many scholars believe that in an efficient market, yield curves should satisfy a property known as the expectations hypothesis. But the evidence indicates that in practice, yield curves fail to satisfy this property, possibly because the most important behavioral element is conservatism. Specifically, anchoring-and-adjustment gives rise to underreaction, particularly in connection with expectations about future rates of inflation. It may be that underreaction interferes with the forces that would otherwise induce yield curves to satisfy the expectations hypothesis.

Case Study: The Orange County Bankruptcy: Setting the Stage

In December 1994, Orange County, California, filed for bankruptcy. The largest municipal bankruptcy in U.S. history occurred as a result of the investment strategy followed by its treasurer, Robert Citron. The case provides an excellent vehicle for a discussion of interest rate forecasts.

One month after the bankruptcy declaration, Robert Citron appeared before California legislators. At that time, he testified that he relied almost exclusively on the advice of Merrill Lynch officials, including the interest rate outlook from its chief investment strategist, Charles Clough. Citron stated that in 1993 Clough had forecast flat or falling interest rates for three to five years.

Charles Clough was known for having made one very important interest rate prediction. Consider figure 14-1, which displays the behavior of the yield on the ten-year Treasury bond between 1985 and 1993. Focus on 1988. In that year, when Treasury bond yields were over 9 percent, Clough forecast a long period of disinflation and said long-term rates would fall further than most people thought possible. As figure 14-1 shows, his forecast turned out to be very accurate. Merrill Lynch heavily promoted the forecast, basing an advertising campaign on it.

In 1988, Robert Citron had already been county treasurer for seventeen years. In a revealing interview with the *Los Angeles Times* that year,

Figure 14-1 Yield on 10-Year Treasury Bond,
November 1985–December 1993

In 1988, Merrill Lynch's Charles Clough predicted a long period of disinflation and said that long-term interest rates would fall further than most people thought at the time. This chart shows him to have been right. Robert Citron, treasurer of Orange County, California, made several leveraged bets based on his belief that interest rates would decline. The chart also shows why his bets paid off handsomely through 1993.

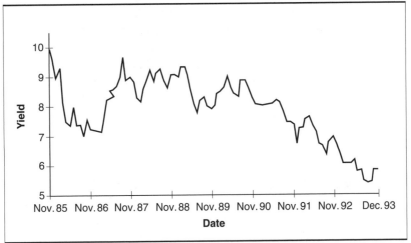

we learn some interesting facts about his trading strategy, and some of the behavioral biases to which he was subject.[1] In the interview, Citron indicated that he had $2.5 billion under management, which he was investing in U.S. Treasuries (bills and two-to-five year notes), U.S. agencies, certificates of deposit, commercial paper, banker's acceptance and medium-term notes, as well as time deposits with banks and S&Ls.

In light of the subsequent bankruptcy, the interview is telling about both Citron's actions and his thinking. Two excerpts follow. In the first Citron discusses the riskiness and performance of his investment strategy.

Q: Do you invest in the stock market?

A: County and city treasurers by state law are not permitted to invest in the equity markets or corporate bonds.

Q: So your money managing decisions revolve around the kinds of notes or bonds you're willing to buy?

A: Yes. I have around $900 million in U.S. government securities, from two to five years in maturity.

Q: Do you actively trade, based on fluctuations in interest rates?

A: I'm not a trader. . . . I buy and hold, and I do matched reverse re-purchase agreements. . . . It's not trading, because the spread is always locked in.

Q: How much money has this technique earned you?

A: Through the first seven months of the fiscal year, we have earned $4.5 million on reverse repos alone.

A: From July 1, 1986, to June 30, 1987, we earned 8% on all the funds. If we hadn't been doing reverse repos, our return would have been only about 7.2%.

Q: How does that 8% return compare to other counties?

A: The state of California has a local agency investment fund in which any local agency, county, city or special district can invest money. . . . (The fund) had an average yield of 7.4% for the fiscal year.

In the second excerpt, Citron provides his predictions for interest rates and the overall economy. As you read this portion of the interview, think back to the discussion in chapter 5 about the strategists' market predictions. See whether you can spot any similarities.

Q: What is your outlook for the economy?

A: The current business cycle has already extended far beyond the average length of three to four years, to over five years. And there's little doubt that a correction is rapidly approaching in the form of a recession. . . .

Q: When can we expect to see a recession?

A: Events in the summer months of 1988 will indicate the beginning of a recessionary period. . . .

Q: What's your outlook for interest rates?

A: We are in a volatile market, so we'll have strong swings. But on average, I think rates will go up.

Q: Why?

A: Because of inflationary pressures. The Fed will react by doing more tightening than loosening.

Q: So we are going to see a recession with rising interest rates?

A: Yes.

Q: Is the Fed going to succeed in dampening inflation with this restrictive monetary policy?

A: Yes, in the summertime.

Overconfidence and Gambler's Fallacy

Were you able to spot examples of heuristic-driven bias in the second excerpt? Citron's 1988 forecast, of a coming recession with rising interest rates that will dampen inflation in the summer, appears to have been made with a great deal of confidence—some might say overconfidence. And why was Citron forecasting a recession in the summer of 1988? Because the economic expansion at that time was a year or so longer than average. Is there a classic bias underlying this forecast? How about gambler's fallacy—the law of small numbers? After tossing five heads in a row using a fair coin, is a tail due? Was a recession due? And did a recession with rising interest rates come about? Yes to rising interest rates, but no to the recession, at least not for two years more.

Well, one out of two may not seem bad. But the overconfident interest rate forecast, in combination with other issues identified in this 1988 interview, combined to produce a disaster. The other issues revolve around Citron's investment strategy. He mentions his use of two- and five-year Treasury securities. Figure 14-2 illustrates the yields on the two- and five-year securities between November 1985 and December 1993. The top curve represents the five-year Treasury yields.

Figure 14-2 Yields on 2-Year and 5-Year Treasury Bonds,
November 1985–December 1993

Robert Citron borrowed at the two-year rate and invested at the five-year rate. The chart shows why, between 1990 and 1993, Orange County's portfolio profited from the widening gap between two-year and five-year yields.

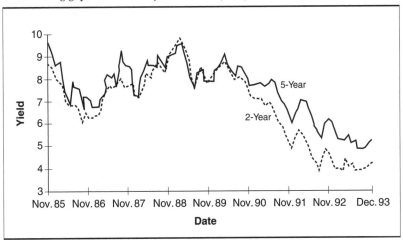

As can be seen from figure 14-2, the spread was typically positive during this period. Citron used a reverse repurchase agreement strategy in which he purchased five-year Treasurys obtained with money borrowed for two years at the two-year rate. So, for example, in December 1993 Citron might have been borrowing at the two-year rate, 4.24 percent, to purchase five-year securities that were yielding 5.2 percent, thereby capturing a spread that was almost 100 basis points. Such leveraging corresponds to purchasing stock on margin.

Overconfidence and Hindsight Bias

The 1988 summer recession predicted by Robert Citron finally arrived in the autumn of 1990. But by 1993, the slowdown was over and the economy was again growing robustly—so much so, in fact, that the Federal Reserve Board was concerned about a rekindling of inflation. In February 1994, the Fed raised short-term interest rates for the first time in five years. It raised them again in March.

On December 6, 1993, Martin Mauro, fixed income strategist at Merrill Lynch, predicted that the Federal Reserve would tighten monetary policy modestly in 1994.[2] Consequently, he expected a flatter yield curve, with higher short-term rates and lower long-term rates. The forecast was way off. Indeed, 1994 was an extraordinary year for the yield curve. In a 1995 survey article that appeared in the *Journal of Economic Perspectives,* John Campbell described what made it so. As short-term interest rates rose throughout the year, so too did long-term rates. Furthermore, the spread stayed about the same.

The behavior of the spread was of considerable importance to the value of the Orange County Investment Pool portfolio. The rising yields reduced the value of both the two-year Treasurys and the five-year Treasurys. A well-known feature of bond prices is that the longer the duration of the bond, the more sensitive the bond price is to a change in yield. Specifically, the prices of five-year Treasurys are more sensitive to yield changes than the prices of two-year Treasurys. Hence, the rise in the yield curve during February and March lowered the value of the Orange County portfolio.

In July 1993, Citron had confidently predicted that interest rates would not go up. In response to a question from an investment banker about how the value of his portfolio would be affected by a rise in interest rates, he responded that interest rates would not rise. When the investment banker asked Citron how he knew this, he is reported to have replied: "I am one of the largest investors in America. I know these things."[3]

Citron described his outlook further in his September 1993 annual report, stating: "We will have level if not lower interest rates through this decade. Certainly, there is nothing on the horizon that would indicate that we will have rising interest rates for a minimum of three years. We believe that our comparative higher interest earning rate yields over the next three fiscal years is insured."

Interestingly, Citron later claimed to have anticipated the February interest rate jump. On March 9, responding to the administrator of the county's public employee retirement system, Citron stated: "The recent increase in rates was not a surprise to us; we expected it and were prepared for it."[4] In light of all the public statements Citron made before February 1994, I find it difficult to believe that he was not surprised. But I do believe that, after the fact, he reconstructed his past beliefs. I believe he displayed hindsight bias. Nevertheless he went on the record that March as saying that he thought further Fed tightening to be likely, with any run-up in interest rates short-lived.

Remember Charles Clough, the Merrill Lynch strategist on whose views Citron was relying. The April 6, 1994, issue of *USA Today* reported Charles Clough's outlook on interest rates, an outlook that resurfaced in court proceedings later.

> Bonds a buy: After the sharp rise in interest rates, Merrill Lynch strategist Charles Clough is bullish on the bond market again. Tuesday, he told clients to start buying 30-year Treasury bonds when their yields are higher than 7.3%. T-bond yields were 7.40% Monday but fell to 7.24 Tuesday. Clough made one of the great bond-market calls ever in 1988, when T-bond yields were over 9%. He forecast a long period of disinflation and said long-term rates would fall further than most people thought possible. . . . "This is entirely different, partly because we're still in an economic expansion so rates don't have that far to fall," Clough says of his renewed call to bonds.
>
> Still, he believes the recent jolt in rates will slow the economy enough to force rates back down late in the year.[5]

Frame Dependence: Reference Points and Layered Pyramids

Later that April, the Federal Reserve increased interest rates again. This lowered the value of Citron's portfolio even more. Now, the

Orange County treasurer's position is an elected one, and 1994 was an election year. Interestingly, for the first time since 1970, Robert Citron found himself with an opponent. Given that the environment of the time was characterized by rising interest rates, I am not surprised that a spirited debate ensued about the merits of using leverage.

Citron's opponent was John Moorlach, later to become his successor. During the campaign, Moorlach wrote a letter to the Orange County Board of Supervisors, criticizing Citron's investment strategy. In his letter, Moorlach stated: "Every prudent investor chooses safety of principal as the top priority," he wrote. "Next comes the need for liquidity. The last priority is achieving yields. . . . Mr. Citron has these priorities inversed."[6] Is this approach reminiscent of a layered pyramid, with a hierarchy of securities matched to a hierarchy of goals? The notion of a layered pyramid forms the behavioral basis for constructing portfolios (see chapter 10).

An article that appeared in the April 30, 1994, issue of the *Los Angeles Times* offers additional insights. The article quotes R. A. Scott, the head of the county's General Services Agency, who has known Citron for more than twenty years and paints the following revealing portrait. "He's competitive, and if he returns a greater rate on short term money than most people, he considers that winning. . . . It's pride. It's being above average. When he's trading, he's all business."[7]

Pride, being above average, and winning: is there a reference point effect here? How about overconfidence about his relative skill? Did Citron's reference point correspond to earning a higher return on short-term money than others earn? We know from chapter 9 that when the probability of ending up below a given reference point is large enough, people tend to *seek risk*. Indeed, the *Los Angeles Times* article points out that Citron "concedes he takes risks but insists they are prudent ones."

Reference points and loss aversion operate in peculiar ways. Despite the risky investment approach he followed in managing the Orange County Investment Pool, Robert Citron never owned a single share of stock in his personal portfolio. Paradoxical? The difference reflects different mental accounts and different reference points.

Forecasts and the Illusion of Validity

What about Citron's interest rate forecast at this point, April 1994? Was it similar to Clough's April perspective? The article states the following:

In recent weeks, Citron has received "collateral calls" that forced him to pony up an additional $215 million in collateral, because the value of the securities he used to borrow money has skidded as interest rates have climbed. His assistant, Matthew R. Raabe, said he expects yet more collateral calls, but he is not worried because the county's $7.5-billion investment pool has about $1 billion in liquid assets.

Citron and Raabe . . . believe interest rates will inch up for a short time and level off. If they are wrong, they say they have a contingency or "exit" plan, although they are unwilling to share the particulars.

Raabe said the only way the county could get into trouble is if "short-term interest rates are going to continue to go up and . . . we don't react. But that's not going to happen."[8]

At this stage, Robert Citron was plagued by a lot of questions: Would he win reelection against John Moorlach? Which investors would withdraw funds from the county pool? In what direction would interest rates move? To whom did Citron turn for guidance? To psychics and a mail-order astrologer. One psychic adviser predicted that Citron would encounter financial difficulties in the month of November, but that these would be over in December.[9] Some of these predictions turned out to be correct. Might there have been some behavioral phenomenon at work here? Indeed, yes: Try the illusion of validity.

Conservatism and Loss Aversion

Still anchored to the downward trend that had brought his investment strategy so much success, Citron appears to have been convinced that short-term rates would level off, so much so that he continued to hold inverse floaters. Inverse floaters are structured to pay lower interest as interest rates rise. The investor makes money when interest rates decline, but loses money when they rise. In fact, it appears that he actually used the inverse floaters as collateral in order to purchase medium-term securities.

Unfortunately, short rates did not level off. The Fed increased rates again in August. The losses to the Orange County portfolio were mounting. Just after Labor Day, a concerned president of one of the local water districts in the county learned that Robert Citron had not reduced the degree of leverage. In fact, quite the opposite. An article appearing in *USA Today* reports that Citron actually increased his borrowing "in a desperate bid to recoup his losses."[10] A few days earlier a piece by Ronald Picur had appeared in the *Chicago Tribune* describing this behavior in the following terms: "True to a gambler's mind-set, Citron increased the size of his 'wagers' by using leveraged funds."[11] According to county records, in March 1993 the principal fund run by Mr. Citron was leveraged 2.4:1. But by August 1994, its leverage had grown to nearly 3:1. By then, Mr. Citron had borrowed nearly $13 billion, using most of the proceeds to purchase notes from Merrill Lynch. (If we needed further convincing about there being a reference point effect at work here, this should do the job.)[12]

A *Wall Street Journal* article on Citron was aptly titled "Hubris and Ambition in Orange County: Robert Citron's Story." The following excerpt describes the effect of loss aversion on Citron's behavior.

> However, the losses were still only on paper, and Mr. Citron was apparently convinced that he could still weather the typhoon. For years, he had boasted about how he almost invariably held securities until maturity, when he could cash them in at face value. That way, he explained, he was able to avoid the losses that come from selling a security that has been adversely affected by a rise in interest rates.
>
> He clung fiercely to that philosophy in his last annual report, on Sept. 26. Mr. Citron noted that there was concern over "paper losses" due to rising interest rates. But he said that the county didn't plan to record any such losses and didn't plan to sell its securities.[13]

In chapter 9 I described why, tax issues aside, the distinction between "paper losses" and "realized losses" is more psychological than real. This is a framing issue. Holding securities to maturity so as not to realize a loss does not imply that wealth has not declined. But the foregone wealth is framed as an opportunity loss, rather than an out-of-pocket loss. The "hold until maturity frame" simply obscures the opportunity loss.[14]

In any event, despite Citron's stated intention not to sell any securities, the reverse occurred. The Fed raised interest rates again in November. Investors who held Orange County Investment Pool securities as collateral anxiously saw those securities decline further in value. In reaction, they began to sell that collateral, thereby forcing Orange County to realize losses. On December 1, Robert Citron and assistant treasurer Matthew Raabe told reporters at a county press conference that the fund faced a $1.5 billion paper loss.

On December 4, Robert Citron resigned as county treasurer. Two days later the county filed for bankruptcy under Chapter 9 of the bankruptcy code, in an attempt to prevent its creditors from liquidating the collateralized securities. This was the largest municipal bankruptcy in U.S. history. At that time, the loss to the Orange County Investment Pool was estimated at $2 billion. On April 28, 1995, Citron pled guilty to six felony counts. He was sentenced to a year in county jail and ordered to pay a $100,000 fine. Matthew Raabe was convicted of the same charges and became the only public official sent to state prison for his role in the bankruptcy. He was sentenced to three years in prison and ordered to pay a $10,000 fine.

Regret, Hindsight Bias, and the Confirmation Bias

Citron's appearance before state legislators in January 1995, offers an example of regret and responsibility shifting. The *Los Angeles Times* reported the issue as follows: "Here was Citron—proclaimed a financial expert for years both by himself and his fawning Board of Supervisors—now reduced to saying how, 'in retrospect,' he would have done a lot of things differently."[15]

Regret is the pain felt from recognizing that one could have done things differently. The intensity of the regret depends on the degree to which a person feels responsible for the decision that was taken. One way people attempt to shift responsibility is by playing the "blame game." This game, whereby a client picks someone regarded as an expert and relies on him or her for advice, is usually set up in advance. If things go well, the client takes the credit, attributing the success to his or her own skill. But if things go badly, then the client can attribute the blame to the expert, thereby reducing *regret* by shifting responsibility for the negative outcome.[16] Of course, for this to work, the person to whom responsibility gets shifted must be seen to have expertise. Otherwise, the client will feel just as much regret for having relied on a novice for advice. In this regard, Citron said during his testimony: "I understood Clough to be the preeminent expert in the field of investment strategy."[17]

In shifting responsibility to Clough, Citron mentioned that he had relied on Clough's 1993 prediction of flat or falling interest rates for three to five years. Even after the Federal Reserve boosted short-term rates in February 1994, Mr. Citron said Mr. Clough told him at a breakfast meeting on March 1 that rate increases were "not sustainable."

However, starting in 1992 officials from Merrill's risk management desk had been urging Citron to lower his leverage. They had even offered to repurchase some of the inverse floaters at a time when these would have produced a profit for the county. Moreover, in February 1994 they warned Citron that the interest rate outlook was uncertain. But Citron disregarded the warning from the risk management group, which conflicted with his own outlook. Instead, he chose Clough's forecast, which confirmed that outlook. He paid attention to confirming evidence while ignoring disconfirming evidence, thereby succumbing to the illusion of validity. When faced with cognitive dissonance, most people resolve the dissonance by choosing the comfortable route.

Subsequently, Orange County played the blame game too, suing a number of parties with whom it had had a relationship. The most notable was Merrill Lynch, against whom it filed both criminal and civil charges, arguing that the firm had provided faulty advice. Both suits were settled. In 1997, Merrill Lynch agreed to pay $30 million to have the criminal suit dropped. In June 1998, it agreed to pay $400 million to have the civil suit dropped, the second largest suit ever involving a brokerage firm.

Orange County also filed suit against the bond-rating agency Standard & Poor's Corp. for having given its top rating to the county. This raises the question of whether or not agencies incur legal liability for misjudgment, an interesting question indeed given the propensity for behavioral biases and errors.

The range of lawsuits filed by Orange County raises the general issue of *fairness*. Events in Orange County featured the misjudgment of Robert Citron, the aggressive sales tactics of some Merrill Lynch employees, the cautious warnings by other Merrill Lynch employees, and the mistaken opinions of bond-rating agencies. Is there a fair way to share the blame? The blame game is a fairness issue with which the investment community repeatedly struggles.

An interesting article appeared in the summer issue of the *Journal of Derivatives*. The article was written by Merton Miller and David Ross (1997) and titled "The Orange County Bankruptcy and Its Aftermath: Some New Evidence." Miller and Ross argue that it was not necessary for Orange County to have declared bankruptcy, since in December 1994 the Orange County Investment Pool was neither insolvent nor illiquid. Moreover, they point out that had the portfolio simply been held rather than liquidated, subsequent interest rate moves would actually have led to a profit. The county would have emerged ahead, recovering the full $21 billion of its portfolio plus $300 million of interest.[18]

Appropriate actions are always clear in hindsight. That's why the phenomenon is called hindsight bias. But Miller and Ross would not accept hindsight bias as a reason. Rather they contend that "the positive cash flows earned in 1995 are fully consistent with expectations based on historical term structure patterns." Or, to put it somewhat differently, they suggest that interest rates are predictable.

Indeed, a December 30, 1994, article that appeared in *Investor's Business Daily* concerning the Orange County fiasco stated: "There is still an incentive to leverage assets at the front end of the yield curve, where very short-term rates are at least 200 basis points lower than two-year rates."[19]

We move now from a discussion about the specific events surrounding the Orange County bankruptcy and the predictability of interest rates in December 1994 to a discussion about the general predictability of interest rates.

The Expectations Hypothesis of the Yield Curve

In his 1995 survey article, John Campbell describes some of the main features associated with yield curves. The most well-known theoretical property is the *expectations hypothesis*. This hypothesis concerns the question of whether future interest rate movements can be predicted based on the yield spread.

To explain the expectations hypothesis, consider a situation like the one that prevailed in 1993 when long-term rates were higher than short-term rates. Look at the right side of figure 14-2. If investors expected the yield curve to remain unchanged through time, they would have an incentive to do what Robert Citron did: Sell the short-term securities short and use the proceeds to purchase the long-term securities.

If all investors thought along these lines, then they would all be following what I'll call a "Citron strategy." So, what expectations would prevent them from behaving in that manner? For one, investors would have to believe that the yield curve would move. But in what direction? Consider an investor with a short time horizon. What kind of expectations would this investor have to hold in order to think twice about a Citron strategy? One possibility is that he would expect long-term yields to rise: The expected capital loss on his long-term securities would provide the disincentive. Another possibility is that although he does not expect long term yields to rise, he perceives the risk that they might as a sufficient deterrent. In other words, he perceives the term premium as insufficient compensation for bearing this risk.

How about an investor with a long time horizon? If she were to think twice about a Citron strategy then she would be expecting short-term rates to rise enough to offset any advantage to the current spread.

Putting the last two points together leads to the following implications. An upward-sloping yield curve reflects investors' expectations that both short-term rates and long-term rates will rise, but long-term rates will rise more. Moreover, the expected return difference between holding long-term bonds and holding three-month Treasury bills would have to be zero. This implication is testable.

The evidence reported by Campbell in connection with this implication is portrayed in figure 14-3, for the period 1952–1991. The upward-sloping curve shows the average yield spread between Treasurys of various maturities and the three-month Treasury bill. The higher the maturity, the greater the spread. The second curve shows how the average holding return varied across different maturities relative to the yield on three-month Treasury bills. According to the expectations hypothesis, the excess return should be zero for all maturities. But in reality, the excess return was positive for most maturities, declining with longer maturities. For the ten-year maturity, the excess return was actually negative.

Campbell also reports that wider spreads tended to be followed by long-term yields moving down rather than up, as the expectations hypothesis predicts. In this respect, he offers the following comment:

> This is exactly the behavior noted by Macaulay (1938) in a classic work on the movements of asset prices in the late nineteenth and early twentieth centuries. Macaulay wrote (p. 33): "The yields of bonds are higher if the highest grade should *fall* during a period in which short-term rates are higher than the yields of the bonds and *rise* during a period in which the short-term rates are lower. Now experience is more nearly the opposite." It is particularly impressive that this finding in the late nineteenth century appears in the late twentieth century as well as in Macaulay's data. (p. 139)

In order to understand why the expectations hypothesis fails, we need to examine investors' expectations, not just the subsequent be-

Figure 14-3 Evidence about the Expectations Hypothesis of the
Term Structure

The upward sloping curve in this figure shows the average spread between the
Treasury yield for a particular maturity and the three-month Treasury bill, for the
period 1952–1991. According to the expectations hypothesis of the yield curve, the
excess return to holding a Treasury security of a given maturity, relative to
Treasury bills, should be zero across all maturities. But the pattern is not flat. It
rises and then falls. Indeed, the return to the ten-year bond was negative over this
period.

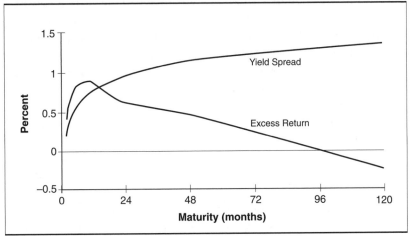

havior of yields of various maturities. Kenneth Froot (1989) undertook
the first study that used investors' interest rate forecasts to examine
this issue. He used data from a survey conducted by the *Goldsmith-
Nagan Bond and Money Market Letter,* now published in the investment
newsletter *Reporting on Governments.*

Froot investigated how future interest rates change in relation to
changes in the forward rate. The forward rate is the yield to maturity
from a Citron strategy involving zero coupon bonds. If the expectations
hypothesis were valid, then interest rates should move one-for-one relative to changes in the forward rate. Froot decomposed the relationship
into three components.

- The effect of prediction errors by investors
- The effect of changing term premia, that is, the compensation required by investors to compensate them for the risk of holding
  bonds
- The one-for-one effect predicted by the expectations hypothesis

Froot confirms that the expectations hypothesis indeed fails. Yields move significantly less in response to forward rates than they would in a one-for-one relationship. Moreover, Froot finds evidence that biased forecasts and varying term premia are both involved. He concludes that for short-term securities, the spread's bias may be entirely due to term premia. However, he also concludes that the "inability of the spread to forecast future long-rate changes is attributable entirely to systematic expectational errors. . . . [E]xpected future rates underreact to changes in the short-rate" (p. 304).

Money Market Services (MMS) is one of the major firms that track interest rate forecasts. MMS surveys investors and economists weekly to obtain forecasts for three maturities and two time horizons. The maturities are three months, two years, and thirty years. The horizons are one week and four weeks. Using weekly data from 1988 through 1997, I find that the forecasts obtained by MMS display the same characteristics reported by Froot.[20]

The MMS interest rate forecasts display a number of interesting features. Suppose we look at the implied forecasts of interest rate changes over the ten-year period 1988–1997. One striking pattern is that for the three-month and thirty-year maturities, forecasted changes were too high relative to actuals. The consensus expectation was that interest rates would be higher than turned out to be the case. For example, forecasters predicted that on average the three-month Treasury bill rate would go up by 13.7 basis points every four weeks, whereas it actually declined by 0.46 basis points. But for the two-year maturity, the reverse was true: the two-year yield fell by less than was expected.

This pattern did not hold in 1994, when interest rates were higher than predicted no matter what the maturity or time horizon. For example, forecasters predicted that on average the three-month Treasury bill rate would go up by 14.5 basis points every four weeks, whereas it actually rose by 19.4 basis points.

And how about expectations about long rates, whose sharp rise throughout 1994 led to the Orange County bankruptcy? Remember that in December 1993 Merrill Lynch fixed income strategist Martin Mauro had predicted that long yields would fall in 1994. Well, Mauro was not alone. This is also what the MMS forecasters predicted for both two-year and thirty-year yields.

Inflation Expectations and the Yield Curve

How important is inflation as a factor in determining yields?[21] In chapter 3, I reported on a study by Eldan Shafir, Peter Diamond, and

Amos Tversky (1997), which found that although people understand the difference between real and nominal changes, framing issues in nominal terms is more natural for them. Therefore, real changes tend to be less salient.

As far as the yield curve is concerned, appreciating the role of inflation is crucial. In a most insightful article, Werner De Bondt and Mary Bange (1992) discuss how the yield curve is affected by expectations about inflation. Their study is based on inflation forecasts for the period 1953 through 1987 that were collected by Joseph Livingston of the *Philadelphia Inquirer.* Beginning in 1946, Joseph Livingston conducted a biannual survey in which he asked respondents to estimate the future rate of inflation over both the next six months and the next twelve months. I have updated the De Bondt–Bange data through June 1998.

A critical question for the determination of yields concerns expectations about inflation. If investors expect high future inflation, they will bid yields up. Hence, a major issue involves the question of accuracy. How accurate have inflationary expectations been?

Figure 14-4 portrays the time series of the six-month-ahead consumer price index (CPI) forecast error, expressed as a percentage of the CPI. The predictable component of an efficient forecast should, of course, be zero. But De Bondt and Bange find that the forecast error in the Livingston survey has a very strong predictable component. It tended to be negative during the 1950s and 1960s, indicating that forecasters underestimated future inflation during this time. The error turned positive in the early 1970s, at the time President Nixon imposed wage and price controls. It turned negative again in the late 1970s, and then entered a phase where it has been positive most of the time. Since 1980, forecasters have consistently overestimated the rate at which the CPI would rise.

Notice that in figure 14-4, inflation forecast errors tend to be negative during periods of rising inflation and positive during periods of falling inflation. De Bondt and Bange argue that this is an underreaction phenomenon. That is, investors underreact to the most recent decline in the inflation rate. Instead, they place too much weight on historical rates.

De Bondt and Bange make a convincing case that errors in inflation forecasts are the major reason why the expectations hypothesis fails. In particular, they focus on the effect of inflation forecast errors. During the 1980s, both long-term rates and spreads were high because investors were too pessimistic about inflation. As investors received positive but *surprising* news about declining inflation, yields on long

Figure 14-4 CPI Forecast Error as Percent of Actual CPI,
          June 1954–June 1998

The time path of the percentage CPI forecast errors between 1954 and 1998 in the
Livingston survey. Efficient forecasts fluctuate randomly about zero. But the
Livingston errors stray from zero for long periods. During periods of declining
inflation they tend to be positive, while during periods of rising inflation they tend
to be negative. The pattern suggests that investors underreact to changing inflation: Their predictions for the CPI are too high when inflation is declining, and too
low when it is rising.

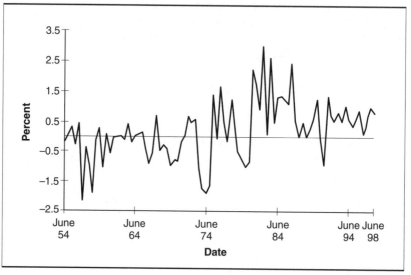

maturities declined. But because investors continued to underreact,
and inflation rates continued to decline, yields on long-term securities
tended to fall, not rise, as the expectations hypothesis would predict.
Moreover, short-term rates fell over the life of long-bonds issued in the
1980s.

Did investors in the 1990s continue to be surprised by how quickly
inflation declined? As can be seen from figure 14-4, the answer is yes.
Here are the opening paragraphs from an article that appeared in the
Wall Street Journal on September 17, 1998.

> Investors sent stock and bond prices soaring in one of Wall Street's
> strongest days this decade.
> The U.S. Treasury market had its biggest rise this year, with the
> bellwether 30-year bond soaring 2 5/32 points, or $21.563 for each
> $1,000 face amount. The yield on the issue, which moves in the oppo-
> site direction of the price, fell to 6.40%. That was the second-largest
> single-day decline in the yield in the 1990s.

The plunge in interest rates unleashed a torrent of buying among the big blue-chip stocks that have been out of favor for the past six weeks. . . .

Behind the powerful rallies was the August consumer-price report, which erased any fears that inflation was about to spring up. This ignited what some traders called a "buying panic" in both stocks and bonds.[22]

Think about this excerpt within the context of figure 14-4. Does it seem like investors continued to underreact to the decline in inflation? It's not that people don't learn. It's that they learn very slowly.

Full Circle

We are coming full circle. What about a Citron strategy? Did it make sense? De Bondt and Bange's findings provide an answer, but it depends on both the magnitude of the spread and past forecast errors about inflation. When spreads are high *and* investors have been underreacting to declining inflation, then a Citron strategy indeed does make sense. This was the case throughout the 1980s and 1990s.

De Bondt and Bange report that there are three important features concerning the link between predictable interest rate movements and inflation forecast errors. First, when the yield spread is above average, inflation forecasts tend to be too high. Second, when the twelve-month-ahead inflation forecast exceeded the six-month-ahead forecast, investors subsequently earned positive excess returns by holding long-term bonds. Third, past inflation errors are positively correlated with future excess returns. This means that not only are excess returns forecastable, they can be predicted by the extent to which investors misjudged recent inflation.

A Citron strategy makes sense because it capitalizes on investor errors. But as we saw very clearly, the strategy is also risky. Why? Not because of uncertainty about what the Federal Reserve might do, but because the strategy's success relies on particular investor errors. In his 1995 survey article, Campbell emphasizes that the 1994 surprise exceeded the extent of Federal Reserve tightening at the short end of the yield curve. In addition, long yields rose by about the same amount as short yields. What hurt the Orange County Investment Pool was the fact that Citron both guessed wrong and chose to be highly leveraged.

Of course, this begs the question as to why long-term rates rose in 1994. Was it heuristic-driven bias? Both Froot and De Bondt–Bange state that as a general matter, long yields do not overreact to changes at the short end. I suppose you could say that 1994 was the exception that proved the rule.

Summary

The first half of this chapter focused on instances of heuristic-driven bias and frame dependence. The second half focused on inefficient markets. In the first half, I discussed events pertaining to the Orange County Investment Pool. These events are replete with behavioral phenomena. At the beginning of the case, gambler's fallacy, betting on trends, and overconfidence figure prominently. As the case progresses, conservatism, the illusion of validity, regret, and loss aversion come to dominate.

Underlying the events associated with Orange County bankruptcy is a general issue—the longtime puzzle concerning the expectations hypothesis of the yield curve. In the second half of the chapter, I explained why the failure of the hypothesis reflects market inefficiency, largely stemming from underreaction to changes in the rate of inflation.

Chapter 15

The Money Management Industry: Framing Effects, Style "Diversification," and Regret

*P*lacing funds with an active money manager is typically a bad bet. Yet institutions continue to hire active money managers. Why?

The short answer is that the individuals who serve on institutional investment committees exhibit frame dependence and heuristic-driven bias. When it comes to framing, committee members tend to think of portfolios as a series of mental accounts, with associated reference points known as benchmarks. Therefore, committee members tend to mistake variety in manager "styles" for true diversification. In addition, reference-point thinking leads people to give opportunity costs less weight than out-of-pocket costs of the same magnitude.

In addition to frame dependence, members of institutional investment committees bear responsibility for the performance of the portfolio. Consequently, they are vulnerable to regret. Choosing active managers enables committee members to shift some of the responsibility for performance onto the managers, thereby reducing their own exposure to regret.

As noted elsewhere, heuristic-driven bias stems mostly from reliance on representativeness. Specifically, representativeness underlies the mistaken belief in hot hands, an effect that leads sponsors to believe, mistakenly, that they have the ability to pick managers who can beat the market.

This chapter discusses the following:

- a case about a university endowment that illustrates how the portfolio is structured as a series of mental accounts

- the effect that regret and representativeness have on the manner in which the endowment portfolio is managed

- some general findings about the performance of active money managers in the tax-exempt money management industry

Case Study: The Management of a University Endowment

In 1998, eight active money managers managed the equity portion of Santa Clara University's endowment portfolio. These managers used a variety of different styles, such as large-cap growth, small-cap value, opportunistic, and emerging markets. The equity portion made up about 75 percent of the portfolio. The remainder was in fixed income securities and cash.[1]

Figure 15-1 is a pie chart that describes how the university's allocation was allocated across money managers at the end of March 1998. The legend in the figure begins with the manager identified with a growth style. The percentage allocation to growth was 7 percent, and resides at the one o'clock position in the pie chart. Proceeding down the figure legend, and clockwise in the chart, we move to opportunistic, diverse, and so on.

Responsibility for overseeing the university's portfolio is entrusted to a sixteen-member investment committee. For advice and monitoring services, the committee uses Cambridge Associates, Inc., which advises many educational institutions. It offers advice on both asset allocation and the selection of specific money managers. In addition, it tracks managers' performance and provides detailed reports to the investment committee.

The investment committee meets on a regular basis with Cambridge once a quarter.[2] Each manager makes a presentation to the committee at least once per year, in order to provide his or her "take on the market." Usually two money managers make presentations at each of the quarterly meetings. The university's vice president for finance also pays a series of visits to managers.

How about goals? As far as long-term return is concerned, the committee set an objective range of 10 to 15 percent per year. The lower

Figure 15-1 Portfolio Style Allocation

The university's portfolio is allocated across a variety of equity styles. Twenty-five percent of the portfolio is maintained in fixed income securities.

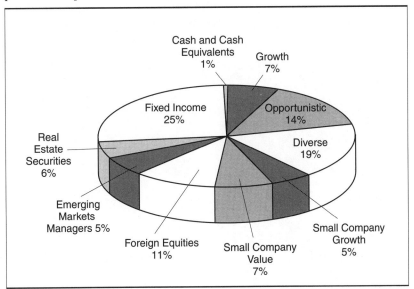

end of this range corresponds to the historical return on equities. In view of the fact that 25 percent of the portfolio is allocated to fixed income securities that have averaged 8.8 percent a year since September 1989, this goal appears to be somewhat aggressive.

How can a goal of 10 to 15 percent be achieved? Higher risk? Just plain good luck? Or superior money management performance? I find little evidence that the investment committee seeks above-average risks: The beta on the equity portion of the portfolio is approximately 1.0. Moreover, a major reason why 25 percent of the portfolio is allocated to fixed-income securities is precisely to achieve some risk reduction.

Instead of counting on risk or good luck, the investment committee counts on above average performance from its money managers. Each manager's performance is compared to the performance of a particular benchmark portfolio. Managers are grouped. Those in the same group are evaluated against the same benchmark. The precise benchmarks used at the university are described in table 15-1. The committee has a secondary goal. It looks for each of the managers to beat the corresponding benchmark by 1 percent a year.

Table 15-1

Style	Benchmark
Growth	S&P Midcap 400
Opportunistic	S&P 500
Diverse	S&P 500
Small-company growth	Russell 2000 Growth
Small-company value	Russell 2000 Value
Foreign equities	GMO EAFE Lite
Emerging markets managers	IFC Investable Composite Index
Real estate securities	NAREIT
Fixed income	Lehman Brothers Aggregate Bond Index
Cash and cash equivalents	US Treasury bills

Behavioral Issues

The first behavioral issue concerns the belief in active money management. Is there reason to believe that active money management delivers superior performance?

The investment committee is guided by a set of principles. One principle concerns risk exposure. This principle stipulates that the way to minimize exposure to risk is to do two things: Allocate a portion of the portfolio to fixed income securities, and choose managers with different styles. Another principle stipulates that the way to superior performance is to choose managers who beat their benchmarks. The two together provide both prudence and superior returns.[3]

In 1998, a vice president of Franklin Resources chaired the committee. By and large, the members of the investment committee believe in active money management. Only one member, the chairman of a local technology firm, has consistently argued for an indexed approach. But his has been a lonely voice. The other external members of the committee include an active money manager, a retired member of the California Supreme Court, a principal in a Chicago commodities trading firm, and a local real estate developer.

Because the committee seeks managers who have the skill to beat their benchmarks, they attribute a below-benchmark performance as much to a money manager's actions as they do to bad luck. Two years of below benchmark performance leads to a manager's being put on notice. Shortly thereafter, if performance does not improve, the manager gets replaced.[4] Is two years enough time to separate out the skill component from overall performance? In chapter 12 I discussed just how difficult a task that can be.

How has the university's active money management strategy worked? Between September 1989 and March 1998 the university's endowment portfolio grew by 13.2 percent a year, within its 10–15 percent target range. During this period, the S&P 500 increased by 17.7 percent a year. In fact, the only domestic benchmark that had a return lower than 13.2 percent was the Russell 2000 Growth Index, which returned 12.1 percent a year. Interestingly, the S&P 500 had a higher rate of return and a lower return standard deviation over this period than any other benchmark. Its Sharpe ratio of 1.1 was higher than that of the Russell 2000 (0.5), the Wilshire 5000 Equity Index (1.1), and the Lehman Brothers Aggregate Bond Index (0.7).

During the three-year period of March 1995 through March 1998, the university's portfolio grew by 21.7 percent a year. Except for the Russell 2000 Growth Index, all the other domestic benchmarks grew by more than 28 percent a year, with the S&P 500 returning 32.8 percent.

I find it difficult to argue that this is superior performance. But was the fact that the university portfolio only returned 21.7 percent cause for concern? Apparently not. The investment committee does not use 32.8 percent as a reference point for comparison.[5] It uses 10–15 percent, its long-term goal. And 21.8 looks mighty good against that reference point. The 6–10 percent difference earned by U.S. equities carried very little weight. Because of the reference point used to evaluate the outcome, this differential is treated as a foregone opportunity, not an out-of-pocket cost. As argued by Daniel Kahneman and Amos Tversky (1979) and Richard Thaler (1991), *opportunity costs typically receive much less weight than out-of-pocket costs.*

Indeed, the committee is quite clear. Members were much more concerned with dampening a less frequent but serious market decline than in taking a chance on capturing the additional return. As one member of the committee put it: "We don't really think about what we are giving up. Comfort level has a lot to do with it."[6]

In many ways, the decision approach followed by committee members conforms to the behavioral paradigm. The committee looks at the portfolio as being segmented into a series of mental accounts, one manager per account. Each account has its own reference point, its own benchmark.[7]

Interestingly, the rapid increase in the value of the portfolio that took place during 1996 and 1997 gave rise to yet another behavioral effect. In early 1996 the value of the university's endowment stood at $225 million. At that time, the president of the university indicated that he hoped the endowment would grow to $300 million by the year 2000.

However, because the market was so strong during the subsequent two years, the endowment crossed the $300 million mark during the first quarter of 1998. Reaching that landmark early is akin to walking into a casino and being handed free gambling chips. Now do people tend to take more risk when they play with chips from the "house" instead of with their own money? As I discussed in chapter 3, Richard Thaler and Eric Johnson (1991) have found that they do. Thaler and Johnson call this tendency the "house money effect."

So, was there a house money effect at the university? Let me answer that question by asking another. Do venture capitalists take greater risks than the average money manager does? How about hedge fund managers? I ask this because shortly after its endowment hit $300 million, the university decided to add venture capital, hedge funds, and private equity placements to its asset allocation mix.

How representative is the university's experience as far as institutional money management is concerned? In a word, very. Take the house money effect. William Sharpe (1987) describes a typical attitude among pension committees by providing an illustrative quote for the case of overfunding: "We're well funded; let's put all our money in stocks—we can afford the risk." However, he also discusses the extent to which the different approaches to money management—for example, strategic asset allocation (match the market) or tactical asset allocation (time the market, pick winners)—are inconsistent with maximizing expected return for a given level of risk.

A Better Mouse Trap?

In chapter 8, I discussed the case of RJF Asset Management, now Fuller and Thaler Asset Management. RJF has always promoted itself as using a behavioral strategy that exploits "mental mistakes" in the market. And since its inception in 1992, RJF has performed well. Yet, for all this talk about hot hands, RJF's assets under management have grown slowly.[8]

If you build a better mousetrap, will people beat a path to your door? RJF argues not. Doug Carlson of Cambridge Associates offers some reasons why.[9] He points out that the composition of sponsor investment committees tends to be similar to those of the university above. Committee members get used to evaluating particular types of managers. In other words, they get used to thinking in terms of a particular frame. In addition, committee members come to hold strong opinions. Carlson suggests that managers who use uncommon approaches face uphill battles with sponsors; and RJF's approach is definitely uncommon. Suppose a sponsor listens to the presentations of two managers with comparable track records. But one manager uses a common style and the other uses an uncommon style. When the sponsor gets ready to make a choice after the presentations, he or she will tend to choose the manager with the common style.

These are behavioral issues, dealing mostly with familiarity and regret. Committee members hold a fiduciary responsibility, and they want to feel comfortable with their choice of money manager. They typically want to "understand" the money manager's strategy. In particular, they recognize that if a manager's performance is poor they will have to explain what happened to the board.

Carlson indicates that unless they "feel a real need to break out of the box," committee members will choose the familiar over the unfamiliar. Choosing the familiar lowers exposure to regret. Perhaps this is the Catch-22 of behavioral finance: Behavioral obstacles get in the way of behaviorally oriented money managers.

General Findings

Joseph Lakonishok, Andrei Shleifer, and Robert Vishny (1992) did a most illuminating study of the tax-exempt money management industry. They focus their discussion on the management of corporate pension funds, which parallels the management of university endowment funds. From their work, we learn the following about both kinds of funds:

- Outside money managers are hired to manage large portfolios.
- Consulting firms are used to select the money managers and monitor their performance.

- The money managers so selected tend to use active strategies within the restrictions of an identifiable style.

- The distribution of betas for the equity portfolios is tightly clustered around 1.0.

- The equity portion of a representative fund underperforms the S&P 500. This underperformance does not take into account fees, or the fact that managers also hold cash. Hence, the returns to sponsors are even worse.

Lakonishok, Shleifer, and Vishny use data obtained from SEI, which at one time was in the consulting business, like Cambridge Associates.[10] The study covers the period 1983–1990. Lakonishok, Shleifer, and Vishny paint the following picture of the industry.

Many corporate pension contracts are defined benefit plans. In this case, the pension assets are set aside to generate benefits promised to employees. Largely, any excess amounts generated relative to these obligations belong to corporate shareholders.

The responsibility for managing corporate pension assets falls to the treasurer's office. This is a major responsibility, and the treasurer's office usually meets it by delegation, using consultants like Cambridge Associates as well as money managers.

Why use active money managers rather than an indexed approach? Lakonishok, Shleifer, and Vishny suggest that the behavior of the treasurer's office must be seen through the lens of self-interest. Overseeing pension assets constitutes a major portion of what this office is charged to do. Surely, the expertise to manage pension assets could be hired and brought in house. Yet, this typically does not happen. Why?

Given the inferior performance of active money managers, the use of index funds would seem to be beneficial to shareholders. But it would also jeopardize much of the raison d'être for the treasurer's office. Therefore, those people employed within the treasurer's office, the outside consultants, and the money managers all benefit if the superiority of an indexed approach happens to be *opaque*. And they foster opaqueness by claiming to generate performance superior to the S&P 500, a style benchmark, or a risk adjusted benchmark.

The money management industry appears to have two segments. The first segment consists of large banks and insurance companies that offer generic products such as index funds, guaranteed income contracts, and annuities. The second segment offers specialized money management for groups that do not believe in the superiority of index funds. Indeed, since people learn slowly, it has not been difficult for active money managers to mask the superiority of index funds.[11] Behavioral phenomena lead people to overattribute investment success to skill rather than luck. Therefore, the treasurer's office acquires the responsibility of selecting superior money managers. This sets up the dynamic of the track record game, as the treasurer's office sets out to chase superior track records.

Is there persistence among active institutional money managers? Do top performers tend to repeat? The interesting thing is that they do, somewhat. Suppose we divide managers into four groups based on their track record from the previous year. If performance is completely random, what are the odds that the top performers from the previous year will continue to excel? In theory, the answer is 25 percent; in actuality, 26 percent of winners repeat. Even more interesting is the fact that the chances a manager will move from the worst group to the best is 32 percent, not the 25 percent predicted by random performance. Persistence is even stronger when viewed over periods of two and three years. For the three-year horizon, the expected benefit from going with past winners rather than past losers is about 110 basis points. But remember, managers travel, meaning they regularly migrate from one performance group to another. Thus, performance is somewhat persistent but mostly unstable.

Because of the persistence effect, successful money managers will tend to have good track records. But they need something else—a good story to tell and a concept to sell. If returns have been poor, the employees at the treasurer's office will have some explaining to do to the sponsor. Consequently, they will need to offer a convincing explanation for what went wrong. And to whom do they turn for an explanation? Money managers. Sponsors have a strong need for reassurance when returns are poor. The ability to provide effective hand-holding and communicate a clear story are the two most important ingredients of "service."

The folks in the treasurer's office who earn their keep playing the active management game spend their time chasing past winners and diversifying across managers. Why diversify? Because, as noted, managers' performance can be highly unstable. The workers in the treasurer's office will be evaluated relative to their counterparts at other sponsors. Therefore, it will pay for these people to diversify across styles. If they avoid value funds, and value funds do well in a particular year, their judgment will be called into question. Therefore, better to use the services of a manager who uses the value style. A similar remark applies to other styles: growth, small cap, emerging funds, and so forth.

Regret and Responsibility

There are interesting differences between institutional money managers and mutual fund managers. Mutual fund managers provide superior returns to investors, but offer no hand-holding. However, the folks in the treasurer's office choose money managers in accordance with their own comfort levels. They need effective hand-holding in order to feel comfortable. An important element of this comfort is exposure to regret.

Meir Statman and I (Shefrin and Statman 1986) discuss the roles of regret and responsibility in the money management industry. Regret, as previously noted, is the psychological pain associated with realizing after the fact that the wrong decision was made (see chapter 3). The magnitude of regret affects the degree to which the person who made the decision feels responsible.

The treasurer's office directs pension assets by transferring the responsibility for investment decisions to money managers. If things go well, employees can pride themselves on having selected top performers. However, if things do not go well, they can mitigate the criticism directed at them by blaming the managers. People look for ways to minimize their exposure to regret. One way is to behave conventionally. Sponsors now routinely diversify across active money managers, even when superior index fund alternatives are available. Sponsors can also make active managers the scapegoat when returns are poor. This also serves to enhance the level of comfort by mitigating possible future regret.

Of course, the pain of regret may also play a role in learning, analogous to the pain experienced by touching a hot stove. The latter experience helps us learn to avoid touching hot objects. However, shifting regret to money managers inhibits learning about the most effective ways of managing the sponsor's assets.

Money managers may not completely understand this part of the game. They too have personal needs for pride and are averse to regret. Consequently, they may take steps to reduce the blame directed at them. For example, many managers engage in "window dressing," hiding the identity of poor investment choices from sponsors by selling them before the end of the reporting period.

Gary Brinson, Randolph Hood, and Gilbert Beebower (1986) analyzed the performances of ninety-one large U.S. pension plans over the period 1974–1983, comparing the performances of these plans to that of strategic asset allocation. Two important numbers came out of that study. The first number was 1.1 percent. That is, the average fund underperformed a strategic asset allocation approach by 1.1 percent.

What does this tell us? Roughly speaking, it suggests that the value paid for scapegoating services is about 1.1 percent. After all, sponsors are perfectly able to use passive management. But they don't, and on average 1.1 percent is what they give up. Of course, that assumes sponsors know how much they are giving up. Another possibility is that because of heuristic-driven bias they do not. Instead, sponsors believe that the active managers *they* hire are likely to outperform strategic asset allocation. This might happen because of a combination of the hot hands phenomenon, stemming from representativeness, and the usual overconfidence.

The second number that came out of the Brinson-Hood-Beebower study was 93.6 percent, which is the R-squared from a regression of pension plan returns on the returns to strategic asset allocation. This second number is often described by saying that strategic asset allocation is "90 percent of the game."[12] But that description is misleading at best, in that it is suggestive of relative performance. The R-squared says nothing about relative performance.

Consider a hypothetical situation in which active pension fund managers always earn returns that are double those of strategic asset allocation. This is what would happen if pension fund managers simply bought the market portfolio on 50 percent margin. In this hypothetical situation, the R-squared for a regression of pension fund returns on strategic asset allocation is 100 percent.

Does this say that strategic asset allocation is "100 percent of the game"? To say so is to admit that little potential value is generated by tactical asset allocation. Yet Statman (1999) points out that over the period 1980–1997, the marginal gain to effective tactical asset allocation would have been 800 basis points. The point is that "93.6 percent" tells us the degree to which pension fund returns move in the same direction as the returns to strategic asset allocation. But that figure says nothing about relative performance.

Summary

The institutional money management industry has a split personality. One half is highly concentrated and stable, consisting of large banks and insurance companies offering generic products. The other half is unstable, consisting of a large number of money managers offering active money management and specialized services. In many ways this segment is like the market for restaurants and beauty salons, with customers always in search of new favorites and the latest hot spots.

A combination of private interests and behavioral phenomena provide the basis for the existence of this active segment. Both frame dependence and heuristic-driven bias play major roles.

Frame dependence occurs as the sponsor divides responsibility for its portfolio across several active money managers. These managers are evaluated relative to benchmarks. The division of the portfolio gives rise to a mental accounting structure with particular reference points. This leads sponsors to react more strongly to outcomes that fall below a reference point than to outcomes that lie above it. Mental accounting also leads to the view that diversification means having variety across styles rather than maximizing expected returns subject to a fixed return variance.

An important aspect of active money management is scapegoating, or shifting regret to, the manager when returns are poor. Given the fact that active managers underperform strategic asset allocation, the amount of underperformance may serve to measure the value of scapegoating.

Scapegoating is one explanation for why sponsors select active money managers. Another is that sponsors are overconfident, believing the active managers *they* hire are likely to outperform strategic asset allocation. This might happen in conjunction with a hot hands phenomenon stemming from representativeness.

PART V

THE INTERFACE BETWEEN CORPORATE FINANCE AND INVESTMENT

Chapter **16**

Corporate Takeovers and the Winner's Curse

Corporate executives suffer from "Lake Wobegon syndrome": Lake Wobegon is the mythical rural Minnesota community where *all* children are above average.[1] Lake Wobegon syndrome pertains to *hubris,* overconfidence about ability. In chapter 4, I mentioned that most people rate themselves as above-average drivers. In this chapter, I discuss how overconfidence affects corporate decisions, mostly associated with mergers and acquisition.

There is general evidence that corporate executives exhibit hubris—they are impressed with their own abilities. Since July 1996, the Financial Executives Institute and Duke University have been jointly surveying corporate executives on a quarterly basis. During the first two years of the survey, executives of companies whose stocks are publicly traded have consistently indicated that their companies were undervalued.[2]

Corporate decisions offer ample examples of heuristic-driven bias and frame dependence. This chapter offers several examples: excessive optimism, the illusion of control, gambler's fallacy, and loss aversion. Hubris, however, is the primary bias involved in corporate takeovers because it leads to the phenomenon of winner's curse, where the acquiring firm overpays for the target. Richard Roll (1983) coined the term *hubris hypothesis* for this effect.

This chapter discusses the following:

- the role of hubris in the decision by American Telephone and Telegraph (AT&T) to take over computer maker NCR

- how after the takeover, loss aversion led AT&T to throw good money after bad

• what the general literature has to say about the winner's curse in corporate takeovers

Case Study: AT&T's Bid for NCR

Let's begin with some history. Once upon a time AT&T thought it would be the premier computer company in the world. Its research arm, Bell Laboratories, had produced truly revolutionary breakthroughs such as the transistor and UNIX, a major operating system. The switching technology that forms the backbone of a telephone network is essentially a computer. Therefore, AT&T had every reason to see itself as the leading computer firm.

But for seven years in the 1950s, AT&T fought an antitrust suit brought by the U.S. Justice Department. When it ended in 1956, AT&T signed a consent decree agreeing not to market its computers outside its own company. This agreement stayed in force until 1984, when a landmark agreement took effect that broke up AT&T's monopoly in the telephone business and created seven independent regional phone companies.

No longer bound by the 1956 agreement, AT&T entered the computer market with a line of medium-range machines that used its UNIX operating system. But AT&T ran into a series of difficulties. It could not produce its machines fast enough to meet consumer demand, or cheaply enough to be especially profitable. In 1986, just two years later, its computer division was generating losses at the rate of $1 billion annually. By the end of the 1980s AT&T was widely recognized as a failure in the computer business, having lost between $2 and $3 billion.

On December 2, 1990, AT&T announced its intention to acquire NCR, at the time the fifth-largest computer maker in the United States. What was AT&T's rationale in choosing NCR?

AT&T's chairman at the time was Robert E. Allen. In Allen's view, corporations, led by banking and retailing, were increasingly coming to rely on permanently connected networks of computers to transact business instantaneously. So from his perspective, AT&T would supply the networking capability and NCR would provide the transaction technology. Allen put it as follows: "It's a natural marriage between our communication services and network skills and their transaction service operations all over the world."[3]

The Behavioral Basis for Winner's Curse

Analysts greeted the announcement with skepticism, viewing the proposed merger as a high-stakes gamble. They pointed out that virtually *every* merger between technology companies in recent years had failed. At the time, the largest technology takeover was Burroughs Inc.'s 1986 $4.8 billion acquisition of Sperry Univac. The entity resulting from that merger was Unisys. Unisys was the product of a hostile takeover and produced a string of losses.

A situation very similar to the AT&T/NCR case was IBM's purchase of Rolm. This deal was designed to produce the same marriage of computers (IBM) and telecommunications (Rolm) that AT&T was pursuing with NCR. When the IBM/Rolm combination failed to create value, IBM sold Rolm to Siemens, the German technology firm, and wrote off its losses.

Robert Kavner was AT&T's top computer executive and the architect of its hostile takeover attempt of NCR. During a news conference that December, Richard Shaffer, a technology analyst and principal of the firm Technologic Partners, put the following issue before Kavner: "It sounds like hyperbole, but no one I know can think of a single example of where a large high-technology merger has been really successful. And it's hard to see how AT&T's play for NCR would be any different."[4] Shaffer then asked Kavner if he could name any high-technology merger, even a friendly one, that had been successful. Apparently embarrassed by the question, Kavner mumbled that he could not.

Why did AT&T executives believe that they could succeed where others had failed? When dealing with similar questions that were posed to Kavner, Robert Allen did acknowledge that "it's going to be tough" not to repeat history. But he argued that the NCR deal offered AT&T unique opportunities to increase its core telecommunications business and enter the emerging market for networked cooperative computing, meaning computers linked by telephone lines.

Consider the behavioral biases here. Were AT&T's executives overconfident? Might they have been unduly optimistic? Did hubris lead them to believe that they could succeed when *all others* had failed? I suggest that the answer to each of these questions is yes.

There may have been other behavioral biases at work as well. Allen commented on the risk attached to his strategy, stating: "This is not a safe world. And we're not looking for safety. Taking the easy, less-risky way is not satisfactory because it won't make us successful."[5]

Think about this statement in light of AT&T's losses in its computer operations. Do you recognize any patterns that have been discussed in earlier chapters? What about loss aversion—taking risks that are unlikely to pay off, especially after having incurred a loss?

Did AT&T suffer from the illusion of control, believing that it was more in control of the situation than, say, IBM had been in dealing with

Rolm? Was AT&T influenced by its experience in previous deals? For example, in January 1988 it had agreed to purchase up to 20 percent of workstation manufacturer Sun Microsystems. One year later, AT&T took a 49 percent stake in AG Communication Systems, a joint venture with GTE Corp. that makes telephone switching equipment. In March 1989, AT&T acquired Paradyne Corp., a manufacturer of data communications equipment, for about $250 million. Twelve months after that it entered the consumer credit card business with the AT&T Universal card, available through either Visa or MasterCard. Some of these deals had shown early promise. However, none were comparable in magnitude to the NCR acquisition.

The Fine Act of Overpaying

Discussions between AT&T and NCR actually began on November 7, 1990. At that time, NCR shares were trading at $48. In private discussions, AT&T had offered to pay $85 per share in a stock swap, a *premium* of 77 percent. When the NCR board rejected this offer, AT&T announced that it planned to acquire NCR shares in a takeover attempt, and increased its bid to $90, an 88 percent premium.

During the previous week, NCR shares had closed at $56.75. How did the market react the day of AT&T's announcement? Well, the price of NCR shares jumped dramatically, surging by $26.50 to $82.25. NCR stock was the second most actively traded issue on the New York Stock Exchange that day. Not surprisingly, the most active issue was AT&T. But unlike NCR, whose stock rose, the price of AT&T shares fell by 2⅛ to $30.

How did the combined market value of the two stocks change as a result of the announcement by AT&T? This is an important issue, in that it reflects investors' collective assessment of the merits of the merger. On the previous Friday, the market value of AT&T's 1.1 billion shares was $35.33 billion, and the market value of NCR's 64.5 million shares was $3.66 billion. The combined value, $39 billion, actually *declined* slightly to $38.3 billion on the day of the announcement![6]

Was Robert Allen doing the shareholders of AT&T a favor? Not on December 2, 1990. What about the shareholders of NCR? It might certainly seem so. Given the small change in combined value, the effect of the announcement was to transfer $1.65 billion from the shareholders of AT&T to the shareholders of NCR.

However, keep in mind that the NCR board had rejected an offer of $85 a share. What were they thinking? Were they still anchored on NCR's 52-week high, which was $104.25? If so, were they reluctant to sell below this reference point? Or were they committing gambler's fallacy by anticipating a reversal? It is worth keeping this point in mind as we trace through the negotiations that ensued over the following months.

In December 1990 the NCR board rejected AT&T's bid of $90 a share, but it expressed a willingness to talk if AT&T would agree to a price of $125 a share. This offer corresponded to a premium of 120 percent, relative to the price of NCR shares just prior to AT&T's announcement. Apparently, AT&T thought the price was too high, and instead of accepting the counteroffer it began a proxy battle to take control of NCR's board. Two days after its $90 offer was rejected, AT&T asked NCR shareholders to hold a special meeting to remove the board.

The proxy battle took place during the first four months of 1991. During the public relations campaign Charles Exley, chairman of NCR, reminded investors that history had shown that such takeovers turned out to be "calamities!" Exley pointed out the difficulties of bringing disparate corporate cultures together, and he stressed the indirect costs associated with having the attention of top-level executives distracted by the merger instead of being focused on the core competencies of the firms. But because technological developments continue to occur, "the competition has a field day at your expense," he was quoted as saying.[7]

On March 28, the day of the shareholders' meeting, AT&T and NCR announced that for tax reasons they had agreed to a stock swap in which AT&T would pay the equivalent of $110 a share.[8] In September 1991, the two companies filed merger papers in Maryland, where NCR had been incorporated, thereby concluding a $7.48 billion dollar deal.

The Chickens Come Home to Roost

AT&T implemented the takeover by having its own computer division absorbed by NCR. In this regard, it focused attention on promoting NCR's high-powered 3000 series of computers. AT&T merged marketing groups, announced phased plans to discontinue a variety of product lines, such as minicomputers and client/server systems, and terminated previous arrangements with firms such as Intel and Sun Microsystems.[9] At the time, the overall cost of this streamlining was estimated at $1.5 billion.

Takeover discussions took place against an interesting financial backdrop for NCR. NCR had been forecasting robust results for 1991 and beyond. It had told AT&T that it was expecting revenue to hit $6.6 billion in 1991, $7.3 billion in 1992, $10.3 billion in 1995, and $16.84 billion by the year 2000. NCR's income forecast was equally upbeat: $386 million in 1991, $545 million in 1992, $897 million in 1995 and $1.56 billion in 2000. However, NCR's 1990 performance had actually been poor. In 1990 NCR posted net income of $369 million, a 10 percent decline from the previous year, on revenue of $6.29 billion, a 6 percent increase. The fourth quarter of 1990 had not ended well. In January 1991, NCR announced earnings of $1.71 per share compared to $2.02 per share a year earlier.

Were NCR's financial projections well founded? Was 1991 going to turn out much better than 1990? On July 17, 1991, NCR stated that it was unlikely its 1991 results would meet 1990 levels. In this regard, NCR cited several factors, including the U.S. recession. About a month later, the company filed a statement with the SEC, saying that its 1991 revenue, income before taxes, and net income would be "materially below" projections made to AT&T during the merger negotiations.

NCR blamed the change in outlook on the slumping market in Europe and on weakening orders for its products in the Pacific region. It indicated that revenues and income from its new line of high-power computers, the 3000 series, would not begin to flow until 1992. However, NCR put its disappointing results into context by pointing out that other computer makers, such as IBM and Digital Equipment Corp., had experienced similar problems.

AT&T's reaction to these disclosures was interesting. It stated that NCR's disclosure had not altered either AT&T's view of the merger or the price it was paying for NCR. An AT&T spokeswoman was quoted in the September 9, 1991 issue of the *Wall Street Journal* as saying: "We're merging with NCR for the long-term strategic fit. Both sides still believe this is a perfect match. We did our homework on this."[10]

Think about NCR's rosy projections through the year 2000. Had AT&T really done its homework? Or did it underreact? Did AT&T ignore disconfirming information about NCR's financial performance during 1991, thereby succumbing to the illusion of validity? Perhaps. Having committed themselves to the takeover, did AT&T also succumb to loss aversion?

Remember Richard Shaffer's asking AT&T's Robert Kavner to name a successful technology merger? Did the AT&T-NCR deal turn out to be a major success story, did it turn out like IBM-Rolm, or was it a "calamity" as Charles Exley had warned? In 1991, many speculated that Robert Allen's legacy at AT&T would be determined by how well the NCR deal worked out. Were they right?

In September 1991, NCR became a unit of AT&T, with a new name—Global Information Services (GIS). The results of 1992 did not match NCR's forecast. AT&T had not done its homework very well. The plan was for GIS to move away from NCR's highly focused strategy and become a computer company with broad appeal. This did not work out favorably. Key managers from the original NCR left GIS, and longtime customers felt abandoned. The competitive environment also changed, shifting toward low-margin personal computers and away from the larger systems in which NCR specialized. In July 1995, AT&T announced a layoff plan for GIS and stated its intention to get out of the consumer goods, transportation, and government markets and concentrate instead on the financial, retail, communications, services, and media markets.

Robert Allen's Legacy

The NCR fiasco did not turn out to be Robert Allen's legacy. His legacy is the second breakup of AT&T, the largest voluntary corporate breakup in history. In September 1995, Allen announced that AT&T was planning to split itself into three separately quoted companies: telecommunications services, telephone equipment manufacturing, and computing.[11] The telecommunications firm retained the name AT&T Corporation, the equipment manufacturing firm took the name Lucent Technologies, and the computing firm was "spun off" under its old name, NCR. (I place "spun off" in quotation marks because it arises as an issue in later discussion about equity carve-outs.)

Between 1993 and 1996, GIS lost over $3.85 billion. The financial press reported that by the time NCR was "spun off" in December 1996, AT&T had lost approximately $7 billion on its investment during the five years AT&T ran the company. From 1993 through 1996, *it threw more than $3 billion in good money after bad.*

AT&T's experience with NCR is a dramatic example of winner's curse, driven by hubris, optimism, the illusion of control, loss aversion, and the illusion of validity. But is the AT&T takeover of NCR case just another interesting story, or does it hold lessons that are more general? Just how typical is it?

Corporate Takeovers and the Winner's Curse: The General Case

The article best known for arguing that hubris leads acquiring firms to suffer from winner's curse is by Richard Roll (1993). He argues that one of the first things an acquiring firm does when examining a potential takeover target is to consider the target's market value. The acquirer then makes its own independent assessment of value, an assessment that would factor in any perceived synergy. If the acquiring firm's own evaluation lies below current market value, then it regards the target as overvalued and would not choose to enter a bid. But if its evaluation lies above market value, then the acquiring firm may choose to enter a bid. Roll points out that this leaves the acquiring firm open to winner's curse because it acquires the target only when its estimate is too high.

A central aspect of this argument involves the accuracy of market value. Market value reflects the collective judgment of many investors, not just the judgment of the acquiring firm's managers. Imagine that this collective judgment is correct and properly reflects all the information known about the target firm, even the information that is held by insiders. In other words, the market is strong-form efficient.[12] Roll suggests that we imagine a world where there are no inefficiencies with respect to operations or management's choice of strategy. He calls this the "frictionless ideal benchmark" from which to judge the evidence. In this type of world, the managers of the acquiring firm incorrectly place greater confidence in their independent estimate of value than in the collective wisdom of all other market participants. They do so because of hubris.

Suppose that the hubris hypothesis is valid, in its strong-form efficient characterization. Think about what would happen to market prices if an acquiring firm made its intentions known through an announcement that had not been anticipated by the market. In this case, the acquiring firm's actions would cause the price of the target firm's stock to rise. But because there is no value to the acquisition in this frictionless ideal world, and there *are* direct takeover costs, rational investors would bid down the price of the acquiring firm's stock. Why? Because the combined entity is worth less than the sum of its parts. Of course, if the acquiring firm were to abandon its bid, then the price would revert. However, if the bid were to prove successful, then the price of the target firm would rise still further, whereas that of the acquiring firm would decline even more.[13]

Recall how the market reacted to AT&T's announcement that it intended to acquire NCR. The price of NCR stock soared, while that of AT&T declined. The combined market values fell slightly. This pattern is consistent with the hubris hypothesis described above. Roll (1993) surveys the evidence about how takeovers affect the market values of acquiring firms, target firms, and the combined entity. Begin with target firms. Michael Bradley, Anand Desai, and E. Han Kim (1983), and Paul Asquith (1983), find that the target's market value goes up by an average of 7 percent on the announcement of a bid. However, if the bid is withdrawn within sixty days, and no further offer is subsequently made for a year, then market value falls back to a little below its starting point.

Evidence about total gains is difficult to measure from returns, especially when the acquiring firm is a lot larger than the target. The conclusion is ambiguous. We do not really know what happens on average. Paul Asquith, Robert Bruner, and David Mullins (1983) find that bidder returns are higher when bidders acquire larger targets, suggesting that this finding is consistent with positive overall gains. Yet Roll is not persuaded by their argument, because their finding could also mean simply that losses tend to be lower for larger targets.

Two other studies suggesting that corporate takeovers generate positive value added are those by Michael Jensen and Richard Ruback (1983) and Steven Kaplan (1989). Kaplan analyzed the largest management buyouts between 1980 and 1986. He finds that three years after a buyout, target firms had big boosts in both income and net cash flow, as well as lower capital expenditures. Shareholders earned an average 42 percent premium gain from the buyout, as measured by the share-price boost between the price two months before the bid and the price upon completion of the buyout. Kaplan found that the efficiencies came from better incentives for management and workers rather than from layoffs.

Bradley, Desai, and Kim (1982) attempt to measure dollar gains directly, rather than by using returns, and conclude that there is an increase in combined market value (though not by a statistically significant amount). They find that the average amount in their study, $17 million, is split into a +$34 million piece for the target and a –$17 million piece for the bidder!

Bradley, Desai, and Kim (1982) exclude offers that are not "control oriented" and find that both bidder and target benefit from increased market value. Paul Malatesta (1983) finds a positive effect for targets but a negative effect for bidders. He studied the period covering the sixty months that preceded approval by the target board. During this period, the increase in combined value turns out to be positive but very small. In addition, targets tend to perform poorly during this period, but bidders appear to do well. Yet during the merger months, the acquiring firms do not increase significantly in value, unlike the target firms.

Using British data, Michael Firth (1980) finds strong evidence for the $-/+/0$ effect in which the value of the acquiring firm declines ($-$), that of the target firm increases ($+$), but the combined value of the two stays the same (0). He finds that the change in combined market value is negative, with over half of the mergers experiencing a combined loss. Specifically, Firth finds that the premium paid by the bidder is proportionally related to the decline in the bidder's market value, suggesting that the market actually understands winner's curse! Nikhil Varaiya (1985) finds a positive but insignificant increase in combined market value, with the bidder losing and the target gaining. Moreover the larger the gain for the target, the worse the loss for the bidder.

What happens on the day of the announcement? Here the evidence is mixed. Asquith finds positive, but insignificant, returns to the bidder on the day of the announcement. However, Peter Dodd (1980) finds the opposite. Carol Eger (1983), studying noncash offers, finds negative returns. Interestingly, Varaiya finds negative returns on announcement day, with the effect stronger when there are rival bidders.

Equity Carve-outs

When AT&T announced that it would split itself into three companies, the price of AT&T's shares rose $2.625 to close at $67.375, a 4.1 percent increase. The average increase is 2.3 percent. John Hand and Terrance Skantz (1997) report that this upsurge is a common occurrence in equity carve-outs. But they also suggest that it is indicative of mispricing, because when the carved-out subsidiary goes public, there is a corresponding mean excess stock return of -2.4 percent. On average, the time between an announcement and the subsequent IPO is forty-five trading days. The situation with AT&T was considerably more complex than most, and took about one year.

Hand and Skantz suggest several possible reasons for this mispricing. One is the tendency of the financial press to describe equity carve-outs as "spinoffs." They state that "[s]pinoffs are more common events that are well known to increase parent stock prices by an average of 3%." A second possible reason stems from accounting changes associated with carve-outs that may mislead investors.

General Biases

The case study involving AT&T documented several behavioral biases that afflict corporate executives, most notably excessive optimism, the illusion of control, and loss aversion. These biases have been addressed in a series of articles.

Meir Statman and David Caldwell (1987) discuss a variety of reasons why executives are reluctant to terminate losing projects. In a follow-up article, Statman and James Sepe (1989) study how the stock price reacts to the announcement of a project termination. They find that stock prices typically rise when a project termination is announced, suggesting that investors greet the announcement as good news. Why good news? Investors are aware that being human, executives suffer from loss aversion and throw good money after bad. This stops with project termination.

The recognition of biases on the part of others is also a theme in the work of Statman and Tyzoon Tyebjee (1985). They find that in an experimental setting, managers seek to offset the optimistic capital budgeting projections made by their corporate colleagues.

J. B. Heaton (1998) has developed a theory of corporate financial decision making, based on optimism. His work builds on the studies of psychologist Neil Weinstein (1980), who finds that excessive optimism is especially pronounced when individuals believe they exert a measure of control (again the illusion of control) and their commitment levels are high. Heaton notes that optimism appears to be most severe among individuals of high intelligence and those who are dealing with career events.[14]

Summary

Corporate executives are vulnerable to both heuristic-driven bias and frame dependence. In particular hubris, a form of overconfidence, predisposes executives engaged in takeovers to overpay for targets. The act of overpaying is called winner's curse.

This is not to say that overpayment is inevitable. In fact, as a general matter, the evidence on the hubris hypothesis is mixed. Nevertheless, corporate executives contemplating a takeover need to be mindful of winner's curse. Most important, they need to think about which other firms have been successful in similar situations, and they must be prepared to justify why they are at least as capable of performing the same feat as these other firms. Executives might also benefit from being more attentive to the red flags that get raised when they announce their intention to acquire the target.[15] It is not that successful takeovers are impossible. But they are more difficult and less frequent than overconfident, optimistic executives tend to believe.

Chapter 17

IPOs: Initial Underpricing, Long-term Underperformance, and "Hot-Issue" Markets

Many investors have experienced an IPO-adrenaline rush on the first trading day as they search for the "next Microsoft." In the case of Internet stocks, the editor of one IPO newsletter has described investor activity as "insanity.com trading."[1]

There are three behavioral phenomena associated with initial public offerings (IPOs). These have been termed (1) *initial underpricing*, (2) *long-term underperformance*, and (3) *"hot-issue" market*. Before explaining what each of these terms means, let me note that there are three main parties to IPOs: the issuing firm, the underwriter, and investors. Although the role of all parties in the three phenomena is discussed, the emphasis is on the role of investors.

Initial underpricing occurs when the offer price is too low. That is, the issue will be underpriced and its price will soar on the first trading day. But price may overshoot fundamental value, in which case, it will fall back over time, giving rise to *long-term underperformance*. IPO activity also appears to move in hot and cold cycles. A *hot-issue market* is a period where investor demand for IPOs is especially high.

Are the three IPO phenomena consistent with market efficiency? I argue not. In a hot-issue market, excessive optimism on the part of investors leads IPO prices to rise above fundamental value on the first trading day and remain so for long periods. This optimism is a manifestation of heuristic-driven bias. Investors may also be affected by other heuristics, including instances of similarity, betting on trends, and representativeness. Also, in a hot-issue market, the possibility of regret looms large in the minds of investors.[2]

This chapter discusses the following:

- two cases, one dealing with Boston Chicken and the other with Netscape Communications. Both cases feature the three IPO phenomena, as well as several behavioral elements
- the general evidence about IPOs
- some theories that explain the three IPO phenomena

Case Study 1: Boston Chicken

Boston Markets is a franchise owned by Boston Chicken, Inc.; Boston Market rotisserie chicken has been a popular dinner choice across the country. Several years ago, Boston Chicken was a favorite among diners and investors alike, appearing attractively priced to both. At most outlets, a quarter chicken, two side items, and corn bread started at $3.99. In a 1996 episode of the NBC sitcom *The Single Guy*, the main character's father describes his few regrets in life: not spending more time with his son and not investing in Boston Chicken stock.

The case of Boston Chicken vividly illustrates initial underpricing and long-term underperformance. The firm went public on November 8, 1993, with a 1.6 million share offering at $20. On its first trading day, Boston Chicken shares soared 142.5 percent, opening at $45.25 and closing at $48.50 per share. This was the best first-day performance for an IPO in the preceding two years.

How did the stock fare over the next five years? Figure 17-1 shows the dramatic rise and fall of the stock, after adjusting the price for a subsequent 2-for-1 split. After a dramatic climb in 1995 and 1996, the stock price closed at $8.47 a share on November 10, 1997. In fact, in 1997 Boston Chicken was among the 10 worst-performing stocks on NASDAQ, declining by 82 percent. Then, on October 5, 1998, Boston Chicken filed for bankruptcy protection and closed 178 restaurants across the country. The price of its stock fell to 46.75 cents.

Consider the elements underlying the movements in Boston Chicken stock, both on the first trading day and subsequently. What made investors so enthusiastic about Boston Chicken shares on that first trading day? Were they subject to heuristic-driven bias? For example, were they betting on trends? To answer this question, consider the following financial highlights, described in Boston Chicken's prospectus and shown in table 17-1.

Figure 17-1 Stock Price of Boston Chicken,
            November 8, 1993–January 25, 1999

The roller-coaster ride of Boston Chicken's stock price, from its offer price on the first day of the IPO through January 1999, including declaring bankruptcy in October 1998.

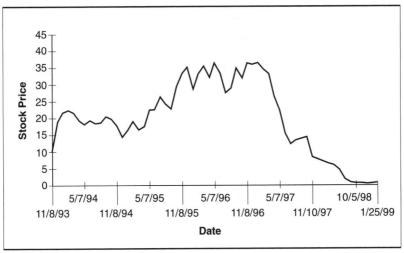

Table 17-1

Source: Boston Chicken Inc. prospectus

	1993 to Date[a]	1992	1991
Revenue	$28.20	$8.30	$5.20
Net income (loss)	$0.30	($5.90)	($2.60)
Stores:			
Company-operated	25	19	5
Franchise	142	64	29
TOTAL:	167	83	34

[a]40 weeks to October 3

Given the figures in table 17-1, trend extrapolation would seem more than a stretch. So, if investors were not basing their optimistic projections on the previous financials, what were they looking at?

The underwriter in the Boston Chicken offering was Merrill Lynch. That year, Merrill Lynch had underwritten two other offerings that had large first-day jumps: indoor-playground operator Discovery Zone, which jumped 61 percent, and golf-club maker Callaway Golf, which jumped 62 percent.

Was there a connection between the Discovery Zone offering and Boston Chicken? Might investors have been basing their projections on the performance of stocks they viewed to be similar? At the time, Robert Natale was emerging-growth analyst for Standard & Poor's. He appears to have thought so. In a pre-IPO report, Natale noted that the Boston Chicken offering would be hot because of small investors who had profited—or wished they had—from buying stock in Discovery Zone.[3]

Notice that the possibility of regret looms large here. Put yourself in the position of an investor who cognitively associates the stock of Boston Chicken with the stock of Discovery Zone. Keep in mind that the price of Discovery Zone shares soared 61 percent the day it went public. How badly would you feel if, having missed out on Discovery Zone, you missed buying Boston Chicken shares, the stock price soared on the first day, and you lost out? How much *regret* would you feel for having failed to act? In hindsight, how obvious would it look to you that you made the wrong decision? If you are prone to regret, then you might have bought Boston Chicken stock on that first day, motivated in part by a desire to avoid blaming *yourself* if history repeated *itself*.

In his pre-IPO report, Robert Natale mentions two additional pertinent points. First, the number of Boston Chicken shares being offered was low—less than two million, about 10 percent of the company. This may have contributed to the first-day price advance, with demand for shares being much higher than supply at the offer price. Second, Boston Chicken's chairman, Scott A. Beck, was a former executive at Blockbuster Entertainment, the video-rental chain, as were other members of management. Given the success of Blockbuster Entertainment around this time, investors may have bet on the Blockbuster Entertainment trend.

Who was buying Boston Chicken stock on that first day? And what were purchasers thinking? An article that appeared on *Dow Jones News Service* on November 24, 1993, offers some insight:[4] "Traders said institutional buyers drove Boston Chicken's stock early in the day, and most retail brokers were shut out. But desire to buy the hot new offering apparently fired interest in two competing companies, Clucker's Wood Roasted Chicken Inc. (CLUK) and Pollo Tropical Inc. (POYO)."

Many institutional investors flipped their shares later in the day. But not all. The article quotes Douglas S. Foreman, portfolio manager of Putnam Investment Management's Specialty Growth Equities Group in Boston, who held on to some of his allocation. He said: "They've got a terrific product. Basically, what they're doing is selling home-cooked meals at fast-food prices."

Underpricing of the initial offer means that Boston Chicken's initial shareholders did not benefit directly from the price surge on the initial day. They did not receive even as much as the offer price, given the seven percent or so spread that Merrill Lynch received and the usual expenses associated with going public. In hindsight, underpricing cost Boston Chicken shareholders 50 percent of what they might have received. Why? Because they had to sell a larger fraction of the company than they would have at a higher price to raise the $35.3 million that they did. In other words, the preissue shareholders suffered from a dilution of their ownership in the company.

Case Study 2: Netscape Communications (and Other Internet Stocks)

Some of the most spectacular IPOs have been associated with Internet stocks. This case provides an opportunity to discuss the three IPO phenomena in connection with Internet stocks.

On August 7, 1995, an article with the headline "Market Sees Netscape Most Savory IPO Since Boston Chicken" appeared in the *Wall Street Journal*.[5] Netscape, of course, refers to Netscape Communications Corp. After Netscape and its investment bankers, Morgan Stanley and Hambrecht & Quist, had issued a preliminary prospectus containing an initial offer range and conducted a marketing campaign—in the process acquiring information about investors' willingness to purchase the issue (bookbuilding)—they were on the verge of setting a final offering price. The next steps would be to issue the final prospectus and wait for SEC clearance before the IPO could become "effective."

The marketing campaign had generated tremendous interest in the offering. Institutional investors had to be turned away at the New York roadshow luncheon when the room reached capacity at nearly 500. Morgan Stanley, the lead underwriter for the offering, was forced to set up a toll-free number to take requests for information on the deal, while comanager Hambrecht & Quist received more than 1,000 calls a day. In 1995, Robert Strawbridge worked as a summer intern at Hambrecht & Quist. He was put in charge of emptying the San Francisco firm's voice mailbox. He found his time fully dedicated to listening to investors' pleas from around the world "People were desperate," Mr.

Strawbridge recalled. "The calls would come in from people saying, 'I've never opened an account before, but this one I have to own. Can someone please, please, call me back?'"

Of course, Morgan Stanley and Hambrecht & Quist were allocating shares to their institutional clients, as well as to some lucky individual investors. And retail brokers were hearing the same kind of pleas. The August 7 *Wall Street Journal* article mentioned earlier describes a retail broker's perspective:

> "Netscape is going to be a monster—probably one of the best new issues of the year," said Steven Samblis, an analyst at Empire Financial Group in Longwood, Fla. "I've got people calling me and saying, 'Is there any way I can get this?' It's almost impossible for a normal guy to receive an allocation of the new issue, but when the market opens, attack it."
>
> Samblis said he expected Netscape's IPO to be priced at about $14 a share with the first trade at about 25. He estimated the stock will go to about 27 the first day and reach the high 30s within 10 days.[6]

Samblis appears to have been predicting underpricing of the initial offer. Was he right about the amount of the offer price, the fact that it would be too low, and the levels to which the stock would move? Partly. At the time, Netscape did indeed plan to offer 3.5 million shares, including 500,000 to international investors, at $12 to $14. However, two days later, on August 9, underwriters doubled the offer price to $28 per share and increased the size of the offering to 5 million. This change did not exactly prevent initial underpricing: The stock opened at $71, quickly jumped to $72.50—far from Samblis' prediction of $25—and closed at $58.25—a far cry from $27.

How about predictions concerning long-term underperformance? Consider remarks made by Robert Natale about both the Boston Chicken offering and the Netscape offering. In the November 10, 1993, "Heard on the Street" column, the day after Boston Chicken went public, Natale was quoted as saying: "You're certainly subscribing to the greater-fool theory if you're looking for a big upside from here in the next six to nine months."[7]

As figure 17-1 shows, Natale turned out to be right on that one. Two years later, the day after Netscape went public, *Dow Jones News Service* quoted Natale on the prospects for Netscape's stock: "However, Natale warned that Netscape's stock 'could tread water for a year or two' while the company puts its business plan in place, but he believes the stock will move higher."[8] Figure 17-2 depicts the time path of

Figure 17-2 Stock Price of Netscape Communications,
August 9, 1995–January 29, 1999

The roller-coaster ride of Netscape Communications's stock price, from its offer
price on the first day of the IPO through January 1999 after being acquired by
America Online.

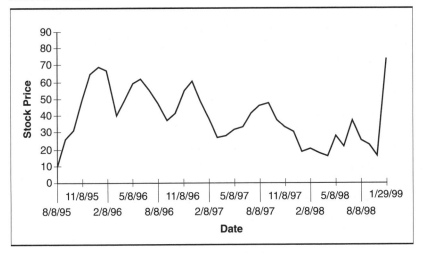

Netscape share prices from August 9, 1995, through January 29, 1999,
adjusted for a subsequent 2-for-1 stock split. Was Natale right? Not on
this one.

Netscape hardly trod water during the first year it went public.
And over the long term it definitely underperformed. On January 6,
1998, the *San Francisco Chronicle* reported that "stock in Netscape Communications fell 20 percent yesterday after the company, staggered by
competition from Microsoft, said it lost money in the fourth quarter
and will lay off an undetermined number of workers. . . . News of the
loss and restructuring knocked the wind out of Netscape's stock, which
fell $4.81 to close at $18.56—the lowest since it went public in August
1995."[9]

Interestingly, the risk posed by Microsoft had been clearly foreseen
in 1995, prior to the offering.[10] In any case, the story of Netscape Communications Corp. ended on November 24, 1998, when it was bought
by America Online (AOL) for about $4.2 billion.

The last four months of 1998 and beginning of 1999 constituted a
very interesting period for IPOs. In early November dozens of companies were postponing or canceling IPOs.[11] Then the IPO market turned
hot overnight. On November 12, Web page provider theglobe.com set a
new record for the biggest first-day gain in IPO history. Starting from
an offer price of $9, the stock price soared as high as $97 before closing

at $63.50, a 606 percent gain for the day. But the best performing IPO for 1998 was eBay, an online auction service. eBay went public on September 23, 1998, at an offer price of $18, and closed 1998 at $241.25, a 1,240.3 percent increase.[12]

Was the end of 1998 the beginning of another hot-issue market for IPOs? Certainly several firms went public during these months and experienced rapid price gains; and they were not all Internet firms. So, is there a general hot-issue market phenomenon? Are there times when investors are unduly optimistic about the prospects for IPOs?

The period that began in November 1998 provides a clearer case of a hot-issue market. On Friday, January 15, 1998, financial news provider MarketWatch.com went public. From an offer price of $17 a share, the stock rose to $130, closing the day at $97.50, a first-day gain of 474 percent. This was the second highest first-day gain for an IPO, behind theglobe.com. MarketWatch.com joined the company of five other recent Internet start-ups whose value tripled or more on the first trading day. Is it safe to call these hot issues?

As for the timing of the Netscape IPO, practitioners held different opinions. On one side, we have Robert Natale, who in August 1995 opined that the timing of the Netscape offering was chosen to exploit a hot-issue market. He stated, "Normally, this company would go public in about a year and half when it's further along in executing its business strategy and earning a profit. But the market is so strong now and the valuation is so high that they're not waiting."[14] Hugh A. Johnson, chief market strategist at First Albany Corp., shared a similar view. He described instances in which the price of stocks doubled virtually overnight as "one of the many warnings signs that we've entered a period of significant speculation."[15]

In contrast, David Menlow, president of the IPO Financial Network in Springfield, New Jersey, expressed the view that Netscape's first-day performance provided no grand insights into the IPO market. "It doesn't say anything about the IPO market at all. It's a singular situation and shouldn't be confused for any frothiness in the market or excessive tendencies of investors." Others concurred. David Shulman, market strategist at Salomon Brothers Inc., commented that "This does not happen with a market where everything is going up."

Before turning to the general discussion, the last word goes to Robert Natale,[16] already quoted in connection with Boston Chicken and Netscape. Here is his comment on MarketWatch.com:[17] "The underwriters priced the deal based on what they thought was fair from a historical perspective. Clearly investors are using a different model."

General Evidence

Let's turn from the specific to the general. What about the academic evidence concerning general underpricing, long-term underperformance, and hot-issue markets? And what are possible explanations, behavioral and otherwise?

I begin with initial underpricing. Figure 17-3 below is taken from Jay Ritter (1998). It shows the distribution of first-day returns to IPOs. Clearly, there is a general underpricing phenomenon. Boston Chicken and Netscape may be extreme cases, but they do illustrate the broad phenomenon.

Why is there an underpricing phenomenon? That is, why as a general matter do underwriters set the offer price too low? And why do the shareholders of the firms going public agree to the offer price, given the likelihood that they will lose out? Ritter (1998) offers several possibilities, of which some are behavioral in nature. I begin with one that is not.

One possible explanation is the *winner's curse hypothesis.* We encountered the issue of winner's curse earlier, in our discussion of corporate takeovers (see chapter 16). With IPOs, the question is not

Figure 17-3 Initial Returns (Percentage Return from Offering Price to First Day Close)

Histogram of initial returns (percentage return from offering price to first day close) for 2,866 IPOs in 1990–96. Units, ADRs, REITs, closed-end funds, and small IPOs are excluded. The average initial return is 14.0%. *Source:* Ritter (1998).

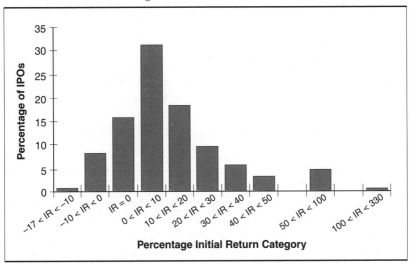

whether investors ignore winner's curse, but rather whether their recognition of it explains initial underpricing.

Suppose that you are an investor with an investment banking firm that is taking a company public. Suppose the investment bank is the fictitious First Public, the firm is a fictitious company called Softtech, and the date is August 1, 1996, a week before the IPO.

As an investor, you are expecting to receive some allocation of shares at the offer price. Today, August 1, you know neither what your allocation will be, nor what the offer price will be. Suppose that you are not in possession of any nonpublic information about Softtech. However, one week later, you learn the following. The offer price is below the low end of the range described in the initial prospectus, the number of shares to be issued is unchanged from the initial prospectus, and you will receive all of the shares you requested.

Would you view this as good news? Normally, the fact that the price has been lowered should be good news to a potential buyer. But why has the price been lowered? Would you be concerned that the reason you will receive all the shares you requested is that other investors with material information have pulled out? They have pulled out because they know that Softtech is no Netscape. According to the winner's curse hypothesis, as a smart investor with no material inside information, the only way you would be willing to take a chance on being stuck with a lemon IPO is if First Public underpriced their offerings as a general matter.

A second explanation is the *bandwagon,* or *fad, effect.* If investors see that a lot of other investors are interested in an issue, then they may scramble to get on board. Hence, the investment banker may underprice issues in order to induce a bandwagon to form. There are two aspects to the bandwagon effect. First, there is belief that the crowd must know something. Second, misery loves company. Because of the potential for regret, there is safety in numbers. In case of a negative outcome, the pain of regret is mitigated by the fact that many others behaved similarly.

A third explanation is the *market feedback hypothesis.* Here the investment banker makes an implicit deal with investors during the bookbuilding process. If, during bookbuilding, regular investors truthfully disclose their valuations of the IPO, then the investment banker will reward them by underpricing the offer: the more favorable the valuation, the greater the underpricing.

Think about Netscape. The offer price doubled from $14 to $28 just before Netscape went public, and yet the stock opened at $71 and closed at $58 on its first day. Ritter (1998) reports that the underpricing is greatest when the offer price adjustment, relative to the range mentioned in the initial prospectus, is greatest. Still, Netscape's investors would have been better off by $174 million[18] (before bankers' fees) had the offer price been $58.25. Why were they so accepting?

Ritter suggests that investors' accepting attitude stems from their prior expectations. A few weeks before the offering, Netscape shareholders were anticipating that the offer would raise about $50 million.[19] Then, just prior to the offer, the offer price was doubled and the number of shares issued increased. So, instead of raising $50 million, they ended up raising $161 million (less fees).

There is an issue of frame dependence lurking here. Suppose that the total size of the value to be captured by Netscape shareholders on August 9, 1995, was $335 million. Shareholders had set themselves a reference point of $50 million. Hence, the $335 million was segregated into three pieces: the *reference amount* of $50 million, the additional *in-the-pocket gain* of $111 million, and the *opportunity loss* of $174 million. As noted elsewhere, it is a standard behavioral finding that psychologically, in-the-pocket amounts loom much larger than opportunity amounts (Thaler 1991). Therefore, investors react much more strongly to the reference amount and in-the-pocket "gravy" than the opportunity loss. Consequently, they evaluate the resulting combination quite favorably.

All of these explanations beg the question of why hot IPOs trade to what Hambrecht & Quist describes as "irrational prices in the aftermarket."[20] It suggests the following distribution for what investors are willing to pay for a hot issue. During the roadshow, H&Q finds that 200 to 300 accounts are willing to pay an amount that is within the range specified in the initial prospectus. If the issue looks attractive, so that the upper end of the range increases, then at the order stage there will be 100 to 200 accounts placing orders. When the offer price is set, at yet a higher amount, there will be 50 to 100 accounts receiving an allocation. In the aftermarket, H&Q suggests that between 10 and 20 accounts will be willing to pay a "reasonable premium." However, when an issue is "hot," it indicates that there will be a few large holders, between 1 and 5 accounts, willing to pay almost "any price." In the view of Hambrecht & Quist, it is this last group that causes the IPO to trade to an irrational price.

Apparently, the SEC has also had an interest in initial underpricing. In 1999, it was investigating several securities firms for "spinning"—distributing underpriced IPO shares to favored clients in hopes of winning future business. One of those firms was Hambrecht & Quist. Interestingly, William Hambrecht, founder and former chief executive of Hambrecht & Quist, claims that the practice of "spinning" motivated him to start a firm that would change things. W. R. Hambrecht + Co. uses the Internet to enable individual investors to participate in IPOs before stock trades on a public exchange.[21] Time will tell if initial underpricing disappears.

What about long-run underperformance? Before asking what causes underperformance, we should ask whether underperformance is a general phenomenon. This is a complicated issue. Looking at anecdotal evidence, such as the Boston Chicken and Netscape IPOs, can be very misleading. The way to establish whether or not there is a special underperformance effect for IPOs is to compare the long-term performance of IPOs with similar firms that have not issued new shares in the time frame under investigation. Figure 17-4, from Tim Loughran and Jay Ritter (1995), suggests that IPOs underperform their comparison group of nonissuers by 7 percent per year in the five years after issuing, where the comparison group is determined by market capitalization (size).

A study by Alon Brav and Paul Gompers (1997) suggests that the underperformance effect is considerably more complicated. They find that underperformance only seems to occur in small firms that are not backed by venture capitalists. They also employ a different matching procedure, where IPO firms are matched not just by market capitalization but also by market-to-book. In chapter 7, I discussed the fact that historically, small stocks with low market-to-book ratios have earned positive abnormal returns. Brav and Gompers argue that the underperformance does not stem from the issue's being an IPO. Rather the low returns stem from the fact that IPOs tend to be high market-to-book stocks. This is because the original backers and investment bankers prefer to take firms public after some demonstration of success, which usually means a high market-to-book ratio.

Either way, the behavioral implications are much the same. As I argued in chapter 7, high market-to-book stocks tend to earn inferior returns because investors *overreact* to the positive events that led to the run-up in stock price. They overweight the recent good news and wind up being disappointed, on average, over the long run.

Robert Shiller (1989) has suggested that the market for IPOs is subject to *fads*, and that investment bankers behave like impresarios who organize rock concerts. To make the concert an "event," the impresario

Figure 17-4 Average Annual Returns for the Five Years after the
                Offering Date

Average annual returns for the five years after the offering date for 5,821 IPOs in
the United States from 1970–1993, and for nonissuing firms that are bought and
sold on the same dates as the IPOs. Nonissuing firms are matched on market
capitalization, have been listed on the CRSP tapes for at least five years, and have
not issued equity in a general cash offer during the prior five years. The returns
(dividends plus capital gains) exclude the first-day returns. Returns for IPOs from
1992–1993 are measured through Dec. 31, 1996. *Source:* Loughran and Ritter (1995),
as updated.

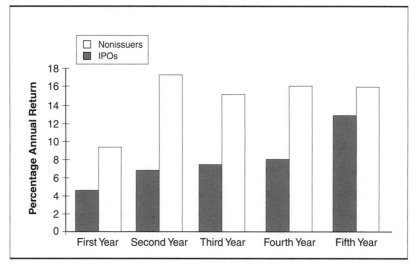

underprices admission charges. On one hand, the strategy does work
to create an event, and for IPOs, it induces investors to overvalue the
offering initially. However, over time, the market will correct its originally optimistic opinion. Therefore, long-run underperformance will
be strongest among stocks with the best initial performance.

Similar reasoning applies to hot-issue markets and *windows of opportunity.* The owners of firms going public clearly hope to obtain the
best price for their shares that they can. Therefore, it will be to their
benefit to time the issue for when sentiment is positive, meaning investors are especially optimistic. The evidence for hot markets is actually strong. Historically, the IPO market has moved in cycles, both for
average initial returns and for the volume of IPOs. Figure 17-5 below
depicts the return cycle, and figure 17-6 depicts the number of deals
cycle.

Figure 17-5

Average initial returns (i.e., on first day) by month for SEC-registered IPOs in the United States during 1977–1998.
Source: Ibbotson, Sindelar, and Ritter (1994), as updated.

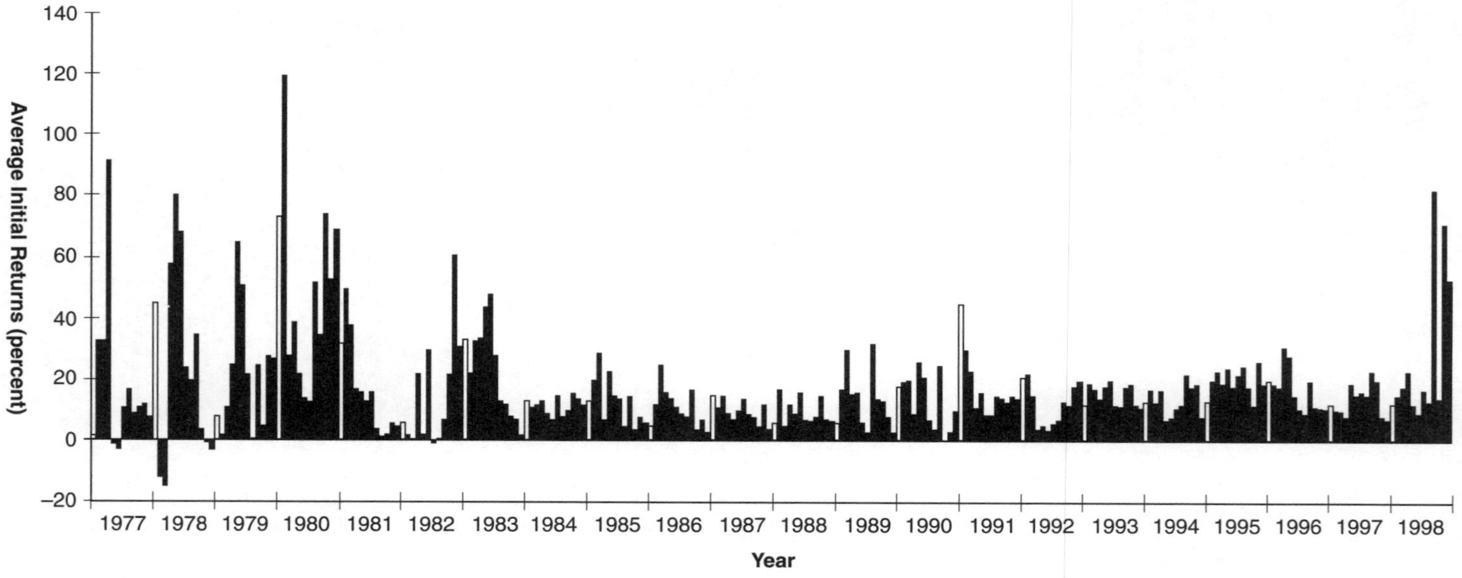

Figure 17-6

The number of IPOs by month in the United States during 1977–1998, excluding closed-end fund IPOs.
Source: Ibbotson, Sindelar, and Ritter (1994), as updated.

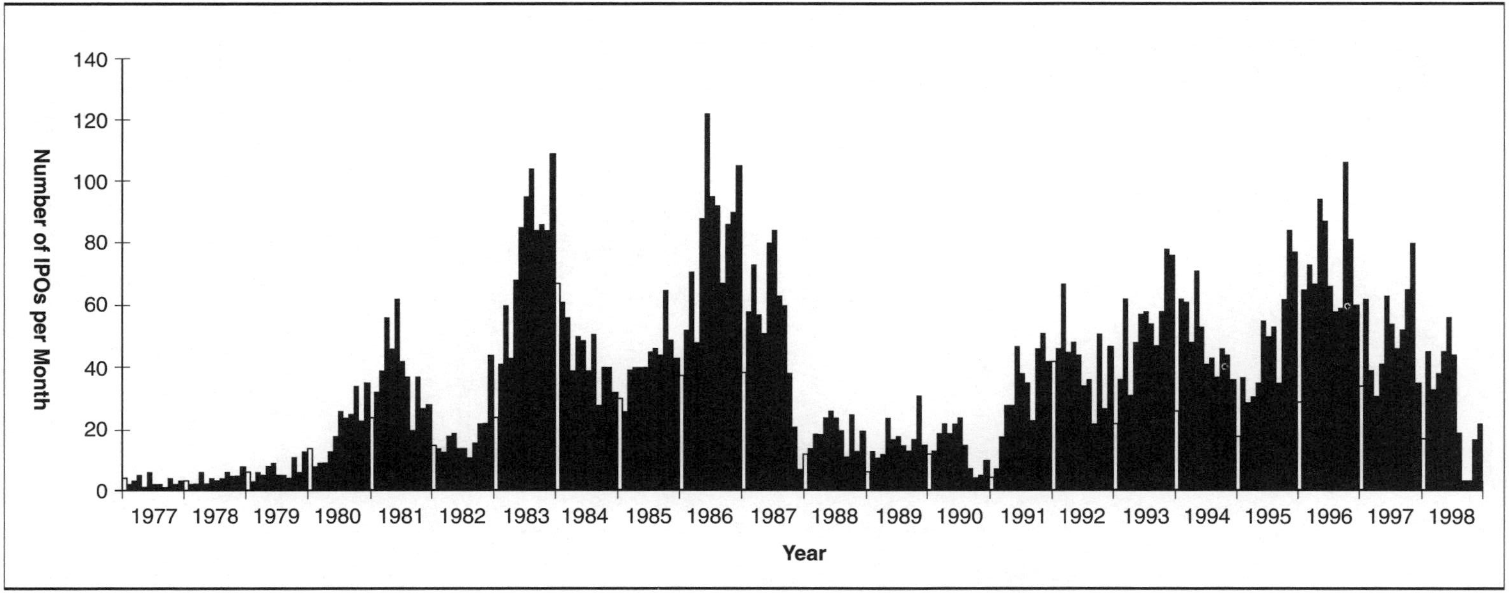

The hot-issue market appears to have become part of the financial landscape. For example, in late January 1998, a *Wall Street Journal* headline read: "Tough Road Is Predicted for IPOs." A tough road means a lukewarm market. The article states: "By the end of last week, underwriters had brought a paltry five new companies to the market. . . . The least appealing deals to investors right now are small deals without lengthy histories."[22] In a similar vein, at the end of 1997 Hambrecht & Quist predicted that the 1998 IPO market would feature fewer but larger deals.

What about seasoned equity offerings, an issue that comes up again in the next chapter? Their story is similar to that of IPOs. Loughran and Ritter (1995) describe the situation for the average case. In the year leading up to the offering, the stock of the average issuing firm has risen dramatically, 72 percent. The profit margin stands at 5.2 percent. Moreover sales have been growing and the firm's managers have been investing heavily in acquiring assets. As we might expect, after the new issue, the managers continue to invest.

Unfortunately, the successful performance that led up to the offering does not continue. Four years later, profit margins have declined from their peak (at issue) to 2.5 percent. Recall that the average IPO underperforms by 7 percent in the five years after issue. For a seasoned equity offering the number is about the same—8 percent.[23]

Why? Are the same factors at work? Consider the situation from the perspective of the firm's management. When will they want to bring out a new issue? When they think that their firm's stock price is undervalued? Hardly—they are more likely to issue when they think they face a window of opportunity and the stock is overvalued. Indeed, if the stock actually is overvalued, then it should come as no surprise that its subsequent returns will be abnormally low.

What about investors? Do they recognize that newly issued shares tend to be overvalued? Or do they instead suffer from excessive optimism? Well, firms that issue new shares tend to have high market-to-book ratios. And as we discussed previously, investors bet on trends. For the most part, they expect continuation, and they overweight the recent past when making long-term projections. As a general matter, high market-to-book stocks and the stocks of firms that have been growing rapidly underperform in the long term. Seasoned equity offerings are part of this group. Interestingly, seasoned equity offerings actually do worse than comparable growth firms do. It is unclear why this occurs. However, a possible explanation centers on the marketing effort by the investment bank bringing out the issue.

Are investors and managers unduly optimistic about the future prospects of the issuing firm? Loughran and Ritter suggest so. As I mentioned in chapter 10, psychological studies document that people are predisposed to be excessively optimistic. When psychologist Neil Weinstein (1980) first studied optimism, he asked people to indicate how likely they were to live past 80, relative to other people of the same age and gender. He also asked them how likely they were to be fired from a job, again, relative to their age and gender. What he found was that most people think that they are more likely to live beyond 80, and less likely to be fired from a job. The subjects in his study were under-graduate students. I have replicated Weinstein's study with MBA students ranging in age from 24 to 45, and find the same pattern he did, though not as strong. It seems that people are predisposed to be opti-mistic, at least until experience leads them to think differently.

Summary

This chapter presented three IPO phenomena: initial underpricing, long-term underperformance, and hot-issue markets. All three are in-dicative of inefficient markets, largely stemming from heuristic-driven bias. Which behavioral elements are involved? Loughran and Ritter suggest that both investors and managers are unduly optimistic about the future prospects of the issuing firm. It may be that similarity, regret, betting on trends, and frame dependence also play key roles in ex-plaining the three phenomena.

Chapter 18

Optimism in Analysts' Earnings Predictions and Stock Recommendations

*I*nvestors are slow to learn that security analysts do not always mean what they say.

Corporate executives, security analysts, and investors play two games, a recommendation game and an earnings prediction game. In both games, analysts follow a company, solicit information from its executives, predict its earnings, and/or issue buy or sell recommendations on its stock. Investors pay attention to the pronouncements of executives and analysts, so these pronouncements affect stock prices. But do the actions of investors lead prices to correctly reflect fundamental values?

Edward Keon Jr. edited the *I/B/E/S Innovator,* a newsletter published by I/B/E/S International, Inc. I/B/E/S collects and disseminates the earnings forecasts and stock recommendations of financial analysts.[1] On August 1, 1997, Keon appeared as a guest on the public television program *Wall $treet Week with Louis Rukeyser.* During that appearance, he made a number of important points about the biases and errors in analysts' recommendations and earnings predictions.

But analysts are not alone in being prone to bias and error. In fact, all three players—executives, analysts, and investors—in the two games exhibit heuristic-driven bias. Moreover, some players appear to exhibit frame dependence as well, with reference-point effects in the earnings game. So, what is the effect of heuristic-driven bias and frame dependence? As usual, market inefficiency.

The two games also have a "wink, wink, nod, nod" character. What investors hear is not always what analysts mean. This is partly because analysts do not always mean what they say. They frequently say "hold" but mean "sell," or say "buy" when they *mean* "hold." But investors often miss the "wink" and misinterpret the "nod."

This chapter discusses the following:

- some short cases that illustrate that the optimism displayed in some analysts' recommendations need to be taken with what Keon calls a "grain of salt"

- general evidence about the recommendations of lead analysts, and the fact that investors underreact to these recommendations

- excessive optimism in the earnings game

- the role of reference points in earnings announcements

The Recommendation Game: Case Studies about Grains of Salt

In order to understand the recommendation game, we need to identify the clients who make use of analysts' services. Retail stockbrokers certainly rely on recommendations to induce trading by individual investors. But the buy-side institutions are also a very important recipient. Not only do they pay attention to analysts' pronouncements, they reward the analysts they value by placing their trades with those analysts' firms. Because of the commissions involved, analysts' activities lie at the center of the action.

But analysts' firms also engage in investment banking. That led Edward Keon, in his *Wall $treet Week with Louis Rukeyser* appearance, to state: "[W]hen there's an investment banking relationship, the analysts are almost always more optimistic than their fellow analysts. So those forecasts of investment bankers who underwrite a company's stock should be taken with a grain of salt."

Here's an example that succinctly describes why such forecasts should be viewed warily. The October 27, 1997, issue of *Fortune* contains the following discussion about underwriters and analyst recommendations:

> Consider the case of Atmel, a small semiconductor company that went public in 1991. Although Alex. Brown was the lead underwriter, bankers from other firms soon began paying regular visits to Atmel's CFO, Chris Chellam, hoping to land the company's next deal. "We were looking for more coverage from Wall Street, and we told that to

all the bankers we talked to," says Chellam. "If they weren't willing to pick up coverage, they were never going to get our banking business." (Nocera 1997)

Did Chellam mean unqualified coverage in exchange for Atmel's banking business, or did he mean buy recommendations? In 1994, Atmel did an equity offering. Prudential was one of the underwriters. Earlier one of its analysts had initiated coverage of the company with a "buy" recommendation. The analyst acknowledged: "We got the banking business because of the research." CFO Chellum put it more succinctly when he said: "We liked his reports."

Keon's warning becomes more valid. Let's return to the year 1991 and underwriter Alex. Brown. On November 1 of that year, Alex. Brown took public a development-stage pharmaceutical company named Alteon.[2] Alteon's prospectus stated that it was "engaged in the discovery and development of novel therapeutic and diagnostic products for the complications of diabetes and aging. . . . Numerous studies have demonstrated that the company's lead compound, aminoguanidine, inhibits AGE formation, cross-linking and the progression of the major complications of diabetes in animals." Alteon's potential market at the time was known to be very large.

Here is how the *Wall Street Journal* reported the first day of trading in Alteon shares:

> If ever there was proof that biotechnology has taken Wall Street by storm, it came Friday with the eye-popping, 92% gain in first-day trading of Alteon Inc., a Northvale, N.J., developer of drugs to treat complications of diabetes and aging.
>
> Though it has just 30-odd employees and no sales in sight, Alteon saw its total market value balloon to more than $316 million by the end of the feverish trading day. The embryonic company's initial offering of three million shares, priced at $15, rose a riveting 13¾ to wind up at 28¾, leaving investors to wonder whether the feeding frenzy signaled madness or genius among biotechnology investors.[3]

How did Alteon's stock do after its rip-roaring first day? Over the ensuing seven weeks Alteon's share price fell to a low of $17.75 on November 25, and then recovered, closing at $24 on Friday, December 20. However, this was still $4.75 below its first-day closing price.

The first twenty-five calendar days after an IPO is a "quiet period." Release #5180 from the SEC precludes the firm and its investment bankers from issuing forecasts and opinions relating to revenues, income, or earnings per share during this period. At the conclusion of the twenty-five days, analysts who work for the underwriter are permitted to issue a stock recommendation.

Recall the statements made by Alex. Brown's client Atmel about what they expect in return for their banking business. Those expectations might involve "booster shots," the issuance of positive recommendations intended to boost the stock price of a new IPO, if the price has been retreating. Indeed, on Monday, December 23, after the quiet period, an Alex. Brown analyst issued a "buy" recommendation on Alteon. The stock immediately rose by $4, closing at $27.75 that day. Apparently investors did not view this recommendation as a booster shot.

Was Alex. Brown's "buy" recommendation intended as a booster shot, or did they actually know something that the market did not? After all, the underwriter would supposedly be especially well informed about Alteon. We cannot say with certainty whether the buy recommendation was information based or intended to boost the price. However, figure 18-1, which depicts the behavior of Alteon's stock price over its first two years, suggests that the recommendation

Figure 18-1 Share Price of Alteon,
            November 1, 1991–October 29, 1993

How the price of Alteon stock behaved during the two years following its IPO. Did the positive recommendation issued by its underwriter Alex. Brown on December 23, 1991, contain positive information about its long-term prospects? Or was it a "booster shot," designed to inflate the price of Alteon shares?

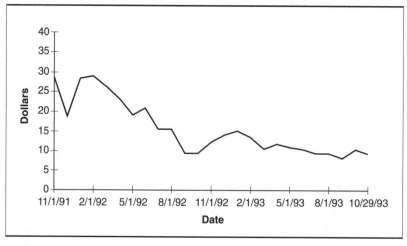

caused the positive price movement for several weeks, and then the "truth played out."

The downward trajectory in figure 18-1 occurred as biotechnology stocks generally fell out of favor in early 1992. But in addition, the Food and Drug Administration had requested more efficacy data on Alteon's main compound aminoguanidine, thereby delaying clinical trials for more than a year.[4]

Is the case of Alteon typical or unusual? An article by Roni Michaely and Kent Womack (1999) demonstrates that the situation with Alteon is in fact typical. Michaely and Womack study "buy" recommendations in the first year after IPOs for the period 1990–1991. They obtained their data from First Call Corporation. First Call collects daily commentary of security analysts, portfolio strategists, and economists at major U.S. and international brokerage firms. It then sells this information to professional investors through an online PC-based system, providing their subscribers with almost instantaneous access to information generated by brokerage firms.

Michaely and Womack's study is a comparison between underwriter "buy" recommendations and nonaffiliated "buy" recommendations for IPOs within their first year of trading. Here is a brief synopsis of what they found.

1. Analysts who work for underwriting firms follow stocks that their firms do not bring to market as well as those they do. Consider a single analyst and suppose we were to divide the stocks for which he issues "buy" recommendations into two groups: (1) companies brought to market by his firm, and (2) all others. Are analysts consistent in the way they follow stocks? Which group do you think does better over the long term? Michaely and Womack find that for twelve of the fourteen analysts in their sample, the second group, "all others," does better. For those suspecting that analysts recommend stocks of firms brought to market by their firms, more favorably, this has the makings of a "smoking gun."

2. In the first month after the quiet period, underwriter analysts issue 50 percent more "buy" recommendations than nonaffiliated analysts do; and they issue them sooner. Moreover, it seems that underwriters do attempt to prop up the share prices of poor performers. Is there a second smoking gun here? It appears so. Consider the thirty days preceding each buy recommendation on a new IPO stock. During this time, the prices of stocks recommended

by non-underwriter analysts have gone up (by 4.1 percent). But the stock prices of firms recommended by underwriter analysts actually have gone *down* on average (by 2.4 percent).

3. Investors' reaction to a buy recommendation actually depends on who issues the buy. The excess return associated with underwriters' "buy" recommendations is 2.8 percent, less than the 4.4 percent associated with nonaffiliated analysts. Yet two years after an IPO, the stocks for which nonaffiliated analysts issued a "buy" recommendation were over 50 percent higher than the stocks for which underwriter analysts issued a recommendation. Taken together, this means that although investors appear to recognize that the recommendations of underwriter analysts need to be taken with a grain of salt, they do not fully discount the effect. If the recommendations of underwriter analysts were superior, because they have access to private information, this should not happen. The underwriter buys should be better predictors of future returns.

4. The IPO stocks that did worst in the 1990–1991 period studied by Michaely and Womack were those that lacked a non-underwriter analyst to corroborate the underwriter analyst recommendation.

5. The cost of subscribing to First Call is substantial. So, it should not be surprising to learn that the market *does* react when an analyst changes his recommendation. Michaely and Womack report that the immediate average price increase to a buy recommendation is 3.6 percent. The immediate reaction to a sell recommendation is a 10.5 percent drop—and, the reaction to a "removed from buy" recommendation is an even stronger 12.7 percent drop. Now the interesting thing is that although investors respond to the change in recommendation, they actually underreact. In the twelve months following the recommendation change, newly recommended "buys" continue their upward march, whereas new "sells" and "removed from buys" continue their downward decline.[5] After twelve months, "removed from buys" are down 15 percent, whereas "sells" are down over 60 percent!

In a sense, we should expect overly optimistic recommendations from the analysts who work for underwriting firms. After all, how easy a time would an underwriter have selling a company's stock if its own analysts withheld their endorsement? But as Michaely and Womack demonstrate, the key behavioral issue is that investors fail to take full account of the bias. To be sure, it's not always easy to sort things out.

Not every "buy" recommendation turns out to be a dud. And investors know that these analysts might have access to superior information.[6]

The Earnings Game:
Optimism in Analysts' Expectations

Now let's consider the earnings game, the second type of game played by corporate executives and analysts. In his 1997 *Wall $treet Week with Louis Rukeyser* guest appearance, Edward Keon stated: "Analysts as a rule historically have tended to be too optimistic in their forecasts, although that's changed in the last five years. For the S&P 500 companies, the analysts have been very accurate, and for quarterly forecasts they've been too pessimistic." What is the historical evidence on *optimism?*

Robert Hansen and Atulya Sarin (1998) have conducted an illuminating study of seasoned equity offerings (SEOs). For the period 1980 through 1991, they examined the behavior of analysts' earnings forecasts concerning SEOs. Hansen and Sarin note that analysts' expectations generally tended to be excessively optimistic in this period, by about 2 percent. This corroborates Keon's characterization and earlier work by Patricia O'Brien.

However, Hansen and Sarin discovered that forecast errors are not uniform across companies. For high earnings-to-price (E/P) stocks, which are where positive earnings surprises tend to get registered, analysts underpredicted earnings by about 3.6 percent. However, for the lowest E/P group, or the high P/E stocks if you prefer, analysts overpredicted earnings by more than 17 percent.

Hansen and Sarin document that companies that issued new stock tended to experience rising earnings during the quarters leading up to the SEO. Figure 18-2, taken from their paper, describes what they found.[7] There are three series plotted in this figure. All are expressed as earnings, normalized by price (E/P ratios). Two are forecasts made of annual earnings for the next fiscal year. One is the median forecast by lead analysts, and a second is the median forecasts made by nonlead analysts. The bottom series is the actual earnings figure corresponding to the forecasts, time-shifted back to facilitate comparison with the forecasts. The fact that the forecast values lie above the actual earnings illustrates the extent of optimism in analysts' forecasts.

Notice that in figure 18-2, earnings (or E/P to be more exact) tended to peak at the time of the SEO. After the SEO, earnings tended to decline. But analysts' forecasts continued to rise, for at least the

Figure 18-2 Comparison of Earnings Forecasts and Actual Earnings around SEOs

The time paths of earnings forecasts for the next fiscal year made by lead under-writers bringing out seasoned equity offerings, and the forecasts of nonlead analysts, relative to actual earnings. Both forecasts are consistently optimistic, but those of the lead underwriter are especially so. Moreover, actual earnings tend to decline after the offering, despite analysts' forecasts that earnings will continue to rise.

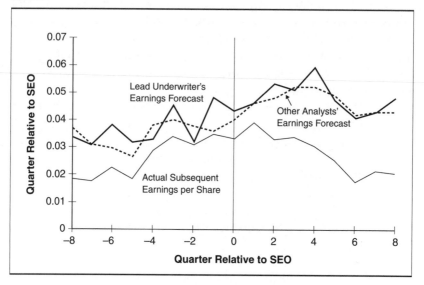

subsequent four quarters. Did analysts overreact to the earnings pattern leading up to the SEO and bet on trends? I suggest that they did.

Were the forecasts of analysts working for the lead underwriter any different than the forecasts of other analysts? Look again at figure 18-2. Notice that both analyst groups were overly optimistic on average, and both continued to project that earnings (E/P) would rise after the SEO.

Hansen and Sarin take pains to point out that forecast optimism is not confined to SEOs. They find that over 70 percent of SEOs are associated with both below-average[8] forecasts and below-average earnings per share. The extent of optimism for members of this group tends to be about 4 percent, regardless of whether or not the firm issued new shares through an SEO. Hence the bias is not special to SEOs but instead is more systemic.

The latter finding does not surprise Hansen and Sarin because analysts have reputations to protect. So a critical issue is the way that analysts get rewarded. And how are analysts rewarded? Interestingly, they are rewarded partly based on their ratings in a survey of buy-side institutions. The magazine *Institutional Investor* runs the survey. But as the October 27, 1997, issue of *Fortune* magazine points out, some analysts also receive a percentage of any investment banking business they help to bring in: Hence the potential for a conflict of interest.

Masako Darrough and Thomas Russell (1998) suggest that by and large, analysts follow a simple, two-stage heuristic when they develop long-range annual earnings forecasts. In the first stage, analysts forecast that the average company's earnings will grow at the overly optimistic rate of 17.2 percent a year. In the second stage, analysts gradually adjust their forecasts downward by 21 cents per month on average as the forecast date arrives.

Interestingly, analysts appear not to deviate systematically from this simple rule, even when new information begins to arrive about ten months or so from the end of FY2, the end of the fiscal year for which earnings are being forecast. So in general, analysts underreact to the arrival of new information, an issue that constitutes the theme of chapter 8.

Trying to Induce Pessimism in Analysts' Earnings Forecasts

During his appearance on *Wall $treet Week with Louis Rukeyser,* Edward Keon mentioned that in recent years, optimism has been disappearing from analysts' forecasts. In fact, he suggested that quarterly earnings forecasts for S&P 500 stocks have actually become pessimistic. Darrough and Russell (1998) do find that this may be the case for the period immediately prior to the announcement of actual earnings. However, outside of the few weeks leading up to the announcement, they remain skeptical that excessive optimism has disappeared from analysts' forecasts.

Pessimistic analyst forecasts are an intriguing part of the earnings game. Analysts are highly dependent on the executives of the companies that they follow for their information. This has led to an interesting situation. In a March 31, 1997 *Fortune* article titled "Learn to Play the Earnings Game (and Wall Street Will *Love* You)," journalist Justin Fox suggests that companies try to downplay analysts' forecasts so that their stock prices will jump when actual earnings exceed expectations.

As an extreme example, Fox presents the case of Microsoft. His article begins by pointing out that for 41 of the 42 quarters since Microsoft went public, its earnings beat analysts' estimates. He describes the reaction to a typical earnings announcement:

The 36 brokerage analysts who make the estimates were, as a group, quite happy about this—the 57 cents per share announced by the software giant was above their consensus of 51 cents, but not so far above as to make them look stupid. . . .

But then Fox continues by describing the following intriguing encounter:

After a typically grim presentation by CEO Bill Gates and sales chief Steve Ballmer at an analysts' meeting two years ago, Goldman Sachs analyst Rick Sherlund ran into the pair outside and said, "Congratulations. You guys scared the hell out of people." Their response? "They gave each other a high five," Sherlund recalls. But Microsoft, unlike some companies less attuned to the rules of this game, also lets analysts know when they're too pessimistic. (Fox 1997)

Here is another example, described by Joseph Nocera in the October 27, 1997 issue of *Fortune*. In January 1997, during the conference call reporting the results of its fourth quarter for 1996, the leading microprocessor firm Intel gave its usual "cautious guidance." But analysts downplayed the caution and raised their estimates for the first half of 1997. The consensus estimate for the second quarter of 1997 jumped from $0.97 per share to $1.05. The market expected that second quarter results would be announced in June. By May the consensus estimate for the second quarter had risen to $1.08. But then Intel preannounced, warning that its second-quarter results might be disappointing. In response, analysts revised their estimates to reflect this new guidance. In less than three weeks, the consensus estimate dropped from $1.08 to $0.90. Of course, so did the stock price, which on May 30 dropped from $82 to $75.75.

So, what did second-quarter earnings actually come in at? $0.92 a share, above the analysts' revised estimates. And how did the market respond? On July 16, the price of Intel stock jumped by $7.50, closing at $88.375. The headline in the *Wall Street Journal* the next day read "Intel's Profit Exceeds Expectations." Figure 18-3 depicts the behavior of Intel's stock price during this period. The two price jumps mentioned above should be quite evident.

Companies have learned that their stock prices go up when actual earnings exceed analysts' forecasts. To the extent that they provide "guidance," many firms now seek to lead analysts to be a little pessimistic, thereby enabling companies to produce positive surprises.

Figure 18-3 Share Price of Intel, January 1, 1997–July 31, 1997

Three events during Intel's earnings game with analysts: (1) In January 1997, analysts downplayed Intel's cautious guidance and the stock price rose in response to their earnings forecasts. (2) Then in May, Intel preannounced that its second-quarter results would be disappointing, and the stock price immediately plummeted. (3) Analysts revised their second quarter forecasts downward, and low enough so that actual earnings came in above the revised consensus forecast. Actual earnings were announced in July, and Intel's stock soared on the news that it had beaten analysts' consensus estimate.

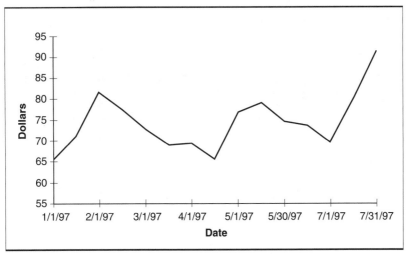

However, analysts' estimates need not reflect their expectations. The earnings game has led to the concept of "whisper earnings" that presumably reflect what analysts really expect. Therefore, stock prices can decline even when announced earnings exceed the consensus estimate. For example, in mid-July 1997, Microsoft's announced earnings barely beat analysts' estimates. Consequently, its stock price fell $8.938, or 6 percent, to close at $140.50. See the July price dip following the June 1997 earnings announcement as depicted in figure 18-4. The figure also depicts the market's reaction for the typical case in which Microsoft's announced earnings are more than a tad above the consensus estimate.

Fox, the author of the *Fortune* earnings game article, points out that because of the conservative way that Microsoft recognizes its shipments, it can engage in earnings manipulation. He quotes Marshall Senk, a Robertson Stephens analyst who follows Microsoft, as saying: "Microsoft does a better job of leveraging accounting—I would almost say it's a competitive weapon—than anybody else in the industry" (Fox 1997).[9]

Figure 18-4 Microsoft Corporation Quarterly Earnings Surprise
Microsoft is able to manage its earnings so that they consistently beat analysts'
forecasts. Investors have become accustomed to the pattern, and if the margin is
too small, as happened in June 1997, the stock price declines on the news. *Source:*
I/B/E/S International.

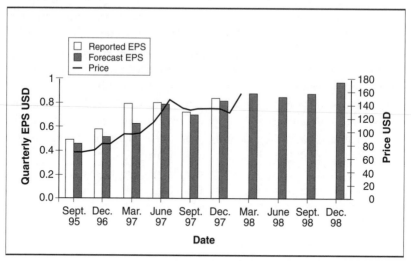

Recognition of Heuristic-Driven Bias?

Are analysts aware of heuristic-driven bias? In 1996, Intel's gross
margins rose approximately 10 percent, and its stock price tripled. But
on February 5, 1997, analyst Mark Edelstone of Morgan Stanley Dean
Witter downgraded Intel to neutral (hold). Why? He changed his recommendation because he was concerned that his fellow analysts had
overreacted to Intel's 1996 success. Edelstone thought that his fellow
analysts were underreacting to a series of potential problems that
might arise from a major product transition and competition from
archrival Advanced Micro Devices.[10] If you recall the discussion about
Intel in the previous section, events proved him correct.[11]

Thresholds in Earnings Manipulation

Francois Degeorge, Jayendu Patel, and Richard Zeckhauser (1997)
argue that the earnings game has led companies to employ threshold
decision making in respect to the way they manage earnings. These authors identify a hierarchy consisting of three specific thresholds:

1. "Red ink," meaning zero earnings;

2. The previous period's earnings; and

3. Analysts' consensus earnings forecasts.

Degeorge, Patel, and Zeckhauser present evidence that suggests managers manipulate earnings in an attempt to surpass all three thresholds if possible. However, suppose that managers anticipate that actual earnings will not surpass analysts' forecasts with respect to the coming announcement. Then, instead of missing earnings by a penny, better to bank those earnings until a later date, and miss by more than a penny. How much more? Well, if a firm can meet the previous period's earnings, then those earnings should be the target. Otherwise, don't miss by a penny, and move down toward zero.

In chapter 3, I discussed the tendency for people to evaluate outcomes relative to a benchmark. As Degeorge, Patel, and Zeckhauser point out, the use of benchmarks leads naturally to a consideration of earnings thresholds. It could be that managers' thought processes are threshold based; or that managers cater to the threshold thinking of investors, or both. Degeorge, Patel, and Zeckhauser also discuss nonpsychological reasons for a threshold structure of earnings management. These mostly have to do with the cost-saving features of discrete indicators.

Do managers actually behave in accordance with these three thresholds? The evidence is quite compelling. Degeorge, Patel, and Zeckhauser show that earnings announcements are not symmetric around thresholds. Rather, they are highly skewed. For example, the number of announcements where earnings are a little less than zero is tiny, whereas the number of announcements where earnings are a little above zero is quite large.

Summary

Corporate executives play two major games with analysts, an earnings game and a recommendation game. But investors are also party to these games. Heuristic-driven bias, and to some extent frame dependence, affect the behavior of the players in these games. The result is market inefficiency.

What type of bias and errors do analysts commit? During a guest appearance on *Wall $treet Week with Louis Rukeyser,* I/B/E/S's Edward

Keon made a series of comments that bear on both games. With respect to the earnings game, he characterized analysts' forecasts as "deeply flawed." He also cautioned that recommendations be taken with a grain of salt when the recommender also wears an investment-banking hat.

The evidence supports both of Keon's contentions. David Dreman (1995) claims that, on average, analysts' earnings recommendations are off by 10 percent. In addition, analysts' forecasts tend to be overly optimistic, except for the period just prior to earnings announcements, when they turn pessimistic. But corporate executives have also learned to play the earnings game. They do so by attempting to induce pessimistic forecasts that they can beat. If necessary, they preannounce; and they manipulate earnings using a threshold-based rule.

With respect to an investment-banking relationship in the recommendation game, the data support Keon's cautionary comments. Interestingly, although investors appear to recognize this feature, they underreact to it.

PART VI

OPTIONS, FUTURES, AND FOREIGN EXCHANGE

Chapter 19

Options: How They're Used, How They're Priced, and How They Reflect Sentiment

*A*nd now for something completely different: In developing the behavioral implications for options, I will not dwell on "hockey stick" charts, binomial trees, or the derivation of the Black-Scholes formula. At most I will remind readers about a few basics, and concentrate on behavioral issues concerning how options are used, priced, and reflect sentiment.

This chapter discusses the following:

- the role played by *frame dependence* in explaining the popularity of covered-call writing

- the role of reference points in determining how employees decide when to exercise company stock options

- how *heuristic-driven bias* moves so-called "implied volatility" away from actual volatility

- two related phenomena, "crashophobia," and the "crash premium," that stem from the effect of the 1987 stock market crash

- how investor sentiment affects and is reflected by option trading

Covered-Call Writing by Individual Investors

An investor who sells a call option on a stock in his portfolio is said to write a covered call. I have a colleague who has been trading options for about thirty years.[1] Most of his option-trading activity involves covered-call writing on stocks in his retirement accounts.[2] He does a good job describing how he uses options. Below I provide his comments using a question-and-answer format.

Q: When did you start trading options, and what strategy did you pursue?

A: Thirty years ago, I would consider a stock. My broker would tell me it looked good, that the analyst rated it as a strong buy. But I wasn't always as sanguine as the analyst. The broker suggested that maybe the options route would be better.

So, I would buy call options on the stock. But my results were mixed using this approach. I won some, lost some, and broke about even.

Q: It sounds like most of the call options that you bought expired worthless. What happened next?

A: So I'm saying, Who's on the other side? Someone is on the other side. Maybe that's the side I should be on.

But I didn't want to sell uncovered calls. So, I asked myself, How do you play it the other way? I found a broker who was doing covered call writing. Now I've been doing it a good twenty-five years.

Q: Can you describe what typically happens when you engage in covered-call writing?

A: Here is a classical success story for me. In February 1998, I bought Cooper Cameron stock at $55.19 a share, including commission. At the same time, I sold a May 60 call for $3.875. The option expired on May 16, when the stock was trading at 62. So I made $3.88 *plus* $4.75 on a $55 stock in three months, more than if I had just bought the stock.

Q: Do they all work out that way?

A: Here's one that didn't work out so well. Boston Chicken:[3] I bought the stock at $12 in October '97. The broker was really hot on it, and the report from Prudential was really good. The price was way down, but I kept hearing that the stock was going to come back. At the same time, I sold the November call at 1.5. Then in November, I sold the January call at 1⁵⁄₁₆. That was a good premium, so I felt I was covered down to 10. It's now at 3. I still have it.

Before continuing with the interview, I want to put some of my colleague's remarks into perspective. Meir Statman and I (Shefrin and Statman 1993a), report that covered-call writing is the most popular option-trading technique that individual investors use. Most investors eventually discover what my colleague realized early on: the majority of call options expire worthless.

A lot of the marketing literature on options that targets individual investors emphasizes covered-call writing. The *Personal Money Guide* published by the Research Institute of America (RIA) suggests that investors think of the premiums they receive from writing calls as "premium dividends." Apparently, brokers too have figured this out. Here is an approach suggested by Leroy Gross (1982) in his manual for stockbrokers.

> *Joe Salesman:* You have told me that you have not been too pleased with the results of your stock market investments.
>
> *John Prospect:* That's right. I am dissatisfied with the return, or lack of it, on my stock portfolio.
>
> *Joe Salesman:* Starting tomorrow, how would you like to have three sources of profit every time you buy a common stock?
>
> *John Prospect:* Three profit sources? What are they?
>
> *Joe Salesman:* First, you could collect a lot of dollars—maybe hundreds, sometimes thousands—for simply agreeing to sell your just-bought stock at a higher price than you paid. This agreement money is paid to you right away, on the very next business day—money that's yours to keep forever. Your second source of profit could be the cash dividends due you as the owner of the stock. The third source of profit would be in the increase in price of the shares from what you paid, to the agreed selling price.
>
> By agreeing to sell at a higher price than you bought, all you are giving up is the unknown, unknowable profit possibility above the agreed price. In return, for relinquishing some of the profit potential you collect a handsome amount of cash that you can immediately spend or reinvest, as you choose. (p. 166)

Individual investors find the lure of three sources of profit appealing. This is a clear case of frame dependence, and it illustrates the concepts I described in chapter 3. Psychologically speaking, many investors savor the three sources of profit separately rather than appreciating the integrated total return. You can see segregation at work in my colleague's Cooper Cameron example, when he reported the two gains from his trading strategy separately. And what about dividends? In behavioral finance, dividends and covered-call writing go hand-in-hand. Here is my colleague's view on that subject.

> Q: Can you explain how you feel about dividends, and why?
> A: I love dividends. They are a very pleasant part of investing. It's real, in my pocket. My family history was tied up with bonds, not stocks. Receiving dividends is like receiving bond coupons.
>
> In prior days, dividends gave a reasonable return. But not today and not on NASDAQ stocks, where I've had to create them for myself. I always like to have some stock in utilities. Like Puget Sound Power and Light. It's given me a 9 percent return. It doubles every seven years, and I've had it for twenty years. Why did I buy it? It was in an area that was growing, in a good regulatory environment, *and* it paid dividends.

Covered-call writing is very appealing to investors who establish target prices for their stocks and plan to sell when the stock price reaches the target. In this respect, the calls they use are far out of the money, with the exercise price corresponding to their objective for the stock. Therefore, covered-call writers tend to let the stock get called away in situations where the market price lies above the exercise price on the expiration date. Of course, they could buy back the call, at a loss, if they wanted to keep those stocks. But if my colleague's behavior is any indication, most do not buy back the option. My colleague says he usually lets the stock go.

The downside to covered-call writing is that the investor can lose out on a big gain if the underlying stock soars. Take Intel, whose stock price went up by a factor of two and a half between December 1995 and June 1998. My colleague tells me he has had Intel called away six times during this period.

Covered-Call Writing by Professional Investors

There are psychological reasons why individual investors find covered-call writing attractive. But the same may not be true for mutual fund managers. It may not be true if their investors focus not on *segregated* gains but on *integrated* returns. An article that appeared in the *Wall Street Journal* describes how covered-call writing adversely impacted the performance of Putnam's Strategic Investments Trust.

Why this poor record? From its launch until 1991, the Putnam fund was a so-called option income fund, which meant it wrote call options against its stock portfolio in an effort to boost the income it paid to shareholders. The trouble was, by writing the options, the fund gave up the chance to earn healthy capital gains. The good stocks got called away by call-option buyers, who had purchased the right to buy the stocks. Meanwhile, the rotten stocks were left.[4]

Employee Stock Options

Employee stock options are especially interesting in that they lead employees to face a classic decision problem studied by psychologists Daniel Kahneman and Amos Tversky (1979). Either (1) exercise the option and take a certain gain, or (2) wait and take the chance that the company stock price will go even higher.

Chip Heath, Steven Huddart, and Mark Lang (1998) have analyzed the way that employees deal with this decision. Note that such employees have high-ranking positions, and so their stakes are considerable. Heath, Huddart, and Lang find that employees tend to exercise options when the stock price moves to a new maximum, relative to some maximum stock price achieved over the preceding eight months.

This behavior conceivably reflects at least three behavioral phenomena. First, employees might believe that little room for improvement remains on the upside, but considerable room remains on the downside, as per Werner De Bondt's (1993) article about betting on trends. Second, employees may recall not having exercised an option at the previous high, and decide to do so now in order to avoid additional regret. Third, employees may be behaving in accordance with prospect theory (Kahneman and Tversky 1979). Heath, Huddart, and Lang suggest that employees set reference points at the eight-month maximum price. According to prospect theory, an employee would exhibit risk-seeking behavior, meaning she would hold the options when the current price was below her reference point, and display risk averse behavior (exercise) when the current price moved above her reference point.

A Practical Perspective on Option Pricing Theory

Academics have developed elaborate and elegant theories about the factors that determine option prices. The best known of these is the option pricing model developed by Fischer Black and Myron Scholes

(1973). Readers will gain little by my specifying the Black-Scholes formula. But I do need to indicate something about the arguments that appear in the formula. The formula stipulates that the price of an option depends on five arguments: the concurrent price of the underlying asset, the return volatility on the underlying asset, the exercise price on the option, the time to expiration, and the risk-free interest rate. Notably, the Black-Scholes formula is based on *assumptions* such as lognormality, constant volatility, and an invariant risk-free rate over the life of the option, a point to which I return below.

The Black-Scholes formula provides an elegant options-pricing theory. That being said, option trader and author Sheldon Natenberg (1988, 1997) suggests that "a trader who becomes a slave to a theoretical pricing model is almost certain to have a short and unhappy trading career."[5]

Option traders face innumerable risks. Natenberg divides these risks into three categories. The first category is *input risk*—risk to be faced when option prices behave in accordance with Black-Scholes. These risks are associated with the option Greeks—delta, gamma, theta, vega, and rho.[6]

The second risk category is *assumption risk*—risk that the theoretical models used to value options are inappropriate. Natenberg mentions several reasons why this might be the case. For example, the underlying price distribution may not be lognormal; or the volatility over the life of the contract may not be constant.

Then there are *practical risks*. Here are two examples. (1) A trader may not have sufficient capital to meet subsequent margin requirements. (2) A short option position may be at-the-money on the expiration date, leading the trader to be uncertain whether or not he will have to supply the underlying security.

Of the different types of risk, the one most relevant to behavioral finance is assumption risk. The Black-Scholes model is indeed very elegant. But when you get right down to it, isn't it just another heuristic, capable of producing heuristic-driven bias? Let's see.

Implied Volatility

Of the five arguments used in the Black-Scholes formula, four are observable and one is not. The unobservable argument is volatility, the standard deviation of the distribution governing the future return on the underlying security. However, one variable that can be observed is the option price, the output from a Black-Scholes formula. This has given rise to the practice of inverting the Black-Scholes formula and using the current option price, together with the four input variables, to infer the market's belief about future volatility. This volatility is known as the *implied volatility* of the option.

Let's consider an example using index options, which are options traded on the S&P 500. On May 19, 1998, the S&P 500 closed at 1108.73. On that day a variety of options were traded on the index. These varied by month of expiration and exercise (strike) price. The expiration months available for trade were June, July, August, September, and December of 1998, and March, June, and December of 1999.

The available exercise prices for each expiration month spanned a wide range. For the June '98 options, the lowest available exercise price was 625, and the highest was 1350. One thing that all the June '98 options shared in common was that they were based on the same underlying asset—the S&P 500. The distribution of future returns on this asset has but one volatility. Therefore, in theory, the implied volatility of all the S&P 500 index options should be the same, regardless of exercise price, and regardless of whether the option is a call or a put.

Figure 19-1 displays two curves of implied volatility relative to exercise price on May 19, 1998, one for June '98 call options, and the other for June '98 put options. In theory, the figure should display a single horizontal line, with one curve lying on top of the other. Is that what we see?

Two features in figure 19-1 are striking. First, the implied volatility curves for call options and put options do not lie on top of each other: The curve for calls is higher. Second, the implied volatility curve is downward sloping. Volatility is high for low exercise prices, declining as the exercise price gets closer to the current price. These curves are very different from a horizontal line, which is the theoretical pattern. Because of its shape, the actual pattern has come to be called a *smile* (a crooked smile perhaps, but a smile nonetheless). The actual smile pattern, in contrast to the theoretical flat pattern, suggests that *assumption risk* is real.

Now take a close look at the magnitudes of the implied volatilities displayed in figure 19-1. Notice that they range from about 100 percent at the left end of the spectrum to less than 20 percent at the right end. What are we to make of such huge discrepancies between numbers that are supposed to be the same, at least in theory?

Figure 19-1 Implied Volatilities for the S&P 500, May 19, 1998

The chart of Black-Scholes implied volatilities, on May 19, 1998, for the S&P 500, across exercise prices. On that day the S&P 500 closed at 1108.73. In theory, there is only one implied volatility that is the same for puts and calls, and all exercise prices. In practice, the pattern has come to be called a smile when it turns up on both the right and left. In this figure, the pattern is closer to a sneer. The steepness of these curves on the left suggests that investors are disproportionately concerned about a sharp drop in the market—in other words, that they suffer from "crashophobia."

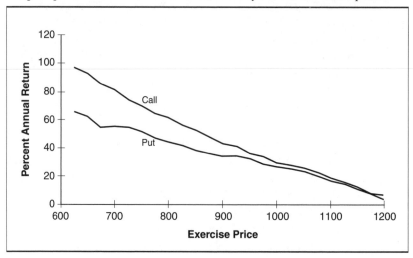

The Impact of the Crash of 1987 on Implied Volatilities

Jens Jackwerth and Mark Rubinstein (1996) point out that historical volatility has been about 20 percent. But volatility is itself volatile. If we were to look at volatility every April during the period 1986–1993, we would see that it fluctuated between 11.8 percent and 23.8 percent when measured over a three-year window. For a twelve-month window, the range was higher, with a low of 10 percent, and a high of 34.8 percent. Note that the 34.8 percent figure, which is exceptionally high, includes October 1997, when the U.S. stock market crashed. The next highest figure is 17 percent. The figures for narrower windows (twenty-eight days and ninety-one days) are similar to those for the twelve-month window.

Figure 19-2 shows how volatility has varied in the period October 1995 through May 1998. The data in this figure should be interpreted as volatility in the S&P 500 index, measured over moving windows that are forty days wide. Notice that actual volatility fluctuated between 8

Figure 19-2 Volatility, S&P 500

How volatile is the return on the S&P 500? Return standard deviation ranged from below 10 percent to above 25 percent between November 1995 and June 1998.

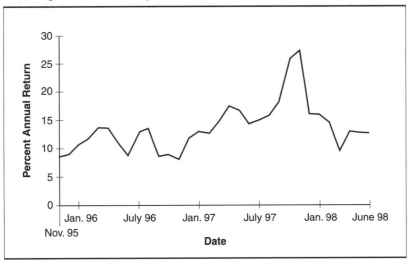

percent and 28 percent during this time, and was actually below 15 percent much of the time. This range is similar to the ranges reported by Jackwerth and Rubinstein.

Take another look at figure 19-1. The implied volatilities for the lowest call exercise prices are near 100 percent.[7] On October 19, 1987, the day of the crash, the two-month S&P futures price declined 29 percent. As was mentioned above, the volatility from April 1987 through April 1988 was 34 percent, far less than 100 percent or even the corresponding 60 percent figure for puts. What is going on?

As Jackwerth and Rubinstein document, the 1987 crash changed a lot of things. Before the crash, implied volatilities were much the same for different exercise prices. After the crash, the smile patterns emerged. What do those smile effects tell us?

One thing they tell us is that option traders do not accept the lognormal assumption in the Black-Scholes framework. Given the range of implied volatilities that existed before 1987, lognormality implies that the magnitude of the decline on October 19, 1987, is almost impossible. In fact, the lognormal assumption with historically observed volatility levels implies that over a twenty-billion-year time span—the life of the universe—the expected number of stock market crashes like the one experienced in 1987 is less than one!

You will observe that 20 billion years is longer than a century. Yet in this century we have observed the 1929 crash, the 1987 crash, and the October 1989 minicrash. In other words, option traders seriously underestimated the probability of a crash. So the challenge is how to reconcile the volatility values we observe with a higher probability of crash events.

The solution is to replace lognormality with a distribution that has a fatter lower tail and is skewed to the left. The high implied volatilities associated with low exercise prices are picking up that fat tail. In other words, the prices of the options are much higher than occur in a Black-Scholes setting, not because of higher volatility but because of skewness. Crashes simply occur more frequently than the Black-Scholes lognormal framework admits.

So what causes crashes? Robert Shiller (1993b) reports the results of a survey he ran within days of the 1987 crash to try and answer this question. What he discovered was the absence of fundamental news to trigger the decline. No precipitating news event sparked the fall. The most frequent response by investors was that "the market was overvalued." I translate that as sentiment.

Implied Volatility as a Forecasting Variable

Linda Canina and Stephen Figlewski (1993) argue that implied volatility is neither a good predictor of future volatility nor a good reflection of past volatility. If so, this suggests that investors are not very good at forecasting market volatility.

Before examining some evidence, recall one of the lessons discussed in chapter 5, concerning the character of efficient forecasts. The point was that forecasts should be less volatile than the variable being forecast. But for many people, their predictions *are about as variable* as the series they are trying to predict, because their predictions are guided by representativeness.

With this in mind, consider the average of the implied volatilities of call options with exercise prices between 900 and 995. Figure 19-3 below shows how the average implied volatility moved over the period April 17, 1997, through May 19, 1998. This was a time when the S&P 500 moved from 768 to over 1100, crossing 1000 on February 2, 1998. The figure also includes a curve of subsequent S&P 500 volatility, measured over a moving window of forty trading days. For each date, the implied volatility curve shows the market's forecast of future

Figure 19-3 Comparison Implied Volatility, 900 Calls versus
Subsequent Realized Volatility

Does implied volatility serve as an efficient forecast for subsequent actual
volatility? In an efficient market, it would. Given the smile or sneer pattern, we
need to figure out *which* implied volatility to use. The most common choice of
implied volatility is the one associated with at-the-money call options. During the
period shown in the chart, implied volatility was higher than actual volatility for
most of the time. It is also very volatile itself: efficient forecasts tend to be less
volatile than the variable being forecast. Representativeness tends to induce
excessive volatility in forecasts.

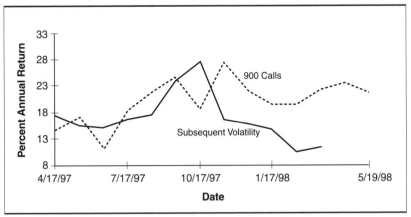

volatility, whereas the subsequent volatility curve shows what volatility turned out to be over the next forty trading days.

Recall that a forecast should fluctuate less than the variable whose
value is being predicted. Does the implied volatility curve in figure
19-3 fluctuate too much relative to actual volatility? I leave that one to
you.

Index Options and Market Swings

David Bates (1991) suggests that in 1987, investors' fears of a crash
could be perceived in index option prices. For comparable exercise
prices, he found considerably higher put-option implied volatilities
than call-option implied volatilities. This led him to construct what he
called a "crash premium."

The summer of 1998 was another interesting period when it comes
to the way index option prices reflect investors' concerns. By the end of
August 1998, the S&P 500 had declined almost 20 percent, relative to
the all-time high it reached just six weeks earlier. *Wall Street Journal*

writer Suzanne McGee suggested that one reason for the stock sell-off might have been the high cost of index options. She also mentions the role that index options played in the 1987 crash, a point to which I return. She wrote:

> In past sell-offs, market participants and analysts have worried that derivative products, designed to protect individual portfolios, have in fact exacerbated market declines. During the stock market crash of October 1987, for instance, money managers seeking to protect their holdings aggressively sold stock index futures even as the market slid, sending indexes to new lows that in turn triggered still more selling.
>
> But this sell-off is different. Some market participants believe it was the absence, rather than the presence, of the right kind of derivative products at an affordable price that made a sell-off almost inevitable.
>
> "By the time Monday arrived, volatility had gone up so much that it was far, far too expensive to buy put options," says Scott Fullman, option-market strategist at Swiss American Securities in New York. . . .
>
> On July 31, when the index closed at 1120.7, investors could buy the right to sell the index at 1010 in or before the third week of September for only $10. That means they could lock in 10% downside for about 1% of the index's value for a period of seven weeks.
>
> By the time the dust settled late Monday, the S&P 500 had fallen to 957.50, below the 1010 strike price, and the option's premium had soared to $68. Yesterday, as the market rebounded, the premium fell back to only $33. Still, to lock in seven weeks' worth of 10% downside protection from yesterday's S&P 500 close would cost $18, or nearly 18%, almost double levels of a month ago.[8]

What does Suzanne McGee's discussion mean in terms of implied volatilities? The implied volatilities associated with a 10 percent decline had gone from under 30 percent to over 40 percent.

At the beginning of the excerpt, McGee describes the sale of stock index futures during the crash of 1987. This instance provides a dramatic illustration of *assumption risk*. Money managers had purchased "portfolio insurance," a synthetic put option that in theory replicates an actual put option through a dynamically adjusted combination of Treasury bills and a short position in index futures. But in the crash of 1987, the unanticipated volume led to major problems with order execution, thereby preventing the synthetic put from being properly formed.

Overreaction

I interviewed soybean trader Sheldon Natenberg about the volatility of implied volatility. His response was instructive: "Markets in general tend to overreact. This is probably true of implied volatility as well. Part of volatile volatility is psychological. But it also has to do with weaknesses in the model."

Jeremy Stein (1989) studied whether the index option market tends to overreact. Specifically, he asked whether long-term options overreact to short-term shocks. For example, a sudden unexpected move in the market may lead to an increase in the implied volatility of options that expire in the month or so. But by the law of averages, the impact on options that expire many months away should be much less. In fact, the longer the time to expiration, the closer the implied volatility should be to the long-term historic volatility of 20 percent.

What does the implied volatility curve look like for long-term options? In May 1998, the longest available options on the S&P 500 expired in December 1999. Figure 19-4 shows the implied volatilities at various exercise prices. Notice that with the exception of the 750 calls, the remaining volatility pattern is quite flat.[9] This pattern is typical for LEAPS, including the dip at the left.

Are implied volatilities for LEAPS stable or do they move too quickly in response to short-term events? This is the essence of the overreaction question. Consider a comparison between the implied

Figure 19-4 S&P 500 Implied Volatility, December 1999 Calls
The pattern for long-term option volatilities tends to be much flatter than the pattern for options expiring in the short term. For very long options, implied volatilities should hover around mean historical volatility. Overreaction occurs if long-term volatilities react to financial news in a comparable way as their short-term counterparts.

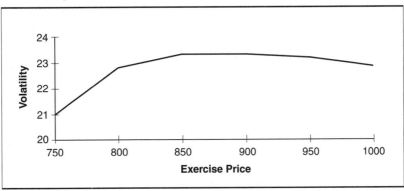

volatilities for the June 1998 calls and December 1999 calls for two dates, roughly one month apart.

On April 21, 1998, the S&P 500 closed at 1126.7. On that date, implied volatility for an at-the-money June call was 19 percent, while implied volatility for the December 1999 LEAPS was about 21 percent. One month later, on May 19, the S&P 500 was a little lower at 1109.52, and implied volatility for an at-the-money June call had fallen to 17 percent. But as we saw in figure 19-4, the implied volatility for December 1999 LEAPS had climbed 2 percent, to 23 percent.

Because the long-term volatilities moved in the opposite direction from their short-term counterparts, I am not sure I would call this an instance of overreaction. But by the same token, I wouldn't call the long-term implied volatilities stable. I should mention that the overreaction issue raised by Stein has produced something of a controversy. A study by Diz and Finucane (1993) using a different time period claims to find no evidence of overreaction.

Using Options to Measure Sentiment

Is there evidence of sentiment in option trading? Natenberg suggests that unlike the case of futures, where traders are content to make the bid-ask spread, "option traders try to create positions that are consistent with their opinions."

The call-put ratio (CPR) is defined as the ratio of open daily call volume to open daily put-option volume. Users of the CPR, mostly technical analysts, believe that when investors become more optimistic, option traders increase their holding of call options relative to put options. Hence, they believe that an abnormally high reading of this index signals considerable optimism. In other words, they believe that the CPR is a sentiment indicator, just like the Bullish Sentiment Index discussed in chapter 6.

As they do with the Bullish Sentiment Index, technical analysts treat the CPR as a contrarian indicator. In his book on technical analysis, Thomas Meyers (1989, 1994) states that a buy signal is generated when the inverse of the CPR, the put/call ratio, exceeds 0.55.[10] Billingsley and Chance (1988) argue that the put/call ratio is in fact positively correlated with returns, thereby supporting the claims advanced by technical analysts.

Consider two questions. First, does the recent evidence support the claim that the CPR is a contrarian indicator? Second, what drives the CPR?

Figure 19-5 Call/Put Ratio and the Subsequent Gains in the S&P 500
Index, January 1995–November 1998

Some technical analysts believe that when investors are unduly optimistic, they
buy more call options than put options. As a result, analysts treat the ratio of open
calls to open puts as a sentiment index, believing that extreme sentiment tends to
be unwarranted. In other words, that when the call/put ratio is low, the market
subsequently tends to rise. The chart plots the subsequent percentage change in
the S&P 500 against the call/put ratio. The gain in the S&P 500 is measured as
1 plus the change. On the whole, the two series tend to move inversely.

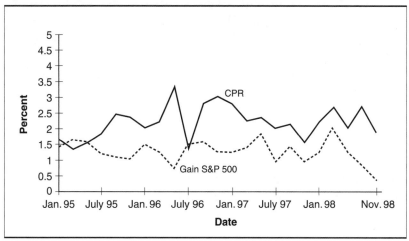

Figure 19-5 displays the comovement of the call/put ratio and the
gain to the S&P 500 over the subsequent 60-day period. The subsequent
movement (60 days later) is vertically aligned with the value of the
CPR. When we look at figure 19-5, it does seem that when the call/put
ratio goes up, the S&P 500 subsequently turns down.[11] Hence the evidence does support the claim that the CPR is a contrarian indicator.

The second question asks about the determinants of the call/put
ratio. For example, when we looked at the Bullish Sentiment Index, we
found that its value was largely driven by past movements in the market. The Bullish Sentiment Index is an excellent predictor of the past. Is
the same true for the call/put ratio? Yes, because technical analysts are
trend followers.

Summary

All three behavioral themes can be identified in option markets.
This chapter explained how options are used and priced, and how they
reflect sentiment.

Usage: Covered-call writing is the most popular option-trading strategy among individual investors. Its popularity largely stems from frame dependence, especially the ability to segregate gains and achieve a psychological counterbalance for losses on the underlying stock. As I indicated, the connection between option premiums and cash dividends is very important for investors inclined to write covered calls.

Pricing: Heuristic-driven bias leads to a smile effect that distorts the connection between implied volatility and actual volatility. The implied volatilities attached to index options with low exercise prices are unrealistically high. Rubinstein (1995) uses the term *crashophobia* to describe one aspect of this effect. Just as other markets do, option markets exhibit overreaction, a consequence of representativeness. Most academic scholars believe that option prices are determined by arbitrage and that therefore prices are free from the influence of sentiment. The behavior of implied volatilities relative to actual volatilities suggests the contrary.

Sentiment: The call/put ratio does appear to capture a key aspect of sentiment. Moreover, the evidence supports an inverse relationship between the call/put ratio and subsequent movements in the market.

Chapter 20

Commodity Futures: Orange Juice and Sentiment

*T*he frantic hand signals that commodity traders use in the trading pits suggests that prices are extremely volatile. Is this impression accurate?

From the perspective of market efficiency, the question about volatility boils down to whether commodity prices overreact to the flow of new material information. From the outside, it is often difficult to judge how germane the flow of information actually is. However, in a very clever article, Richard Roll (1984) suggests that we can use one commodity market to evaluate those information flows. That commodity is orange juice concentrate, where the most relevant fundamental variables that change on a day-to-day basis are the weather around Orlando, Florida, and the supply of oranges from Brazil.

There are many kinds of players in the market for orange juice concentrate:

- large fruit companies such as UniMark,
- beverage companies like Tropicana and Coca Cola (maker of Minute Maid orange juice),
- large funds speculating on the direction of commodity prices,
- "paper guys"—traders in the ring who handle orders from account executives or trade for their own accounts, and
- those in search of what orange juice trader Frank Tesoriero calls a "cheap coffee analogy."[1]

The bottom line is that heuristic-driven bias by these traders causes the price of orange juice concentrate to be excessively volatile relative to the underlying fundamentals. In other words, sentiment impacts the market for concentrate. Usually, excess volatility is a manifestation of trader overreaction, either to news that has occurred or to the absence of news altogether.

This chapter discusses the following:

- the institutional structure of the concentrate market
- the importance of Orlando weather
- the volatility of prices for orange juice concentrate
- four short cases about the reaction of concentrate prices to changes in Florida weather, events in Brazil, and nothing at all

The Institutional Structure of the Market for Orange Juice Concentrate

Orange juice concentrate is traded on the floor of the New York Cotton Exchange. At any one time there are usually nine futures contracts being traded, with the delivery dates being two months apart. For example, on July 26, 1997, contracts were available for delivery in September 1997, November 1997, January 1998, and so on up through January 1999. A single contract is for 15,000 lbs. of orange solids, standardized by concentration (termed "degrees Brix"). Prices are quoted in cents per pound. For example, on July 26, 1997, the closing price for the March 1998 contract was 82.55¢ per pound.

Why Florida Weather Is So Important

What makes orange juice futures so special, as far as studying volatility is concerned, is that almost all of the U.S. orange crop—more than 98 percent—used to manufacture concentrate is grown in a single geographic location: near Orlando, Florida. As we shall see later, oranges grown in Brazil are also used to make orange juice concentrate. However, the important point is that this highly localized production enables us to track much of the key information flows about the supply of oranges.

With the current technology, natural conditions impair producers from making short-term adjustments to capacity. Why? Because it takes between five and fifteen years before a newly planted orange tree is mature enough to produce fruit. So most of the time, markets will witness little day-to-day variation in the supply of oranges to the market.

Orange juice concentrate is, of course, the key ingredient in orange juice, be it fresh or frozen. So, it is reasonable to expect that the retail price of orange juice would play a key role in the price of concentrate. The factors that drive the retail price of orange juice tend to be quite stable—consumer tastes, consumer incomes, the different ways to consume orange juice, and the prices of substitute products such as apple juice. Roll reports that these factors do not exhibit a lot of day-to-day variation.

So, where does this leave us? Demand conditions appear to be quite stable. The retail price of orange juice is quite stable. Production capacity is quite stable. How about Florida weather?

The most critical weather events for a citrus crop are freezes. A severe freeze can destroy the entire crop. In fact, an 1895 freeze not only destroyed the crop, but also killed almost every tree. Today, advances in technology have made Florida citrus trees more resistant to freezing temperatures. However, several successive days of below-freezing temperatures can still wreak havoc on the crop. The harvesting of oranges occurs from autumn through early summer. A freeze will damage fruit, prompting trees to drop significant amounts prematurely.

Historically, the most important source of information about Orlando weather, particularly temperature and rainfall, has come from the U.S. Weather Service reporting station in Orlando. When Roll first wrote about orange juice futures in 1984, this station issued two reports daily. These reports contained forecasts covering the next thirty-six hours. Since that time technological advances have extended the time horizon out to as long as fourteen days, although short-term forecasts continue to be the most reliable. Forecasts are made for maximum daily temperature, minimum daily temperature, and precipitation.[2]

Commodity Price Volatility

The size of the orange crop depends on a number of weather factors: temperature, sunshine, amount of rain, and frequency of storms. In fact, weather is the single most important factor impacting the supply of oranges to the market for concentrate. Figure 20-1 illustrates the time path of the spot contract from October 19, 1995, to January 20,

Figure 20-1 Spot Price for Orange Juice Concentrate

The volatile time path of the spot price for orange juice concentrate. Where's the news driving orange juice futures?

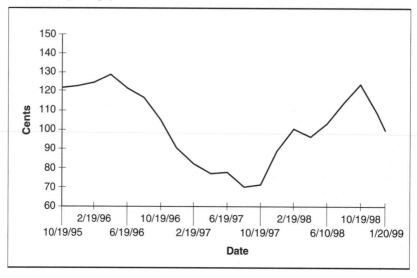

1999. The figure makes clear that the spot price for orange juice concentrate is quite volatile. Is the weather around Orlando as variable?

Case Study 1: A December 1997 Cold Front

To gain some insight into the relationship between Florida weather and the market price for orange juice concentrate, consider some examples. On the afternoon of Tuesday, December 2, the following forecast was issued for the current evening and subsequent four days, as shown in table 20-1.

Notice that on Tuesday, December 2, rain had been forecast to occur in and around Orlando beginning as showers the next day and intensifying on Thursday. Note also that temperatures were predicted to drop over the course of the next few days, dipping below 40 °F on the weekend.

On Thursday, December 4, a cold front passed through Florida. On the same day the price of concentrate jumped. Below are descriptions of two events, one concerning weather, and the other regarding the movement of orange juice futures on December 4.

WEATHER 12/5/97[3]

Intense Thunderstorms Drench Southern Half of Florida

Widespread moderate to heavy rain fell over the southern half of Florida Wednesday night.

A cold front is pushing southeastward through the state, and a moist, subtropical jet has put itself in the front's path. Intense thunderstorms developed Thursday afternoon over the lower Florida Keys and moved northeastward to bring another round of heavy rain to the region.

Key West had a heavy thunderstorm on top of already almost an inch of rain Wednesday night. Other rain totals included Miami with 1.10 inches, Sarasota with 1.76 inches and Tampa with 2.03 inches.

The threat of a freeze is enough to drive the price of concentrate up very quickly. Consider the behavior of prices for the March 1998 contract on Thursday, December 4, 1997. Trading began at 10:15 EST, with the opening price at 84.4¢. Prices hovered just below 84¢ for most of the day. However, at 13:55 prices jumped above 85¢, closing just below 86¢. Figure 20-2 below depicts the time path of these price changes.

The *Dow Jones News Service* offers a daily feature titled "World Commodities Summary." This feature highlights the most active commodities markets every trading day and describes the events that

Table 20-1 Five-Day Forecast for Orlando, Florida, Tuesday, December 2, 1997

Today	Wednesday	Thursday	Friday	Saturday
Partly sunny and pleasant; breezy	A shower in the afternoon	Rain in the morning	Clouds and sun; breezy	Partly sunny and breezy
High: 77 Low: 59	High: 78 Low: 62	High: 76 Low: 54	High: 66 Low: 43	High: 55 Low: 38

Current Conditions			
Time	5:00 P.M.	**Wind direction**	E/NE
Temperature	73	**Wind speed**	4 mph
Humidity	56%	**Visibility**	10 miles
Pressure	30.07"	**Weather**	Partly cloudy

Figure 20-2 Price Path of March 1998 Contract, December 4, 1997

An illustration of intraday volatility: What happened between 13:00 and 14:00 on December 4, 1997?

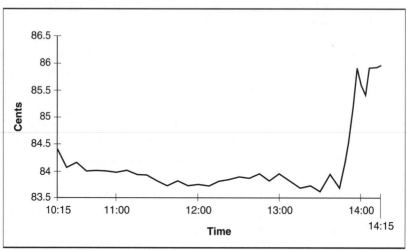

affected prices. What do we learn from the December 4 "World Commodities Summary" about the events that moved orange juice prices that day?[4] Absolutely nothing: Not a single mention is made of the cold front sweeping through the state that day. In fact, this article makes no mention of orange juice prices at all. In contrast, consider the following description of the events affecting soybean prices the same day.

> Nearby CBOT soybeans tested support levels just under $7 a bushel at midday Thursday, and finally toppled during the closing minutes. The session almost mirrored Tuesday's, when the contract suffered more than half its daily losses just before the closing bell rang. Although technical factors were the main reason for Thursday's dip, demand worries also played a role.
>
> The U.S. Department of Agriculture said Thursday that U.S. soybean sales for the week ended Nov. 27 totaled 361,700 metric tons— down 50% from the previous week and down 39% from the four-week average.
>
> "The sales were half of what they were the previous week," Henderson of Stewart-Peterson said. "That shows a slowdown in demand."

The contrast between the paucity of news and the volatility of orange juice futures is striking. And it's not an isolated event. One interesting aspect of news about prices of orange juice futures is its relative *nonexistence.* On a typical trading day, there are about five hundred stories about commodities that are available through *Dow Jones News Service.* Of these, there may be one or two about orange juice, and they usually concern nothing more than opening and closing prices.

This paucity of news led Roll to ask some obvious questions. To what are traders in orange juice futures reacting? Is it information not being picked up by the news wires? Or are they just reacting to themselves? Are they simply reacting to each other's trades? In his 1985 presidential address to the American Finance Association, the late Fischer Black suggested that many traders cannot distinguish between relevant information and irrelevant information. He called irrelevant information "noise," and labeled those who trade on "noise" instead of "information" *noise traders.* Are orange juice traders noise traders? Is noise-trader sentiment the driving force behind the price of orange juice futures?

Looking at December 4, it is clear that despite the absence of a report about Florida weather in the commodities news stories, there was an event. So, a skeptical reader may be reluctant to condemn orange juice traders as noise traders.

Case Study 2: A Typical July

But now let's look at a summer month such as July, rather than a winter month such as December. Consider table 20-2, which shows the weather forecast for Orlando that was issued on the evening of July 1, 1997.

This is a typical forecast for July, with high temperatures in the 90s and low temperatures in the 70s. There was no indication of a possible weather event that might damage the orange crop in this report. Moreover, the only information about orange juice futures that appeared in the many *Dow Jones News Service* stories about commodities[5] from June 30 through July 7, 1997, concerned the opening and closing prices of orange juice contracts. Yet, consider the September 1997 futures. As can be seen in figure 20-3, prices were quite volatile throughout, even into the calm, "uneventful" summer months. The low price for July 3 was 76.45¢ cents, the high price was 77.5¢, and the closing price was 77.45¢. The difference between high and low, relative to the close, was 1.36 percent. That change is typical for the S&P 500, where the information flows are quite substantial on a daily basis. But for the September orange juice contract, in July?! Not to put too fine a point on it, but was

Table 20-2 Five-Day Forecast for Orlando, Florida, Tuesday, July 1, 1997

Today	Wednesday	Thursday	Friday	Saturday
Showers in the afternoon	Clouds and sun; breezy	Partly sunny and hot	Partly sunny and hot	Partly sunny and hot
High: 92 Low: 73	High: 92 Low: 74	High: 94 Low: 75	High: 94 Low: 76	High: 93 Low: 75

Current Conditions

Time	11:00 P.M.	**Wind direction**	W
Temperature	82	**Wind speed**	11 mph
Humidity	73%	**Visibility**	10 miles
Pressure	29.92"	**Weather**	Mild and clear

Figure 20-3 Price Path of September 1997 Orange Juice Contract

The volatile time path of prices for the September 1997 contract. Is the market any less volatile in summer months, when there is less chance of a Florida freeze?

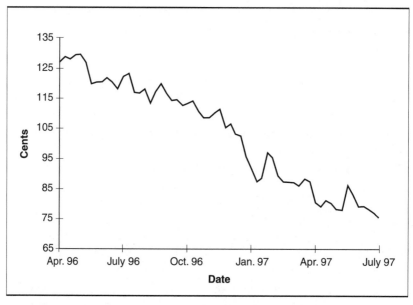

there some unreported hint of a summer freeze before September? To paraphrase a fast food television commercial from the 1980s: Where's the news?!

Case Study 3: Genuine News

In case you are thinking that the news services simply do not report news that is genuinely germane to orange juice contracts, here are two examples that they do. The first example is a news story that highlights the two major events that impact the market for orange juice concentrate—Florida weather and events in Brazil.[6] Despite the emphasis on fundamentals, note the references to sentiment as you read the following excerpts.

> Orange juice futures on the New York Cotton Exchange settled higher on Wednesday the day after the trade as buyers came in for the second session in a row, analysts said . . .
>
> Heavy rains in Florida citrus regions over the past week may have caused some fruit to drop, and traders are buying as a result of the talk, said Jack Scoville, analyst with LIT Price Group, a brokerage in Chicago. . . . Bullish sentiment has increased because the trade has been a buyer this week, Scoville said. "The trade had been covering shorts," early this week, he said. "They turned buyers' Tuesday," he said, and "they were buyers in the first half (of Wednesday's session)."
>
> Many traders are still bullish because of Brazil's projection last Friday of a drop in its 1998–99 orange crop to 325 million boxes from 380 million this season, Scoville said.
>
> "We've changed fundamentals around 100% because we're looking at sharply lower production from Brazil the coming year," he said. Gains in futures have been limited this year because USDA last October projected this season's Florida orange crop at a record 254 million boxes, he said.

Here is yet one more example of genuine news. On February 10, 1999, the United States Department of Agriculture (USDA) issued a report that stunned the orange juice futures market.[7] In its *World Agricultural Supply and Demand Estimates,* the USDA predicted that the 1998 U.S. orange crop would be 194 million boxes, above the expected range of 185 to 190 boxes. In addition, the report predicted a record yield of juice per box: 1.60 gallons, up from the 1.57 yield of 1997.

The price of the March contract fell by 7.95 cents on the report, closing at 92.25 cents.

Commodities analyst Jack Scoville,[8] quoted earlier, made an interesting statement about the reaction to the USDA report: "They got them coming and going." Coming and going—the hallmark of volatility.

Case Study 4: The View from the Trading Floor

How about the view of those who actually trade orange juice futures? In June 1998 I interviewed Frank Tesoriero, an orange juice futures trader who at the time was also president of the Citrus Associates, a subsidiary owned by the NYCE.[9] I asked him for his view on what drives the price of orange juice concentrate. We spoke about both sentiment and fundamentals, and began with a specific instance.

On June 24, 1998, the price for the July contract opened at 105 cents and dropped to 103 within the first ten minutes. In response to my question about what had precipitated the drop, Tesoriero stated: "It went down on absolutely nothing." He went on to explain that it may have been "locals trying to pick each other's pockets," that when it comes to market price, "locals will try to whip it around."

As for Brazil, Tesoriero described the difficulty of obtaining reliable and timely information, because those in possession of the information engage in strategic release. Moreover, those releases may come at times during the day that are difficult to anticipate. He noted that when it comes to providing information nonstrategically, Brazil has no counterpart to the USDA.

Recall that figure 20-1 illustrates the volatility of the spot price for orange juice. Notice that the second half of 1998 was even *more* volatile than the first half, with the price fluctuating between 98 cents and 123 cents.

Summary

The price of orange juice concentrate appears to be excessively volatile relative to the underlying fundamentals. The major fundamentals that affect the market for orange juice concentrate are the weather conditions in Florida and the supply of oranges from Brazil. Major news events about either one typically cause large changes in the prices of orange juice concentrate futures. However, the fact that volatility occurs in the absence of news about altered fundamentals is evidence of heuristic-driven bias and market inefficiency.

Chapter *21*

Excessive Speculation in Foreign Exchange Markets

*F*oreign exchange traders engage in excessive speculation. So, why do traders speculate so much? Is it because they trade on strongly held, but erroneous, opinions? The evidence suggests that this is the case, and that psychological issues figure prominently.

This chapter discusses the following:

- a case based on the Asian crisis of 1997 and 1998, when the financial press reported that exchange rates were determined, not by economic fundamentals, but by psychology
- the general findings about excessive speculation in foreign exchange markets

Case Study: The Asian Crisis that "Began" in 1997

The statement about psychology mentioned above was part of a front-page story that appeared in the August 24, 1998, issue of the *Wall Street Journal*. Below is an excerpt from the article.

Frightened investors and quick-moving speculators in markets as far apart and different as Brazil and Hong Kong, Canada and Russia, Japan and Venezuela are scurrying to exchange local currencies for the U.S. dollar. . . .

Hopes that the crisis, ignited by the July 1997 devaluation of the Thai baht, would soon burn itself out have been dashed. . . .

In theory, a currency's value mirrors the fundamental strength of its underlying economy, relative to other economies. But in the current white-knuckled climate, traders and lenders are trying to guess what every other trader thinks. While traders use the most modern communications, they act by fight-or-flee instincts. If they expect others are about to sell the Brazilian real for U.S. dollars, they try to sell their real first. It isn't just economics at work now; it's a psychology that at times borders on panic.[1]

The statements about "psychology that at times borders on panic," "fight-or-flee instincts," and "expecting others to sell" recall an issue that was discussed in the first chapter. Remember the pick-a-number game? Its attendant lesson for practitioners was to factor in the importance of others' errors.

Here is a thumbnail sketch of the events leading up to this near panic. In thirty years, the Asian tigers—Hong Kong, Singapore, South Korea, and Taiwan—achieved what the United States had taken a century to accomplish. These countries managed to increase fourfold the standard of living of their citizens. From 1994 though the first half of 1997, Asia accounted for one half of global economic growth. In order to integrate their economies into the global market, these countries established fixed exchange-rate policies against the U.S. dollar.

During the first quarter of 1997, the forecast for the tigers, as well as for the would-be tigers (Thailand, Indonesia, Malaysia, and the Philippines) appeared promising. Then, in the second quarter, the possibility of some problem loans in Thailand led investors to speculate that the Thais would be unable to maintain the value of their currency, the baht, against the dollar. However, investors did not anticipate that the second half of 1997 would bring major chaos to Asian financial markets.

Take the case of Indonesia. At the beginning of July 1997, the Indonesian rupiah was trading at 2,450 to the dollar. Prior to that, the rupiah had been very steady. But by early January 1998, it had moved to 10,225—an 80 percent decline in value!

Heuristic-Driven Bias by Borrowers

The following excerpts from the December 30, 1997, issue of the *Wall Street Journal* describe the problem facing Indonesian borrowers.[2] As you read, keep in mind that most predictions are made by extrapolating recent trends—what Werner De Bondt (1993) calls "betting on trends." In addition, people tend to be overconfident in their predictions. This leads them to be surprised more frequently than they had anticipated. The first paragraph of the article provides the background.

Counting on continued growth and a predictable currency, Indonesian nonfinancial companies more than doubled their foreign borrowing from the end of 1995 to mid-1997, according to Standard & Poor's. As of Sept. 30, according to President Suharto's new special adviser on debt, Radius Prawiro, Indonesia's total foreign debt was $133.3 billion, of which $65.6 billion was owed by private companies.

The next portion of the article discusses the way in which Indonesian borrowers speculated.

Indonesian borrowers faced a simple choice. They could borrow rupiah at 18% or 20% and not worry about the exchange rate. Or they could borrow dollars at 9% or 10% a year and then convert the proceeds to rupiah. A year later, they figured, it would take 4% or 5% more rupiah to buy the dollars needed to repay the loan, but the cost still was less. . . .

The central bank, Bank Indonesia, had trouble keeping track of all the short-term foreign borrowing Indonesians were doing, but it knew this borrowing was heavy. "The currency was on a steady course," Mr. Soedradjad notes. "And we had all these banks from all over the world landing here and handing out the money."

Speculation can go either way. How did this one go? The article continues:

It is now clear that Indonesian companies made a huge bet that went bad: Few executives took seriously the possibility that Bank Indonesia would let the rupiah fall sharply. Even fewer were willing to pay the cost of hedging, insurance that banks and investments houses sell to protect against currency collapse.

In late July and early August, Goldman, Sachs & Co. surveyed 34 Indonesian chief financial officers. Two-thirds had more than 40% of their debt in foreign currencies; of those, half were completely unhedged, and most of the rest had well under half of their debt hedged. That proved a costly mistake.

Indonesian business people extrapolated a trend and then speculated on it. Most were surprised when they ended up with serious losses. In other words, these investors were overconfident as well.

Opaque Framing

Were there warning signs about the deteriorating situation in the Asian economies that were ignored by overconfident investors? Economist Paul Krugman argues that this was in fact the case. In 1994, he wrote an article in *Foreign Affairs* that generated a major controversy. The article summarized work by economists Lawrence Lau of Stanford University and Alwyn Young of Boston University, who suggested that the sources of growth in the Asian economies were declining. Consequently, economic growth in these countries was likely to slow.

These economists argued that the Asian economic miracle was not a product of an "Asian system" where farsighted Asian governments promoted specific industries and technologies. Rather, it was the result of more run-of-the-mill changes such as high savings rates, good education, and the movement of underemployed peasants into the modern sector. If these arguments are true, then growth will slow when, for example, few underemployed peasants are left to move into the modern sector. This feature is truer of an economy like Singapore's than of one like China's. So, in short, Lau and Young, and then Krugman, argued that investors were looking at Asian economies through an *opaque* frame, not a *transparent* one.

In the conventional economic view, investors gradually adjust their expectations about Asian economic growth as information about changing fundamentals appears. But the adjustment in 1997 was hardly gradual. Consider some hard questions. Had investors been unduly exuberant about investing in Asia, particularly in emerging markets? Did they have available to them information that would enable them to make informed decisions? Did they underreact to the economic statistics that were available? Or did they simply extrapolate past growth rates and succumb to the optimism bias? Did undue optimism lead to widespread investments in negative net present value projects all across Asia, projects that could not produce positive returns, let alone the kinds of returns investors had imagined? These are important questions. For a sense of the answers, consider the following.

In a later article for *Fortune* magazine Krugman (1997) discussed investors' sudden realization that they had been ignoring important statistics like the trade deficit. He stated: "By last year it became clear that South Korea's and Thailand's torrid growth rates of the first half of the 1990s had to end—wages were rising faster than productivity; overheated domestic markets were spilling over into imports, creating massive trade deficits. . . . And international capital markets have suddenly noticed that countries throughout the region have been running world-class trade deficits—bigger relative to their economies than Mexico's was just before the big peso collapse."

Krugman's article appeared in August 1997. Perhaps I myself am committing hindsight bias, but let me point out that two months later, managers of most mutual and pension funds were still oblivious. Then, in October, the financial markets in Hong Kong suffered a sudden jolt. Between October 20 and 23, Hong Kong's stock market lost nearly a quarter of its value on fears concerning interest rates and pressures on the Hong Kong dollar. In the above cited *Wall Street Journal* article, Bill Sutton, who monitors Asian currency markets for Merrill Lynch, stated that "the vast majority of hedge funds, real-money funds and other institutional investors were fully invested in the rupiah." Julian Robertson Jr.'s Tiger Management Corp. was a prominent example. The *Wall Street Journal* reported on Tiger Management's experience in October as follows:

> Tiger Management decided to buy, figuring the rupiah, down to around 3,800 to the dollar, was due for a rebound. Tiger says it snapped up $975 million in rupiah in early October. This wasn't a big sum for the hedge fund, but it was for the rupiah market, and it pushed up the currency—briefly.
>
> "Our people were very bullish on the rupiah," Tiger's Mr. Robertson says. But he is the boss, and "finally I just said, 'I don't want to be long any of this crap.'" Tiger held its position about three weeks and sold most of it in $150 million chunks at the end of October, plus the final piece at the end of November.[3]

What began as a decline in Asian currencies eventually engulfed those of Latin America and Russia, not to mention Canada, illustrating the point I made earlier that excessive speculation—driven by psychology and panic—is a major issue. In the September 7, 1998, issue of *Fortune*, Krugman called for the controversial action of implementing exchange controls. Here is how he put it.

> In short, Asia is stuck: Its economies are dead in the water, but trying to do anything major to get them moving risks provoking another wave of capital flight and a worse crisis. In effect, the region's economic policy has become hostage to skittish investors. Is there any way out? Yes, there is, but it is a solution so unfashionable, so

stigmatized, that hardly anyone has dared suggest it. The unsayable words are "exchange controls."

"Skittish investors"? Time to consider the general findings about excessive speculation.

The General Case

Economists Kenneth Froot and Jeffrey Frankel (1993) have documented that excessive speculation occurs in normal times just as it does in extraordinary times. They focus on the determinants of forward discounts in foreign exchange markets.

Consider the following example. On Monday, March 27, 1995, the Japanese yen was trading at 86.4 to the U.S. dollar. Speculators who wanted yen 30 days later, on Wednesday, April 26, could pursue one of the following two alternatives. They could exchange dollars for yen on March 27 at 86.4, take delivery of the yen a month before, and invest for the proceeds for one month at the short-term Japanese interest rate. Or, they could purchase the yen forward, at the thirty-day forward rate of 86.049. In the second case, the exchange of dollars for yen would take place on April 26, not March 27.

Notice that the March 27 forward rate was less favorable than the corresponding spot rate, because a dollar bought fewer April 26 yen than it did March 27 yen. On a per yen basis, the forward dollar value of the yen was more than the dollar spot value. In other words, the yen was trading at a premium on March 27.

What does this mean? For one thing, Japanese interest rates were lower than U.S. rates. On March 27, 1995, the thirty-day Japanese interest rate was only 1.72 percent, whereas the corresponding U.S. rate was 6.16 percent. If the yen did not trade at a premium, then investors could make large arbitrage profits very easily. They could borrow yen at the low Japanese rate, purchase dollars at the spot rate, and invest the dollars at the higher U.S. rate for thirty days. Of course, they would have to repay their yen loan on April 26. But if the yen were not trading at a premium on March 27, they could lock in a favorable rate by converting their dollars back into yen in April. Most important, the rate they locked in would enable them to earn a guaranteed profit by borrowing at a low interest rate and investing the proceeds of that loan at a higher interest rate.

When the yen trades at a discount, does that mean that investors expect the yen to depreciate over the next thirty days? Perhaps, but not necessarily. Money Market Services (MMS) is one of the major firms that track investor expectations about currency rates. It reported that on March 27, 1995, investors expected that in thirty days time, the yen would move to 90.[4] So, although the yen was trading at a premium, investors expected that it would depreciate over the next thirty days. In fact, the yen appreciated to 84 over that period.

How frequently do investors' expectations about exchange-rate movements run in the opposite direction from the forward discount? It happened 42 percent of the time during the period March 27, 1995, through January 5, 1998, in the thirty-day forward yen market.

It definitely appears that investors are willing to bet against the direction implied by the forward discount. Is this sensible? It depends on how well the forward discount does as a predictor of future movements in the spot rate. If, over time, the spot rate tends to move by about the amount predicted by the forward discount, then it would be foolish to bet against the forward discount. However, the truth is that during the period August 8, 1994, through January 5, 1998, the yen depreciated against the dollar despite the yen's trading at a premium throughout this entire period. Figure 21-1 shows the behavior of the yen (per dollar).

How would traders have made money speculating against the forward discount? When should they buy low, and when should they sell

Figure 21-1 Time Series of Yen per U.S. Dollar
How has the dollar value of the yen fluctuated between 1994 and 1998?

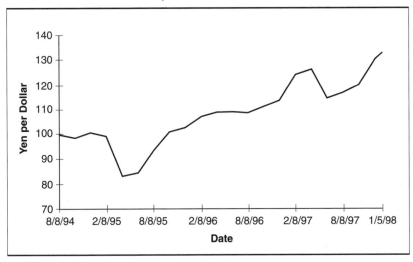

high? If they expect the yen to depreciate over the next thirty days, then selling high means selling the yen forward today, since the forward yen trades at a premium. They could then plan to buy low by buying yen in thirty days time at the April 26 spot rate, whatever that turns out to be.

How would it have turned out? Speculators could have sold yen at 86 on March 27, agreeing to deliver 86 yen in exchange for one dollar. Then on April 26, they would have expected to purchase yen for immediate delivery at a rate of 90, which would have been good news. Traders would expect only to have to spend $0.96 to purchase the 86 yen that they promised to deliver, and would receive $1.00 in return. So, they would expect to make a 4-cent profit per yen in completing their forward transaction. But the news on April 26 was bad, not good. The yen had fallen to 84. Hence, speculators would have had to spend $1.02, more than a dollar, to purchase the 86 yen they committed to deliver a month earlier, thereby losing 2 cents per yen instead of making 4 cents.

Is betting against the forward discount speculative? If so, is it *excessively* speculative? To answer that question, Froot and Frankel point out that investors form their expectations about exchange-rate movements by considering the contemporaneous spot rate and a host of other variables. They ask whether we can tell if investors should place more or less weight on the spot rate.

To answer the question, they suggest comparing the accuracy of investors' predictions to their forecasts. They measure accuracy as the difference between the forecasted change in the exchange rate and the actual change. The point is that if investors make rational use of information, then accuracy at any date should be a matter of luck. On the other hand, suppose that investors tend to be too extreme in their predictions. Then their forecasts will not be rational. When they predict appreciation, they predict too much appreciation; when they predict depreciation, they predict too much depreciation. In short, investors overreact. In this case, we could improve their forecasts by toning down the predicted size of the changes being forecast.

Froot and Frankel find that as a general matter, investors' predictions about exchange-rate changes are too extreme. How about their yen forecasts during the period we have been discussing? The MMS forecasts fit the general pattern of excessive speculation.

Moreover, forecast errors tend to be highly predictable. You can make a good guess about how far off investors' predicted change in the exchange rate would be. This is because forecast errors tend to be

Figure 21-2 Forecast Errors in Yen Appreciation

The time pattern of MMS forecast errors concerning the value of the Japanese yen. An efficient forecast is not excessively volatile, and it fluctuates randomly around zero. But once positive, the yen forecasts tend to stay positive, and once negative they tend to stay negative.

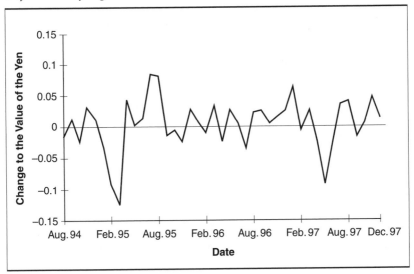

highly persistent. You can see this feature in figure 21-2. Notice that the prediction error tends to move in cycles. When the error is positive, it tends to stay positive for a while before turning negative. Once negative, it stays negative for a while.

There is a long-standing question about whether the presence of a risk premium inhibits the forward discount from predicting future spot-currency rates. The *risk premium* is defined as the difference between the forward discount and the predicted change in the spot rate. In theory, the risk premium should explain some portion of the discount. Of course, when the yen trades at a premium, and investors predict that the currency will depreciate, as was the case on March 27, 1995, the risk premium exceeds the value of the discount.

Froot and Frankel indicate that there may well be a nonzero risk premium. But they argue that the behavior of the risk premium is not the major impediment preventing the forward discount from serving as an efficient predictor of future spot rates. In fact, for the period under discussion, the correlation between the risk premium and the forward discount prediction error is very close to zero.

Summary

Foreign-exchange traders engage in excessive speculation, stemming from heuristic-driven bias. In particular, foreign-exchange traders seem to overreact, bet on trends, and be overconfident. Therefore, the foreign-exchange market shares similar features with the pick-a-number game described in chapter 1. Foreign-exchange rates are affected by both fundamental economic factors and by sentiment. This is yet one more instance where heuristic-driven bias leads to market inefficiency.

Final Remarks

Behavioral finance is everywhere that people make financial decisions. Psychology is hard to escape; it touches every corner of the financial landscape, and it's important. Financial practitioners need to understand the impact that psychology has on them and on those around them. Practitioners ignore psychology at their peril.

I began this book with an excerpt from a quotation about a "change in psychology" that reads: "Well, I was worried about the change in the attitude of investors, particularly portfolio managers. . . . So, it was a decided change in psychology. There's no change in the fundamentals. I'm still bullish long term."[1]

You will have read the same point again, in the last chapter. There I included a quotation, invoking psychology, that read: "It isn't just economics at work now; it's a psychology that at times borders on panic."[2]

The two quotes pertain to different financial settings, one the market for U.S. equities and the other the market for foreign exchange. The quotations, coming from the first and last chapter, symbolically make the point that psychology is everywhere. Moreover, both quotations clearly indicate that psychology matters. What the authors of these and similar quotations are less clear about is what *psychology* means.

The goal of this book has been to explain the current state of thinking about what psychology means for finance. To accomplish this task, I organized the subject matter of behavioral finance into three broad themes: heuristic-driven bias, frame dependence, and inefficient markets. For the moment, let's focus on the first two. Heuristic-driven bias concerns the biases to which people are prone because they rely on heuristic rules of thumb. Frame dependence concerns issues of form and substance: People are very sensitive to issues of form, and so form can become substantive.

I wrote this book about practitioner psychology for a practitioner audience. Practitioners who read the book should learn to recognize heuristic-driven bias and frame dependence in themselves and in others. Both heuristic-driven bias and frame dependence predispose practitioners to commit specific errors. Recognizing behavior is the first step towards modifying behavior.

A place for final remarks is no place to recapitulate details about gambler's fallacy, loss aversion, or self-control. However, when it comes to the third theme, inefficient markets, I do want to reiterate a word about overconfidence.

An inefficient market means that price differs from fundamental value. The evidence that markets are inefficient is, by now, compelling. But behavioral finance emphasizes that smart-money investors, who are free from overconfidence, do not try to exploit every mispricing opportunity that they see. The smart-money investor:

- distinguishes luck from skill;
- recognizes that the mistakes of other traders produce an extra source of risk as well as a potential profit opportunity; and
- knows that only some risks are worth taking.

Overconfident investors who know only a *little* of behavioral finance can do themselves great harm trying to exploit market inefficiencies.

So, to the overconfident, and that means most of us:

Forewarned is forearmed.

Notes

Chapter 1

1. This occurred on the August 18, 1998, program *Wall $treet Week with Louis Rukeyser.*

2. A synonym for traditional finance is "standard finance." Meir Statman (1995a) wrote an intriguing 1995 article that he titled "Behavioral Finance vs. Standard Finance."

3. Proponents of traditional finance accept minor violations of error-free beliefs and frame independence, but argue that errors cancel out at the level of the market. For example, the errors by investors who are overly bullish get offset by the errors of investors who are excessively bearish. So the market finds just the right middle ground.

4. "Financial Planning: Win a Flight to the U.S." *Financial Times,* May 10, 1997.

5. Zero is also an equilibrium choice in this model.

6. There were 1,468 entries in this contest, and the average response was 18.91. There were 31 entries with the winning guess of 13.

7. Scholes has since left LTCM.

8. LTCM's returns were 19.9 percent in 1994, 42.8 percent in 1995, 40.8 percent in 1996, and 17.1 percent in 1997.

9. Royal Dutch shares are included in the S&P 500, and Shell is included in the FTSE (Financial Times Allshare Index). Notably, Royal Dutch share prices appear to be driven by the factors that drive the S&P 500, while Shell prices are driven by the factors that drive the FTSE 100.

10. Robert C. Merton, the Nobel laureate, is the son of Robert K. Merton, the well-known behaviorist whose 1948 work constitutes an important contribution to the understanding of self-fulfilling prophecies.

11. De Bondt–Thaler prescribes buying losers, whereas Shefrin-Statman points out that investors are reluctant to sell losers. This struck Merton as contradictory, and he stated that a "rational" investor would "find himself 'convicted' by his actions of one or the other cognitive failures." I remember Bob Merton telling me that he was especially struck by the fact that the two articles appeared back-to-back in the same journal issue.

12. In Shefrin-Statman, losers are portfolio specific, and reflect initial purchase price for the investor. In De Bondt–Thaler, losers are the worst-performing stocks during the past thirty-six months. A Shefrin-Statman loser may not be a De Bondt–Thaler loser, and vice versa.

Chapter 2

1. In case it's not clear: *Availability* is the principle; judging the frequency of occurrence by the number of instances that come readily to mind is the *heuristic rule of thumb*; being predisposed to ease of recall resulting from distortions in media coverage is the *bias*; and judging homicide to be a more frequent cause of death than stroke is the *error*.

2. I thank Barbara Stewart, Santa Clara University, for providing these data.

3. Keep in mind that the question pertains to those who graduate college.

4. Readers will see that representativeness plays a major role in many of the issues discussed in this volume. Some of the most important applications are predicting the market, picking stocks, choosing mutual funds, selecting money managers, and investing in initial public offerings (IPOs) and seasoned equity offerings (SEOs).

5. There is a technical issue about predicting autocorrelated time series. Is the autocorrelation positive or negative? Most economic and financial series feature positive autocorrelation, whereby above-average performance tends to be followed by above-average performance; likewise, below-average performance tends to be followed by below-average performance.

6. Michael Siconolfi, Anita Raghavan, and Mitchell Pacelle, "All Bets Are Off: How the Salesmanship and Brainpower Failed at Long-Term Capital," *Wall Street Journal*, 16 November 1998.

7. Jonathan Clements, "Getting Going: Behavioral Specialists Put Investors on Couch," *Wall Street Journal*, 28 November 1995.

Chapter 3

1. Miller made this statement at the University of Chicago conference on behavioral finance in October 1986, on the day the Nobel Prize committee announced that Franco Modigliani was to receive the prize for that year.

2. Loss aversion implies that people have a *predisposition* toward avoiding a certain loss. But I note that loss aversion can be counterbalanced by panic. In an interview with *Forbes* magazine titled "Management, Strategies, Trends: Living with the Bull, Preparing for the Bear," fund manager Martin Zweig compared his own behavior with that of Warren Buffett, stating: "I could never do what he does. He buys things and holds forever—correctly, because he recognizes that if you sell and pay taxes, it cuts your return. But my problem is, I can't sit through bear markets. Buffett says, if you can't afford to see your stock go down 30% or 40%, you shouldn't be in it. I can't take the pain. I built my technique based on what I can handle personally. This means I have to be in and out a lot. My main thing is, I want to survive. I want to be there, and when the big bear market comes, I don't want to get chewed up" (Brimelow 1998).

3. "Today's Rogue Traders Just Want to Save Face," *Associated Press*, 13 September 1995.

4. I thank Bob Saltmarsh, who was treasurer at Apple during this period, for sharing his insights about the Newton with me.

5. Jim Carlton, "Apple Drops Newton, an Idea Ahead of Its Time," *Wall Street Journal*, 2 March 1998.

6. Because their studies used students, Thaler and Johnson employed stakes that were smaller by a factor of 100.

7. So called because gamblers who receive a gift of chips from the house tend to be more tolerant of risk, since they begin by seeing themselves ahead.

Chapter 4

1. Michael Siconolfi, Anita Raghavan, and Mitchell Pacelle, "All Bets Are Off: How Salesmanship and Brainpower Failed at Long-Term Capital," *Wall Street Journal*, 16 November 1998.

2. Ibid.

3. I thank Jacob Thomas, coauthor of Bernard and Thomas (1989) for providing me with the data for this figure.

4. The questions that I used involved stakes that were near the historical growth rates of real personal consumption expenditures.

5. In replicating the Shiller-Pound survey in 1998, I obtained a similar result, almost 40 minutes.

6. I thank Bob Shiller for providing me with this data, updated to 1999.

7. Although he did not shock his audience, most of whom were nodding off at Greenspan's after-dinner speech at the American Enterprise Institute, according to an unnamed source from the Securities and Exchange Commission who was present that evening.

8. Along with interest rates, inflation, and tolerance for risk.

9. In chapter 2 I indicated that the 1998 closing value of the Dow was 9181, but would have been 652,230 if dividends were taken into account.

10. As can be seen from figure 4-3, the low D/P does not stem from low D, but from high P!

11. In chapter 2, I discussed gambler's fallacy in connection with Robert Farrell's predictions for below-average stock returns. Although Campbell and Shiller consider mean reversion, and predict below-average stock returns over the next ten years, they do not succumb to gambler's fallacy. Their analysis is based on the relationship between valuation measures and subsequent returns. I hasten to emphasize that from a statistical perspective, the confidence associated with the 1996 Campbell-Shiller prediction for the 1997–2006 period is very low. This is because the value of P/E at year-end 1996 was at the extreme end of its historical range, which is where prediction confidence is lowest. It is worth noting that the *Wall Street Journal* reported John Campbell to have been very confident in his analysis. Campbell hedged his entire stock portfolio using futures, as a means of

selling his stocks without triggering capital gains. See "The Outlook: Sometimes Stocks Go Nowhere for Years," by David Wessel, January 13, 1997. At the end of 1996, the Dow Jones Industrial Average stood at 6448. It crossed 11,000 on May 3, 1999.

12. Shiller's work, and that of LeRoy and Porter (1981), which was published at the same time, was based on some controversial technical assumptions. Much of the debate has centered on some of these assumptions. In addition, his measure of fundamental value is based on a time invariant expected real interest rate and the stream of future dividends. Yet, managers appear to smooth dividends over time. See Alan Kleidon (1986) and Robert Merton (1987b).

13. The *Wall Street Journal* makes the same point in connection with a sharp market drop that took place in August 1998 (see chapter 5).

14. What is wrong with this picture? From year-end 1993 through year-end 1998, earnings on the S&P 500 grew at 11.9 percent a year and dividends grew at 4.2 percent a year, but the return on the S&P 500 was 24 percent a year. Earnings in 1997 and 1998 earnings grew at 3 percent and –4 percent at a time when the S&P 500 returned 33.3 percent and 28.4 percent. What dramatic differences are investors expecting in future earnings, dividends, interest rates, or rates of inflation?

15. The leading P/E ratio was 26.46.

16. The high P/E environment in the U.S. market, relative to the historical norm, reminds me of the Japanese stock market in the 1980s. In February 1999, the Nikkei stood at 14,232. But it was over three times as high a decade earlier when the P/E on Japanese stocks was over 50. During 1986 and 1987, the Nikkei had risen by more than 28 percent a year. In January, 1988 concerns about the Japanese market being in a bubble started to surface: see Kenneth French and James Poterba (1991). But despite being overvalued the Japanese market rose by a further 64 percent over the next two years. But what about the long-term return? One hundred yen invested in the Nikkei in January 1988 would have been worth 71 yen in March 1999. Yet an investor who pulled out of Japanese stocks in January, 1988, would have spent the next two years kicking himself.

17. During the market's strong performance in 1997 and 1998, *Wall $treet Week with Louis Rukeyser* host Louis Rukeyser continually chided panelist Gail Dudack, the most bearish of all the panelists on his program.

18. E. S. Browning, "Stock Market's New Year's Party Keeps Going," *Wall Street Journal*, 11 January 1999.

19. Browning, "Market's New Year's Party."

20. As of January 1999, Behavioral Value had been operating for three years, during which time it posted returns of 18.3 percent, net of fees. The Russell 2000 returned 14.4 percent in the same period.

21. Russ Fuller, interview by author, February 2, 1999. Fuller and Thaler apply a screening procedure to the De Bondt–Thaler losers, in order to select stocks for the Behavioral Value fund. A generic De Bondt–Thaler strategy

has an excess return (alpha) of between 3 and 4 percent. Fuller tells me that his screening procedure sifts out the most underpriced 10 percent, with the resulting alpha being 11 percent.

Chapter 5

1. Earnings had grown by 11 percent and 14 percent respectively. The yield on the 30-year Treasury bond had fallen from above 8 percent to 6.6 percent.

2. This is a much-quoted phrase from a speech given by Greenspan on December 5 at the American Enterprise Institute.

3. Jonathan Laing, "High Anxiety: As Market Gurus Debate, Investors Watch Nervously After Last Week's Slide," *Barron's*, 10 August 1998.

4. Unless we are dealing with negative autocorrelation, which is not the case with stock market returns.

5. Abby Cohen's predictions were certainly higher than average, but below the historical average. During her appearance on the program *Wall $treet Week with Louis Rukeyser,* on January 8, 1999, program host Louis Rukeyser mentioned that her actual predictions appeared to be on the low side. Cohen responded by saying that Goldman Sachs announces prediction levels that they believe to be attainable.

6. De Bondt's study also examines the predictions for future inflation and the growth of industrial production.

7. Greg Ip, "The Final Bears May Be Giving Up: Bull's Victory Prompts Fears," *Wall Street Journal*, 13 April 1998.

8. This finding is statistically significant at the 5 percent level.

9. Greg Ip, "It's Official: Stock Market's Pups Are Likely to Be Bulls," *Wall Street Journal,* 8 July 1998.

10. This quiz is a variant of the one found in Russo and Schoemaker (1989).

11. Lauren R. Rublin, "A Very Good Year," *Barron's*, 30 December 1996.

12. Lauren R. Rublin, "Another Chance," *Barron's*, 23 June 1997.

13. Ibid.

14. Lauren R. Rublin, "Sober Salute: It Was a Great Market Year, So Why All the Frowns?" *Barron's*, 5 January 1998.

15. An analogous statement holds when the market has been declining. They believe there is only a little room left for movement on the downside, but a lot of room left for movement on the upside.

16. The data on individual investors comes from the Association of Individual Investors (AAII).

17. Steven Mufson wrote the article.

18. On the television program *Wall $treet Week with Louis Rukeyser,* 27 December 1996.

19. Notice that Acampora had retreated from his prediction of 10,000, in fact pushing it out to 1999.

20. Jonathan Laing, "High Anxiety: As Market Gurus Debate, Investors Watch Nervously After Last Week's Slide," *Barron's,* 10 August 1998.

21. For a discussion of events pertaining to Asia, see chapter 21.

22. Leslie Scism and E. S. Browning, "Heard on the Street: In Battle of the Stock Market Gurus, Bulls Win a Round," *Wall Street Journal,* 6 August 1988.

23. In chapter 6, I discuss in further detail the way that technical analysts treat measures of sentiment.

24. Greg Ip and Aaron Lucchetti, "Mood Swing: Stock Market Plunges as Negative Sentiment Spreads to Blue Chips," *Wall Street Journal,* 5 August 1998.

25. Michael Santoli, "A Ray of Sunshine," *Barron's,* 31 August 1998. Those interviewed were Marshall Acuff (Salomon Smith Barney), Byron Wien (Morgan Stanley Dean Witter), Douglas Cliggott (J. P. Morgan), Abby Joseph Cohen (Goldman Sachs), and Elizabeth Mackay (Bear Stearns). Acuff stated that this was not the end of the bull market, but rather a cyclical correction. Wien described it as a temporary bottom from which to rally. Cliggott restated his target of 1065 for the S&P 500 at year-end. Cohen restated her target of 1150 for the S&P 500 at year-end. Mackay predicted that returns from stocks would lie in the historically normal range.

26. A friend of mine learned this lesson, but not by tossing coins. He recently welcomed the birth of his first son after five daughters.

27. Some may feel that a situation involving tosses of a fair coin produces the least predictability, making it an inappropriate analogy for a financial market. Here is a variant that might come closer. Let there be two coins: a gold coin where the probability of tossing a head is 80 percent, and a silver coin where the probability of tossing a tail is 80 percent. Suppose that after every head we toss the gold coin, and after every tail we toss the silver coin. That makes long runs much more likely than when a fair coin is tossed. More important, it makes short-run predictions reliable. If the last toss was a head, and you predict that the next toss will be a head, you will be right four out of five times, much better than what Wall Street strategists do. But how about the long term? Suppose I begin by tossing the gold coin. What is the probability that a head will appear on the fifth toss? It is definitely more that 50 percent—in fact, the answer is 53.9 percent. On the tenth toss, the probability is down to 50.3 percent, not much different than with a fair coin. The point is that predictability evaporates very quickly.

28. Moreover, Acampora tends to change his long-term forecasts quite frequently. He justifies these changes by saying, "People say, 'It sounds like one day you say one thing and another day you say another thing,' but

that's what they pay me to do: call significant turns. And we've had some very significant turns in a very short time. See Mufson, "Joe Investor."

29. Santoli, "Ray of Sunshine."

30. Lauren R. Rublin, "Another Chance," *Barron's*, 23 June 1997.

Chapter 6

1. In chapter 5, I discussed Richard Bernstein's work showing that an index of recommended allocations by strategists is negatively correlated with subsequent returns. However, there is no such relationship to speak of when it comes to the predictions made by newsletter writers.

2. Greg Ip, "The Final Bears May Be Giving Up: Bull's Victory Prompts Fears," *Wall Street Journal*, 13 April 1998.

3. *Investors Intelligence*, November 26, 1984.

4. Ip, "Final Bears."

5. Greg Ip, "Market's Logic," *Wall Street Journal*, 17 May 1997.

6. Greg Ip's *Wall Street Journal* article, "Final Bears," mentions that sentiment indicators are usually used to time short-term moves in the market. The character of figure 6-1 is no different when it comes to short term moves as when it comes to long term rates.

7. John Dorfman, "Your Money Matters," *Wall Street Journal*, 26 January 1989.

8. Clements, Jonathan, "Getting Going," *Wall Street Journal*, 12 May 1998. "The Truth Investors Don't Want to Hear on Index Funds and Market Soothsayers."

9. Specifically, when advisors are bearish, the market is no more likely to go up than down.

10. In a fascinating article, Leda Cosmides and John Tooby (1992) differentiate this heuristic from another heuristic that efficiently tests for evidence of cheating on social contracts. In some circumstances, the latter leads to the right algorithm for testing the validity of "If P, then Q." For example, suppose P is "drink an alcoholic beverage" and Q is "underage." If your job is to enforce this rule in a bar, whom must you check? People you know to be underage (not-Q) and those you know to be drinking alcoholic beverages (P).

11. The following experiment by psychologist Peter Wason (1960) illustrates the point. Imagine that I show you four cards. I tell you that each card has a letter on one side and an integer on the other. But when I show you the cards for the first time, you get to see only one side. The four cards I show you have on them *A, B,* 2, and 3. Consider an if-P-then-Q hypothesis about these four cards: Every card with a vowel on one side (P) has an even number on the other side (Q). The hypothesis may or may not be true. Your task is to verify whether the hypothesis is true by turning over as *few*

cards as possible. Most people who play this game choose *A* and 2, or *A* alone. They do so because turning these cards provides *confirming* evidence. But this is the wrong way to go. The efficient way of examining the hypothesis is to turn over cards that might *falsify* the hypothesis. Consider the falsification potential of each card in turn. Suppose we turn the card featuring an *A*. We will find either an even number or an odd number. If we find an even number, we have evidence supporting the hypothesis. However, if we find an odd number we know that the hypothesis is false. Next, suppose we turn over the card with the letter *B*. This card provides us with no evidence to judge the veracity of the hypothesis, since the hypothesis says nothing about cards featuring consonants. Next, consider the card featuring a 2. If we turn it over, we might find a vowel. This would be consistent with the hypothesis. Alternatively, we might find a consonant. That would be irrelevant to the hypothesis. Hence, this card offers no opportunity for falsification. Last, suppose we turn over the card featuring a 3. If we find a vowel, we know that the hypothesis is false. A consonant provides no information to support or falsify the hypothesis. So the two cards that offer the potential for falsification feature *A* and 3; i.e., P and not Q. However, as mentioned, most subjects choose *A* and 2, or *A* alone. Notice that while *A* allows for both support and falsification, 2 allows for support only.

12. There is a flip side to this story, one that also holds little validity. Suppose we look at the periods associated with market tops, and ask whether sentiment tends to be especially bullish at these times. The answer is no more bullish or bearish than at other times.

13. Ip, "Final Bears."

14. See the discussion about Werner De Bondt's (1993) "betting on trends" concept in chapter 5.

15. The reaction to the Dow is a little different. Before the crash, a 10 percent increase in the Dow led to a 6.7 percent increase in the Bullish Sentiment Index, whereas the same increase afterward only led to a 3.6 percent increase.

16. Less than they would have been in a less volatile market, that is.

17. The correlations between the different sentiment indicators are quite low, somewhere around 25 to 35 percent for most pairs of indexes. The strongest correlation is 40 percent, and it is between the discount on an equally weighted portfolio of closed-end equity funds and the AAII sentiment index. I thank Bhaskaran Swaminathan for providing me with historical data on closed-end fund discounts, and Meir Statman for historical data on the advisory sentiment index and AAII sentiment index.

Chapter 7

1. I thank Rich Dubroff, executive producer of *Wall $treet Week with Louis Rukeyser,* and writer Georgette Jasen of the *Wall Street Journal* for furnishing me with the data underlying these claims.

2. See Andrei Shleifer and Robert Vishny (1997) for a discussion of the limits to arbitrage.

3. There is varying terminology used to describe analysts' recommendations. Most use a 5-point scale: strong buy, buy, neutral, sell, strong sell. First Call uses buy, buy/hold, hold, hold/sell, sell.

4. Examples of the three types are Raymond James Financial in St. Petersburg, Florida (local), A.G. Edwards in St. Louis (regional), and Travellers/Salomon/Smith Barney in New York (national).

5. John Dorfman, "How Stock-Pick Prowess of the Brokers Is Judged," *Wall Street Journal*, 2 February 1990.

6. John Dorfman, "Edwards Wins '88 Stock-Picking Crown With Shearson Tops for 30-Month Period," *Wall Street Journal*, 3 February 1989.

7. John Dorfman, "Brokerage Firms Beat the Market with Stock Picks," *Wall Street Journal*, 25 February 1993.

8. I am grateful to Rick Chrabaszewski at Zacks for preparing and providing me with this data.

9. There is always a question of survivorship bias: whether we are focusing only on the winners and ignoring the losers because they drop out. However, the results reported over the period 1993–1997 are based on a stable group of brokerage firms.

10. Brad Barber, Reuven Lehavy, Maureen McNichols, and Brett Trueman (1998) confirm Womack's findings. Their study covers the wider period 1986–1996.

11. "Intel Stk up; Merrill Sees Declining 80386 Inventories," February 1, 1989, Dow Jones News Service Ticker. I thank Kent Womack for kindly sharing his data with me.

12. Kurlak cited evidence that the excess inventory of 80386 microprocessors had been worked down by Intel customers, that IBM was increasing its orders to Intel, and that Intel's own inventory was also declining to more normal levels.

13. John Dorfman, "Your Money Matters: Few Brokerage Firms Beat the Market Last Year," *Wall Street Journal*, 8 February 1996.

14. John Dorfman, "Your Money Matters: Latest Stock Picks of Brokers Fare Poorly," *Wall Street Journal*, 22 May 1997.

15. Geert Rouwenhorst (1997) documents that the momentum effect occurs on global markets.

16. I discuss this issue in more detail in chapter 5.

17. John Dorfman, "Your Money Matters: Weekend Report: Following a Broker's Advice Can Reap Nice Gains—Until You Get the Tax Bill," *Wall Street Journal*, 15 August 1997.

18. In an article by Daniel P. Wiener that appeared in the June 19, 1989 issue of *U.S. News & World Report*, the author indicated that all participating

brokerage firms recommended only five stocks. The article was titled "News You Can Use; Investing. What to Do When Your Broker Says 'Buy.' A Stock Awarded a Thumbs Up by Wall Street May Be the Last Investment You Should Be Considering."

19. John Dorfman, "Your Money Matters: Stock Pickers Do Well, Even If Their Employers Don't," *Wall Street Journal*, 9 May 1989.

20. John Dorfman, "Wall Street Beat the Market in Third Quarter," *Wall Street Journal*, 8 November 1995. My reading of the data shows that the PaineWebber recommended stocks were about as volatile as the average recommended stock. Compared to the S&P 500, PaineWebber stocks were 25.7 percent more volatile. The most volatile recommendations were those of Alex. Brown, which were 64 percent more volatile than the S&P 500.

21. John Dorfman, "Your Money Matters: Successful Stock Pickers in Quarter Avoided High Tech," Wall Street Journal, 7 November 1988.

22. John Dorfman, "Edwards Wins '88 Stock-Picking Crown, with Shearson Tops for 30-Month Period," *Wall Street Journal*, 3 February 1989.

23. De Bondt and Thaler (1994) credit Humphrey Neill (1954) for having popularized the term *contrarian*, Neill in turn credits economist William Stanley Jevons.

24. When I ran my investor expectations survey, I also included the *Fortune* magazine questionnaire. I obtained results very similar to the results reported by *Fortune* magazine.

25. Subject to the qualification that P/E is not negative. Negative earnings present some complications.

26. The winner-loser effect has other puzzles associated with it. First, although past losers tend to outperform the market for five consecutive years, all the action takes place in January. This is surprising—and troubling. If price movements are truly driven by overreaction, then it is difficult to understand why the correction only occurs one month in the year, and always the same month. The small-firm effect, which has not reappeared with the strength it exhibited prior to 1980, also appears to be a January phenomenon.

27. By growth stocks, I mean stocks with a low book-to-market ratio.

28. Like Lakonishok, Shleifer, and Vishny, we control for size and market-to-book equity.

29. Fama's argument reminds me of a story about a retired attorney who is writing his memoirs. The attorney recalls the time when he was young and inexperienced, and because of this was losing cases he should have won. But as time goes on, he learns from his mistakes, so much so that in later years he wins cases he feels he should rightly have lost. Thus, he concludes his memoirs by stating that on average, justice was done. By the same token, markets are efficient.

30. Barbara Donnelly, "Your Money Matters: Investors' Overreactions May Yield Opportunities in the Stock Market," *Wall Street Journal*, 7 January 1988.

31. A study by Paul Griffen, Jennifer Jones, and Mark Zmijewski (1995) finds that the stocks recommended on *Wall $treet Week with Louis Rukeyser* do indeed outperform the market by 4 percent, and that the recommendations on the program have been large, low beta, high price-to-book stocks.

Chapter 8

1. "Stephens Inc. Starts Plexus Corp. with Buy Rating," *Dow Jones*, 2 February 1997.

2. Jay Palmer, "Growth Versus Value: Computer Searches Turn Up Promising Stock Picks for Both Persuasions," *Barron's*, 2 June 1997.

3. A December 18 report on the *Dow Jones News Service* offered similar remarks: "According to A.G. Edwards & Sons analyst Mark Jordan, the company's projection is 'about $10 million' below his estimate. He attributed the shortfall to weak orders and volumes from 'one large customer,' as well as a general 'tightening of order flow' in the electronics industry. Jordan, who rates the company maintain, said he thinks it is 'solidly profitable, with margins under control,'" but he also expects slower sales growth for the second quarter."

4. Kathleen Gallagher, "Plexus Shares Take 44 Percent Nose-Dive," *Milwaukee Journal Sentinel*, 19 December 1997. The next three excerpts are also from this article.

5. I am grateful to Fred Stanske and Russ Fuller of Fuller and Thaler Asset Management for their help in preparing this chapter.

6. Leslie P. Norton, "Mutual Funds: Fund of Information. Bad Behavior: If It Looks Like a Duck, Don't Buy It; The Cold Hand of Sheldon Jacob," *Barron's*, 5 January 1998.

7. See the discussion in chapter 2 on the illusion of validity.

8. This is consistent with work by Kent Womack (1996).

9. The size effect is consistent with evidence provided by Bernard and Thomas (1989) that post-earnings-announcement drift is stronger for smaller firms. And larger firms do have more analyst coverage. The Plexus case illustrates something about the process by which analyst coverage grows with firm size.

Chapter 9

1. Robert McGough and Michael Siconolfi, "Buy and Hold: Their Money's Fleeing, But Some Investors Just Keep Holding On," *Wall Street Journal*, 18

June 1997. Their article also describes the case of Melvin Klahr discussed here. The quotes by Klahr are from this article.

2. Ibid. McGough and Siconolfi attribute this statement to Wall Street historians.

3. Robert McGough, "At Dead-Last Steadman, Past Is Prologue," *Wall Street Journal*, 15 April 1997.

Chapter 10

1. Dread is extreme anxiety.

2. O'Neill has changed the names to preserve anonymity.

3. The time period for O'Neill's study was the late 1980s, so the income figure would have to be adjusted up significantly to place it into current dollars.

4. Jonathan Clements, "Getting Going: If Santa Had This List, He'd Be Wiser, Wealthier and Ready for the New Year," *Wall Street Journal*, 23 December 1997.

5. Jonathan Clements, "Getting Going: How Much Should You Invest in Stocks? It All Depends on Goals and Time Frame," *Wall Street Journal*, 11 February 1997.

6. Ibid.

7. Jonathan Clements, "Getting Going: Need Cash in Five Years? Dumping Stocks Isn't Always the Best Investment Strategy," *Wall Street Journal*, 7 January 1997.

8. The investors varied in location, age (mid-twenties to their mid-fifties), income ($30,000 to upwards of $500,000 per year), and wealth. The responses across all three groups were similar.

9. In my survey, I also examined how the choice of securities depended on the time horizon attached to a given goal. I found that when the time horizon is short, such as for a vacation or a home remodel, and investors feel close to being able to fund the goal at the end of their horizon, then the tendency is to invest in low-risk securities such as money market funds. Those investors who indicated that they do not currently have the resources to fund a goal said that they relied on stock options and commodities to provide the necessary funds. This was particularly true for luxury items such as boats and jewelry.

10. In the interest of disclosure, I should mention that I served as a consultant in the design of the Financial Engines software.

11. There are numerous other examples of securities designed to appeal to cautiously hopeful investors. Merrill Lynch offers S&P 500 Market Index Target-Term Securities (MITTS), which mature in five years and pay the principal but no interest. Instead of interest, they pay 115 percent of the S&P 500 gain, if there is any. Another example involves so-called Click

Funds, which offer index-linked investments with specific downside protection. These funds have recently become very popular in the Netherlands. See Smid and Tempelaar (1997). Investors have also been known to simulate securities such as these. John McConnell and Eduardo Schwartz (1992) report that some Merrill Lynch investors held large balances in their money market accounts, and used the interest to buy call options.

12. I discussed the issue of skewed confidence intervals in chapter 5.

13. At least, these are the types of stocks they hold.

14. The broad issues involve the role of financial market regulation as a means of dealing with potential conflicts between fairness and efficiency.

15. Rebecca Buckman, "These Days, Online Trading Can Become an Addiction," *Wall Street Journal*, 1 February 1999.

Chapter 11

1. Not their real names. Ira and Jeannie engaged the services of a financial planner, and their case became part of a financial-planning database.

2. These statistics come from the financial-planning database containing Ira and Jeannie's case.

3. Greg Ip, "It's Official: Stock Market's Pups Are Likely to Be Bulls," *Wall Street Journal*, 8 July 1998.

4. This question is based on an actual situation. In 1974, the utility Consolidated Edison did omit a quarterly dividend, and many of its shareholders complained, indicating that they would be forced to cut consumption expenditures.

5. There are other puzzles about dividends. Roni Michaely, Richard Thaler, and Kent Womack (1995) study the price reaction to dividend initiations and omissions. Investors react positively to initiations, and negatively to omissions. But the reaction to omissions is larger. In both cases, investors appear to underreact, in that the full price impact takes many months. Interestingly, they find little evidence of a clientele effect, meaning that investors do not move in and out of stocks sharply in response to dividend initiations and omissions. Shlomo Benartzi, Roni Michaely, and Richard Thaler (1997) show that firms raise their dividends when their earnings have been rising, and reduce them when their earnings have been falling. However, these changes carry little predictive power about future earnings growth, with one exception. Firms that increase their dividends are less likely to experience a drop in future earnings.

Chapter 12

1. The folks at Fidelity Investments certainly hope so. In 1998, they used Peter Lynch in a series of television and newspaper advertisements, teaming him up with well-known comedians such as Lily Tomlin.

2. Gerard Achstatter, "Fidelity's Peter Lynch: How He Conducted the Research That Made His Fund Best," *Investor's Business Daily*, 2 February 1998.

3. I am grateful to Tisha Findeison at Vanguard Fiduciary Trust for providing me with this statistic.

4. Achstatter, "Peter Lynch."

5. By my rough estimate. There are over 6,500 funds that the *Wall Street Journal* screens in consort with Lipper Analytical Services, Inc.

6. The evidence on this point is reviewed in Goetzmann and Peles (1994).

7. Jonathan Clements, "Looking to Find the Next Peter Lynch—Try Luck and Ask the Right Questions," *Wall Street Journal*, 27 January 1998.

8. Personal interview; 3 March 1998.

9. Adam Shell, "Making Money in Mutuals: Should You Sell a Fund That's Past Its Prime?" Investor's Business Daily, 3 March 1998.

10. Jeffrey M. Laderman with Geoffrey Smith, "The Best Mutual Funds: BW's Ratings Tell You Who Gave the Best Returns—with the Least Amount of Risk," *Business Week*, 2 February 1998.

11. See Tom Petruno, "Your Money: Who is the Typical Fund Owner?" *Los Angeles Times*, 1 August 1996. This article summarized the findings of both the ICI study and the Vanguard study.

12. Jonathan Clements, "Abracadabra, and a Putnam Fund Disappears," *Wall Street Journal*, 5 May 1993.

13. There are survivorship issues that arise in this connection and paint an overly positive picture of the mutual fund industry. See Brown and Goetzmann (1992).

14. Charles Gasparino, "SEC Chairman Levitt to Criticize Fund Industry over Fee Disclosure," *Wall Street Journal*, 15 May 1998.

15. Andrew Bary, "The Trader: Fund Managers Get Rich, But Not Their Customers," *Barron's*, 29 December 1997.

16. Kathryn Haines, "Fund Attracts Attention: Gets High Ratings," *Wall Street Journal*, 13 June 1997.

17. Eric J. Savitz, "Silicon Values: An Interview with Kevin Landis and Ken Kam," *Barron's*, 23 June 1997.

Chapter 13

1. I am grateful to William Kehr, Andrew Schell, and Brad Shaw of John R. Nuveen and Company for their helpful comments on this material.

2. Andrew Bary, "After Rout, Many Muni Funds Sell at Steep Discounts," *Barron's*, 29 November 1993.

3. In fact, 1993 was an extremely active year for the introduction of new closed-end funds. During 1993, 126 new funds were brought to market at a value of $19.1 billion. Among those was Nuveen Premium Income Fund 4 (NPT), which began trading on February 17, 1993, at an initial price of—can you guess?—$15.

4. Leslie Scism, "Quarterly Mutual Funds Review: Closed-end Bond Funds Look Cheap," *Wall Street Journal*, 7 January 1994.

5. Andrew Bary, "After Rout."

6. Ibid.

7. Russ Wiles, "Mutual Funds: Your Money: Automatic Opening for a Closed-end Portfolio," *Los Angeles Times*, 11 May 1997.

8. Deborah Lohse, "Small Stock Focus," *Wall Street Journal*, 28 July 1997.

9. Peter C. DuBois, "Closed-end Mania Is Ba-a-a-ack," *Barron's*, 3 January 1994.

10. Michael Sesit, "Capital Floods into Germany at Frantic Pace," *Wall Street Journal*, 8 January 1990.

11. Andrew Bary, "After Rout."

12. The 150 percent comes from the 2-to-1 ratio of common to preferred: $150\% = (2+1)/2$.

13. Bary, "After Rout."

Chapter 14

1. Eric Schine, "Interview with Robert Citron," *Los Angeles Times*, 18 April 1988.

2. Downloaded from Dow Jones News Service. "Merrill Lynch Forecasts: Yld Curve May Invert Next Year, " 6 December 1994.

3. Sarah Lubman and John R. Emshwiller, "Hubris and Ambition in Orange County: Robert Citron's Story," *Wall Street Journal*, 18 January 1995.

4. David Lynch, "Orange County/How it happened/How golden touch turned into crisis," *USA Today*, 23 December 1994.

5. Daniel Kadlec, "Some Warning Signs to Remember," *USA Today*, 6 April 1994.

6. Lou Cannon, "The Great Orange County Bust," *The Washington Post*, 28 December 1994.

7. Mark Platte and Jeff Brazil, "O. C. Treasurer Thrust into Spotlight over Risk Claims," *Los Angeles Times*, 30 April 1994.

8. *Los Angeles Times*, same as footnote 7.

9. These events were documented in the *Los Angeles Times*. See Tracy Weber

and Dexter Filkins, "Woes in Advance, Panel Told," *Los Angeles Times*, 29 December 1995.

10. David J. Lynch, "Orange County: How It Happened," *USA Today*, 23 December 1994.

11. Ronald D. Picur, "The $2 Billion Gamble: A Step-by-Step Guide on How to Prevent the Orange County Debacle from Occurring in Your Neighborhood," *Chicago Tribune*, 19 December 1994.

12. See chapter 9 for a more detailed discussion of this issue.

13. Lubman and Emshwiller, "Hubris and Ambition."

14. Moreover, Citron did not make it a policy to hold all securities to maturity. The April 5, 1995, issue of the *Wall Street Journal* reports that his portfolio turned over at the rate of 250 percent a year between 1990 and 1993.

15. Dana Parsons, "The Wizard Himself Peels Back Layers of His Own Legend," *Los Angeles Times*, 18 January 1995.

16. Self-attribution bias is the term used to describe conditional attribution. A positive outcome is attributed to the self, a negative outcome to bad luck or a scapegoat.

17. William Power, "Heard on the Street: Investment Strategists Rally to Defend Merrill Expert," *Wall Street Journal*, 18 January 1995.

18. Brad Shaw from John R. Nuveen tells me that events such as those that occurred in Orange County lead to mispricing of otherwise sound municipal bonds because of "guilt by association." In these circumstances, companies like Nuveen are able to purchase underpriced bonds, another instance of inefficient markets. Telephone interview, 22 February 1999.

19. Bernice Napach, "Orange County: Lessons in Risk Management," *Investor's Business Daily*, 30 December 1994.

20. I thank Kim Rupert and Louis Radovich of MMS for graciously providing me with data on interest-rate forecasts.

21. Actually, let me first ask a related question. Suppose we look at how frequently stories have appeared in English language publications since 1970. On the topics of sex, inflation, and unemployment, which topic appeared most frequently, and which topic appeared least frequently? Economist Robert Shiller (1995) reports that inflation topped the list, followed by sex and unemployment. Most people find that fact pretty striking.

22. Suzanne McGee and Gregory Zuckerman, "Stocks and Bonds Catch Fire as Inflation Cools," *Wall Street Journal*, 17 September 1998.

Chapter 15

1. I thank Harry Fong, associate vice president for finance, and Robert Warren, vice president for finance, for their insights about the management of Santa Clara University's endowment portfolio.

2. The committee also holds emergency meetings. For example, the university was invested with Barings Bank at the time it collapsed as a result of trading losses by Nicholas Leeson. By moving quickly the committee was able to liquidate the university's position and reduce the magnitude of loss incurred.

3. This is a message committee members say they constantly hear: Be averse to risk and diversify. The general feeling of the committee is that both actions would reduce the impact of a severe decline in the market on the university's portfolio.

4. In a recent incident, a money manager was replaced because the committee was concerned that he did not spend enough time visiting companies. They also noted that they were disappointed with the "service" he provided.

5. See chapters 1, 6, and 7 in connection with other reference-point effects.

6. Personal interview with associate vice president for finance, 20 May 1998.

7. Although members of the investment committee focus their attention on which managers beat their benchmarks, Cambridge Associates does look at covariance (the extent to which the different managers' performance covary with each other). They do so because they want to avoid managers performing in lockstep with each other.

8. At the end of 1996, RJF had $66 million under management. This figure grew to $163 million at the end of 1997, and to $428 million at the end of 1998.

9. Personal telephone interview, 17 February 1999.

10. SEI has since moved on to run a family of mutual funds.

11. Many of the reasons were covered in chapter 12, which discussed open-ended mutual funds.

12. For example, the 1997 PBS television documentary series *Beyond Wall Street: The Art of Investing*, cohosted by Jane Bryant Quinn and Andrew Tobias, featured an episode titled "90% of the Game."

Chapter 16

1. Garrison Keillor, of the radio show *Prairie Home Companion,* created Lake Wobegon.

2. The mean response is 57.2 percent, and the range has been 48.7 percent to 67.7 percent.

3. Carla Lazzareschi, "AT&T's Allen Bets Legacy on Computer Deal," *Los Angeles Times,* 14 May 1991.

4. Carla Lazzareschi, "High-Tech Hybrids: The Rocky Results of Such Mergers Raise Questions About AT&T's Bid for NCR," *Los Angeles Times,* 30 December 1990.

5. Carla Lazzareschi, "AT&T's Allen Bets Legacy on Computer Deal," *Los Angeles Times*, 14 May 1991.

6. Note that the Dow Jones industrial average rose by 5.94 that day, closing at 2,565.59.

7. Lazzareschi, "High-Tech Hybrids."

8. AT&T felt able to meet NCR's $110 price because the market had increased dramatically since it had first offered $90. But it also agreed to pay this price even if the market fell before the agreement was completed.

9. John J. Keller, "AT&T Sells Stake in Sun Microsystems, Which Buys Back Five Million Shares," *Wall Street Journal*, 4 June 1991.

10. John J. Keller, "NCR '91 Talks to Be 'Materially Below' Forecasts Made to AT&T During Talks," *Wall Street Journal*, 9 September 1991.

11. A fourth business, AT&T Capital Corporation, was sold to the public under a different name.

12. A financial market is strong-form efficient when prices correctly reflect *all* available information, both public and private.

13. There may be complicating factors that deal with information transmitted during the bidding process. Investors may learn something positive about the acquiring firm through the fact that it is bidding (e.g., it has money to spend on acquisitions), or negative if the bid is abandoned (e.g., it does not have the money).

14. This finding is from Klaczynski and Fauth (1996).

15. As I began work on this chapter in January 1998, Compaq Computer Corp. announced its intention to acquire Digital Equipment Corp. Journalist Raju Narisetti raised a host of red flags when he reviewed the history of similar attempts in an article titled "History Holds Some Hard Lessons for Compaq," which appeared in the January 28, 1998, issue of the *Wall Street Journal*. The list of failed ventures that were similar now included AT&T's takeover of NCR, IBM's takeover of Rolm, Silicon Graphics' takeover of the supercomputer firm Cray, and Hewlett-Packard's takeover of workstation manufacturer Apollo.

Chapter 17

1. Aaron Lucchetti, "Marketwatch's IPO Continues the Boom in Web Stocks," *Wall Street Journal*, 15 January 1999.

2. I thank Jay Ritter for his very helpful comments on this chapter.

3. William Power, "Heard on the Street: Boston Chicken Soars 143% on Its First IPO Day," *Wall Street Journal*, 10 November 1993.

4. See "IPO Focus -2: Hot Stocks, If You Can Get Them," *Dow Jones News Service—Ticker*, 24 November 1993.

5. The author was Scott Reeves.

6. Reeves, "Market Sees Netscape."

7. William Power, "Heard on the Street: Boston Chicken Soars 143% on Its First IPO Day," *Wall Street Journal*, 10 November 1993.

8. Scott Reeves, "Netscape's IPO: Brokers Say Demand Very High." *Dow Jones News Service*, 9 August 1995.

9. David Einstein, "Netscape Slides 20%, Layoffs Loom," *San Francisco Chronicle*, 6 January 1998.

10. Molly Baker and Joan E. Rigdon, "Netscape's IPO Gets an Explosive Welcome," *Wall Street Journal*, 8 August 1995.

11. Aaron Lucchetti, "EarthWeb and theglobe.com Defy IPO Gravity," *Wall Street Journal*, 16 November 1998.

12. AOL's takeover of Netscape also took place in the midst of a major antitrust trial against Microsoft. Attorneys for the Justice Department and twenty states charged Microsoft with inflicting harm on Netscape by employing anticompetitive practices in the browser market.

13. John Fitzgibbon, an editor at the newsletter *IPO Reporter,* describes these events as "insanity.com trading."

14. Reeves, "Netscape's IPO."

15. Robert O'Brien, "Netscape's Rise May Be Sign of Frothy Times in Market," *Dow Jones News Service*, 9 August 1995.

16. By then Natale had moved on to become a portfolio manager at Bear Stearns.

17. Lucchetti, "Marketwatch's IPO."

18. This figure includes 750,000 overallotment shares.

19. 3.5 million shares at $12–$14 per share.

20. Described in a private presentation to Financial Executives Institute, Santa Clara Valley Chapter, 20 January 1998.

21. See Lisa Bransten and Nick Wingfield, "New Company Aims to Shift IPO Playing Field," *Wall Street Journal*, 8 February 1999.

22. Deborah Lohse, "Tough Road Is Predicted for IPOs," *Wall Street Journal*, 26 January 1998.

23. As with the IPOs, the comparison group involves nonissuing firms with the same market value of equity. Also, there may be an issue about size here: The effect may be absent for NYSE-traded stocks, which tend to be older and larger, but present for NASDAQ-traded stocks.

Chapter 18

1. I/B/E/S is the Institutional Brokers Estimate System. Keon has since left I/B/E/S and moved to Prudential Securities.

2. I am grateful to Kent Womack for kindly providing me with this example.

3. Anne Newman, "Biotech Stock Alteon Skyrockets in IPO," *Wall Street Journal*, 4 November 1991.

4. In November 1993, Robertson, Stephens & Co. analyst Michael Walsh initiated coverage of Alteon with a "buy" rating, saying that the clinical trial delays had created "an exceptional buying opportunity." He placed Alteon's fair value at $16 per share. Was the motivation for this recommendation in the spirit of Prudential's motivation for initiating coverage of Atmel? Alas, it took almost another two years before Alteon's share price rose above $10, and it didn't cross $16 until the last trading day of 1995.

5. These comparisons are made relevant to the stocks of similarly sized firms for which there has been no change in recommendation.

6. Is conflict of interest the only reason for the bias? Perhaps, but it may be that cognitive biases also play a role. Here are some possibilities: (1) Analysts who work for the underwriting firm may be focused on the initial positive information that led to the decision to go public. Recall the discussion on the *illusion of validity* in chapter 6. People have a tendency to search for evidence that confirms their prior views, while downplaying or even ignoring evidence inconsistent with those views. (2) Analysts suffer from *self-attribution bias*. They may attribute past successes to their own efforts but blame their past failures on a combination of bad luck and the mistakes of others. Since their firm took the IPO public, they may be *overconfident* in their own abilities or their colleagues' abilities. (3) Analysts who work for the underwriting firm tend to be especially close to the new IPO. Hence they may overweight the information specific to the IPO and underweight *base rate* information relating to the way things generally work out.

7. I am grateful to Rob Hansen and Atulya Sarin for providing me with the data for this figure.

8. Actually, below median.

9. Most companies are not in the advantageous position in which Microsoft finds itself. In his *Fortune* article, Fox lists some techniques currently in use: (1) Companies such as General Electric time asset sales or store openings to keep earnings rising smoothly. (2) For some assets such as software, there are no clear guidelines about the length of time the asset should be depreciated. America Online was known to depreciate software quite aggressively. (3) Some companies will take a restructuring cost today, with the intention of shifting earnings into the future. IBM is a case in point.

10. There have been times when executives at Intel have rolled their eyes after hearing the pronouncements of a security analyst who follows their company. On August 22, 1997, Thomas Kurlak of Merrill Lynch downgraded Intel from buy to neutral. Yet, on the *same* day, Edelstone upgraded Intel from neutral to outperform.

11. Not to take anything away from Tom Kurlak: In the October 27, 1997, issue of *Fortune*, Joseph Nocera points out that Kurlak appears to have consistently been more astute than his fellow analysts in tracking the semiconductor industry's "inventory cycle." See chapter 8.

Chapter 19

1. Jerry Shapiro, professor of counseling psychology at Santa Clara University. I thank Jerry for his help in preparing the material on covered-call writing for this chapter, in a conversation held on 19 May 1998.

2. A call option confers on its owner the right, but not the obligation, to buy a stock at a particular price, the exercise price, on or before the expiration date. When an investor owns a stock and sells a call option on that stock, he is said to have written a covered call. The stock he holds covers the option he sells. The investor who writes a call receives a premium, the price paid by the buyer of the call option. If the price of the stock subsequently lies above the exercise price when the option expires, the investor who wrote the call will find that the stock gets called away. The writer of the call will then sell the call and receive the exercise price, not the current market price of the stock.

3. See the discussion about Boston Chicken in chapter 17.

4. Jonathan Clements, "Abracadabra and a Putnam Fund Disappears," *Wall Street Journal*, 5 May 1993.

5. Personal interview. Telephone interview, 25 May 1998.

6. For example, Natenberg describes delta risk as the "risk that the underlying contract will move in one direction rather than another." He describes gamma risk as the "risk that the underlying contract will make a swift move, regardless of the direction."

7. I have benefited from discussions with SPX traders Chris Bernard, Al Wilkenson, and Rick Angell about the subtleties involved in using implied volatility data. They stress that for exercise prices well below the price of the underlying asset, it is better to focus on put options rather than call options. Also, the underlying asset for SPX options is the S&P 500 futures, as opposed to the cash.

8. Suzanne McGee, "Did the High Cost of Derivatives Spark Monday's Stock Sell-Off?" *Wall Street Journal*, 2 September 1998.

9. SPX trader Chris Bernard indicates that from the perspective of the trading pit, the pattern is completely flat.

10. The 0.55 value may be somewhat high relative to the period following publication of his book, which was first published in 1989 and reprinted in 1994.

11. Statistically, the observations in figure 19-5 are daily. Hence, the observations overlap. If we restrict attention to nonoverlapping observations the strength of the effect is considerably weakened, but is still negative.

Chapter 20

1. During the 1990s, there have been more incidents of dramatic price increases with coffee futures than with orange juice futures. In 1994, two freezes in Brazil severely damaged the coffee crop. In 1997, the memory of

1994, some threatening weather, and dock strikes in South American ports combined to induce another surge in coffee prices. The "cheap coffee analogy" is about *similarity bias*—the similarity between coffee and orange juice based, for example, on the fact that both are crops grown in Brazil. Note that in the mid-1980s, when Roll wrote his article, orange juice prices were much more volatile than coffee prices. Telephone interview, 26 June 1998.

2. Until 1995, the National Weather Service issued specialized agricultural forecasts, notably a "fruit and frost forecast," a special bulletin that was issued to signal the threat of a frost. This service was cut from the U.S. budget in 1995, and is now provided by private forecasting firms.

3. Dow Jones News Service, 5 December 1997. (Weather service no longer available.)

4. Daniel Rosenberg and Robin K. Taylor, "CBOT Soybeans Fall to 1-Mo Low."

5. These were accessed through Dow Jones News Service, using the //WIRES N/CMD command in *terminal* mode.

6. Stephen Cox, "NYCE Orange Juice Settles Higher: Trade Enters Buying," Dow Jones Commodities Service, 28 January 1998.

7. Margarita Palatnik, "Orange-Juice Prices Get Squeezed Lower on Unexpectedly Bearish U.S. Report," *Wall Street Journal*, 11 February 1999.

8. Ibid. Scoville is identified as an analyst with Chicago-based Price Group Futures, Inc.

9. Telephone interview, 26 June 1998.

Chapter 21

1. Bob Davis, Jonathan Friedland, and Matt Moffett, "Epidemic: As Currency Crisis Spreads, Need of a Cure Grows More Pressing," *Wall Street Journal*, 24 August 1998.

2. David Wessel, Darren McDermott, and Greg Ip, "Money Trail: Speculators Didn't Sink Indonesian Currency; Local Borrowing Did," *Wall Street Journal*, 30 December 1997.

3. Ibid.

4. I thank Kim Rupert and Louis Radovich of MMS for graciously providing me with data on investor forecasts of currency rates.

Chapter 22

1. This occurred on the August 18, 1998, program *Wall $treet Week with Louis Rukeyser.* The speaker was Frank Cappiello.

2. Bob Davis, Jonathan Friedland, and Matt Moffett, "Epidemic: As Currency Crisis Spreads," *Wall Street Journal*, 24 August 1998.

References

Abarbanell, Jeffrey, and Victor Bernard. 1992. "Tests of Analysts' Overreaction/Underreaction to Earnings Information as an Explanation for Anomalous Stock Price Behavior." *Journal of Finance* 47, no. 3: 1181–1208.

Amir, Eli, and Yoav Ganzach. 1998. "Overreaction and Underreaction in Analysts' Forecasts." *Journal of Economic Behavior & Organization* 37: 333–347.

Anderson, J. 1979. "Perspective on Models of Uncertain Decisions." In *Risk, Uncertainty, and Agricultural Development*, edited by J. A. Roumasset, J. M. Boussard, and I. Singh, 39–62. New York: Agricultural Development Council.

Andreassen, Paul. 1990. "Judgmental Extrapolation and Market Overreaction: On the Use and Disuse of News." *Journal of Behavioral Decision Making* 3: 153–174.

Andreassen, Paul, and Steven J. Kraus. 1990. "Judgmental Extrapolation and the Salience of Change." *Journal of Forecasting* 9: 347–372.

Asquith, Paul. 1983. "Merger Bids, Uncertainty, and Stockholder Returns." *Journal of Financial Economics* 11: 51–83.

Balduzzi, Pierluigi, Edwin Elton, and T. Clifford Green. 1997. "Economic News and the Yield Curve: Evidence from the U.S. Treasury Market." Working paper, New York University, New York, N.Y.

Ball, Ray, and S. P. Kothari. 1989. "Non-Stationary Expected Returns: Implications for Tests of Market Efficiency and Serial Correlation in Returns." *Journal of Financial Economics* 25: 51–74.

Banz, R. W. 1981. "The Relation Between Return and Market Value of Common Stocks. *Journal of Financial Economics* 9: 3–18.

Barber, Brad, Reuven Lehavy, Maureen McNichols, and Brett Trueman. 1998. "Can Investors Profit from the Prophets? Consensus Analyst Recommendations and Stock Returns." Working paper, University of California, Berkeley.

Barber, Brad, and Terrance Odean. 1998a. "Boys Will Be Boys: Gender, Overconfidence, and Common Stock Investment." Working paper, University of California, Davis.

———. 1998b. "The Common Stock Investment Performance of Individual Investors." Working paper, University of California, Davis.

Barberis, N., A. Shleifer, and R. Vishny. 1997. "A Model of Investor Sentiment." *Journal of Financial Economics* 49, no. 3: 307–344.

Barsky, Robert, F. Thomas Juster, Miles Kimball, and Matthew Shapiro. 1997. "Preference Parameters and Behavioral Heterogeneity: An Experimental Approach in the Health and Retirement Survey." *Quarterly Journal of Economics* 112, no. 2: pp. 537–580.

Basu, S. 1983. "The Relationship Between Earnings Yield, Market Value, and Return for NYSE Common Stocks: Further Evidence." *Journal of Financial Economics* 12: 129–156.

Bates, David. 1991. "The Crash of 87: Was It Expected? The Evidence from Options Markets." *Journal of Finance* 46, no. 3: 1009–1044.

———. 1996. "Testing Option Pricing Models." In *Statistical Methods in Finance/ Handbook of Statistics*, edited by G. S. Maddala and C. R. Rao. Amsterdam: Elsevier. 567–611.

———. 1995. "Post-'87 Crash Fears in S&P 500 Futures Options." Working paper, Wharton School and National Bureau of Economic Research.

Benartzi, Shlomo, and Richard Thaler. 1995. "Myopic Loss Aversion and the Equity Premium Puzzle." *Quarterly Journal of Economics* 110, no. 1: 73–92.

———. 1998. "Illusionary Diversification and Its Implications for the U.S. and Chilean Retirement Systems." Working paper, University of California, Los Angeles.

———. 1999. "Risk Aversion or Myopia? Choices in Repeated Gambles and Retirement Investments." *Management Science*, forthcoming.

Bernard, Victor. 1993. "Stock Price Reactions to Earnings Announcements: A Summary of Recent Anomalous Evidence and Possible Explanations." In *Advances in Behavioral Finance*, edited by Richard H. Thaler, 303–340. New York: Russell Sage Foundation.

Bernard, Victor, and Jacob Thomas. 1989. "Post-Earnings-Announcement Drift: Delayed Price Response or Risk Premium?" *Journal of Accounting Research* 27: 1–36.

———. 1990. "Evidence That Stock Prices Do Not Fully Reflect the Implications of Current Earnings for Future Earnings." *Journal of Accounting and Economics* 13: 305–340.

Bernheim, B. Douglas, Jonathan Skinner, and Steven Weinberg. 1997. "What Accounts for the Variation in Retirement Wealth Among U.S. House-holds?" Working paper, National Bureau of Economic Research, Cambridge, Mass.

Bernstein, Peter. 1996. *Against the Gods: The Remarkable Story of Risk*. New York: John Wiley & Sons.

Bernstein, Richard. 1995. "Quantitative Viewpoint." *Merrill Lynch, Pierce, Fenner, and Smith Newsletter*. New York: Merrill Lynch, Pierce, Fenner, and Smith.

Billingsley, Randall S., and Donald Chance. 1988. "Put-Call Ratios and Market Timing Effectiveness." *Journal of Portfolio Management* (fall) 15, no. 1: 25–28.

Black, Fischer. 1993. "Noise." In *Advances in Behavioral Finance*, edited by Richard H. Thaler, 3–22. New York: Russell Sage Foundation.

Black, Fischer, and Myron Scholes. 1973. "The Pricing of Options and Corporate Liabilities." *Journal of Political Economy* 81 (May–June): 637–659.

Blume, Marshall, J. Crockett, and Irwin Friend. 1974. "Stock Ownership in the United States: Characteristics and Trends." *Survey of Current Business* 54 (November): 16–40.

Blume, Marshall, and Irwin Friend. 1975. "The Asset Structure of Individual Portfolios and Some Implications for Utility Functions." *Journal of Finance* 30 (May): 585–603.

———. 1978. *The Changing Role of the Individual Investor: A Twentieth Century Fund Report.* New York: John Wiley & Sons.

Bodurtha, James N. Jr., Dong-Soon Kim, and Charles M. C. Lee. 1995. "Closed-End Country Funds and U.S. Market Sentiment." *Review of Financial Studies* 8, no. 3: 879–918.

Bowen, John J. Jr., and Meir Statman. 1997. "Performance Games." *Financial Analysts Journal* 23, no. 2: 8–15.

Bradley, Michael, Anand Desai, and E. Han Kim. 1983. "The Rationale Behind Interfirm Tender Offers." *Journal of Financial Economics* 11, no. 1, 183–206.

Brav, Alon, and Paul Gompers. 1997. "Myth or Reality? The Long-Run Underperformance of Initial Public Offerings: Evidence from Venture and Nonventure Capital-Backed Companies." *Journal of Finance* 52: 1791–1823.

Brinson, Gary P., L. Randolph Hood, and Gilbert L. Beebower. 1986. "Determinants of Portfolio Performance." *Financial Analysts Journal* 42 (July–August), no. 4: 39–44.

Brinson, Gary P., Brian D. Singer, and Gilbert L. Beebower. 1991. "Determinants of Portfolio Performance II: An Update." *Financial Analysts Journal* 51 (May–June), no. 1: 40–48.

Brown, Keith, Van Harlow, and Laura Starks. 1996. "Of Tournaments and Temptations: An Analysis of Managerial Incentives in the Mutual Fund Industry." *Journal of Finance* 51: 85–110.

Brown, Roger H., and Stephen M. Schaefer. 1994. "The Term Structure of Real Interest Rates and the Cox, Ingersoll, and Ross Model." *Journal of Financial Economics* 35: 3–42.

Camerer, Colin. 1989. "Does the Basketball Market Believe in the Hot Hand?" *American Economic Review* 79, no. 5: 1257–1261.

Campbell, John Y. 1995. "Some Lessons from the Yield Curve." *Journal of Economics Perspectives* 9: 129–152.

Campbell, John Y., Andrew W. Lo, and A. Craig MacKinlay. 1997. *The Econometrics of Financial Markets.* Princeton, N.J.: Princeton University Press.

Campbell, J. Y., and R. J. Shiller. 1988. "Stock Prices, Earnings, and Expected Dividends." *Journal of Finance* 43, no. 3: 661–676.

Canner, Niko, N. Gregory Mankiw, and David N. Weil. 1997. "An Asset Allocation Puzzle." *American Economic Review* 87, no. 1: 181–191.

Canina, Linda, and Stephen Figlewski. 1993. "The Informational Content of Implied Volatility." *Review of Financial Studies* 6, no. 3: 659–681.

Carhart, Mark. 1997. "On Persistence in Mutual Fund Performance." *Journal of Finance* 52, no. 1: 57–82.

Chan, L. K. C., and J. Lakonishok. 1993. "Are the Reports of Beta's Death Premature?" *The Journal of Portfolio Management* 19, no. 4: 51–62.

Chen, Nai-Fu, Raymond Kan, and Merton H. Miller. 1993. "Are the Discounts on Closed-End Funds a Sentiment Index?" *Journal of Finance* 48, no. 2: 795–800; and (with Navin Chopra) "A Rejoinder," 809–810.

Chodia, Tarun. 1996. "The Structure of Mutual Fund Charges." *Journal of Financial Economics* 41: 3–39.

Chopra, Navin, Josef Lakonishok, and Jay Ritter. 1993. "Measuring Abnormal Performance: Do Stocks Overreact?" In *Advances in Behavioral Finance*, edited by Richard H. Thaler, 265–302. New York: Russell Sage Foundation.

Chopra, Navin, Charles M. C. Lee, Andrei Shleifer, and Richard H. Thaler. 1993. "Yes, Discounts on Closed-End Funds Are a Sentiment Index." *Journal of Finance* 48, no. 2: 801–808; and "Summing Up," 811–812.

Clarke, Roger G., and Meir Statman. 1998. "Bullish or Bearish? The Patterns of Investor Forecasts." *Financial Analysts Journal* (May/June): 63–72.

———. 1999. "The DJIA Crossed 652,230 (in 1998)." Working paper, Santa Clara University, Santa Clara, Calif.

Constantinides, George. 1983a. "Capital Market Equilibrium with Personal Tax." *Econometrica* 51: 611–636.

———. 1983b. "A Note on the Sub-Optimality of Dollar-Cost Averaging as an Investment Policy." *Journal of Financial and Quantitative Analysis* 14, no. 2: 443–450.

———. 1984. "Optimal Stock Trading with Personal Taxes: Implications for Prices and Abnormal January Returns." *Journal of Financial Economics* 9: 221–235.

Cooley, Philip L. 1977. "A Multidimensional Analysis of Institutional Investor Perception of Risk." *Journal of Finance* 32: 67–78.

Cosmides, Lena, and John Tooby. 1992. "Cognitive Adaptations for Social Exchange." In *The Adapted Mind: Evolutionary Psychology and the Generation of Culture*, edited by Jerome Bankow, Lena Cosmides, and John Tooby. New York: Oxford University Press.

Cutler, David, James Poterba, and Lawrence Summers. 1993. "What Moves Stock Prices." In *Advances in Behavioral Finance*, edited by Richard H. Thaler, 133–152. New York: Russell Sage Foundation.

Daniel, Kent, David Hirshleifer, and Avanidhar Subrahmanyam. 1998. "A Theory of Overconfidence, Self-Attribution, and Security Market Under- and Over-reactions." *Journal of Finance* 53: 1839–1886.

———. 1999. "Investor Overconfidence, Covariance Risk, and Predictors of Securities Returns." Working paper, University of Michigan, Ann Arbor.

Darrough, Masako, and Thomas Russell. 1998. "A Behavioral Model of Earnings Forecasts: Top Down Versus Bottom Up." Working paper, University of California, Davis.

De Bondt, Werner. 1989. "Stock Price Reversals and Overreaction to News Events: A Survey of Theory and Evidence." In *A Reappraisal of the Efficiency of Financial Markets*, edited by S. J. Taylor et al. New York: Springer Verlag.

———. 1991. "What Do Economists Know About the Stock Market?" *Journal of Portfolio Management* 17, no. 2: 84–91.

———. 1992. *Earnings Forecasts and Share Price Reversals*. Charlottesville, Va.: Research Foundation of the Institute of Chartered Financial Analysts.

———. 1993. "Betting on Trends: Intuitive Forecasts of Financial Risk and Return." *International Journal of Forecasting* 9: 355–371.

———. 1998. "A Portrait of the Individual Investor." *European Economic Review* 42: 831–844.

De Bondt, Werner, and Mary Bange. 1992. "Inflation, Money Illusion, and Time Variation in Term Premia." *Journal of Financial and Quantitative Analysis* 27, no. 4: 479–496.

De Bondt, Werner, and Anil Makhija. 1988. "Throwing Good Money After Bad? Nuclear Power Plant Decisions and the Relevance of Sunk Costs." *Journal of Economic Behavior and Organization* 10: 173–199

De Bondt, Werner, and Richard Thaler. 1985. "Does the Stock Market Overreact?" *Journal of Finance* 40: 793–805.

———. 1987. "Further Evidence on Investor Overreaction and Stock Market Seasonality." *Journal of Finance* 42: 557–581.

———. 1989. "A Mean Reverting Walk Down Wall Street." *Journal of Economic Perspectives* 3, no. 1: 189–202.

———. 1990. "Do Security Analysts Overreact?" *American Economic Review* 80, no. 2: 52–57.

———. 1995. "Financial Decision Making in Markets and Firms." In *Finance, Series of Handbooks in Operations Research and Management Science*, edited by R. Jarrow, V. Maksimovic, and W. T. Ziemba. Amsterdam: Elsevier–Science: 385–410.

De Long, J. Bradford, Andrei Shleifer, Lawrence Summers, and Robert J. Waldmann. 1989. "The Size and Incidence of the Losses from Noise Trading." *Journal of Finance* 44, no. 3: 681–696.

———. 1990. "Positive Feedback Investment Strategies and Destabilizing Rational Expectations." *Journal of Finance* 45, no. 2: 379–395.

———. 1993. "Noise Trader Risk in Financial Markets." In *Advances in Behavioral Finance*, edited by Richard H. Thaler, 23–58. New York: Russell Sage Foundation.

Degeorge, Francois, Jayendu Patel, and Richard Zeckhauser. 1997. "Earnings Manipulation to Exceed Thresholds." Working paper, Harvard University, Cambridge, Mass.

Del Guercio, Diane. 1996. "The Distorting Effect of the Prudent Man Law on Pension Fund Equity Investments." *Journal of Financial Economics* 40, no. 1: 31–62.

Diz, Fernando, and Thomas J. Finucane. 1993. "Do the Options Markets Really Overreact?" *Journal of Futures Markets* 13: 298–312.

Dodd, Peter. 1980. "Merger Proposals, Managerial Discretion, and Stockholder Wealth." *Journal of Financial Economics* 8: 105–138.

Dreman, David N. 1995. "Exploiting Behavioral Finance: Portfolio Strategy and Construction." In *Behavioral Finance and Decision Theory in Investment Management,* edited by Arnold S. Wood. Charlottesville, Va.: Association for Investment Management and Research: 42–49.

————. 1998. *Contrarian Investment Strategies: The Next Generation: Beat the Market by Going Against the Crowd.* New York: Simon & Schuster.

Dreman, David N., and Michael Berry. 1995. "Analyst Forecasting Errors and Their Implications for Security Analysts." *Financial Analysts Journal* 51, no. 3: 30–41.

Edwards, Ward. 1982. "Conservatism in Human Information Processing." In *Judgment Under Uncertainty: Heuristics and Biases,* edited by Daniel Kahneman, Paul Slovic, and Amos Tversky. New York: Cambridge University Press.

Eger, Carol E. 1983. "An Empirical Test of the Redistributive Effect in Pure Exchange Mergers." *Journal of Financial and Quantitative Analysis* 18: 547–572.

Einhorn, H. J., and R. Hogarth. 1978. "Confidence in Judgment: Persistence in the Illusion of Validity." *Psychological Review* 85, no. 5: 395–416.

Fama, Eugene. 1970. "Efficient Capital Markets: A Review of Theory and Empirical Work." *Journal of Finance* 25, no. 2: 383–417.

————. 1991. "Efficient Capital Markets: II." *Journal of Finance* 46, no. 5: 1575–1618.

————. 1998a. "Efficiency Survives the Attack of the Anomalies." *GSB Chicago* (winter): 14–16.

————. 1998b. "Market-Efficiency, Long-Term Returns, and Behavioral Finance." *Journal of Financial Economics* 49, no. 3: 283–306.

Fama, Eugene R., and Kenneth R. French. 1988. "Permanent and Temporary Components of Stock Prices." *Journal of Political Economy* 96: 246–273.

————. 1992. "The Cross-Section of Expected Stock Returns." *Journal of Finance* 47: 427–465.

————. 1996. "Multifactor Explanations of Asset Pricing Anomalies." *Journal of Finance* 51, no. 1: 55–84.

Firth, Michael. 1980. "Takeovers, Shareholder Returns, and the Theory of the Firm." *Quarterly Journal of Economics* 94, no. 2: 235–260.

Fisher, Kenneth, and Meir Statman. 1997. "Investment Advice from Mutual Fund Companies." *Journal of Portfolio Management* (fall): 9–25.

———. 1999a. "A Behavioral Framework for Time Diversification." *Financial Analysts Journal*, forthcoming.

———. 1999b. "The Sentiment of Investors, Large and Small." Working paper, Santa Clara University, Santa Clara, Calif.

French, Kenneth, and James Poterba. 1991. "Are Japanese Stock Prices Too High?" *Journal of Financial Economics* 29, no. 2: 337–364.

———. 1993. "Investor Diversification and International Equity Markets." In *Advances in Behavioral Finance*, edited by Richard H. Thaler, 383–392. New York: Russell Sage Foundation.

Fridson, Martin. 1998. *It Was a Very Good Year.* New York: John Wiley and Sons.

Friedman, Milton, and Leonard J. Savage. 1948. "The Utility Analysis of Choices Involving Risk." *Journal of Political Economy* 56: 279–304.

Froot, Kenneth. 1989. "New Hope for the Expectations Hypothesis of the Term Structure of Interest Rates." *Journal of Finance* 44: 283–305.

Froot, Kenneth, and Jeffrey A. Frankel. 1993. "Forward Risk Bias: Is It an Exchange Risk Premium?" In *Advances in Behavioral Finance*, edited by Richard H. Thaler, 359–382. New York: Russell Sage Foundation.

Froot, Kenneth, and Andre Perold. 1996. "Global Equity Markets: The Case of Royal Dutch and Shell." Case N9-296-077. Boston: Harvard Business School.

Fuller, Russ. 1995. "Behavioral Biases and Alphas." In *Behavioral Finance and Decision Theory in Investment Management*, edited by Arnold S. Wood. Charlottesville, Va.: Association for Investment Management and Research: 31–34.

Galloway, Tim, Claudio Lauderer, and Dennis Sheehan. 1998. "What Does the Market Learn from Stock Offering Revisions?" *Financial Management* 27, no. 1: 5–16.

Gilovich, Thomas R., and Victoria Husted-Medvec. 1993. "The Experience of Regret: What, When, and Why." *Psychological Review* 102, no. 2: 379–395.

Gilovich, Thomas R., Robert Vallone, and Amos Tversky. 1985. "The Hot Hand in Basketball: On the Misperception of Random Sequences." *Cognitive Psychology* 17: 295–314.

Glick, Ira. 1957. "A Psychological Study of Futures Trading." Ph.D. diss., University of Chicago.

Goetzmann, William, B. Greenwald, and Gur Huberman. 1992. "Market Response to Mutual Fund Performance." Working paper, Columbia University, New York, N.Y.

Goetzmann, William N., and Roger G. Ibbotson. 1994a. "Do Winners Repeat?" *Journal of Portfolio Management* (winter): 9–18.

———. 1994b. "Games Mutual Fund Companies Play: Strategic Response to Investor Beliefs in the Mutual Fund Industry." Working paper, Yale University, New Haven, Conn.

Goetzmann, William N., and Phillipe Jorion. 1999. "A Century of Global Stock Markets." *Journal of Finance*, forthcoming.

Goetzmann, William N., and Nadav Peles. 1994. "Cognitive Dissonance and Mutual Fund Investors." Working paper, Yale University, New Haven, Conn.

Gokhale, Jagadeesh, Laurence J. Kotlikoff, and John Sabelhaus. 1996. "Understanding the Post-War Decline in U.S. Saving: A Cohort Analysis." Working paper 5571, National Bureau of Economic Research, Cambridge, Mass.

Gompers, Paul, and Andrew Metrick. 1998. "How Are Large Institutions Different from Other Investors? Why Do These Differences Matter?" Working paper, Harvard University and National Bureau of Economic Research, Cambridge, Mass.

Goodman, Jordan E. 1998. *Everyone's Money Book.* 2nd ed. Chicago: Dearborn Financial Publishing.

Graham, Benjamin, and David Dodd. 1934. *Security Analysis.* New York: McGraw-Hill.

Griffen, Paul, Jennifer J. Jones, and Mark E. Zmijewski. 1995. "How Useful Are Wall $treet Week Recommendations?" *Journal of Financial Statement Analysis* 1, no. 1: 33–52.

Grinblatt, Mark, and Sheridan Titman. 1989. "Mutual Fund Performance: An Analysis of Quarterly Portfolio Holdings." *Journal of Business* 42: 1977–1984.

Grinblatt, Mark, Sheridan Titman, and Russ Wermers. 1995. "Momentum Investment Strategies, Portfolio Performance, and Herding: A Study of Mutual Fund Behavior." *American Economic Review* 85: 1088–1105.

Gross, Leroy. 1982. *The Art of Selling Intangibles: How to Make Your Million($) by Investing Other People's Money.* New York: New York Institute of Finance.

Gruber, Elton J., Sanjiv Das, and Matt Hlavka. 1993. "Efficiency with Costly Information: A Reinterpretation of Evidence from Managed Portfolios. *Review of Financial Studies* 6: 1–21.

Gruber, Martin. 1996. "Another Puzzle: The Growth in Actively Managed Mutual Funds." *Journal of Finance* 51, no. 3: 783–810.

Hand, John R. M., and Terrance R. Skantz. 1997. "Noise Traders in Event Studies? The Case of Equity Carve-outs." Working paper, University of North Carolina, Chapel Hill, N.C.

Hanley, Kathleen Weiss, Charles M. C. Lee, and Paul Seguin. 1996. "The Marketing of Closed-end Fund IPOs: Evidence from Transaction Data." *Journal of Financial Intermediation* 5: 127–159.

Hansen, Robert S., and Atulya Sarin. 1997. "Is Honesty the Best Policy? An Examination of Security Analysts' Forecast Behavior Around Seasoned Equity Offerings." Working paper, Virginia Polytechnic Institute, Blacksburg, Va.

Hawawini, G., and Donald Keim. 1995. "On the Predictability of Common Stock Returns: World-Wide Evidence." In *Finance, Series of Handbooks in Operations Research and Management Science,* edited by R. Jarrow, V. Maksimovic, and W. T. Ziemba. Amsterdam: Elsevier-Science: 497–544.

Heath, Chip, Steven Huddart, and Mark Lang. 1998. "Psychological Factors and Stock Option Exercise." Working paper, University of North Carolina, Chapel Hill.

Heaton, J. B. 1998. "Managerial Optimism and Corporate Finance." Working paper, University of Chicago, Ill.

Heisler, Jeffrey. 1994. "Loss Aversion in a Futures Market: An Empirical Test." *The Review of Futures Markets* 13, no. 3: 793–822.

Hendricks, Darryl, Jayendu Patel, and Richard Zeckhauser. 1993. "Hot Hands in Mutual Funds: Short-run Persistence of Performance." *Journal of Finance* 48: 93–130.

———. 1995. "The J-Shape of Performance Persistance Given Survivorship Bias." Working paper, Harvard University, Cambridge, Mass.

Hong, Harrison, Terence Lim, and Jeremy Stein. 1999. "Bad News Travels Slowly: Size, Analyst Coverage, and the Profitability of Momentum Strategies." *Journal of Finance,* forthcoming.

Huberman, Gur. 1997. "Familiarity Breeds Investment." Working paper, Columbia University, New York, N.Y.

Ippolito, Richard A. 1989. "Efficiency with Costly Information: A Study of Mutual Fund Performance." *Quarterly Journal of Economics* 104, no. 1: 1–23.

Jackwerth, Jens Carsten, and Mark Rubinstein. 1996. "Recovering Probability Distributions from Contemporaneous Security Prices." *Journal of Finance* 51, no. 5: 1611–1631.

Jacob, Nancy. L. 1974. "A Limited-Diversification Portfolio Selection Model for the Small Investor." *Journal of Finance* 29: 837–857.

Jahnke, William W. 1997. "The Asset Allocation Hoax." *Journal of Financial Planning* (February): 109–113.

Jegadeesh, Narasimhan, and Sheridan Titman. 1993. "Returns to Buying Winners and Selling Losers: Implications for Stock Market Efficiency." *Journal of Finance* 48: 65–91.

Jensen, Michael C. 1968. "The Performance of Mutual Funds in the Period 1945–1964." *Journal of Finance* 389–416.

———. 1994. "Self-Interest, Altruism, Incentives, and Agency Theory." *Journal of Applied Corporate Finance* 7, no. 2: 40–45.

Jensen, Michael C., and William H. Meckling. 1976. "Theory of the Firm: Managerial Behavior, Agency Costs and Ownership Structure." *Journal of Financial Economics* 3, no. 4: 305–360.

Jensen, Michael C., and Richard S. Ruback. 1983. "The Market for Corporate Control." *Journal of Financial Economics* 11: 5–50.

Kahneman, Daniel, Jack Knetsch, and Richard Thaler. 1991. "Fairness as a Constraint on Profit Seeking: Entitlements in the Market." In *Quasi-Rational Economics,* edited by Richard Thaler. New York: Russell Sage Foundation: 199–219.

Kahneman, Daniel, and Mark W. Riepe. 1998. "The Psychology of the Non-Professional Investor." *Journal of Portfolio Management* 24, no. 4: 52–65.

Kahneman, Daniel, Paul Slovic, and Amos Tversky. 1982. *Judgment Under Uncertainty: Heuristics and Biases.* New York: Cambridge University Press.

Kahneman, Daniel, and Amos Tversky. 1979. "Prospect Theory: An Analysis of Decision Making Under Risk." *Econometrica* 47, no. 2: 263–291.

Kandel, Shmuel, and Robert Stambaugh. 1991. "Asset Returns and Intertemporal Preferences." *Journal of Monetary Economics* 27: 39–71.

Kaplan, Steven. 1989. "The Effects of Management Buyouts on Operating Performance and Value." *Journal of Financial Economics* 24: 217–254.

Kennickell, Arthur, Martha Starr-McCluer, and Annika E. Sunden. 1997. "Household Saving and Financial Planning: Some Findings from a Focus Group." *Financial Counseling and Planning* 8, no. 1: 1–17.

King, M. A., and J. L. Leape. 1984. "Wealth and Portfolio Composition: Theory and Evidence." Working paper 1468, National Bureau of Economic Research, Cambridge, Mass.

Klaczynski, Paul A., and James M. Fauth. 1996. "Intellectual Ability, Rationality, and Intuitiveness as Predictors of Warranted and Unwarranted Optimism for Future Life Events." *Journal of Youth & Adolescence* 25, no. 6: 755–773.

Kleidon, Alan. 1986. "Anomalies in Financial Economics: Blueprint for Change?" *Journal of Business* 59, no. 4, part 2: 469–499.

Klein, April. 1990. "A Direct Test of the Cognitive Bias Theory of Share Price Reversals." *Journal of Accounting and Economics* 13, no. 2: 155–166.

Klibanoff, Peter, Owen Lamont, and Thierry A. Wizman. 1998. "Investor Reaction to Salient News in Closed-end Country Funds." *Journal of Finance* 53: 673–700.

Krigman, Laurie, Wayne H. Shaw, and Kent L. Womack. 1999. "The Persistence of IPO Mispricing and the Predictive Power of Flipping." *Journal of Finance,* forthcoming.

Kroll, Y. H. Levy, and A. Rapoport. 1988. "Experimental Tests of the Separation Theorem and the Capital Asset Pricing Model." *American Economic Review* 78, no. 3: 500–518.

Kyle, A. 1985. "Continuous Auctions and Insider Trading." *Econometrica* 53: 1315–1336.

La Porta, Rafael. 1996. "Expectations and the Cross Section of Stock Returns." *Journal of Finance* 51, no. 5: 1715–1742.

Lakonishok, Josef, Andrei Shleifer, Richard H. Thaler, and Robert Vishny. 1991. "Window Dressing by Pension Fund Managers." *American Economic Review* 81, no. 2: 227–231.

Lakonishok, Josef, Andrei Shleifer, and Robert Vishny. 1992. "The Structure and Performance of the Money Management Industry." Brookings Papers on Economic Activity. Washington, D.C.: Brookings Institution: 331–339.

———. 1994. "Contrarian Investment, Extrapolation, and Risk." *Journal of Finance* 49, no. 5: 1541–1578.

Lakonishok, Josef, and Seymour Smidt. 1986a. "Are Seasonal Anomalies Real? A Ninety-Year Perspective." *Review of Financial Studies* 1, no. 4: 403–425.

———. 1986b. "Capital Gain Taxation and Volume of Trading." *Journal of Finance* 41: 951–974.

Lease, R. C., W. Lewellen, and G. Schlarbaum. 1976. "Market Segmentation: Evidence on the Individual Investor." *Financial Analysts Journal* 32: 53–60.

Lee, Charles, James Myers, and Bhaskaran Swaminathan. 1999. "What Is the Intrinsic Value of the Dow?" *Journal of Finance,* forthcoming.

Lee, Charles, Andrei Shleifer, and Richard Thaler. 1991. "Investor Sentiment and the Closed-End Puzzle." *Journal of Finance* 46: 75–109.

Lee, Charles, and Bhaskaran Swaminathan. 1998. "Price Momentum and Trading Volume." Working paper, Cornell University, Ithaca, N.Y.

Lehmann, Bruce. 1990. "Fads, Martingales, and Market Efficiency." *Quarterly Journal of Economics* 105: 1–28.

LeRoy, S., and R. Porter. 1981. "The Present-Value Relation: Tests Based on Implied Variance Bounds." *Econometrica* 49: 555–674.

Levin, Laurence. 1992. "Are Assets Fungible? Testing Alternative Theories of Life-Cycle Savings." Working paper, Santa Clara University, Santa Clara, Calif.

Levy, Haim. 1978. "Equilibrium in an Imperfect Market: A Constraint on the Number of Securities in the Portfolio." *American Economic Review* 68, no. 4: 643–658.

Lichtenstein, Sarah, Baruch Fischoff, and Lawrence Phillips. 1982. "Calibration of Probabilities: The State of the Art to 1980." In *Judgment Under Uncertainty: Heuristics and Biases,* edited by Daniel Kahneman, Paul Slovic, and Amos Tversky. New York: Cambridge University Press: 336–334.

Lo, Andrew, and A. Craig MacKinley. 1988. "Stock Market Prices Do Not Follow Random Walks: Evidence from a Simple Specification Test." *Review of Financial Studies* 1, no. 1: 41–66.

Lopes, Lola. 1987. "Between Hope and Fear: The Psychology of Risk." *Advances in Experimental Social Psychology* 20: 255–295.

Loughran, Tim, and Jay Ritter. 1995. "The New Issues Puzzle." *Journal of Finance* 50: 23–51.

Lynch, Peter. 1989. *One Up on Wall Street*. New York: Simon & Schuster.

———. 1993. *Beating the Street*. New York: Simon & Schuster.

Lyon, Andrew. 1984. "Money Market Funds and Shareholder Dilution." *Journal of Finance* 39, no. 4: 1011–1020.

Macaulay, Frederick R. 1938. *Some Theoretical Problems Suggested by the Movements of Interest Rates, Bond Yields and Stock Prices in the United States Since 1856*. New York: National Bureau of Economic Research.

Malatesta, Paul. 1983. "The Wealth Effect of Merger Activity and the Objective Functions of Merging Firms." *Journal of Financial Economics* 11: 155–181.

Markowitz, Harry M. 1952a. "The Utility of Wealth." *Journal of Political Economy* 60: 151–158.

———. 1952b. "Portfolio Selection." *Journal of Finance* 6: 77–91.

———. 1959. *Portfolio Selection: Efficient Diversification of Investment*, 2nd ed. New York: John Wiley & Sons. New Haven, Conn.: Yale University Press, 1970.

Marsh, Terry, and Robert Merton. 1986. "Dividend Variability and Variance Bounds Tests for the Rationality of Stock Market Prices." *American Economic Review* 76, no. 3: 483–498.

Mayers, Thomas A. 1989. *The Technical Analysis Course*. Chicago: Irwin.

McConnell, John, and Eduardo Schwartz. 1992. "The Origin of LYONs: A Case Study in Financial Innovation." *Journal of Applied Corporate Finance* 4, no. 4: 40–47.

Mehra, R., and Edward C. Prescott. 1985. "The Equity Premium Puzzle." *Journal of Monetary Economics* 40, no. 2: 145–161.

Mendenhall, Richard. 1991. "Evidence on the Possible Underweighting of Earnings-Related Information." *Journal of Accounting Research* 29, no. 1: 170–179.

Merton, Robert C. 1987a. "On the Current State of the Stock Market Rationality Hypothesis." In *Macroeconomics and Finance: Essays in Honor of Franco Modigliani*, edited by R. Dornbusch, S. Fischer, and J. Bossons. Cambridge, Mass.: MIT Press.

———. 1987b. "A Simple Model of Capital Market Equilibrium with Incomplete Information." *Journal of Finance* 42, no. 3: 483–510.

Metrick, Andrew. 1999. "Performance Evaluation with Transaction Cost Data: The Stock Selection of Investment Newsletters." *Journal of Finance*, forthcoming.

Michaely, Roni, Richard Thaler, and Kent Womack. 1997. "Price Reactions to Dividend Initiations and Omissions: Overreaction or Drift?" *Journal of Finance* 52, no. 3: 573–608.

Michaely, Roni, and Kent Womack. 1999. "Conflict of Interest and the Credibility of Underwriter Analyst Recommendations." *Review of Financial Studies* 12, no. 3, forthcoming.

Miller, Merton H. 1986. "Behavioral Rationality in Finance: The Case of Dividends." *Journal of Business* 59: S451–468.

Miller, Merton H., and David J. Ross. 1997. "The Orange County Bankruptcy and its Aftermath: Some New Evidence." *Journal of Derivatives* 4, no. 4: 51–60.

Modigliani, Franco, and Richard Cohn. 1979. "Inflation and the Stock Market." *Financial Analysts Journal* 35, no. 2: 24–44.

Natenberg, Sheldon. 1988. *Option Volatility and Pricing Strategies: Advanced Trading Techniques for Professionals.* Chicago: Probus Publishing.

———. 1997. "Option Trading—Theory and Practice." Presented at the 32d annual conference of the Western Finance Association, San Diego, Calif.

O'Brien, Patricia C. 1988. "Analysts' Forecasts as Earnings Expectations." *Journal of Accounting and Economics* 10: 53–83.

Odean, Terrance. 1998a. "Are Investors Reluctant to Realize Their Losses?" *Journal of Finance* 53: 1775–1798.

———. 1998b. "Volume, Volatility, Price, and Profit When All Traders Are Above Average." *Journal of Finance* 53: 1887–1934.

Olsen, Robert. 1998. "Behavioral Finance and Its Implications for Stock-Price Volatility." *Financial Analysts Journal* 54, no. 2: 10–18.

O'Neill, Barbara. 1990. *How Real People Handle Their Money.* Newton, N.J: Rutgers Cooperative Extension.

Palomino, Frederic. 1996. "Noise Trading in Small Markets." *Journal of Finance* 51, no. 4: 1537–1550.

Patel, Jay, Richard Zeckhauser, and Darryl Hendricks. 1997. "Investment Flows and Performance: Evidence from Mutual Funds, Cross Border Investments and New Issues." Working paper, Harvard University, Cambridge, Mass.

Pontiff, Jeffrey. 1995. "Closed-End Fund Premia and Returns: Implications for Financial Market Equilibrium." *Journal of Financial Economics* 37, no.3: 341–370.

———. 1996. "Costly Arbitrage: Evidence from Closed-End Funds." *Quarterly Journal of Economics* 111, no. 4: 1135–1151.

———. 1997. "Excess Volatility and Closed-End Funds." *American Economic Review* 87, no. 1: 155–169.

Pope, Robin. 1983. "The Pre-outcome Period and the Utility of Gambling." In *Foundations of Utility and Risk Theory with Applications,* edited by B. P. Stigum and F. Wenst, 137–177. Dordrecht, Netherlands: Reidel.

Porter, David, and Vernon Smith. 1994. "Stock Market Bubbles in the Laboratory." *Applied Mathematical Finance* 1: 111–127.

Poterba, James, Steven F. Venti, and David A. Wise. 1996. "How Retirement Saving Programs Increase Saving." *Journal of Economic Perspectives* 10, no. 4: 91–112.

Ritter, Jay. 1988. "The Buying and Selling Behavior of Individuals at the Turn of the Year." *Journal of Finance* 43, no. 3: 701–717.

———. 1991. "The Long-Run Performance of Initial Public Offerings." *Journal of Business* 46: 3–28.

———. 1998. "Initial Public Offerings." In *Contemporary Finance Digest, FMA International/CIBC World Markets* 2, no. 1: 5–30.

Rogalski, Richard, and Seha Tinic. 1986. "The January Size Effect: Anomaly or Risk Mismeasurement?" *Financial Analysts Journal* 42, no. 6: 63–70.

Roll, Richard. 1984. "Orange Juice and Weather." *American Economic Review* 74, no. 5: 861–880.

———. 1993. "The Hubris Hypothesis of Corporate Takeovers." In *Advances in Behavioral Finance,* edited by Richard H. Thaler, 437–458. New York: Russell Sage Foundation.

Ross, Stephen A. 1989. "Institutional Markets, Financial Marketing, and Financial Innovation." *Journal of Finance* 44: 541–556.

Rouwenhorst, K. Geert. 1998. "International Momentum Strategies." *Journal of Finance* 53, no. 1: 267–284.

Roy, Andrew. 1952. "Safety First and the Holding of Assets." *Econometrica* 20, no. 3: 431–449.

Rozeff, Michael S. 1994. "Lump-Sum Investing Versus Dollar-Averaging." *Journal of Portfolio Management* (winter): 45–50.

Rubinstein, Mark. 1994. "Implied Binomial Trees." *Journal of Finance* 49, no. 3, 771–818.

Russo, Edward, and Paul Schoemaker. 1989. *Decision Traps.* New York: Simon & Schuster.

Samuelson, Paul A. 1965. "Proof That Properly Anticipated Prices Fluctuate Randomly." *Industrial Management Review* 6 (spring): 41–49.

———. 1989. "The Judgment of Economic Science on Rational Portfolio Management: Indexing, Timing, and Long Horizon Effects." *Journal of Portfolio Management* (fall): 4–12.

Samwick, Andrew A., and Jonathan Skinner. 1996. "Abandoning the Nest Egg? 401(k) Plans and Inadequate Pension Saving." Working paper 5568, National Bureau of Economic Research, Cambridge, Mass.

Saunders, Edward M. 1993. "Stock Prices and Wall Street Weather." *American Economic Review* 83, no. 5: 1337–1345.

Schlarbaum, Gary G., Wilbur G. Lewellen, and Ronald C. Lease. 1978. "Realizing Returns on Common Stock Investments." *Journal of Business* 51: 299–325.

Schwed, Fred, Jr. 1967. *Space Age Edition of Where Are the Customers' Yachts? or A Good Hard Look at Wall Street*. Springfield, Mass.: John Magee.

Shafir, Eldan, Peter Diamond, and Amos Tversky. 1997. "Money Illusion." *Quarterly Journal of Economics* 112, no. 2: 341–374.

Sharpe, William F. 1964. "Capital Asset Prices: A Theory of Market Equilibrium Under Conditions of Risk." *Journal of Finance* 19, no. 3: 425–442.

———. 1987. "The Risk Factor: Identifying and Adapting to the Risk Capacity of the Client." In *Asset Allocation for Institutional Portfolios*, edited by Michael D. Joehnk. Chicago, Ill.: Dow Jones Irwin, 35–45.

Shefrin, Hersh. 1984. "Inferior Forecasters, Cycles, and the Efficient-Markets Hypothesis: A Comment." *Journal of Political Economy* 92: 156–161.

Shefrin, Hersh, and Meir Statman. 1984. "Explaining Investor Preference for Cash Dividends." *Journal of Financial Economics* 13, no. 2: 253–282.

———. 1985. "The Disposition to Sell Winners Too Early and Ride Losers Too Long: Theory and Evidence." *Journal of Finance* 40: 777–790.

———. 1986. "How Not to Make Money in the Stock Market." *Psychology Today*, February, 52–57.

———. 1993a. "Behavioral Aspects of the Design and Marketing of Financial Products." *Financial Management* 22, no. 2: 123–134.

———. 1993b. "Ethics, Fairness and Efficiency in Financial Markets." *Financial Analysts Journal* 49, no. 6: 21–29.

———. 1994. "Behavioral Capital Asset Pricing Theory." *Journal of Financial and Quantitative Analysis* 29, no. 3: 323–349.

———. 1995. "Making Sense of Beta, Size, and Book-to-Market." *Journal of Portfolio Management* 21, no. 2: 26-34.

———. 1998. "Comparing Return Expectations with Realized Returns." Working paper, Santa Clara University, Santa Clara, Calif.

———. 1999. "Behavioral Portfolio Theory." Working paper, Santa Clara University, Santa Clara, Calif.

Shefrin, Hersh, and Richard Thaler. 1988. "The Behavioral Life Cycle Hypothesis." *Economic Inquiry* 24: 609–643.

Shiller, Robert. 1979. "The Volatility of Long-term Interest Rates and Expectations Models of the Term-Structure." *Journal of Political Economy* 87: 1190–1219.

————. 1993a. "Do Stock Prices Move Too Much to Be Justified by Subsequent Changes in Dividends." In *Advances in Behavioral Finance*, edited by Richard H. Thaler, 107–132. New York: Russell Sage Foundation.

————. 1993b. "Speculative Prices and Popular Models." In *Advances in Behavioral Finance*, edited by Richard H. Thaler, 493–506. New York: Russell Sage Foundation.

————. 1993c. "Stock Prices and Social Dynamics." In *Advances in Behavioral Finance*, edited by Richard H. Thaler, 167–218. New York: Russell Sage Foundation.

————. 1995. "Why Do People Dislike Inflation?" Working paper, Yale University, New Haven, Conn.

Shiller, Robert, and John Campbell. 1998. "Valuation Ratios and the Long-Run Stock Market Outlook." *Journal of Portfolio Management* 24, no. 2: 11–26.

Shiller, Robert, and John Pound. 1989. "Survey Evidence on Diffusion of Interest and Information Among Investors." *Journal of Economic Behavior and Organization* 12: 47–66.

Shleifer, Andrei, and Robert Vishny. 1997. "The Limits of Arbitrage." *Journal of Finance* 52: 35–56.

Sirri, Erik, and Peter Tufano. 1992. "The Demand for Mutual Fund Services by Individual Investors." Working paper, Harvard Business School, Boston, Mass.

Slovic, Paul. 1969. "Analyzing the Expert Judge: A Study of a Stockbroker's Decision Process." *Journal of Applied Psychology* 27: 255–263.

————. 1972. "Psychological Study of Human Judgment: Implications for Investment Decision Making." *Journal of Finance* 27: 779–801.

Slovic, Paul, Baruch Fischoff, and Sarah Lichtenstein. 1979. "Rating the Risks." *Environment* 21, no. 3: 61–74.

————. 1982. "Facts Versus Fears: Understanding Perceived Risk." In *Judgment Under Uncertainty: Heuristics and Biases*, edited by Daniel Kahneman, Paul Slovic, and Amos Tversky, 463–492. New York: Cambridge University Press.

Smid, Peter, and Frans Tempelaar. 1997. "Click Funds in the Netherlands: The How and Why of an Index-Linked Financial Innovation." Working paper, University of Groningen, Netherlands.

Solt, Michael, and Meir Statman. 1989a. "Good Companies, Bad Stocks." *Journal of Portfolio Management* 15, no. 4: 39–44.

————. 1989b. "How Useful Is the Sentiment Index?" *Financial Analysts Journal* 44, no. 5: 45–55.

Starr-McCluer, Martha. 1995. "Tax Losses and the Stock Portfolios of Individual Investors." Working paper, Federal Reserve Board of Governors, Washington, D.C.

Statman, Meir. 1987. "How Many Stocks Make a Diversified Portfolio?" *Journal of Financial and Quantitative Analysis* 22, no. 3: 353–364.

———. 1995a. "A Behavioral Framework for Dollar Cost Averaging." *Journal of Portfolio Management* (fall): 70–78.

———. 1995b. "Behavioral Finance Versus Standard Finance." In *Behavioral Finance and Decision Theory in Investment Management,* edited by Arnold S. Wood. Charlottesville, Va.: Association for Investment Management and Research.

———. 1998. "The Numbers Racket Rages On." *Financial Planning* (April): 105–108.

———. 1999. "The 93.6% Question of Financial Advisors." Working paper, Santa Clara University, Santa Clara, Calif.

Statman, Meir, and David Caldwell. 1987. "Applying Behavioral Finance to Capital Budgeting: Project Termination." *Financial Management* (winter): 7–15.

Statman, Meir, and James Sepe. 1989. "Project Termination Announcements and the Market Value of the Firm." *Financial Management* (winter): 1–8.

Statman, Meir, and Tyzoon Tyebjee. 1985. "Optimistic Capital Budgeting Forecasts: An Experiment." *Financial Management* (autumn): 27–33.

Stein, Jeremy. 1989. "Overreactions in the Options Market." *Journal of Finance* 44, no. 4: 1011–1023.

Stewart, James B. 1996. *Blood Sport: The President and His Adversaries.* New York: Simon & Schuster.

Summers, Lawrence. 1993. "Does the Stock Market Rationally Reflect Fundamental Values?" In *Advances in Behavioral Finance,* edited by Richard H. Thaler, 153–166. New York: Russell Sage Foundation.

Swaminathan, Bhaskaran. 1996. "Time-Varying Expected Small Firm Returns and Closed-End Fund Discounts." *Review of Financial Studies* 9, no. 3: 845–887.

Thaler, Richard. 1985. "Mental Accounting and Consumer Choice." *Marketing Science* 4, no. 3: 199–214.

———. 1991. "Toward a Positive Theory of Consumer Choice." In *Quasi-Rational Economics,* edited by Richard H. Thaler, 3–24. New York: Russell Sage Foundation.

———. 1993a. *The Winner's Curse.* New York: Russell Sage Foundation.

———, ed. 1993b. *Advances in Behavioral Finance.* New York: Russell Sage Foundation.

Thaler, Richard, and Eric Johnson. 1991. "Gambling with the House Money and Trying to Break Even: The Effects of Prior Outcomes on Risky Choice." In *Quasi-Rational Economics,* edited by Richard H. Thaler, 48–73. New York: Russell Sage Foundation.

Thaler, Richard, and Hersh Shefrin. 1981. "An Economic Theory of Self Control." *Journal of Political Economy* 89, no. 2: 392–406.

Tversky, Amos, and Daniel Kahneman. 1971. "Belief in the Law of Small Numbers." *Psychological Bulletin,* 105–110.

———. 1974. "Judgment Under Uncertainty: Heuristics and Biases." *Science* (185): 1124–1131.

———. 1986. "Rational Choice and the Framing of Decisions." *Journal of Business* 59, no. 4, part 2: 251–278.

———. 1992. "Advances in Prospect Theory: Cumulative Representation of Uncertainty." *Journal of Risk and Uncertainty* 5: 297–323.

Varaiya, Nikhil. 1985. "A Test of Roll's Hubris Hypothesis of Corporate Takeovers." Working paper, Southern Methodist University, Dallas, Tex.

Wall, Ginita, 1993. *The Way to Save.* New York: Henry Holt.

———. 1995. *The Way to Invest.* New York: Henry Holt.

Wasik, John F. 1995. *The Investment Club Book.* New York: Warner Books.

Weinstein, Neil. 1980. "Unrealistic Optimism About Future Life Events." *Journal of Personality and Social Psychology* 39, no. 5: 806–820.

Wiggins, James B. 1991. "Do Misperceptions About the Earnings Process Contribute to Post-Earnings-Announcement Drift?" Working paper, Cornell University, Ithaca, N.Y.

Womack, Kent. 1996. "Do Brokerage Analysts' Recommendations Have Investment Value?" *Journal of Finance* 51, no. 1: 137–168.

Credits

Jay Palmer, "Technical Havoc: Chartists Predict Dow Will Keep Falling; Next Stop 5000?" from *Barron's*, August 31, 1998. Copyright © 1998 by Dow Jones & Company, Inc. All rights reserved worldwide. Reprinted by permission of *Barron's*.

Dana Parsons, "The Wizard Himself Peels Back Layers of His Own Legend" from *Los Angeles Times*, January 18, 1995. Copyright © 1995 by *Los Angeles Times*. Reprinted by permission.

David Pettit, "Logged On" from *The Wall Street Journal*, September 8, 1998. Copyright © 1998 by Dow Jones & Company, Inc. All rights reserved worldwide. Reprinted by permission of *The Wall Street Journal*.

Ronald D. Picur, "The $2 Billion Gamble: A Step-by-Step Guide on How to Prevent the Orange County Debacle from Occurring in Your Neighborhood" from *The Chicago Tribune*, December 19, 1994. Copyright © 1994 by Ronald D. Picur. Reprinted by permission of the author.

Mark Platte and Jeff Brazil, "O.C. Treasurer Thrust into Spotlight Over Risk Claims" from *Los Angeles Times*, April 30, 1998. Copyright © 1998 by *Los Angeles Times*. Reprinted by permission.

William Power "Heard on the Street: Boston Chicken Soars 143% on Its First IPO Day" from *The Wall Street Journal*, November 10, 1993. Copyright © 1993 by Dow Jones & Company, Inc. All rights reserved worldwide. Reprinted by permission of *The Wall Street Journal*.

William Power "Heard on the Street: Investment Strategists Rally to Defend Merrill Expert" from *The Wall Street Journal*, January 18, 1995. Copyright © 1995 by Dow Jones & Company, Inc. All rights reserved worldwide. Reprinted by permission of *The Wall Street Journal*.

Scott Reeves, "IPO Focus" from *The Wall Street Journal*, November 24, 1993. Copyright © 1993 by Dow Jones & Company, Inc. All rights reserved worldwide. Reprinted by permission of *The Wall Street Journal*.

Scott Reeves, "Market Sees Netscape Most Savory IPO Since Boston Chicken" from *Dow Jones Interactive*, August 7, 1995. Copyright © 1995 by Dow Jones & Company, Inc. All rights reserved worldwide. Reprinted by permission of the *Dow Jones Interactive*.

Scott Reeves, "Netscape's IPO -2-: Brokers Say Demand Very High" from *Dow Jones Interactive*, August 9, 1995. Copyright © 1995 by Dow Jones & Company, Inc. All rights reserved worldwide. Reprinted by permission of the *Dow Jones Interactive*.

From *RIAG's Personal Money Guide*. Reprinted by permission of the publisher, Research Institute of America Group.

Jay Ritter, "Initial Public Offerings" from *Contemporary Finance Digest*, Spring 1998. Copyright © 1998 by Warren, Gorham & Lamont, 31 St. James Street, Boston, MA. Reprinted by permission.

Doug Rogers, "Making Money in Mutuals" from *Investor's Business Daily*, December 15 1997. Copyright © 1997. Reprinted by permission of *Investor's Business Daily*.

Daniel Rosenberg and Robin K. Taylor. "World Commodities Summary: CBOT Soybeans Fall to 1-Mo Low" from *Dow Jones Interactive*, December 4, 1997. Copyright © 1997 by Dow Jones & Company, Inc. All rights reserved worldwide. Reprinted by permission of the *Dow Jones Interactive*.

Lauren R. Rublin, "A Very Good Year" from *Barron's*, December 30, 1996. Copyright © 1996 by Dow Jones & Company, Inc. All rights reserved worldwide. Reprinted by permission of *Barron's*.

Lauren R. Rublin, "Another Chance" from *Barron's*, June 23, 1997. Copyright © 1997 by Dow Jones & Company, Inc. Reprinted by permission of *Barron's*.

Rutgers Cooperative Education, Case study developed by Barbara O'Neill. Reprinted with permission from Rutgers Cooperative Extension.

Eric Savitz, "Silicon Values: An Interview with Kevin Landis and Ken Kam" from *Bar-*

Index